Philip Johnson.
The Constancy of Change.

PHILIP JOHNSON. THE CONSTANCY OF CHANGE.

Edited by Emmanuel Petit

Foreword by Robert A. M. Stern

Essays by Beatriz Colomina, Peter Eisenman, Kurt W. Forster, Mark Jarzombek,
Charles Jencks, Phyllis Lambert, Reinhold Martin, Detlef Mertins,
Stanislaus von Moos, Joan Ockman, Terence Riley, Vincent Scully, Michael Sorkin,
Kazys Varnelis, Ujjval Vyas, Mark Wigley

Yale University Press / New Haven and London
in association with the Yale University School of Architecture

Photography for "The New Canaan Estate: A Gallery" copyright © Paul Warchol.

Designed by Pentagram
Set in Avenir and Egyptienne by Yve Ludwig
Printed in China through World Print

Library of Congress Cataloging-in-Publication Data

Philip Johnson : the constancy of change / edited by Emmanuel Petit ; foreword by Robert A. M. Stern ; essays by Beatriz Colomina . . . [et al.].
p. cm.
Includes index.
ISBN 978-0-300-12181-0 (cloth : alk. paper)
1. Johnson, Philip, 1906–2005—Criticism and interpretation.
I. Petit, Emmanuel, 1973– II. Colomina, Beatriz.
NA737.J6P57 2009
720.92—dc22
[B]
2008021330

A catalogue record for this book is available from the British Library.

This paper meets the requirements of ANSI/NISO Z39.48-1992 (Permanence of Paper).

10 9 8 7 6 5 4 3 2 1

Page x: Philip Johnson hidden behind door lintel
Page 13: Philip Johnson, Doghouse, 1998
Cover: Johnson in the Glass House, 1998. © Richard Schulman, www.schulmanphotography.com

Contents

Foreword

Philip Johnson (1906–2005) was one of the exceptional talents of the postwar generation of American architects. For over six decades Johnson helped shape architectural culture as we know it today, in the United States as well as internationally. Possessed of a brilliant intellect, he was a compulsive truth teller, never failing to challenge the accepted canon of architecture. He was an unapologetic aesthete who took pleasure in testing new ideas. At a time when most professionals regarded architecture as the direct consequence of functional and technological problem solving, Johnson embraced the precedence of form. He measured contemporary work against the highest accomplishments from the past, proclaiming that sentient architects "cannot not know history."

Although Johnson was educated at Harvard, in his maturity he was very much, as used to be said, a Yale man. His multifaceted affiliation with Yale began in 1950 when George Howe (1886–1955), newly appointed chair of the department of architecture, hired him as part-time studio critic and public lecturer. Johnson perfectly suited Howe's mission to reform the curriculum, integrating the compositional theories of the International Style with those of the Western classical tradition as a whole, and Johnson's impact on Yale's architecture program was immediate. He was featured in 1952 on the pages of the first issue of Yale's architectural journal, *Perspecta,* with the student editors presenting his work alongside that of Paul Rudolph and Buckminster Fuller. In the next issue his piercing intelligence can be seen in a roundtable discussion with Louis Kahn, Vincent Scully, Pietro Belluschi, and Paul Weiss. In subsequent issues of *Perspecta*, Johnson published two of his most important texts, "The Seven Crutches of Modern Architecture" (*Perspecta* 3) and "Whence and Wither: The Processional Element in Architecture" (*Perspecta* 9/10). Johnson continued his association with the School of Architecture over his long career, as a frequent critic on juries of student work and as public lecturer. Toward the end of his life, in 1999, he accepted an invitation to serve as Eero Saarinen Visiting Professor in the School of Architecture, sharing the responsibility with Peter Eisenman. Johnson was also architect for a number of important Yale buildings, including Kline Geology Laboratory (1963), Kline Chemistry Laboratory (1964), and Kline Biology Tower (1965), as well as the Laboratory of Epidemiology and Public Health (1964). In 1978 the university recognized Johnson with an honorary degree, citing his "combined passion for the new with an appreciation for the excellence of the past" and going on to state that his "generous dedication to others in the profession has inspired greatness in them."

At Johnson's request, there was to be no memorial event following his death. But with the consent of David Whitney (1939–2005), Johnson's companion of over thirty years, Yale, in association with the Museum of Modern Art, the other cultural institution with which Johnson was intimately associated, undertook to evaluate his legacy at a symposium in February 2006. The essays here amplify that evaluation of the historical, theoretical, and political significance of this key architect, and they are thoughtfully edited by Emmanuel Petit, assistant professor at the Yale School of Architecture, and beautifully designed by Michael Bierut. It is my great good pleasure to thank them both.

Robert A. M. Stern
Dean and J. M. Hoppin Professor of Architecture, Yale University

Acknowledgments

This book was made possible by the very generous support of a number of institutions and individuals. I would like to thank the Graham Foundation for Advanced Studies in the Fine Arts, which offered a substantial grant for the project and reconfirmed its dedication to promoting the public dialogue about architecture's role in the arts, culture, and society.

I want to express my appreciation to Elise Jaffe + Jeffrey Brown for critical financial support for this book, enthusiastic dedication to the culture of architectural education, and esteemed friendship. I am grateful to the Whitney Center for the Humanities at Yale, which made available resources from the A. Whitney Griswold Faculty Research Fund to help finance research for the volume. And I also want to thank Terence Riley for a donation to help realize the project.

I extend my gratitude to Yale University Press for publishing this volume. In particular, I thank Michelle Komie, editor, for her enthusiasm for the project, her optimism, and her friendship, and for ushering me through the labyrinth of publishing; Heidi Downey, senior manuscript editor, for her incredible attention to detail during the copyediting process; John Long, photo editor and assistant production coordinator, for his patience and dedication in excavating image material from the library archives. I also thank Emily Schlemowitz for image research in the early stages of the project.

In the School of Architecture, I am grateful to John Jacobson, associate dean, Monica C. Robinson, director of development, Rosemary Watts, office assistant to the business manager, and to Lillian Smith, financial administrator, for managing the resources and finances for the project.

I am grateful to the Museum of Modern Art, New York, and to the Getty Center, Santa Monica, California, for allowing me to do research in their archives.

I thank Dean Robert A. M. Stern for his intense and continuous support throughout this project, and for allowing me to participate in his vision for architectural culture.

I am grateful to Ralitza for her loving dedication to a common project, in architecture and beyond.

Emmanuel Petit

Introduction

Emmanuel Petit

Because I was there, I can talk about things the experts do not know anything about, and they do not dare contradict me, whether I am right or wrong.
—Philip Johnson

How long does an architect live? Ninety-eight years, like Philip Johnson when he died in January 2005? Eternally, like Imhotep? What constitutes the life span of an architect? Does his existence comprise his person, his public persona, a series of ideas and concepts, the *oeuvre complète* of his buildings, or a network of people who contribute to the making of an architect's discourse? With Johnson in particular, the answer to this question is anything but straightforward, and, therefore, allows for unique insights into the multifaceted reality of the world of architects and architecture. Whoever hopes to reconstruct the phenomenon of Philip Johnson from these pages, however, will inevitably encounter the limits of historiography: the illustrious *aura* of the life of Johnson cannot be transcribed or reproduced on paper, yet much of the fascination with Johnson can be ascribed to precisely his charisma and poise.

This collection of texts on Philip Johnson analyzes the cultural influence of the architect beyond the half-life of his person; sixteen scholars, historians, theorists, and practicing architects reflect on this American icon's eclectic and erudite rapport with history, his endorsement of different versions of architectural modernism, his tactical use of rhetoric and the mass media as an architectural modus operandi, his social persona and politics of patronage, as well as his cultural and architectural legacy. Johnson was well aware of the historical process, which he saw himself immersed in, and which he envisioned with metaphors borrowed from Heraclitus, the pre-Socratic philosopher who said: "One cannot step twice into the same river, for the water into which you first stepped has flowed on."[1] In order to enact this credo of constant change—endemic also to the very idea of modernity since the Enlightenment—Johnson relished generating a contradictory Weltanschauung under the banner of Art. The architectural scene *happened to be* the stage on which he could be both impresario and protagonist in this theater of change.

"The practice of architecture is the most delightful of all pursuits," Johnson declared in the inaugural passage of his 1979 acceptance speech for the first Pritzker Prize ever to be awarded. The term "delightful" reveals his bias for architecture as a nontheoretical and nonmethodical art practice. With some philosophical backing from the satirical and poetic Friedrich Nietzsche, Johnson is said to have had no faith in the power of long explanations and intellectual exposés, preferring to leave the technicalities and complications of a coherent architectural theory to others. Every built and written statement of his invokes new inspirations, which he quickly picked up and just as rapidly exchanged with other ideas. As a consequence of this lack of patience, his oeuvre is full of *ideas* even though it shuns the cerebral consistency of *concepts,* which would make his thinking both recognizable and teachable. While keeping theory at a distance, however, Johnson paradoxically liked to keep some of its protagonists close—if not to be instructed by them, then at least to be diverted and aesthetically inspired for his art in a mode of aristocratic, and at times facile, *sprezzatura.* Herein he assumed the role of a "symposiarch," assembling a select group of devoted dialecticians and overseeing the dynamic dialogues between them—a role that he readily assumed when hosting lunches and dinners at the Four Seasons Restaurant (which he designed in New York City), as well as on the academic platform.

In this role Johnson never missed an opportunity to express his playful and amusingly mocking relationship to the value of epistemological systems, cooked up and defended by the so-called experts—historians, theorists, architects, philosophers alike—and suggested that his long-lived experience made him into a connoisseur of a unique kind. The views of Geoffrey Scott helped him argue that artistic judgment was to transcend formulaic theory, and to be just as variable and unpredictable as art itself.[2] What is more, his secure financial and social situation made it possible for him to use the eccentric *mal mot* characteristic of an enfant terrible to express his verdicts on the contemporary experimentations with architectural form; this was part and parcel of a particular worldview, as well as of a marketing strategy for his flamboyant personality.[3] As such, in the mid-1970s he declared: "I don't believe that architecture is ennobling or that music is ennobling. To me, it's merely a matter of kicks. It enhances whatever you're thinking of at that moment.... I think that architecture can give you a kick and it's much like the kick from cocaine I suppose—I never tried it. But a kick is a kick."[4]

This nonchalant approach was at times tainted with brattish and posh cynicism. Nevertheless, his attitude is also attributable to an existentialist streak of thinking that inhabited him. His stance was borrowed from Albert Camus, who declared in *The Fall* that only those who have no character must resort to a method; even though the detached demeanor of Johnson's persona did not ever really create a fundamental anxiety within the discipline of architecture, it nonetheless teased the latter's different intellectual institutions to the point where they had to at least reassess the meaning of their traditions as a "serious, all too serious," discipline— a discipline always refracted in the aura of Johnson's mocking criticism. Johnson played no negligible role in reconfirming the saga of the celebrity-architect, whose judgment in matters of architecture in the form of his endorsement or veto could either make or break whole careers.

For Johnson, only "characters" could make art, and within his worldview, truth is not *found,* but *made* by strong personalities, whose aesthetic sensibility transcends the cognitive faculty of the masses: "Architecture in the main is something that is more apt to be run by popes, kings and generals than by public vote," Johnson stated, "and so I got interested in getting things done in a grand way."[5]

With this confidence in an elite taste and judgment in mind, Johnson liked to freely roam through history in search of the strong "characters" in architecture, which for him were mostly to be found in the Greco-German classical tradition, which he knew well from both his family upbringing and from his early education in the classics and in philosophy at Harvard. Trusting in the judgment of the select few, Johnson saw architecture as an art for the *eyes*—one of the traditional loci of "subjective" perspectivalism, and primordially as a problem of the phenomenal reality: "Eyes are better informers than ears," says Heraclitus.[6] Johnson was thus attracted to the teachings of the architecture historian, who taught him how to "see" history, and designated Henry-Russell Hitchcock the "eye scholar."[7]

Johnson's overt focus on the subjective and aesthetic dimensions of the modern zeitgeist architecture, which he and Hitchcock discovered together in modernist Europe in the late 1920s and early 1930s, opens up some of the most consequential challenges to historiography: what is the relationship between subjects and objects in the construction of a critical historical narrative? In other words, what is the status of Johnson's biography and of the terms of his aesthetic and ethical judgments in determining the significance of his ideas in architecture? The question is critical for a book like the present one, since a great part of the literature on Johnson concentrates on his person, whereas his architecture is often invoked as a mere illustration of his traits of character and persona, or considered of less interest than his colorful life altogether. As a consequence, much of the writing belongs either to the realm of anecdotal hagiography prefaced by Johnson himself, or, much less frequently, to an indiscriminate condemnation of Johnson's detached eclecticism, reaching from accusations of facileness to cynicism.[8] There is a reason for this biography-centered writing on Johnson; this reason is related not only to the idiosyncrasies of the commentators but also to the architect himself in that he understood how to present himself to the media.

While Johnson's most famous and visible moment might well have been when his portrait appeared on the cover page of *Time* magazine in January 1979, holding a model of the newly commissioned AT&T headquarters building, there is an impressive number of newspaper commentaries, film documentaries, and radio and television interviews in which he could broadcast both his character and his ideas to a broad spectrum of spectators. Among the more important documentaries is an early black-and-white film from 1965, directed by Merrill Brockway, entitled "This is Philip Johnson." Johnson's lively and energetic demeanor structures the entire short film, while his architecture is invoked as a sort of by-product of his personality; in particular, the enticing jest and anecdotal humor emerging from his short attention span describe an out-of-the-ordinary architect noticeably lacking the sternness of some of his generational peers, including Skidmore Owings & Merrill's Gordon Bunshaft, Louis I. Kahn, or the slightly younger Paul Rudolph and I. M. Pei. Without a doubt, the medium of the moving picture is singularly suited to capturing this character, who was passionate about constantly relating his thoughts through words, gestures, and grimaces. It is as if the narrative aspect of the film medium duplicated his idea of "procession" in architecture, always leading from one surprising and entertaining event to the next, never standing still. A significant number of short films followed, including "Philip Johnson: Self Portrait" by John Musili in 1985, "The Artist at Work: Philip Johnson" from the Museum of Television and Radio Seminar

Series in September 1991, the BBC's "Philip Johnson: The Godfather of American Architecture" from 1994, "Philip Johnson: Diary of an Eccentric Architect" by Barbara Wolf in 1996, and "Beyond Utopia: Changing Attitudes in American Architecture" by Michael Blackwood Productions in 1997. Many of the narratives in these films focus on Johnson's sharing his memories of architectural history and his views on architecture against the backdrop of his New Canaan compound, the pavilions of which he erected between 1949 (his famous "Miesian" Glass House) and 1998 (the little fan-shaped Dog House). On the one hand, the dense web of his stories, descriptions, and recollections in these films makes architecture appear as the architect's internal monologue turned inside out, presenting the viewer with a lively demonstration of how images move in his head. The collection of buildings on the estate, on the other hand, materializes as his autobiographical storybook and, at the same time, as his architectural memoirs "written" in brick, stucco, steel, and glass. "Clients are so awful," he said. "There is only one good client: that's me." Being an architect, he adds, is "such fun" that each building added to his estate "has been more fun than the last."[9]

In addition to these documentary films Johnson made several appearances on PBS's *Charlie Rose Show* between 1993 and 1996, paired with some of his younger protégés—the "kids," including Frank Gehry, Peter Eisenman, and Charles Gwathmey—and also on the occasion of his ninetieth birthday. Johnson's persona was perfectly geared to television, where colorful and prompt statements are needed and valued.

In hindsight, it almost appears as a comic episode of history that Johnson's friend and professor of architecture at Pratt Institute, Sibyl Moholy-Nagy, would address to him the following question in response to one of his more well-known texts, "The Seven Crutches of Architecture" (1954), in which he dismantled seven central themes of modernist architectural methodology.[10] Moholy-Nagy asked Johnson: "Would you consider to add to your 'Seven Crutches of Architecture' an eighth one: The Crutch of Publicity, with God being less and less in the details and more and more in the advertising copy, and the prerequisite for creating 'significant architecture' less and less a passage through the clouds but more and more a passage through the Journals? Oh, Philip, has this really to be? I am much disturbed."[11]

Moholy-Nagy's expression of dismay against the aesthetic arbitration of the emerging media culture in architecture was addressed to Johnson in a letter dated 1957; little did she know what a skillful media performer Johnson would turn into, and how much the "significance" of his architecture would ultimately be defined through the mechanisms of his media appearance and publicity.

Without a doubt, Johnson argued for the aesthetic basis of the buildings he designed or admired even as he constructed and publicized his own persona *in analogy to* an artistic creation. His self-fashioning in a way emulated the poetic freedom of the aesthetic object—the aesthetic phenomenon, which gives law to itself, and which is self-governing as much as self-canceling. The apparent contradictoriness of much of Johnson's rhetoric, including his self-denigrating and ironic statements about his own person as well as about his architectural talent, is therefore utterly consistent with his faith in an aesthetic ideology.[12] In unspecific attempts to be "spirited" he freely constructed a seemingly inconsistent persona—equally enigmatic as an artifice or an art object. In particular, the quick wit, for which he was so renowned, is in line with this belief in aesthetics, as wit is a rhetorical form of detachment and aloofness that both constructs and depends on its own criteria of "truth." While often creating in his audience a frustrating sense of being played, Johnson also constantly invited his audience to stay tuned for the next episode of "the new him." The aesthetic "object" of the architect's media persona turns into a topic of historiography even more than his buildings do.

The cyclical logic of positing and dissolving—so characteristic of conversational and anecdotal wit—permeated Johnson's worldview. Numerous examples of this apparent indifference and aloofness can be discovered throughout his writings and statements: when he reflected on the International Style exhibition in the context of its fiftieth anniversary, for instance, he claimed that the architect's beliefs are not really part of any operative dimension in the process of architectural design. "We knew that in 1932 architecture was not a question of morals—especially not German political morals. We were anti–Social Democratic to the core, but we never made that into an overt intellectual position. It wasn't necessary, because, as Hitchcock and I have always said, *it makes no difference what the architect believes.* One of the very best of the intellectual architects was Hannes Meyer, who was also the best Communist, and we were *not* pro-Communist."[13]

His tongue-in-cheek attitude is more than apparent in this passage. Elsewhere, Johnson would reinforce his seeming intellectual apathy by emphasizing the necessity for an architect to have strong convictions—even faith—without caring much about a possible "content" of belief: "You have to get away from the straightjacket of the thought process of the early part of the century.... I have never heard of an architect who was broad-minded, because that means shallow, and *you just cannot design without convictions.* I don't know how many Moslems there are present, but *I am sure that faith would help* just as much as being a Marxist or an existentialist."[14]

Here, all beliefs are considered equivalent and exchangeable for the purpose of an architect's creativity; Johnson's pluralism and eclecticism can no doubt be interpreted as his way of defusing the zeitgeist approach of the modern avant-gardes by mocking the importance of the ideological fervor in the architectural process. In this sense, Johnson constructs his worldview systematically in opposition to the status quo where and when it helps to liberate the artistic dimensions of architecture: "We thought that architecture was still an art; that it was something you could look at; that, therefore, architects should not be worried about the social implications, but about whether the work looked good or not. In that sense we had only three allies in the Modern Movement: Le Corbusier, Oud and Mies. Talking to Gropius was a dead end because he would still mouth the Giedionesque platitudes of social discipline and revolution; that is, in Corbusier's phrase, 'if you have enough glass walls, you become free.'"[15]

In addition, Johnson's eclecticism has another very different dimension, in that it has to be read as a symptom of a society oriented toward the market, in which the exchangeability of all goods—including cultural and metaphysical ones—is the highest ideal, and based on the principle of *indifference of beliefs;* let us recall that Karl Marx saw money as a purely aesthetic phenomenon: self-breeding, self-referential, and self-propagating.[16] Very similarly, Johnson's formalism of belief was purged of content, allowing both religious faiths and materially based convictions to be likened to one another: they all turned into the materials with which he built his *Weltanschauung*. The element of change underlying the latter is linked to an unspoken, quasi-Bergsonian trust in the creative potential of intuition; unlike the intellect, intuition is here seen as life-giving and inherently creative without necessarily being progressive or evolutionary.[17] Change is seen as sheer passage or flux without resolution, devoid of any sense of progress. This, too, is part of the aesthetic ideology mentioned earlier, and while Johnson's worldview arguably coalesced in his specific brand of eclecticism as an architect, it also had some bearing on other aspects of his intellectual life.

In particular, Johnson's confidence in elite leadership, combined with a naive fascination with the aesthetics of the spectacle during his early twenties, motivated his controversial political allegiances throughout the nineteen-thirties, when he acted as a German wartime correspondent to Father Coughlin's extreme right-wing paper *Social Justice*.[18] In hindsight, Johnson ascribed this episode to juvenile stupidity, and he dismisses the idea that he went to see a Hitler rally in 1931 or attended one of the Nuremberg Nazi meetings in 1932 for political reasons. Instead, in a series of interviews fifty years later with one of his protégés, Peter Eisenman, Johnson explained that at the time he was a political analphabet, and he blamed these mistakes on his innocent hunger for "total excitement" and his "lust for power."[19] He related that as a young man in Berlin, and far away from home, he felt really free for the first time, and consequently, he saw the Hitler rally as "just one exciting evening," which made him feel "like going to *La Bohème*."[20] Furthermore, he explained that Hitler's authoritarianism impressed him, yet added that "Stalin would have done just as well."[21] Johnson was admittedly under the spell of the spectacular aesthetics of Fascist politics. At the same time, he would insist in interviews that, when he attended the Nazi rallies, the Jewish question had not been in the open yet; this fact was to grant him at least partial redemption. Nevertheless, as Father Coughlin's correspondent as late as 1939—at the brink of Hitler's invasion of Poland—any political naiveté seemed unlikely, and Johnson was clearly sensitive to the presence of Jews in the deserted streets of Polish villages when he wrote: "But here was a real boundary once on the Polish side. I thought at first that I must be in the region of some awful plague. The fields were nothing but stone, there were no trees, mere paths instead of roads. In the towns there were no shops, no automobiles, no pavements and again no trees. There were not even any Poles to be seen in the streets, only Jews!"[22] It is hard to miss certain analogies between the images used in Johnson's description and Camus's metaphors in *The Plague* almost ten years later.

Even one of Johnson's close friends from the Harvard years in the 1920s— the writer, arts advocate, and ballet impresario Lincoln Kirstein, in whose honor Johnson erected a landscape "event" at his New Canaan estate in 1985—would turn antagonistic toward him when Kirstein learned in May 1934 that Johnson and Alan Blackburn had launched a Fascist group called the Gray Shirts, later renamed Young Nationalists. A recent Kirstein biography reveals Kirstein's reaction to Johnson's political attitudes, and the fact that Kirstein urged Alfred Barr to avoid the risk of associating MoMA with certain ideologies. Kirstein even advised Nelson Rockefeller to stay "strictly clear of the pair [Johnson and Alan Blackburn], that otherwise both his family and the MoMA could become tarred with the Fascist brush."[23]

For these early misjudgments—be they ideological or "merely" aesthetic in nature—Johnson has never been as vehemently and openly criticized as other intellectuals with a comparable past, notably the literary critic and Yale professor Paul de Man. De Man had contributed about two hundred articles to the collaborationist papers *Le Soir* and *Het Vlaansche Land* when he was only thirty years of age. It is true that voices were raised and some fingers were pointed at Johnson, notably by Michael Sorkin, Peter Eisenman, and Charles Jencks. Johnson even paid a considerable kill fee to Eisenman so that the interviews the latter conducted with him in 1982 would not be published as Johnson's autobiography until after his own passing and also after the death of his companion David Whitney, the art collector and curator.[24] In de Man's case, the posthumous discovery in the mid-1980s of his early political essays stirred an intellectual scandal of a different kind; the controversy linked de Man's rightist political stance to his formalist approach to the question of language, such as the idea of the ironic incommensurability of all language and the conceptual aporia at the basis of language's aesthetic "effects." What followed was a fierce debate, between de Man's detractors and supporters, about the ethical consequences of aesthetic autonomy. His supporters included Jacques Derrida, who already had come to the defense of Martin Heidegger's divisive acceptance of the Heidelberg University deanship under National Socialism in 1933.[25]

But beyond any moral verdicts, both the Heidegger controversy and the debate around de Man opened unprecedented types of intellectual arguments on the nature and relationship of the aesthetic and the ethic realms in the thinking of artistic form. The foregrounding of the "question of aesthetics" in de Man makes the comparison with Johnson more than relevant, even though Johnson wrote many fewer rightist articles than did de Man. De Man found his nemesis in Marxist theorist Terry Eagleton, among others, and, more specifically, in Eagleton's *Ideology of the Aesthetic.*[26] Conversely, in Johnson's case, the ideological counterattack was never as acutely theorized, and as a consequence his body of thought has not had as disturbing and critical an effect on architectural discourse as de Man had on the interpretation of literature.

This type of intellectual debate is long overdue in the context of an individual who held a key role in the cultural milieu of the American intelligentsia for a large part of the twentieth century. With almost no exceptions, the books on Johnson so far have been of a documentary nature, and have stayed away from speculative and critical considerations of his legacy. Many of them seem even docile and, tellingly, contain a foreword, an interview series, or a postscript by Johnson himself. Even though this book contains no such text, it does not entirely escape his sway; a definite sense of *Nachleben,* or "memory effect," can be felt in many of the contributions; this, however, is unavoidable in the cultural, institutional, and temporal contexts in which this volume appears.

A few significant books on the study of Johnson should be mentioned here. Importantly, a unique volume from 1979 entitled *Philip Johnson: Writings* brings together many of Johnson's own essays from 1931 to 1975.[27] Johnson's texts are put in context in a foreword by Vincent Scully, an introduction by Peter Eisenman, and text commentaries by Robert A. M. Stern. *Writings* remains the most comprehensive collection of Johnson's texts, and it is a valuable primary source for the scholarship on this architect. The essays in this collection allow the reader to follow many of the shifts in Johnson's thinking from the International Style to his advocacy of "traditionalism" and the beginning of his historic revival in architecture. The variety of themes and positions in the book is overwhelming and not reducible in any way—a "quality," which, in his foreword, Scully amusingly attributes to Johnson's "attitudinizings" throughout the thirty-three texts.[28]

Then, Franz Schulze, who had already written a biography on Mies van der Rohe in 1985, published one on Johnson entitled *Philip Johnson: Life and Work* in 1994.[29] This very thorough life story was intended for publication only posthumously, but Johnson finally agreed to have it published in the mid-nineties. The book is structured around five time periods of Johnson's life, highlighting Johnson's childhood in Cleveland, his classical education at the Hackley School and at Harvard College, his first trips to Europe, the struggle with his homosexuality, his infatuation with extreme rightist politics both in the United States and in Europe, his involvement with the Museum of Modern Art, his return to Harvard to study at its Graduate School of Design, the relationships with his main clients and office partners, his break with modernism, and his rise to superstardom. Schulze's meticulous collection of facts about Johnson's life is explicitly narrative, and the author abstains from appraising his significance for architectural discourse.

In 1998, the Museum of Modern Art devoted an issue of its *Studies in Modern Art* to Johnson, one of its central curators, donors, and architects.[30] This strictly historical review discusses the content of the twenty-two hundred works that he donated to the museum's collection between 1932 and 1966, the landmark exhibitions he curated, and the architectural projects he both conceived and executed for the museum, including the Abby Aldrich Rockefeller Sculpture Garden in 1953, his proposal for the museum's extension in 1970, and the Rockefeller Guest House from 1950.

Then, Frank D. Welch published *Philip Johnson and Texas* in 2000, documenting Johnson's special relationship to the state, where some of his largest and most prominent buildings were erected, including the classicizing Amon Carter Museum in 1961, the sculptural and monolithic Art Museum of South Texas in Corpus Christi in 1972, the trapezoid-shaped Pennzoil twin towers in Houston in 1976, the obelisk-like Transco Tower in Houston in 1983, the multi-gabled RepublicBank Center in Houston in 1984, the Gerald D. Hines College of Architecture at the University of Houston in 1985 (a close interpretation of Claude-Nicolas Ledoux's House of Education from 1779), and the barrel-vault-roofed Momentum Place in Dallas in 1987.[31] Furthermore, Welch illustrates Johnson's relationship with his wealthy clients, including Dominique de Menil, Ruth Carter Stevenson, and the developer Gerald D. Hines.

Autonomy and Ideology: Positioning an Avant-Garde in America, edited by Robert Somol, deserves special mention here.[32] The book pulls together the proceedings of a conference in New York City in 1996, organized by Phyllis Lambert and Peter Eisenman and convened by Somol. The conference put to debate the development of architectural discourse in America in the first half of the twentieth century, with special focus on the impact of the European polemics around modern architecture on the United States. While this book is not *on* Philip Johnson properly speaking, it nevertheless acknowledges his crucial presence in animating these discussions for a good part of the century. This scholarly study on the idiosyncrasies and consequences of avant-garde thinking is among the rare theoretical documents to help understand Johnson's context of action and thinking.

Closest in spirit to this last book, the present volume engages in a different type of debate. It is an early attempt to understand the conceptual breadth of Johnson's endeavors in architectural culture during his lifetime, as well as of his legacy following his death; in addition, the theoretical themes and conceptual questions that arise from the extensive analysis of Johnson, the architect, have yielded a barometer of the contemporary debate in architectural thinking. The figure of Johnson prompts some of the field's leading intellectuals to both refine their understanding of "the modern" at the beginning of the new millennium and lay bare their expectations and desires about what can be accomplished with architecture today. In particular, while some of the notions stirred by this debate—including "history," "taste," "power," "sensibility," "*Stimmung,*" "imitation"—might evoke the intellectual atmosphere of the eighteenth century, it becomes clear that Johnson nests them within twentieth-century modernism and discloses his historical moment as ceaselessly elastic and absorptive: Johnson is a paradigm of an assimilative modernism, and he symptomatically assumes a dialectical role in the history of modern architecture; his love for paradox and contradiction already holds an assigned place within our dialectic understanding of history since the Enlightenment.

The first group of chapters in this book deals with Johnson's relationship with history, and his aptitude to appropriate different moments of history and shape them into a personal narrative of self-discovery and self-promotion.

Vincent Scully presents Johnson as an ambivalent modern figure who built his Glass House as the ideal environment for the liberation of the individual. Johnson here is seen as a lonely, existential character whose only community in architectural terms was his series of pavilions and follies, which are inspired by his vivid and personal interest in history, and which are subjectively sited in nature to be viewed from the Glass House. Scully traces parallels between Johnson's architectural intuitions and those of both Frank Lloyd Wright and the architecture of the Roman emperor Hadrian; furthermore, Scully reviews Johnson's formal proclivities, which, as he explains, all served the purpose of seeing history, modernism, and architecture *as art.* Then, Johnson's endorsement of individual judgment, subjective memory, and autobiography as gauges for beauty and as key criteria for art is evident in Kurt W. Forster's consideration of Johnson's New Canaan estate as a museum of personal memories, which inscribes itself in a long series of autobiographical houses throughout the history of architecture, from Giulio Romano to John Soane, and from Thomas Jefferson to Frank Gehry. The creator's self-fashioning impulse makes history appear in the light of the latter's individual experiences, and it allows Forster to draw analogies between the person of Johnson and the atmosphere he created in New Canaan. Forster contends that the best image to describe the atmosphere of Johnson's architecture is the lonely person sitting quietly in the Glass House at night, reflecting. Terence Riley dissects Johnson's letters to his parents during the 1920s and '30s, and shows how Johnson is both influenced by and diverted from Henry-Russell Hitchcock's ideas on modern architecture. Riley also reviews Johnson's impact on the Museum of Modern Art in New York as its first architectural curator, from 1930–34, and discusses a series of exhibitions that Johnson curated, including *Modern Architecture: International Exhibition, Early Modern Architecture: Chicago 1870–1910, Objects: 1900 and Today, Young Architects from the Midwest,* and

Machine Art, as well as the critical reactions to these shows. Beatriz Colomina then focuses on the Glass House in New Canaan and argues that this personal project is to be seen as Johnson's platform on both the professional and the popular media, and as a kind of TV broadcasting studio for the advertisement and promotion of his ideas throughout time. Johnson turned the New Canaan park into a stage on which he could experiment with ever-newer stage sets in the form of his many pavilions, which are set apart from one another both in space and in time. The Glass House, Colomina argues, holds a special position within the history of modern architecture in that it fulfills two recurring visionary dreams of the twentieth century, the all-glass house and television.

The next group of chapters focuses on Johnson's position in society, his political opinions, and his patronage of architects and artists.

Joan Ockman maintains that, despite the apparently shifting point of view in his rhetoric, Johnson had a steady worldview throughout his career, which revolved around two principles: the primacy of art and beauty, and the superiority of the will over reason. Ockman connects these principles to Johnson's ideological and political conservatism and his interest in right-wing thinking and Fascist politics. She analyzes Johnson's rapport with his numerous Jewish friends and with Jewish artists, whose work he collected, and contends that art could have functioned as a means for his moral catharsis. Next, Reinhold Martin concentrates on a particular building of Johnson's, and considers the "pure shapes" of the Pennzoil Twin Towers in Houston as symptoms of a certain market-constellation in a transnational oil economy. For Martin, these shapes tell the story of liquidity and circulation—a tale that can help defuse the fiction of the intra-architectural narrative of the historical transition from "modern" to "postmodern." At Pennzoil, architecture turns into the fetish of oil, with Johnson as the enabler of its promulgation. In a similar effort to read the power structures behind the forms of a building, Kazys Varnelis uses the case study of the AT&T headquarters to discuss the nature and limits of Johnson's networking ability. Varnelis parallels Johnson's network of artists and patrons to the AT&T corporation's network under its chairman John deButts, and speculates that these forms of centralized power structures remain unique to the late seventies and early eighties; today, he argues, the power relations in the global system of architectural culture are much more dispersed, and do not have a place for another Philip Johnson. According to Charles Jencks's text, Johnson's interest in constantly scanning the cultural horizon for the "greatest" men and architects is an imperative of capitalism. Johnson learns the power of the lists—his "Listomania"—both from the idea of the Nietzschean superman and from the modern media, and he promotes it with his own lists, which include groups like "The Five Architects," the eight "Deconstructivists," and "P3." As a consequence, Johnson's contribution is as an impresario of architects in the younger generation, and as a facilitator of the marriage of American money to good architects. Yet ultimately, Jencks argues, Johnson's belief in the Greats "froze his thought and stilled his pen." After that, for his satirical and biting evaluation of Johnson's legacy, Michael Sorkin parodies the architect in a fictional history as imagined in Philip Roth's *Plot Against America*—a novel about the struggles of a Jewish family in 1940 in an imaginary American context, in which Charles Lindbergh, the flying hero who crossed the

Atlantic in 1927, is elected president. This false memoir is embellished by Sorkin's caustic tale of Johnson, who finds himself caught up in a White House initiative to adopt for the United States some principles of the Nazi reconstruction of Germany. Helped by Disney scenographers, Johnson appears as one of the leaders of the New American Villages program, which pilots the implementation of two towns for the harmonious segregation of Negroes and Jews: "New Plantation" in Alabama and "New Warsaw" in Arizona.

The self-understanding of modernism in architecture changed considerably during Johnson's long lifetime, and he himself took an active part in constantly redefining its premise. Four chapters address the question of these transformations.

Detlef Mertins identifies "taste" as an integral part of modernist cultural practices, illustrating how the particular alterations of Johnson's conceptions of taste throughout his life reflect certain shifts within modernism's overall history. Mertins herein pinpoints the change from the understanding of a "commonality" in taste to one of individual preference and personal emancipation. Stanislaus von Moos then finds within the notions of taste and style the core conceptual disagreements among four thinkers of a modern architecture in steady alteration, between Sigfried Giedion, Philip Johnson, Robert Venturi, and Denise Scott Brown. Giedion's overt gendering and degrading of "style" as a "playboy" sensibility only opens a chain of debates between the messianic historian of modernism, the gay and apolitical curator of modern architecture, and the *engagé* architect, who is concerned with the value of popular taste. Giving attention to one particular moment of Johnson's anachronism within the history of modernism, Phyllis Lambert reviews his first break from the International Style in the 1950s and 1960s and situates it in the design of the Four Seasons Restaurant at the Seagram Building, opening in 1959. Here, Johnson introduced into his architecture the notions of sensual and dramatic atmosphere, or *Stimmung,* as a way to supersede Mies's cold rationalism. Mark Wigley then searches for correspondence between the character of Johnson and the type of modernity he stands for: self-promotion and the promotion of a movement are defined as one and the same thing. "Reaction" is used as the key term to define the strategy both of Johnson and of the modern—a reaction, which is neither progressive nor regressive, and which always rewrites the history of the *recent* past as "the modern."

The final section of this book addresses more specifically theoretical questions concerning the notions of aesthetics, of the avant-garde, and of the hegemony of the individual in historical space.

Peter Eisenman addresses the intellectual dissimilarities between Johnson and Hitchcock, and draws comparisons between Johnson's ideological strategies, which brought about two of his most influential exhibitions at the Museum of Modern Art: *Modern Architecture: International Exhibition* and *Deconstructivist Architecture.* In particular, Eisenman attributes Johnson's mindset to the realm of the perception-based "aesthetic" and opposes it to Eisenman's own interest in the theoretical and "formal." He argues that the former is a category of perception leading to historical narratives, while the latter is a category of conception and theory. Therefore, the aestheticization of architecture in Johnson's curatorship should be interpreted not as purging architecture of political content, but, rather, as enacting his rightist political stance against "theory," which he saw as an instrument of the Left. Ujjval Vyas then identifies Johnson's reaction against the zeitgeist fundamentalism that the latter perceived at the basis of twentieth-century artistic production. For Johnson, Vyas argues, the search for "beauty" was the prime engine of artistic renewal—a discourse that eschewed the historical progressivism and moralist undertone of the different forms of avant-gardism, which devote themselves to the search for Truth. Consequently, Johnson's esteem of Mies and J. J. P. Oud can be attributed to their interest in beautiful architectural form and their rebuff of historical, functionalist, and social messianism. And finally, the hegemony of the individual, to which Johnson adds a chapter in history, complicates the architect's relationship to the epistemological spaces of theory and history. Mark Jarzombek evaluates Johnson's role in the long-lasting historical project of the Enlightenment by unraveling the link between ego and architecture. Discussing the historical roles of *Arbeit*/work and Opus—as established by Immanuel Kant—Jarzombek argues that Johnson undoes this distinction with the excess of ease and "fun" that Johnson claims as the foundation of his design "work." Jarzombek concludes that this inclination toward facileness finds its philosophical legitimacy in the deconstructions of the Enlightenment, and Johnson emerges as a figure and symptom within this crisis of the post-Enlightenment.

Notes

Epigraph. From Robert E. Somol, ed., *Ideology and Autonomy: Positioning an Avant-Garde in America* (New York: Monacelli, 1997), 42.

1. Herakleitos, Fragment 21, *Herakleitos & Diogenes,* trans. Guy Davenport (San Francisco: Grey Fox), 14.

2. In a speech at Barnard College on April 30, 1955, Johnson makes clear the difference between the world of "words" and the world of art as he understands it, and which he sees as "anti-word": "Therefore, as a prejudiced practitioner of the art, I can be free to be as non-intellectual and uninhibited as I wish. I must explain the word 'non-intellectual.' I really mean anti-*word,* because the word kills art. The word is abstraction, and art is concrete. The word is old, loaded with accreted meanings from usage. Art is new. The word is general—art is specific. Words are mind—art is eyes. Words are thought—art is feeling." "Style and the International Style," in Johnson, *Philip Johnson: Writings,* foreword by Vincent Scully, introduction by Peter Eisenman, commentary by Robert A. M. Stern (New York: Oxford University Press, 1979), 73.

3. In 1924, Johnson's father, Homer, gave Philip speculative stocks of the Aluminum Corporation of America; at the end of the 1920s, the Alcoa stocks soared and made Philip Johnson a millionaire.

4. Philip Johnson, interviewed by Lee Radziwill, "Fancy Speaking: Architect Philip Johnson Indulges the Lady in a Great Conversation," *Esquire,* December 1974, p. 160; IV.7, Philip Johnson Papers, Museum of Modern Art Archives, New York (hereafter PJ, MoMA Archive).

5. Quotation from *International Herald Tribune,* December 5–6, 1992: Michael Z. Wise, "The Latest Incarnation of Philip Johnson."

6. Herakleitos, Fragment 12, *Herakleitos & Diogenes,* 13.

7. Johnson designates Henry-Russell Hitchcock an eye scholar in the "Hitchcock Festschrift," Architectural History Foundation, Inc., July 1982; 980060.38.6, Philip Johnson Papers, Getty Center Archive, Santa Monica, Calif. (hereafter PJ, Getty Center Archive).

8. *ANY* magazine published its special issue number 90, the "Philip Johnson festschrift," for Johnson's ninetieth birthday in 1996. While both the choice and large number of authors in the volume demonstrated Johnson's connectedness, virtually all the contributions appear as insider stories and anecdotes, none of which were very informative on a factual and historical level, nor did they contain any critical arguments about architecture. While this problem might be symptomatic of festschrifts in general, this *ANY* issue is an example of the emphasis of Johnson's person and biography in the writing about this architect. The contributors to this journal were Cynthia Davidson, Wolf Prix, Francesco dal Co, Jean-Louis Cohen, James Rosenquist, Suzanne Stevens, David Childs, Robert A. M. Stern, Robert Rosenblum, David Salle, Hans Hollein, Kevin Roche, Frank Gehry, Richard Meier, Arata Isozaki, Michael Graves, Charles Gwathmey, Rem Koolhaas, Charles Jencks, Jeffrey Kipnis, Jacquelin Taylor, Phyllis Lambert, Fritz Neumeyer, Paul Rudolph, Daniel Libeskind, Richard Serra, Stanley Tigerman, Herbert Muschamp, Zaha Hadid, Terence Riley, Paul Goldberger, Peter Eisenman, Vincent Scully, and Henry Cobb.

Another example of a mere collection of anecdotes about Johnson is *Layout Philip Johnson: In Conversation with Rem Koolhaas and Hans Ulrich Obrist;* the volume was published by Walther König in Cologne in 2003, and it seems geared toward demonstrating Johnson's elusiveness in replying to interviewers' questions.

9. Philip Johnson quotation from an interview in the documentary "Philip Johnson: Diary of an Eccentric Architect" (New York: Checkerboard Film Foundation, 1996).

10. The arguments in Johnson's "Seven Crutches of Architecture" were first delivered as an informal talk to students at Harvard in December 1954, and then published in *Perspecta* 3.

11. Sibyl Moholy-Nagy, Letter to Philip Johnson on March 30, 1957; IV.5, PJ, MoMA Archive.

12. I purposefully choose the expression "aesthetic ideology" here in reference to the formalist literary critic Paul de Man's collection of essays published as *Aesthetic Ideology,* edited with an introduction by Andrzej Warminski (Minneapolis: University of Minnesota Press, 1996). Philip Johnson and Paul de Man share a number of biographical attributes and ideological convictions, which I will address in the text.

13. "Johnson Is Interviewed by Peter Eisenman," *Skyline,* February 1982, p. 14 (emphasis added); 980060.38.1, PJ, Getty Center Archive.

14. *Philip Johnson: Writings,* 230 (emphases added).

15. "Johnson Is Interviewed," *Skyline,* p. 14; 980060.38.1, PJ, Getty Center Archive.

16. See this idea developed in Terry Eagleton, *The Ideology of the Aesthetic* (Oxford: Basil Blackwell, 1990), 201.

17. In *Creative Evolution* (original French in 1907, English translation in 1911), Henri Bergson sees intellect and intuition as opposite facets of the work of consciousness. He argues that intuition goes in the very direction of life, whereas intellect goes in the inverse direction.

18. Among Johnson's articles in *Social Justice* were "Letter from Munich" (September 2, 1939), "Poland's Choice Between War and Bolshevism Is a 'Deal' with Germany" (September 11, 1939), "This 'Sitdown' War. Heavy Engagements of the Fortnight Have Been on Economic and Moral Front" (November 6, 1939), "War and the Press: Propagandists Who Fight with Lies Always Lose When Truth Attacks" (November 6, 1939).

19. Peter Eisenman, transcript of an interview with Philip Johnson, October 1982, p. 10; 980060.38.2–4, PJ, Getty Center Archive.

20. Ibid., 69.

21. Ibid., 9.

22. Johnson, "Poland's Choice Between War and Bolshevism"; 980060.36.3, PJ, Getty Center Archive.

23. Kirstein is quoted in Martin Duberman, *The Worlds of Lincoln Kirstein* (New York: Knopf, 2007), 236.

24. Eisenman taped this series of interviews with Johnson in October 1982, intending to use them as a basis for Johnson's autobiography: it was planned that Eisenman's voice would be removed from the transcript, and that the text would be written in Johnson's first person. The kill fee paid by Johnson was $10,000. Later, in 1994, Franz Schulze released a comprehensive version of Johnson's biography entitled *Philip Johnson: Life and Work* (New York: Knopf, 1994). In Eisenman's interview series, Johnson liked to be elusive about the motivations behind his decision to attend a Hitler rally; in particular, he disconnected the realms of politics and aesthetics, but he also added remarks that confused the distinction between the two: To Eisenman's question as to the connection between aesthetics and his more personal motivations, Johnson replied: "No. You see, the three never mixed: the politics, sex, and the architecture" (pp. 57–58). But a few sentences later, upon Eisenman's insistence on the topic, Johnson says in his usual paradoxical rhetoric: "The only connection was a nonconnection, which is amusing" (p. 61), and adds then: "Those little anecdotes will help." 980060.38.2–4, PJ, Getty Center Archive.

25. See Richard Wolin, ed., *The Heidegger Controversy: A Critical Reader* (Cambridge, Mass.: MIT Press, 1993).

26. Terry Eagleton, *The Ideology of the Aesthetic* (Oxford: Basil Blackwell, 1990).

27. *Philip Johnson: Writings.*

28. The selection of thirty-three texts to stand for Johnson's ideas appears to be another "formalist" play of the editors of the book on the year 1933, when Hitler was voted into power.

29. Schulze, *Life and Work.*

30. John Elderfield, ed., *Philip Johnson and the Museum of Modern Art,* Studies in Modern Art 6 (New York: Museum of Modern Art and Harry N. Abrams, 1998).

31. Frank D. Welch, *Philip Johnson and Texas* (Austin: University of Texas Press, 2000).

32. Robert E. Somol, ed., *Autonomy and Ideology: Positioning an Avant-Garde in America* (New York: Monacelli, 1997).

ROAMING THROUGH HISTORY.

Philip Johnson: Art and Irony

Vincent Scully

Philip Johnson was the most emblematic of modern men, the most Protean of figures, always changing, and living almost a hundred years, brilliant, elusive, ambiguous to the last. A true work of modern art himself. In the end, what is the meaning of that long career? The hypothetical syllabus of a course on modern architecture might read:

Philip Johnson, 1906–2005
The International Style and Its Collapse
History. Postmodernism. Neomodernism and Expressionism.

All that seems accurate enough. But it doesn't begin to do justice to Johnson, whose unique presence on the architectural scene was hardly confined to his work as a practicing architect. He was a character, a special kind of cultural presence, like Frank Lloyd Wright, whose successor, perhaps in a more sociological than architectural way, and in the popular mind, he almost was. But the times were different. Wright remained a turn-of-the-century radical throughout his life while, late in the century, Johnson became a kind of power broker on the architectural scene.

Still, despite the obvious differences between them, they had much in common (fig. 1). Both were American confidence men, adept at self-promotion and the flattery of clients. One was surely a great architect, the other perhaps not, but at the very beginning of his career, and probably outdoing anything he was to accomplish later, Johnson somehow managed to build what may well turn out to be the most conceptually important house of the century, and when he visited Taliesin West back then, Wright said: "The prince is visiting the king."

But this was the occasion at Yale in 1955 when Wright, grumbling about not having been met at the train station, came upon Johnson at the obligatory cocktail party in Hendrie Hall and said, "Why, Philip, I thought you were dead." And then, still grumbling, he turned back toward Philip, now abashed and trying to hide among the students across the room, and in a stentorian voice that rang throughout the hall, cried, "Why, Philip, little Phil, all grown up, building buildings and leaving them out in the rain." Later that night Johnson gave Wright the finest introduction I have ever heard, describing the ritual procession through Taliesin West and, coming at last to the fire burning in the heart of the desert, said, "I wept." Johnson often wept for Art, never for himself that I know of, and rarely for mankind. His services, like those of most architects, and for which he called himself a whore, were for the rich, not the poor. It was all Acropolis for him, never really the town, for whose complex problems his attention span was too short and his impatience too demanding. Community was not for him: he was fundamentally lonely, the existential individual on guard in the world.

But they aged in dramatically different ways. The elderly Wright was aglow with nineteenth-century self-satisfaction, but Johnson grew fragile, vulnerable, worn down physically, and perhaps spiritually, by the many transformations of his life, standing near the end of it in the mournful shadows of a cavernous building designed by him but totally different from the Glass House of his youth, and directly inspired by the work of much younger men. Brendan Gill wrote that Wright wore many masks. So did Johnson. But we know who Wright was. Who was Johnson? That question is not easy to answer, and I am not sure that I answer it adequately here. I think—perhaps unsettled by some of the facts his biographer Franz Schulze forces us to consider—that I haven't properly conveyed my own personal experience of him, which was of personal charm, quickness of mind, kindness, and professional generosity. I thought of him as a friend.

And I rashly agreed to write this essay because I felt that he had not been fairly treated in most of his obituaries. These tended to focus on his unsavory political alliances of the 1930s, which, utterly ineffectual and thus essentially harmless as they turned out to be, still suggested some cruel flaws of character, but for the foolishness of which so long ago one can hardly feel other than dismay, regret, and compassion now. But Schulze comes down so heavily on those events and on Johnson's sexual life that I feel compelled to try to confront some of the issues they raise—though avoiding, I hope, an evaluation of art to fit the character of the artist, as is all too common today. I want to focus on Johnson's long, strange, often spectacular career as an architect, beginning well after his early prominence as historian, curator, and critic at the Museum of Modern Art, and especially on the early days of the 1940s and 1950s, when his words and buildings had an important

fig. 1 Philip Johnson with Frank Lloyd Wright, c. 1953

effect upon the thought and practice of my generation, especially at Yale, and certainly upon me as an art historian when I began. It was he who insisted from the beginning, and never throughout his life ceased to insist, that architecture was an art. That sounds banal enough today, thanks partly to him, but it didn't then. When he stood up in old Room 100 about 1950 and said, "I'd rather sleep in the nave of Chartres Cathedral with the nearest john three blocks down the street than I would in a Harvard house with back-to-back bathrooms," it was a liberation for many of us.[1] It broke through the very real limitations imposed upon thought and perception by the dull functionalism of Walter Gropius and the obsessed technocracy of Buckminster Fuller, and it permanently enraged the followers of both those men. Even for me at the time it had a slightly sacrilegious sound, and one was always a little wary of Johnson. He didn't think quite like the rest of us—perhaps because he was not only much richer but also much better educated in Greek and philosophy (and at Harvard) than most of us were. And his manners, with their deceptively self-deprecating tone and their inveterate irony, were, like his early prejudices, a result of the gentlemanly education of an earlier day. Still, his classical pessimism, even his existential detachment, seemed products more of the pagan than of the Christian centuries. He thought, however flippantly, in pitiless realities, like a classic Greek or a Stoic Roman of the Empire, a born rhetorician, witty, truly funny, an incomparable demagogue on the lecture platform.

The century's "will to power" was certainly his. We can leave it to Schulze to ascribe that set of mind to Johnson's early reading of Nietzsche, along with his focus upon art, which was for Nietzsche the most perfect expression of the will to power (as it clearly was in Antiquity), and also his engrossing belief in the necessity for change, upon which Nietzsche most vehemently insisted. Both ideas were disastrously if temporarily transferred to political action in the 1930s. But, as Walter Benjamin so brilliantly noted at the time, Fascism literally aestheticized politics, and we may surmise that it was so for Johnson. It was all art, German art—Speer's overwhelming ceremonies, the uniforms, the classic Mercedes—that did for him rather more, I think, than the ideas of Nietzsche and Ortega. Art and the inevitability of change. "I have no faith whatever in anything," Johnson said many times. "The only actuality is change." Out of that cast of mind Johnson's life-long belief in the young surely came. It was they who best embodied change, after all, and he was unusually kind and generous to younger colleagues throughout his life, and, we might add, gave a good deal up toward the end of it to follow them—though some might say that he also hoped to co-opt their movement and direct its course himself. He was indeed a fast follower and an inspired co-opter throughout his life. His many stylistic "changes," unlike those of Picasso, were never initiated by him, but represented his emulation of the forms and objectives of other men: Mies, the Emperor Hadrian, Stern, Venturi, Eisenman, Gehry, and the others. Nor, within each phase of change, does Johnson's work show any development to speak of. It is all there at first and, when used up, can only be discarded for something else. That's why Johnson was especially supportive of the young. They were the engine of his life.

He was certainly kind to me when I met him in New Canaan in 1948. The Glass House was in building, the Glass House which, scandalously at the time, seemed directly to imitate the work of a master, as architects had normally begun their careers by doing in the past. Believing, as he always said, that it was better to be

fig. 2 Ludwig Mies van der Rohe, collage for Resor House, Jackson Hole, Wyoming, c. 1937

good than to be original, and perhaps understanding his own limitations, Johnson had submitted to the forms of Mies rather than the pedagogy of Gropius. But he never had the manual facility to draw very well, whether in 1942 or so at Harvard or late in life. When, years later, I asked him why he had terminated his postmodern phase, he at once replied, "Because I couldn't draw well enough." Therefore, we are not surprised when Gehry tells us how eagerly Johnson took to the magic of the computer. He had badly needed all the highly skilled people who had drawn and drafted for him over the years, and had relieved him of many other professional chores, among them Landis Gores, Richard Foster, John Burgee, John Manley, and many others who rarely have been credited for their work. In this sense Johnson was always a kind of amateur—or the historian as architect, as he sometimes called himself. He was a conceptual artist who communicated his unusually clear and highly intelligent vision of form to his staff with rough sketches and pictorial words. It was all empathy for him, the physical identification of the viewer with the object viewed, which he had learned from his reading of Geoffrey Scott and found in the purest and most basic of forms in Mies.

Mies differentiates so beautifully between sculpture and architecture. He defines them. It is a classic vision: sculpture is body, architecture is space. With sculpture, human beings embody their presence and their acts; with architecture they shape the environment for that presence and those acts. In the Barcelona Pavilion, the human act is even shown to create the environment. With the courthouses of the thirties, the body becomes quiet. Calm, solid Maillol is set in a frame of perfect space, the ideal environment for the individual, cut off from the chaos of community outside. That's what Johnson wanted. Hence his courthouse in Cambridge. But then Mies goes further. In the Resor project in the heart of the Rockies, he opens out the individual's environment to the whole of the visible world, indeed to nature at its most awesome and sublime, the Grand Tetons filling the horizon (fig. 2). It is most moving, almost nothing, but everything. The European abandons his closed garden to embrace the vast new continent, the new world. Neil Levine has called it the

fig. 3 Nicolas Poussin, *Landscape with the Funeral of Phocion,* 1648

"architecture of exile." Johnson picks that up, in a sense domesticates it or, perhaps like the Museum of Modern Art as a whole, makes it livable and comfortably middle class. Now a gentle frame of trees shapes the boundaries of the space, his "wallpaper," as Johnson called them. Mies's classic figure, now rather louche, is there. And now the inhabitant is open to nature on all four sides but is still alone, and he has to own enough of the natural world to ensure his privacy. He has to be alone. No community group of buildings can be built on this model unless they retreat to the closed court.

Of course Mies had already done almost the same thing in the Farnsworth House. But how different the two buildings are. As many have pointed out, Mies emphasizes the structural frame, subordinates the glass. Johnson does the opposite. His frame is substantial but neutral.

The glass dominates. It is given a plate rail, a dado, which makes us feel it as containing a volume. So Mies's building can be read traditionally, as a structural body, and can also recall, in the special elements of its design, the porch and the stairs, great loggias and monumental stairways. Johnson gives all that up. His house is simply space for a person, not an active force. It recalls almost nothing. So one of the basic desires of modern architecture—the liberation of the individual—is achieved here. That liberation had been central to modern art as a whole; freeing the individual from society, from family, from history, and leaving him alone with nature so long as he can plug into the going sources of power. Between him and nature is only a glass wall.

Johnson also makes his house big enough to live in, which the Farnsworth House barely is. And he has the Brick House to retreat to when necessary. In both the Glass House and the Brick House, however, the circle is an element that catches our eye and seems different from everything else. It seems very important to Johnson all through the studies of the Glass House, in which circular forms constantly reappear. He keeps working on them over time, and finally he tells us in the famous publication of the Glass House in the *Architectural Review* that he derives the circle from a painting by Malevich. In that same publication he says the following, which caught the eye of Peter Eisenman years ago as it also caught mine. He writes, "The cylinder, made of the same brick as the platform from which it springs, forming the main *motif* of the house, was not derived from Mies, but rather from a burnt wooden village I saw once where nothing was left but foundations and chimneys of brick. Over the chimney I slipped a steel cage with a glass skin. The chimney forms the anchor."

Where had Johnson been likely to see a burnt village if not in Poland, into which he traveled with the German invasion in 1939 as a correspondent for Father Coughlin's anti-Semitic rag *Social Justice*? And he did refer in writing to the burning of Warsaw as a "stirring spectacle." If so, what is this thing doing here? Is Johnson exorcizing it all through art, expiating it, as we might like to believe? Or, more likely, is it merely the amoral working in him of the artistic process, ruthlessly making use of whatever is useful to itself? Whatever the case, he seems compelled to refer to it, and his associational reactions, as he sat in front of his fireplace, must have been far more shadowed and complex than any visitor could imagine. In his liberation to nature he had not managed to leave memory behind.

Peter Eisenman told me that when he wrote about this, Johnson talked to him on the phone and said that he wept when he read it. So maybe there was some real sorrow, some regret, inside him about it all. Whatever the case, I had no such associations in 1950 when I wanted to build the cheapest possible house I could (and it was cheap: 1,800 square feet built for $17,500), I based it on Johnson's model, modified as a wooden frame structure open around a central cinder block core which, I am sorry to say, had to be much larger than Johnson's brick chimney. It housed a family with three children, and while Johnson's house is not intended for family life, my take on it worked out quite well for us. I had, of course, to put in some exterior wall bracing because I could not afford rigid joints in welded steel at the corners. So I built diagonally braced planes of wall at intervals, derived, visually at least, from the screens that Johnson used, especially at that time, to move around against the sun. I tried to make them look as if they could slide on the plate. On the other hand, the house clearly shows that although it may work for a family, it is really not right for that function. The Glass House model is for one person alone. Still, its elegant simplicity makes it a truly minimal type as well, the least expensive of structures, a fine camp, a barn. But there is more than that to the experience of Johnson's house. It involves the painting that is still right there next to the hearth, and Johnson contemplated the two together throughout his life. It is either by Nicolas Poussin himself, or is a very fine seventeenth-century replica (of which there were several). It is called *Landscape with the Funeral of Phocion* (fig. 3). Philip knew all about Phocion from Plutarch, who tells us that Phocion was a conservative Athenian statesman of the fourth century, an oligarch and a friend of Philip and Alexander of Macedon, thus in effect a collaborator with Macedon in its conquest of Greece. After the death of Alexander, the restored Athenian democracy forced him to drink the hemlock, and decreed that he be buried outside the borders of Attica, which is what is happening here. And here is Johnson, a kind of would-be oligarch, a far-right-wing politician who leaves New York (perhaps in imagination banished from it) and is now sitting out here in the country in what can be thought of as a self-imposed exile. Plutarch clearly believed that the execution was unjust. Maybe Philip did too, and perhaps he felt that the painting offered, if not a justification, at least a kind of explanation of it all. Certainly he treasured it throughout his life, refusing on several occasions to replace it with a more contemporary abstract work.

fig. 4 George C. Oneto House, Irvington-on-Hudson, New York, 1951

fig. 5 Robert C. Leonhardt House, Lloyd's Neck, Long Island, New York, 1956

And there is even more: Poussin painted another scene that Plutarch describes, in which Phocion's widow gathers up his ashes and smuggles them back into Athens, where she buries them near the family hearth. And here is Johnson looking at painting and hearth together, like talismans.

Whatever the case, all these events and associations usher in what may, in fact, have been the most wholly satisfactory part of Philip's career, the only one that was entirely within his limitations, the one he could handily control. And he did so, designing beautiful, quite small houses out in the country (one thinks, ruefully, of the degraded megamansions of today), some of which might fit right into Poussin's painting itself: the Oneto House on the Hudson, very close to Mies, like a miniaturization of the great Resor project; or, equally close, the cantilevered Leonhardt House, which is based directly on a famous drawing by Mies (figs. 4, 5). Others, like the Wiley House, are more playful (fig. 6). Wright's comment about leaving buildings out in the rain might have been suggested by this toylike building. Mies did not like it either. He felt that the living room ceiling was much too high. But then this inspired Phocion-Johnson ventures back into town and builds for his oligarchical friends at the Museum of Modern Art, especially the gem of the Rockefeller Guest House with its wonderful interior courtyard, and then, by 1954, the incomparable sculpture garden at the museum itself, which has survived all the subsequent changes in that institution and its manifold re-buildings (figs. 7, 8). It is truly urbane, with an elegance that no other architect, I think, could have equaled at that period. For the first time in postwar American architecture, it brought what amounted to a traditional urban garden back into the heart of the city.

It was about this period in Johnson's life that I wrote in 1961, "Johnson, at his best, is admirably lucid, unsentimental, and abstract, with the most ruthlessly aristocratic, highly studied taste of anyone practicing in America today. All that nervous sensibility, lively intelligence, and a stored mind can do, he does. One must take him as he is."[2] It is a qualified endorsement, clearly implying some brittleness and limit, but it was sincerely meant as a tribute to what seemed to be Johnson's

unique qualities at the time. But instantly, by the early 1950s, Johnson became impatient, and he turned toward Rome, especially toward Hadrian's Villa, to which he went in the summer of 1952. I know he did because my wife and I met him in Venice, by chance, in the spring of that year and told him he had to. I had just spent a wonderful year under the influence of the great archaeologist Frank E. Brown of the American Academy in Rome. Brown was making a whole new generation of artists and historians realize that Roman architecture was not at all the dreary affair of soulless engineering that the beaux-artists and the modernists alike seemed to have regarded it as being, but rather a poetry of columns and water, vaulting and light (fig. 9). Brown was making some of the key people in modern architecture see Rome afresh. At the same time, Marguerite Yourcenar was writing her beautiful book *Memoires d'Hadrien,* an incomparable biography, and Eleanor Clark her *Rome and a Villa,* in which she dedicated the chapter about Hadrian's Villa to Brown.

fig. 6 Robert C. Wiley House, New Canaan, Connecticut, 1953

fig. 7 Rockefeller Guest House, New York, interior, 1950 [AD140]

fig. 8 Abby Aldrich Rockefeller Sculpture Garden, east view, Museum of Modern Art, New York, 1953 [PA245]

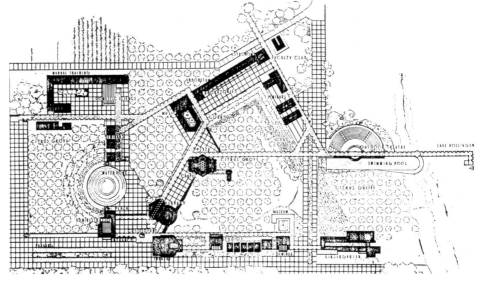

Johnson and Hadrian had a lot in common. First of all, Hadrian is the most Hellenic, the most scholarly, the most archaeological of all the great Antonines. He was a philosopher, and the first Roman emperor to have himself shown with a beard, which had marked the philosopher since Hellenistic times. Hadrian was also the first to have the sculptor cut the pupils of his eyeballs so that there seemed to be a live intelligence behind them. He was a scholar in Greek, Latin, and Etruscan. He must have been one of the last people in the world to learn that old language. His consuming passion, though, was architecture. Like Philip, he took that passion outside the city: to Tivoli, just under the Apennines. In that archetypal location, below the mountain, among Latium's gardens, vineyards, and wheat, he built an elaborate speculation upon the whole history of architecture, and a living memorial to its sacredness in the past. It was believed, in his time, that most of his buildings directly referred to earlier models, usually invoking some ancient sacred site, and that may be largely true. But the Villa is most of all an arrangement of courtyards and gardens, running out on free diagonals across the landscape, flowing with water, canopied with fantastic vaults. The site as a whole, as Frank Brown once put it, "is the first place in Latium where one can stand on tip toe and just barely not see Rome." It has abandoned the city. And the most eloquent drawing ever made of that idea, looking out toward Rome along the so-called philosopher's walk, is by Le Corbusier, made when he visited there in 1910. In it we perceive that empty horizon far off, and somehow Rome just under it. More than that, the major building around which everything else at the Villa seems to spin is that circle in the center of the plan which is an island surrounded by water, with a Greek library on one side and a Latin library on the other. It has normally been called the Maritime Theater, without much reason, and it sets up a musical pattern of columns fanning out from the center of the island, causing it to spin within the circle of water. It is beyond question that the whole plan of the villa and that circle in particular had an enormous effect on Frank Lloyd Wright when he was putting Florida Southern College together in the 1930s (fig. 10). He transforms the circle into what he calls a water dome and sends a simplified edition of Hadrian's diagonals out from it into space. Indeed, Hadrian's apparently very free, almost anarchic diagonals, suggesting contemporary deconstructivist planning, later became very typical of Roman villas and country houses. Hadrian is the first to develop them. We cannot help but see that Wright, too, thought he could use them himself.

I suspect that there is a little touch of them in Taliesin West, where it is all diagonals, and when we finally arrive at the climactic view, it turns out to be one in which, like Le Corbusier standing on tiptoe, we were intended to be just barely not able to see Phoenix. Now, of course, Phoenix has intruded upon it. But the most common kind of building that Hadrian built tends to be voluminously enclosed on the Roman model, like his *triclinium,* the grand banquet hall, whose columns rise within the hollows filled with water and light, and support some incomprehensible canopy of vaulting up above. It was surely believed in Hadrian's time that there is an image in these magical enclosures of the ancient pre-Roman Mediterranean worship of the goddesses of the earth, so appropriate there at the villa, as we find them in the Neolithic temples of Malta, for example, a pre-Greek Demeter and Persephone, those same female shapes. The male column stands inside them. Wright did exactly this late in life, in his own Roman phase. In his Martin Spence project, for example, the circles, the enclosures, the columns inside and the water all recall Hadrian. And Johnson, right away in his Lucas project of 1953, uses circular forms and columns that clearly relate to Wright and probably also to Hadrian (fig. 11).

But the building that Johnson first designed under the influence of the villa is related not to the dining hall but to the so-called Small Baths just behind it, where we find an oval antechamber off the main vault with a vertical black void down its center (fig. 12). That is exactly what Johnson re-created in his synagogue at Port Chester, New York, of 1954, as the entrance to the main body of the building, within which he employed hung vaults that are made to look hollow and weightless and held up by air (fig. 13). It's what the Romans wanted in general: an image of heaven, as Karl Lehmann-Hartleben pointed out long ago, as found in the wind-blown canopies

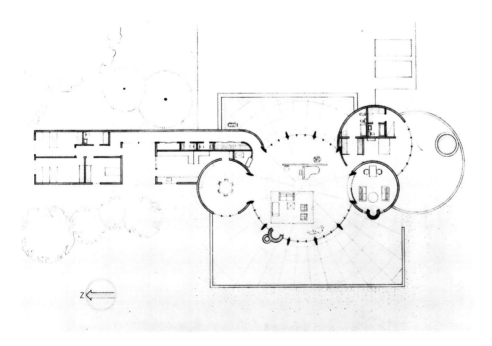

fig. 11 John Lucas House, Nantucket, Massachusetts, 1953

fig. 12 Small baths behind Hadrian's Villa

fig. 13 Kneses Tifereth Israel Synagogue, hung vaults, Port Chester, New York, 1956

of Etruscan mirrors. The Roman vaults, actually of heavy concrete, were all detailed so that if there were columns involved, as in the Baths of Caracalla and Pennsylvania Station, they looked as if they were holding the vaults down in tension, not supporting them. And to Johnson's credit, I think he recognized that in Pennsylvania Station; he was almost the only architect, along with John Lindsay, a congressman at that time, and Aline Louchheim, Eero Saarinen's second wife, to picket its mindless demolition in 1963. Most of the rest of us, I am sorry to say, did not seem to care.

Nevertheless, most of Johnson's work inspired by Roman vaulting, like his redesign of the guest bedroom in the Brick House, was undeniably small in scale. Many people have noted the relationship of these thin-shelled vaults to the work of Soane, and it is true that their little wind-blown canopies seem superficial when compared to their models. And that tended to be our view of Johnson and Rome, partly because Louis Kahn was also under the spell of Frank Brown at that time, and he worked with Roman ruins in a way that was sterner than Johnson's, much more concerned with structure and mass. Although he did go to the villa, Kahn was also involved with Brown's more proletarian examples of Roman brick and concrete construction, like Ostia and Trajan's Market. From these Kahn seemed to be making a powerful and primitive new architecture, indeed to be rediscovering modern architecture's beginnings in Piranesi and the eighteenth-century sublime. There was a deep archaic power that Johnson did not possess. However, Johnson seems to do pretty well with Rome when compared with other architects of the time. Saarinen, for example—also touched by Rome in these years—set his chapel at MIT within a circular moat, almost re-creating the Maritime Theater. He also seems to be trying to make his interior wall undulate, and he did the same thing, even more obviously, at Brandeis, also part of his Roman series. One tends to think that what he had in mind here was one of those great combinations from the villa, especially the so-called Piazza D'Oro, where Hadrian started with one of what Trajan called his "pumpkins," and then directs a colonnaded courtyard to the wonderful, climactic dance of the Nyphaeum's undulating walls.

But Saarinen's is a very feeble attempt at re-creating all this, whereas Johnson, working on exactly the same forms, does rather better, and in an appropriate place, in New Harmony, Indiana, for Robert Owen's gentle community. Johnson called the ensemble an outdoor church, and it is in fact a courtyard, like one of Hadrian's, invoking a sacred temenos. The curvilinear building that terminates the precinct does seem to have grown out of the earth, as though from the wheat fields that stretch out below it. And here in that culminating, even germinating, form, which is so much closer to Hadrian in shape and intention than any of Saarinen's ever were, Johnson, was surely making use of the skills and interests of a young Yale graduate named James Jarrett (at that time James Padavic), a brilliant student who traveled with me in Greece in the summer of 1955 and became deeply committed to Frank Brown, working on archaeological digs in Italy and then in Johnson's office. Again there is a connection of Johnson with someone very young—in this case, an intermediary between Hadrian and himself. And at this point, Johnson was very pleased with what he was doing, as he asserted at Yale in 1959, in a talk that he called "Whither Away—Non-Miesian Directions."

> *The idea that clarity, simplicity, logic and honesty is the best policy, that these "virtues" will get you anywhere, falls down in many ways, and in other fields than architecture. The emergence of existentialism, with its noble philosophy that cuts across Christian and atheist thought [He should, I think, have said "Antique thought"], has changed some of our most cherished values....*
>
> > *My passion is history. I pick up anything, any old point in time or place. I couldn't design without history at my elbow all the time.... I would propose it as a substitute for the debacle of the International Style, which is now in ruins around us.... I think we are getting to a splitting up that is fantastic. I think we are all galloping off in all directions, and all I can say is, "Here we go! Let's all go to the races and have fun!" My own particular thing is "Hurray for history, and thank God for Hadrian, for Bernini, for Le Corbusier..."*[3]

fig. 14 Amon Carter Museum of Art, Fort Worth, Texas, 1961

fig. 15 Aerial view of Lincoln Center, New York

Then, in 1960 he says something very revealing in a talk at the Architectural Association in London—that is, to people who took architecture very seriously in sociological and political terms. He says, "I am too far gone in my relativistic approach to the world. . . . I have no faith whatever in anything. It neither helps nor hurts my architecture." And then, something rather sad but perfect for his audience: "Where there are political passions it is easier to have architectural passions. Since passion is absent, let us do as we please."

And what he pleased to do was build a nuclear reactor for Israel, political passion apparently all spent. He was proud to insist that he and Teddy Kollek, the famous mayor of Jerusalem, were good friends, as he was with many other Israelis. What he gave them was again Hadrianic: the courtyard of the Piazza D'Oro, now with its colonnade, climaxing in the closest approximation one can get in a nuclear reactor to its undulating sanctuary. It seems a rather powerful take on Hadrian, who also had some anti-Semitism in his record, and it was very important to Johnson.

On the other hand, right at that time and clearly responding to the villa, he tried to expand the scale of his compound at the Glass House, making it a kind of villa itself, a generous garden. So he built his little folly in the pool far below the house, and to make it look even farther away he did so at miniature scale. It is not as high as a human being is tall. He loved to be photographed all scrunched up inside it. All this aroused the ire of some of our most conspicuous critics, again British, who discerned a kind of evil in it, and described it as "effete" and "decadent." Philip replied to them in a very dignified way. He wrote, "I designed and built the pavilion for two reasons. The place needed a gazebo, and, secondly, I wanted deliberately to fly in the face of the 'Modern' tradition of functionalist architecture by tying on to an older, nobler, tradition of garden architecture." That might have been all right, but he then went on to say, "The domes in my guest room [which was earlier, remember: 1953] are ten feet high against the five and a half in the pavilion. They have a calming, quieting effect on the guests—most enjoyable." The guest room does in fact look a good deal like something run up by Hadrian to entertain his friend Antinous. And now the cries of "effete" and "decadent," both code words, were joined by the cry of "ballet," here intended in the same way. Therefore the kind of work Johnson then did, like the rather *en pointe* columns of the Amon Carter Museum, are described as being of Johnson's Ballet School, with a sense that they are inconsequential and odd and a little effeminate (figs. 14, 15).

Still, whatever the shapes of the columns, Johnson was now always concerned with an architectural element that he had most directly imbibed from Hadrian, which is the courtyard, and he proposed one for Lincoln Center. A critic of the time condemned him for it, saying in effect that Johnson thought that architecture was the shaping of space. I can't imagine how one would formulate a better definition of architecture, but that is what he said. And the way Bauhaus spaces were invariably cut up at that time, by intrusive buildings functioning as anarchic objects, suggests that the concept of architecture as space- and place-making was very weak in that period. Whatever the case, it is because of Johnson that we have a great urban place in Lincoln Center, which we otherwise would not have had. At first Johnson intended to frame it by a strange, attenuated version of his Ballet School colonnade. But that never happened. Still, the place is there. The buildings shape it but do not intrude upon it. Johnson's New York State Theater is surely the best of them, worthy to house George Balanchine's classic choreography of gorgeous women and leonine men.

Its columns come down like the massive spikes of Balanchine's male dancers. The building's monumental solidity had not been typical of Johnson's design in those years, and we may guess that the influence of Louis I. Kahn, for whose architecture he never normally expressed much admiration, had something to do with it.

If we look at Johnson's Boissonnas House of this period, we can see that its big brick piers and the plan are derived from Kahn's studies of a few years before in houses like that of the De Vore Project (fig. 16). Johnson throws out that wonderful agonized shifting of the four-column square bays in relation to each other that Kahn so lovingly explored. Johnson's is a much more conventional shaping of space, but they are Kahn's spaces, and they recall the proportions of some of Kahn's very few houses of this time. The building has a grandeur new to Johnson.

Much the same thing is true of the Kline Biology Tower in New Haven (fig. 17). It has a solid bulk perhaps more Kahn-Roman than Johnson-Roman hitherto was. It is also successful in shaping another courtyard at the open summit of the hill that Saarinen and Schweikher had intelligently left open by placing the Gibbs laboratory to one side. Johnson might very well have set his building on that summit, on the very axis of Hillhouse Avenue, but he did not do so. He placed it well to the left so that the eye can go freely where it should—that is, to the top of the hill and into the courtyard, and to the mountain beyond it. As in Lincoln Center, Johnson is making a place as he did in the original scheme for Lincoln Center, surrounded by a rather problematical but very lively colonnade.

One wonders what effect the Seagram Building, where Philip was in collaboration with Mies van der Rohe, had on his design of the Kline Biology Tower. I once thought that the siting of Seagram, which is set back from the street but complementing its direction and creating a very reasonable urban plaza, was Johnson's idea rather than Mies's. But when I asked him, Johnson adamantly said, "Absolutely not. As a matter of fact, I was going to turn it in the opposite direction"— which would have been disastrous and was perhaps not even true. It was at least an excellent example of Johnson's deferring to Mies. Clearly, they were both trying to avoid cutting a meaningless hole in the avenue, as Lever Brothers had done just up the street a couple of years before. So they set the slab back to make a useable space respecting the avenue. And they made the face of the slab as homogeneous as possible by suppressing the columns and emphasizing the vertical continuity of the close-set mullions: a typically Miesian device in such circumstances, one which is achieved in the Kline Biology Tower by the closely stacked, vertically continuous brick cylinders. In this way Mies and Johnson turn a surface that is normally read as a skeleton into a plane which is solid enough to be read as defining a space. The way Seagram is sited, directly opposite the Racquet Club, with its monumentally arched entrance, further dignifies that urban relationship.

So we can take Seagram, which everybody loves and approves of, and go on to 1980 and the AT&T Building, which not everybody admires, and we can see that Johnson is developing exactly the same themes. He incorporates, as it were, the entrance to the Racquet Club into the building itself, and he gives the frontality of the slab an even greater emphasis by the use of the Chippendale Highboy top, which Denise Scott Brown was certainly correct in assigning to her and Robert Venturi's work earlier in the decade, but which is surely used here with considerable effect. Indeed, in its relationship to Madison Avenue the building not only powerfully defines

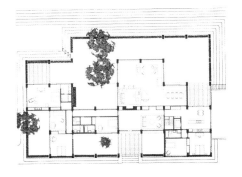

fig. 16 Plan of Eric Boissonas House, New Canaan, Connecticut, 1956

fig. 17 Kline Biology Tower, Yale University, New Haven, Connecticut, 1965

fig. 18 Lipstick Building,
885 Third Avenue, New York, 1985

fig. 19 500 Boylston Street
Building, Boston, 1989

that much narrower street but also takes its own block of it and turns it into a special event, a kind of plaza. All that is surely preferable to what Citicorp does, not far away, where the street level is utterly lost and total urban confusion ensues. And AT&T can also rise up decisively as a frontal slab to its apex and remain street architecture because it is not tall enough to reach the skyline, where slabs have shown themselves to be inadequate as midspace elements, while Citicorp raises its flaccid shaft high enough to become an ambiguous and feeble element in the city's profile.

At the same time, AT&T also ushers in that phase of Johnson's career that I and almost everybody else have found to be the least sympathetic. During that period he himself was certainly less sympathetic to historians and critics. In it he was playing the big-time, tough architect, a very false role for him, and one that he adored. John Burgee was in fact doing his dirty work, running interference with the corporate bosses and so on, in the series of high-rises that they produced together. That series has never been much appreciated, and it does tend to decline in quality from AT&T's intelligently conceived false front to the careless effrontery of the apartment house facade across Fifth Avenue from the Metropolitan Museum of Art. But if we look at some of the basic skyscrapers of this period, such as Pennzoil and the RepublicBank building next to it in Houston, it is obvious that Johnson understands exactly how those buildings are meant to be seen and precisely what their urban situation and function are. They are basic one-liners that we glimpse as we whiz by on the freeway, especially in Houston, where there is no street life and the freeway is close by. We are always in an automobile or underground. So Pennzoil exploits that situation in the rather wonderful slot between its two halves, shifting in relation to each other as the car speeds by. The RepublicBank—though based, it would seem, on the second Finnish entry to the Chicago Tribune Competition of 1922—is another eye-catcher, a stepped-back mountain mass.[4] And it was during this period that Johnson spoke well of the New York skyscrapers of the twenties and thirties, of which this is essentially one. If such choices seem superficial, one can only note that there is a kind of dumbness and superficiality built into the architectural program itself; the skyscraper office building is a comparatively dull type with which to crown a city, compared with a temple or a cathedral or a citadel or a city hall. It means little; it might as well be fanciful. So in Pittsburgh, Johnson's contribution to the type can be at once all Gothic and all glass, shining and shimmering in the great view of it that explodes upon our attention as we burst from the hills above the two rivers in our approach to the city from the north. Conversely, the Lipstick Building on Third Avenue in New York is in a very different urban position and is so shaped and sited that it seems to be sliding forward of the other buildings and picking up the dynamism of that tough commercial street itself (fig. 18).

As time went on, Johnson's conceptions of these tours de force became more and more perfunctory and even careless, and here we feel the lack of drawing most poignantly. His 500 Boylston Street in Boston is an example of this (fig. 19). Only one was built out of two buildings projected; the client was so dissatisfied with it that he took the second one away and gave it to Robert A. M. Stern. Finally there was the unmitigated disaster in Dallas of 1985. It is supposedly Second Empire in style, but the details are not really drawn. Something had gone very wrong. Apparently Johnson realized as much. You will remember that he later said that he stopped

doing this kind of work because he "couldn't draw well enough," and this was true.
So in 1988 with his inveterate instinct for survival through change and through the
young, Johnson managed to organize his deconstructivist exhibition in New York.
This event has been well documented and evaluated by Mark Wigley, and Johnson
himself turned more or less to deconstructivism for a while, as is shown in the whole
sequence from Second Empire to deconstructivist that marks his fairly appalling
projects for Times Square. At the same time he liked to get himself up as a kind of
kidnap victim of the young, and in a truly abominable photograph of 1991 he seems
to contemplate with some equanimity violation at the hands of what appears to
be the Mafia, with Frank Gehry as the rather benign boss on the right, and Peter
Eisenman, the enforcer, on the left (fig. 20).

Nevertheless, in his own foreword to Wigley's catalogue for the deconstructivist
exhibition (which is itself a complement to Wigley's massive and fascinating study
of deconstructivism as a philosophy in relation to architecture as a whole), Johnson
writes very intelligently about the whole thing and notes that as far as architecture
is concerned, deconstructivism is fundamentally Russian constructivism, revived.
Consequently, it is logical that he should go on to do a fine, diagonally activist,
Russian constructivist scheme for Seton Hall, and he indeed builds what we might
call the historical climax of Russian constructivism in the monumentally leaning
towers of the Puerta de Europa in Madrid (fig. 21). But if we follow his work and
come to almost the final examples of it, like the Lauder project for a desert camp, we
cannot help but feel that old influences are still active in him, especially those from
Frank Lloyd Wright, as in his first desert camp in Arizona. But then we see Johnson's
Speyer project. It seems shockingly un-Johnsonian until we think of Johnson as
still the lover of German art, now working his way back beyond the International
Style to the roots of German expressionism, first in Gaudí and culminating in *The
Cabinet of Dr. Caligari.* Johnson found his way back to a time just before he began
and just antedating the style he had helped to name so long before. Even when

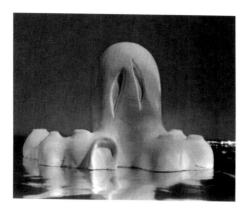

we are confronted by his Octopus Project we easily detect the German expressionist works behind it, like Steiner's *Goetheanum* and, even more strikingly, Hermann Finsterlin's sculptural figures of the mid-twenties. Finsterlin's guppy-like form, with all its excrescences, is developed by Johnson in a much more classical way, coming to resemble a dome with radiating chapels. It is true that we wonder what Johnson really was thinking all this time, especially as he engaged in convoluted theoretical conversations with his newfound friends, he who had consistently deprecated architectural theory throughout his life. He had in fact worked his way from the almost Platonic conceptions of Mies all the way back to animal form. But he was obviously continuing to exercise his passion to change, to try everything, most of all to be out in front of everybody else with the youngest innovators he could assemble around him. Yet it is always German art, and to the very last.

Still, if we look at Johnson's plan for his Octopus Project, we can't help but recognize that it is simply a rather squashed version of the plan of the Small Baths at Hadrian's Villa (fig. 22). And the mention of the villa reminds us that the Glass House and its environs always had a landscape setting that became more and more elaborate over time. At first it was rather suburban: a limited plot, just big enough for privacy on all sides, with the Glass House, the Brick House, the circular swimming pool, and the sculpture by Lipchitz populating and shaping the space. Then, as we have seen, Johnson extended the scale of all this in 1959–62 when he built his miniature garden pavilion down below and openly invoked the tradition of landscape architecture. We can see why he made it so small. It not only looks like a wonderful folly, magical in a garden, but also makes us feel the bigness of the place, and by this time, Johnson was opening it all up by cutting more and more of his trees (opposed at every step by those of us who love trees). But Johnson was driven to keep removing them, and finally it was no longer suburban New Canaan but the bare bones of tough old farmers' Connecticut before everybody left for Ohio and the second-growth timber came in. There are the stone walls evoking the hardscrabble farms and the rocky fields; we have a lean place of tragic dignity and breadth. This was perhaps surprising for Johnson, but no more so than Edith Wharton's writing *Ethan Frome*. So if Hadrian's great villa is all Italy under the Apennines, and Taliesin West is the Sonoran Desert of Arizona, this is Connecticut at its most resonant hour.

As at the villa, where Hadrian built buildings that reflected older monuments in various ways, so here we have Johnson's underground picture gallery, a conical mound of earth, a tholos tomb, like the so-called Tomb of Agamemnon at Mycenae. Inside, Johnson's plan, tomblike itself, is in fact a kind of distillation of the tholos plan and of those neolithic temples on Malta, dedicated to the goddesses of the earth, some of them open to the sky. And that is the way Johnson's sculpture court is conceived: open above but spiraling down in sharp diagonals like those of a little Italian hill town into the earth itself. But in photograph after photograph Johnson sits at the dining table in the Glass House itself, looking toward the view that the visitor sees as he descends into the site from the road well uphill. And because he is the liberated individual, all alone, he cannot look out on other houses by other architects. There cannot be another Glass House. Surely one of the foremost problems with which modern architecture has had to be concerned from that time to the present has been how to develop a viable kind of building, a type out of which a community of interactive dwellings can be created. It was precisely community that Johnson had always avoided. So he has to make his surroundings all by himself, whatever he is to see through his glass. For his view from that dining table he built his library and study, a little monument that recalls the forms of Aldo Rossi, especially his mysterious cones. With those cones in Rossi's work came the red Italian palazzo with its hollow windows, which Johnson must have realized that his friend Frank Gehry had twisted and made his own. More than that, the little building's two vertical elements, as they reach toward each other, strike me as a personal monument to friendship (fig. 23). So are, for example, Johnson's monument nearby to his friend Lincoln Kirstein, an unclimbable Russian constructivist conceit, and his ghostly wire-mesh house for his friend Frank Gehry. From these, looking up

fig. 24 Philip Johnson at the Glass House, c. 2003

the slope along that emblematic stone wall toward the entrance to the site, Johnson's so-called Monsta appears, surprisingly beautiful in the landscape from this point of view. Above, though, we see its entrance side and its dark, Caligari-like twisted door with, inside, the space that reminds me of a tomb. It is first seen as one enters the site under a gate upon which Johnson worked for decades, and which suggests the entrance to a cemetery.

Johnson lived among his monuments for a long, long time, almost as enduring, it began to seem, as nature itself (fig. 24). All the ancient associations and memories, whatever they were, lay behind him as he looked out at his monuments, his friends. At the same time, by his own individual will, there was nothing between him and nature. It was right there, and he watched the seasons change, and die, and be reborn, as if eternally, and he must have felt as if he were surely going to make it himself to his century at least, and all of a sudden he was gone.

People have asked me what I thought Johnson's legacy is. What can one say? Part of it is all around us in the buildings of some of our most important architects, so many of whom were directly aided by him, and who are working now in so many different languages, most of which Johnson had tried himself at one time or another. And the major causes he championed, history, modernism, architecture as art, are all flourishing in one way or another today. What the whole of his legacy may be will become apparent only over time, and in the garden he loved so well and where so much of his best work is found. Visitors to the house, maintained by the National Trust for Historic Preservation, will number many thousands, probably more and more every year. And as time goes on they will weave their myths about the place, and misread it wonderfully, and it will become a place of pilgrimage, sacred ground. How Johnson would laugh. But his ghost will always haunt the place. It's too bad that our architecture doesn't encourage us, as Palladio's did, to crown its roofs with images of our heroes, our gods, our souls, ourselves. Hadrian knew all about that; and just before his own death he wrote a poem to his soul, which may be translated more or less as follows:

> *Little soul, winsome, wanderer,*
> *The body's comrade and guest,*
> *You will now depart to places,*
> *Pallid, rigid, bare,*
> *Without your usual jest.*

It might have been written by Philip himself, who said more than once that he intended to retire to Rome at age one hundred, and that everything always sounds better in Latin anyway, which it probably does:

> Animula, vagula, blandula,
> Hospes comesque corporis,
> Quae nunc abibis in loca,
> Pallidula, rigida, nudula,
> Nec ut soles dabis jocos.

Notes

1. Johnson first said this in a lecture at Yale in 1949; see Vincent Scully, "Doldrums in the Suburbs," *Journal of the Society of Architectural Historians* 24, no. 1 (March 1965): 46–47.

2. Vincent J. Scully, *Modern Architecture: The Architecture of Democracy* (New York: G. Braziller, 1961), 140n41.

3. Philip Johnson, *Philip Johnson: Writings,* foreword by Vincent Scully, introduction by Peter Eisenman, commentary by Robert A. M. Stern (New York: Oxford University Press, 1979), 227–240. Comment by the editor: The end of this quote reads: "Hurray for history, and thank God for Hadrian, for Bernini, for Le Corbusier, and Vincent Scully!"

4. The project is by Elinar Sjostrom and Jarl Eklund from Helsingfors, Finland.

The Autobiographical House:
Around a Haunted Hearth

Kurt W. Forster

The estate of Philip Johnson at New Canaan undoubtedly belongs to the category of dwellings designed by artists and architects for their own use and enjoyment. However, the architect himself took the first step in the opposite direction by publishing his work in America's most prestigious professional journal, the *Architectural Review*.[1] Not to be overlooked is Johnson's ambivalent impulse to seek a private retreat while publicizing the house he designed for himself as a benchmark in the history of architecture.

For hundreds of years the residences of artists have combined privacy with publicity, mutually defining their purposes: the house shields the artist from the public (and permits him to indulge himself in a purely private world) while advertising his special status and the dignity of his art. As the addressee, the artist comes to be identified with a specific place—where he may continue to be commemorated for centuries—and as an address, the house assumes a life of its own and may even achieve the status of a museum.[2] The residence of a Giulio Romano, a Zuccari, or a Rubens, like those of other famous artists and architects, served as a kind of frontispiece on which sculptural and pictorial ideas exulted their owner's eminence.[3] Balancing allegory with personal representation, such residences assume the guise of autobiographical constructs. As such they relinquish generic claims about art and accrue interest for uniquely personal reasons. Such celebrated examples as John Soane's house in London tilted the balance in favor of constantly evolving ideas that were intimately bound up with the owner's life and career.[4]

Since the Renaissance, artists and architects have recognized and frequently underscored the dual nature of their private dwellings. For the public, such houses serve as virtual billboards of the artist's accomplishments; for their owners, they afford a haven in which certain traits are shielded from the public eye and sometimes even from the artists themselves. Behind eloquent facades an artist's intimate persona can leave its mark and keep later generations guessing. Giulio Romano, one of the most famous Italian artists/architects of his time, and one who enjoyed an international reputation, built a house in Mantua (fig. 1).[5] The facade summarizes, as on a frontispiece, the principal ancient sources of Giulio's own architecture. The full scope of building technology is drafted into service: stone, imitation stone, stucco, terracotta ornament, painting, and sculpture all resound in a fully orchestrated "union of the arts."[6] Each of these elements, while conferring a singular status onto the house amid the architecture of the city, also carries precise associations. As an ensemble, they constitute the tropes of its design and submit to the artist as *metteur en scène*.[7]

The facade centers on a piece of sculpture, classically niched, that proudly presides over the doorway. Giulio, who dealt in antiques throughout his career, supplied the statue's missing limbs and head, fashioning an elegant figure of Mercury from a mere torso.[8] As the patron deity of artists—not to mention currency dealers, thieves, and vagrants—Mercury plays swift messenger for the powers that be. He obliges them as a glib persuader and quicksilvery media wizard. As an artifact, however, this Mercury advertises Giulio Romano's exceptional talents in handling antiques. The painter and historian Giorgio Vasari, who knew Giulio and his work intimately, having spent three days in Mantua as his guest, described the treasures of the house and their studied arrangement. Giulio not only owned drawings of all relevant antiquities, but every one of his numerous projects was documented so that his clever transformation of ancient sources—which were at hand in the form of fragments, coins, medals, drawings, and codices—might be fully appreciated. Giulio had also inherited significant works of art, such as a rarefied painting on linen that Albrecht Dürer had sent to Raphael, Giulio's revered teacher. A nearly life-size portrait of Giulio himself—by the hand of Titian, the eminent painter who also portrayed Giulio's patron, Federico Gonzaga—placed the house under the gaze of an artist who would reveal his art with the same assurance as he unfurls a drawing in his portrait.[9] More than just a residence and studio, the Mantuan house was also one of the early museums whose treasures formed a kind of prelude to the owner's art. Vasari picked up a clever phrase from Pietro Aretino when he summed up Giulio's talent and trademark work as being "modern when judged according to the ancients and antique in the eyes of the moderns" ("anticamente moderno e modernamente antico"),[10] an emblematic description whose felicity is confirmed by the statue of Mercury in the guise of an ancient work, deceptively re-created from a genuine torso and modern limbs.[11] Inside the house, in his stately *salone,* however, Giulio lets *Prometheus* take the place of Mercury, striding away from the hearth as he makes off with the fire of the gods under their very own eyes (fig. 2).[12] Suddenly, the artist who advertised his obedient services, not to say his servility, turns to the arch-rebel Prometheus when he decided to vent his feelings of hubris and suffering.

When biography informs not only the physical shell of the house but also its contents and display, we enter the realm of autobiography proper. Among near contemporaries of Philip Johnson, two European writers created dwellings that invite analysis as autobiographical edifices: the literary historian Mario Praz (1896–1982) and the writer Curzio Malaparte (1898–1957). Praz coined the expression *casa della vita* for an elaborate account of how he assembled, in the course of a lifetime, the neoclassical furnishings and works of art in his quarters at Piazza de' Ricci in Rome (fig. 3).[13] Malaparte, who had a conflicted relationship with power, politics, and the public, has more than a little in common with the attitudes of Philip Johnson. And like Johnson, Malaparte created a unique private retreat occupying a rocky spur on the island of Capri. Pointedly, he dubbed the building a *casa come me.*[14]

The interiors of Praz's Roman apartment and of Malaparte's island dwelling are predicated on specific autobiographical moments. They display ideas of their authors rather than obey the plans of professional architects.[15] In these two dwellings, however much they differ from one another, the array of parts and objects derives from, and symbolically reconfigures, the memory of key experiences

fig. 1 Giulio Romano, the artist's house in Mantua, facade, 1540, and statue of Mercury over the doorway of Romano's house in Mantua, 1540

fig. 2 Giulio Romano, Prometheus, fresco in the salon of Romano's house in Mantua, 1540s

in the lives of their creators.[16] As exquisitely personal artifacts, they preserve, like death masks, the physiognomies of individuals who ardently wished to be memorialized; as architectural ensembles, they transcend the mere assembly of memorabilia and erect theaters of memory. They re-create, as if *en miniature,* the references and geographies of a lifetime.

That Praz and Malaparte were not architects is of little moment in our reflection on the category of autobiographical dwellings. Thomas Jefferson acted as his own architect at Monticello, where the client-architect relationship was conflated in the design of an exemplary estate for the new nation (fig. 4). In accordance with the president's vision of a quasi-physiocratic economy, his estate became a monument of national significance.[17] To the extent that Jefferson's own urbanity stood in opposition to his distrust of cities, Monticello assumed the problematic character of a *villa suburbana* rather than remaining a productive rural estate. Its technical refinements and its cultural riches—from the library[18] to the wine cellar, from the imported French paper to the English drafting instruments—belied its independence from the culture Jefferson regarded with suspicion.[19] A comparable case might be made for the Hudson River estate of landscape painter Frederic Edwin Church (1826—1900), who built Olana in the early 1870s on a promontory overlooking the river. The site's geography lent its name to the group of painters so famously represented by the fashionable and often exotic views that were Church's pride (fig. 5). As a "piece of paradise," and what's more, a privately owned one, Olana embodied a modern notion of the idyll: easily reached by transportation, dramatically sited for effect yet secluded in "unspoiled nature," the estate improbably imposes an international culture on a canvas of perfect innocence.[20] From its various windows, loggias, and balconies, the surrounding landscape collapses into images, while the rooms beckon with the exotic trophies the painter gathered during his travels through distant parts of the world. Olana is unthinkable without the urban culture that produced it, and the urban oligarchs who financed it, but it would have been unobtainable

fig. 3 Drawing room (*saletta di passaggio*) in Mario Praz's house on Piazza de' Ricci, Rome, 1970s

fig. 4 Thomas Jefferson's bedroom and study at Monticello as it may have been in the 1820s

within the city itself. It may not be obvious what the painter had in mind when he appointed his various rooms in a variety of quasi-ethnographic styles, except to say that he instantly changed the experience of the interiors as much as the impression of the land beyond, inducing in the observer a state of imaginary travel. The secret of his intervention lies in the displacement of the viewer and the consequent transformation of the views. Church's estate intrigues as the perfect escape from, and the ultimate destination of, nineteenth-century art in America.[21]

While amateur architects occasionally build houses for themselves, professional architects sometimes create surrogate houses for clients who may be among their closest relatives: Robert Venturi designed one of his most memorable early projects for his mother.[22] More than a surrogate for himself, Vanna Venturi's house aims to be the mother of the American house *tout court*. Whether a house springs from an amateur's desire or from an architect's rendition of an *idée fixe*, it can assume the character of an autobiographical site. In a word, the criterion lies not so much in occupancy or even design, but in the imaginary construct of the house as the evolving shell of a life.[23]

Curzio Malaparte, born Kurt Suckert, chose a nom de plume that defiantly challenged Napoleon's.[24] Unhesitatingly he altered the design for a house that he had obtained from Adalberto Libera in 1938, modeling the steep flight of stairs that leads to the rooftop after the entrance to the church of Santa Maria dell'Annunziata on the island of Lipari, where, having fallen into disfavor with Mussolini in 1933, he spent several years under house arrest (fig. 6).[25] Back on Capri, he rendered the facades in stucco, removing any hint of the familiar hierarchy that architects liked to invoke with rubble stone facing and classical symmetry.[26] Inside the house he inserted Tyrolian wooden stairs and railings that strike one as completely incongruous with the Mediterranean setting. Only as an allusion to his northern origins do they make any sense, just as the V-shaped flight of stairs leading to the roof terrace was "transported" to Capri as a memorial to Malaparte's exile on another island.

The full extent of Malaparte's clash with the Fascist regime, and his desire to contravene it while exploiting conflict among its exponents, reveals itself when we

fig. 5 Olana, the estate of the painter Frederic Edwin Church on the Hudson, 1870s

fig. 6 View of La casa come me, Curzio Malaparte's house on Capri, 1940

fig. 7 View of the sea and pine
trees through a tripartite window
in Malaparte's house on Capri

fig. 8 View through the fireplace
of Malaparte's house on Capri

learn that he insisted on locating his villa in a zone of the island where any kind
of construction was legally prohibited. With the help of Count Ciano, Mussolini's
son-in-law, and Minister of Culture Giuseppe Bottai, Malaparte was able to
circumvent the law and build a house that is the manifest memory of exile (within
his own country) and of his "foreign" (German) paternity.[27] The Allies landed on
the island in September 1943, just as the house was completed, and after a brief
incarceration Malaparte was able to receive the head of the Communist party,
Palmiro Togliatti. In short order Malaparte became a liaison officer of the American
Forces, and on his deathbed in 1957 deeded the house to artists from the People's
Republic of China (Philip Johnson may have been less than steadfast in his
politics, but his about-turns seem mere pecadillos by comparison with Malaparte's
chameleonic career.)

The key to the autobiographical meaning of the *casa come me,* if one need
look for one at all, lies in the notion of the permanent "wreckage of the ship of life,"
which, though stranded, is held in place by the sheer weight of its biographical
ballast.[28] The wide, tripartite windows of the living space frame old *pini marini*
almost in the manner of a Japanese folding screen, an impression rendered even
more evocative by several rocks arising from the sea nearby (fig. 7). But the space
also embraces a wooden relief of over-life-size figures intertwined in carnal abandon.
Malaparte's is a dwelling replete with memories of incarceration, alpine refuge,
Mediterranean hideaways, and exotic seaports.[29] Looking out from the loft-like living
space through a large plate of glass at the back of the fireplace, the flames in the
hearth appear to lap at the wine-colored sea (fig. 8). One can almost hear the hissing
of burning logs crashing on the waves, just as one will sense the tension between
John Soane's heroes over the fireplace of his residence at Lincoln's Inn Fields in
London. Bonaparte haunts both Malaparte and Soane, casting a spell on the identity
of the former and a long shadow over an artistic hero of the latter: Soane placed a
cast of Michelangelo's *Tondo Mattei* above the bust of Napoleon in his house (fig. 9).
To harbor the effigy of England's most overt enemy in his London residence, and to
place it above a wrought-iron seashell on his hearth, betrays the searing intensity of
Soane's feelings.[30] The elemental conflict of water and fire, ignited by a flame behind
a cast-iron ornament in Soane's house, bursts open in the villa where Malaparte
wanted to face the flaming logs in full view of the sea.

Though dignified by stone facing in contrast to the ubiquitous brick facades of
adjacent houses, Soane's residence resembles a warren of spaces over-brimming

with images, drawings, models, and fragments, framed and festooned by mementos and stuffed with documents and collectibles—whatever Soane deemed apt to stoke his imagination. This labyrinth of riches quickly turns into a bewildering storehouse of things that often seem incongruous, even incompatible, to the modern viewer. Throughout his interminable labors the collector sought to render them responsive to his inner vision. His roving eye, ever avid and alert, would vault over the cracks gaping among the disparate objects, sifting through the wreckage of distant civilizations. Only when seen impassively from a distance would the collected fragments hold still and submit to their arranger's desire.[31]

Ample use of mirrored glass, indirect lighting, perforated surfaces, and nested spaces, even concealed cupboards with hinged panels for the display of paintings, allowed Soane to achieve one thing above all else: the *specular* array of his mournful mass of objects and images (fig. 10). Gradually, Soane laid down a symbolic geography inside his house by shifting things around, opening top-lit wells and connecting them with catwalks. His spaces were designed to transport the viewer into a meta-time that permitted one to embrace what is disjointed and dislocated in reality within a unifying vision. At the price of illusion, a specular mirage alone could harbor the intellectual chattel of a lifetime. Seeing is believing, believing in seeing history in the dimensions of one man's experiences, although that history always threatens to decay overnight into an inert accumulation. But there are explosive moments, such as that juxtaposition of the *Tondo Mattei* with the head of Napoleon above the fireplace, in which Soane ardently, if controversially, conjoined what he considered superior forces in art and life. Such confrontations must have held exemplary meaning for Soane, who clung to the notion of art and architecture as edifying activities.[32]

In a jump-cut that takes us from Giulio Romano to Frank Gehry, we find our enfant terrible cutting up a turn-of-the-century house in Santa Monica in 1977–78, almost in the manner of Gordon Matta-Clark.[33] Gehry stripped it down inside

fig. 9 Console table in the ante-room to the Picture Room in John Soane's house, Lincoln's Inn Fields, London, 1820s

fig. 10 Breakfast room in John Soane's house, Lincoln's Inn Fields

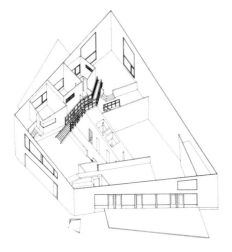

fig. 11 Frank O. Gehry's house in Santa Monica, late 1970s

fig. 12 Frank Gehry, axonometric drawing of the studio house for the painter Ronald Davis in Malibu, 1972

and out, shielding its flanks while gutting its walls, laying down a few randomly assembled steps of cement and plywood in front of the doorway and petitioning Rudolf Schindler for a nod of approval (fig. 11). He appealed to remote but beloved constructivist art with a wire-glass hood over the kitchen but retained many details of the original building. His disassembly is superseded by a vertiginous arrest of time in a moment of . . . *explosante-fixe* . . .—the title Pierre Boulez, one of Frank's friends, gave to a composition he kept elaborating throughout the 1970s and beyond, allowing for variable groups of musicians and alternate modes of performance, a moment that arrests the parts within the time of their assembly.[34] At the Gehry house, the impression is similarly cleft as two movements occur simultaneously, almost corporeal in power but fleeting in manifestation: one, a sudden transformation at the speed of demolition; the other, an improvisational mounting of pieces at a more intermittent yet deliberate pace.

Gehry garnered a second chance at being an architect when artist friends requested designs for houses and ateliers on rock-bottom budgets. Among the earliest such commissions is a house in rural northern California for the painter Ronald Davis, who was then producing multilayered images built up from folded planes and strips embedded in resin. Taking his cue straight from his friend's work, Gehry enfolded the interior of the house as if it were an imaginary extension of Davis's paintings (fig. 12). Simultaneously, the architect yielded to an interest that was distinctly his own, an interest in connecting all spaces inside a house by means of staggered platforms and folding passages. Years later, when he moved into the domain of curvilinear surfaces and billowing volumes, his friendship with the sculptors Claes Oldenburg and Coosje van Bruggen helped him outgrow the orthogonal regimentation of a traditional architect's mind.

The Gehry residence comes across as a prime example of an autobiographical house, from the circumstances of its inception (a second marriage and the launch of a newly independent career) to its periodic transformation; its furnishings, consisting chiefly of the works of artist friends and the results of many ad hoc experiments by Gehry himself; and its probable designation as a "landmark building" after the architect has vacated it. Every corner, every material, and every intervention speaks of "self-fashioning," conveying something that exists yet needs to be constantly revised. A house that time built to make it stand still, in a word, a veritable casa della vita. What emerges from the Gehry house with the "force of nature" is the fact that an autobiographical house can never stand still while its author is alive. Gehry has now "outlived" the house of the 1970s and will consequently move to a new one in nearby Venice.[35] The plan of the new residential complex is so configured as to be easily split up again into the three separate lots that Gehry bought and united in the first place. Whereas he is merely keeping an eye on the economics of real estate (and the financial future of his descendents), the childless Johnson worried only about fame and glory, assuring the survival of his creation in perpetuity as a monument on the list of historic houses maintained by the National Trust.[36]

I doubt that I can synthesize the character of Philip Johnson's estate at New Canaan in the thumbnail fashion I've applied to the residences of Giulio Romano, John Soane, and Frank Gehry (admittedly closing my eyes to dozens of other examples). Johnson clung to his estate for half a century and expanded it periodically, adding seven structures and creating over the years a park of his architectural

ideas.[37] One of the distinctive qualities of Johnson's estate lies in its sheer extent, amounting as it does to a veritable park in which the owner appropriated certain natural features and created others outright (fig. 13). The initial project consisted of two houses, one for the day (1949), the other for the night (1949, altered in 1953), and, at a delay of a few years, a shallow circular pool. Over the years Johnson added other structures, ranging from a subterranean gallery to a tower. In the process, some features, such as a sculpture by Jacques Lipchitz, were eliminated, while others, such as the lakelet below the house, were enlarged and contoured; still others, such as rubble stone enclosures, were modified and the grounds replanted. Gradually, the geography of the estate changed, resembling an ever wider clearing dotted with structures and crisscrossed by paths (fig. 14). A series of pavilions appeared over the years, each of them catering to another whim and exalting another part of the property. More than just offering a free assortment of stations in the landscape, the outlying buildings also parse the evolution of postwar architecture in the United States.[38] Each takes up what had just been proposed by other architects, be it the cloverleaf pattern of the subterranean gallery or the tongue-in-cheek use of chain link for the Ghost House (which, ironically, is no house at all). The gallery shares its affinity for cryptlike spaces with Franco Albini's widely published Treasury of the Cathedral of San Lorenzo in Genova (1952–56), which conjoins four cylindrical spaces of varying diameter around a hexagonal hall, making the most of a sheltered condition in a heavily bombed city. Johnson cast a web of references, naming some of the additions, such as the Lincoln Kirstein Tower or the Gehry Ghost House, after friends. The Ghost House gives a slightly irreverent nod to a colleague who became known for his trademark chain link on some of his early houses, but the last addition to the estate, the Visitor's Booth, called Da Monsta, is both more deferential (to Gehry and Frank Stella) and less sure than any of the other follies. For that is what they all are, pavilions and follies in a park in which references to atomic shelters, viewing towers, and waterworks abound. No definite path guides visitors and assures them that they have hit upon every interesting spot. For example, the Study of 1980 must

fig. 13 Glass House, Guest House, and pond at Johnson's estate in New Canaan, Connecticut, c. 1950 be reached by strolling across the grass, and the Gehry Ghost House may escape attention altogether because it is deeply shaded by beech trees. Johnson placed its gossamer shape on foundations that barely emerge from the ground. These remains of farm buildings are not the only ones. Others hibernate in the parkland, awakening in the unending story of the Johnson estate as it trails off into the future.

It is tempting to think of another autobiographical park created by another *monstre sacré*, the Italian poet Giuseppe D'Annunzio, who labored for years on his Vittoriale above Lake Garda (fig. 15). He dotted the slopes with prows of actual ships, built a Greek theater overlooking the lake, transported rock formations from alpine theaters of war, installed the biplane he piloted over Vienna to drop leaflets into the enemy capital, and permanently moored the boat in which he hit the shore at

fig. 14 Map of Johnson's estate at New Canaan, Connecticut, 1995

Fiume during a rebel expedition: "Everything," he asserted, "created and transfigured by me."[39] D'Annunzio's Vittoriale embraces the landscape, and a spectacular one to boot. Its fluid paths skirt the slopes and always lead back to the *prioria,* or priory, a private museum in which the most execrable and the most exquisite objects rest side by side, as if caught in the rigor mortis of time itself (fig. 16).[40] Eccentric and blatant, irrelevant and melodramatic, Vittoriale transfigures the aesthetic of the English park and rewrites its parts in a score of whistling shells, whirling propellers, and dramatic recitals swirling around a hideout whose atmosphere is scented with gunpowder and musty embroidery. Nonetheless, as an autobiographical site that inflates the private house to the scale of the landscape, the Vittoriale is a piece of searing kitsch not to be missed.

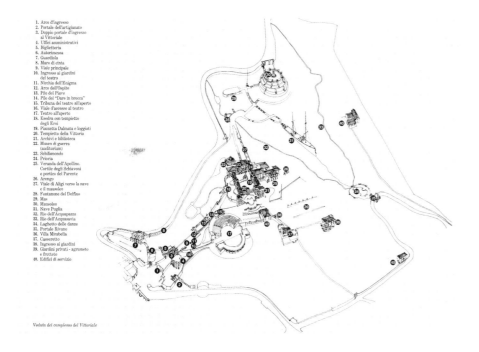

1. Arco d'ingresso
2. Portale dell'artigianato
3. Doppio portale d'ingresso al Vittoriale
4. Uffici amministrativi
5. Biglietteria
6. Autorimessa
7. Guardiola
8. Muro di cinta
9. Viale principale
10. Ingresso ai giardini del teatro
11. Nicchia dell'Enigma
12. Arco dell'Ospite
13. Pilo del Piave
14. Pilo del "Dare in brocca"
15. Tribuna del teatro all'aperto
16. Viale d'accesso al teatro
17. Teatro all'aperto
18. Esedra con tempietto degli Eroi
19. Piazzetta Dalmata e loggiati
20. Tempietto della Vittoria
21. Archivi e biblioteca
22. Museo di guerra (auditorium)
23. Schifamondo
24. Prioria
25. Veranda dell'Apollino. Cortile degli Schiavoni e portico del Parente
26. Arengo
27. Viale di Aligi verso la nave e il mausoleo
28. Fontanone del Delfino
29. Mas
30. Mausoleo
31. Nave Puglia
32. Rio dell'Acquapazza
33. Rio dell'Acquasavia
34. Laghetto delle danze
35. Portale Rivano
36. Villa Mirabella
37. Casseretto
38. Ingresso ai giardini
39. Giardini privati - agrumeto e frutteto
40. Edifici di servizio

Veduta del complesso del Vittoriale

fig. 15 Map of Il Vittoriale, the estate of Gabriele D'Annunzio on Lake Garda

fig. 16 The *officina* (study) of Gabriele D'Annunzio at his Vittoriale

5 Karl Friedrich Schinkel: Casino in Glienicke Park near Potsdam c. 1830. Entrance façade.

The site relation of my house is pure Neo-Classic Romantic—more specifically, Schinkelesque. Like his Casino my house is approached on dead-level and, like his, faces its principal (rear) façade toward a sharp bluff.

6 Karl Friedrich Schinkel: Casino in Glienicke Park near Potsdam c. 1830. Terrace overlooking the Havel.

The Eighteenth Century preferred more regular sites than this and the Post-Romantic Revivalists preferred hill tops to the cliff edges or shelves of the Romantics (Frank Lloyd Wright, that great Romantic, prefers shelves or hillsides).

7 Claude Nicholas Ledoux: Maison des Gardes Agricoles, at Maupertuis c. 1780.

The cubic, "absolute" form of my glass house, and the separation of functional units into two absolute shapes rather than a major and minor massing of parts comes directly from Ledoux, the Eighteenth Century father of modern architecture. (See Emil Kaufmann's excellent study Von Ledoux bis Le Corbusier.) The cube and the sphere, the pure mathematical shapes, were dear to the hearts of those intellectual revolutionaries from the Baroque, and we are their descendants.

8 Mies van der Rohe: Farnsworth House, 1947. (Now under construction near Chicago).

*The idea of a glass house comes from Mies van der Rohe. Mies had mentioned to me as early as 1945 how easy it would be to build a house entirely of large sheets of glass. I was sceptical at the time, and it was not until I had seen the sketches of the **Farnsworth House** that I started the three-year work of designing my glass house. My debt is therefore clear, in spite of obvious difference in composition and relation to the ground.*

9 Philip C. Johnson: Johnson House. New Canaan. 1949. Section at corner

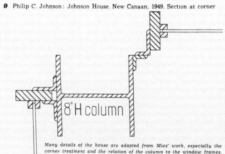

8"H column

Many details of the house are adapted from Mies' work, especially the corner treatment and the relation of the column to the window frames. This use of standard steel sections to make a strong and at the same time decorative finish to the façade design is typical of Mies' Chicago work. Perhaps if there is ever to be "decoration" in our architecture it may come from manipulation of stock structural elements such as this (may not Mannerism be next?).

10 Kasimir Malevitch: Suprematist Element: Circle—1913.

Although I had forgotten the Malevitch picture, it is obviously the inspiration for the plan of the glass house. Malevitch proved what interesting surrounding areas could be created by correctly placing a circle in a rectangle. Abstract painting of forty years ago remains even today the strongest single aesthetic influence on the grammar of architecture.

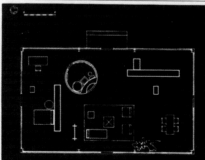

11 Johnson House: Plan of Glass Unit.

North end, sleeping and writing; brick cylinder, washing and w.c.; south-east, cooking; south-west, eating; west, sitting

Except for the cylinder, the plan of the house is Miesian. The use of 6 foot closets to divide yet unite space is his. The grouping of the furniture asymmetrically around a coffee table is his. The relation of cabinets to the cylinder, however, is more "painterly" than Mies would sanction.

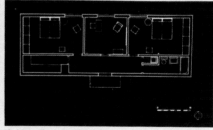

12 Johnson House: Plan of Brick Unit.

Two double guests' bedrooms with study between; combined entrance hall-picture gallery with storage room at one end; bathroom and shower at the other.

The guest house with Baroque plan central corridor and three symmetrically placed rooms, was derived from Mies' designs. The three round windows in the rear of the façade are a Renaissance approach to a Miesian motif. Mies uses the round window as a method of admitting light in a long brick wall in a manner least to disturb the continuity of the wall. A rectangular hole would compete in direction with the shape of the wall itself. I used the round windows for the same reason, with a totally different compositional effect.

From the outset, Philip Johnson claimed his estate as a domain of ideas rather than a private exhibition space.[41] His is virtually the only case of a midcentury American architect publishing his first independent work in a quasi-scholarly article, detailing its genesis and its sources with numerous illustrations (fig. 17). Johnson's article of 1950 would be well worth examining for itself, because its brand of "historicism" was definitely going out of fashion when it appeared.[42] It may have worked not only because it catered to a certain voyeuristic interest but also because Johnson was, after all, historicizing modernism—not only himself. Yet, as a piece of fictional history it continues to puzzle. Craig Owens discovered an "autobiographical ego" at work in the invention of an elaborate genealogy of the buildings, and Peter Eisenman found it "paradoxical," to cite only two readers.[43]

Johnson's article is an exceptional piece of montage, invoking and refuting both obvious and unknown aspects of his work. The way he chose to tabulate his models, selectively indicating citations and elucidating connections to other buildings and ideas, strikes me as disarming and cunning. His hints resemble the commentaries one finds on labels of bottled wine, which often leave their real properties unaccounted for. Owens is right in arguing that Johnson's montage of historical references is in fact completely at odds with the nature of historical analysis. I would go so far as to say that Johnson distracts readers with facts and disarms them with "false clues." He is the more disarming for the utter nonchalance of his performance. Historical learning, never too obscure or too trite, wears thin after a page or two, when claims for the lasting significance of abstract painting in contemporary architecture or intimations of a new age of "mannerism" confuse the issues further.[44] Johnson drops too many hints and names, dividing up what is and what is not Miesian. These hair-splitting distinctions make one more doubtful by the very aplomb with which they are delivered.[45] Readers are thrown for a loop by such claims as "the grouping of my buildings follows Choisy"—the Choisy who coaxed the monuments on the Athenian Acropolis into geometrical alignment. Choisy's plan of the Acropolis was familiar from its numerous appearances in the pages of Le Corbusier's publications, and his terse characterization is worth quoting: "The different masses of the buildings, being asymmetrically arranged, create an intense rhythm. The whole composition is massive, elastic, living, terribly sharp and keen and dominating."[46] These last words, *tel quel,* would make an apt characterization of what Johnson had in mind. But it is difficult to see where he was headed with his simultaneous admissions of a love for the baroque, a desire to emulate the Romantics, and a wish for Miesian sanction. To the extent that Johnson traps readers inside his *marché des antiquaires,* he manages to keep them at bay and well outside his own biography. Eisenman observed as much when he construed the house as the site of a paradox between the edifice and the person—a paradox woven into the veil of the text by "metaphors" that charm inimical concepts into unlikely consonance. "How are we to interpret such a metaphor?" Eisenman asks.[47] But before I continue the thread of his argument, let us return to the "paradox."

Johnson glossed his work, citing a bewildering variety of influences, carefully suppressing some of the more obvious ones. To pick out only one example of the kind of thing Johnson was eager to forget, consider the simple fact that his approach to all buildings on his estate suggests a desire to treat them as autonomous entities, so that what was traditionally a secondary, or subsidiary, part of a larger residence

fig. 18 Interior of the Glass House

fig. 19 Walter Gropius, screened porch of his house in Lincoln, Massachusetts, 1938

gained independence (fig. 18). Kenneth Frampton touched briefly on this issue when he argued that the Glass House derives from the typology of the loggia or belvedere, usually connected to a villa rather than allowed to stand apart.[48] If one considers the prevalent use of Johnson's Glass House as a daytime pavilion, it is important not to overlook the fact that Walter Gropius, dean at Harvard when Johnson was a student there, had just such a pavilion attached to his own house at Lincoln, Massachusetts (fig. 19). Raised on a low rectangular plinth and perfectly symmetrical in plan, the porch need only be detached from the southern flank of the Gropius House to suggest a miniature version of the Glass House, including its stone flooring, flat roof, and steel posts.[49] Even the chair rail is there to lend scale and to recall, if remotely, ancient systems of interior wall partitions. Vertical sunscreens provide, as they do at the Glass House, the only privacy. A charming photograph of Walter and Ise Gropius enjoying breakfast on their "porch" completes the impression of a daytime pavilion so dear to Johnson. Still another peculiarity of the dean's house may have settled in Johnson's mind: one approaches the Gropius house along a path angled to the right and aiming straight at the center of its northern facade! Johnson's well-known animus toward Gropius has been undermined by the very power his teacher's mind continued to exercise over the student.

Johnson's explanations of his work hold more interesting things in store: among all twenty-two captions to the photographs, for that is what he chose to write, only one changes register altogether and ventriloquizes in the manner of a fable when he speaks of a *"burnt village I saw once"* (fig. 20). Is this a memory so remote that no name and no time can be attached to it? In fact, the event so obliquely mentioned had occurred only a decade before the publication of this article. In the fall of 1939, Johnson was among guests of the Wehrmacht information office trailing behind the front in Poland.[50] Devastation was all around them, as village after village had been put to the torch, their inhabitants apprehended at will or summarily executed by special commandoes. To be sure, journalists were kept safely behind the lines, and the invasion was in its last days when Johnson reached Poland. Wehrmacht propaganda wanted to impress the correspondents with the triumphant advance of German forces, whose Blitzkrieg tactics combined aerial and artillery bombardment with motorized infantry. No surprise then that "nothing was left [of the burnt wooden village]" after the German assault "but foundations and chimneys of brick" (fig. 21).

The photograph captioned by Johnson with a reference to the burnt village shows an enchanting night view of the glass house under a full moon, with indirect light in the trees and clouds drifting across the sky. When image and text are so consciously matched, their effect, haunted by Romantic formulas and crackling with the memory of modern devastation, cannot but produce a frisson. It is as if the appeal of the image—perhaps too perfectly fabricated to correspond to an actual impression—resulted from a terrible memory that injects a disturbing ambivalence into every one of its aspects: illuminated as if set ablaze, lost in a pitch-black forest under leaden clouds, the glass house virtually bursts apart as an object. Reduced to its stark frame and silhouetted against the trees, the house appears paradoxical in itself—not just paradoxical in its relationship to its author, as Eisenman suggested. It is irreconcilable with any of the other images, all of which dwell on its idyllic setting, its serene atmosphere, its formal clarity and technical finish. To think it a coincidence that Johnson matched the "frightfully beautiful" image with the only autobiographical hint at devastation and death would shortchange him, but most of all, it would miss the nature of its beauty. Ever since experiences of the sublime gained aesthetic status, the beautiful remains amalgamated with the terrifying, the harmonious haunted by chaos, the accomplished forever in flight from irredeemable failure. Because the image in question is a nighttime view under a full moon, it drifts into the realm of reverie, even of nightmare. Instead of remaining an abode, the Glass House dematerializes into an image, a nocturne, a picture under the spell of Romantic night views and their disquieting atmosphere. Curzio Malaparte described a similar impression from his own house: "I open the window and the night is over the sea at Capri, and when I close the window, the night envelops my lonely house perched on the island, an Italian night descending on my books and my paintings in my library.... When I open the window again, it will soon be daybreak."[51]

The quintessential experience of the house coincides not with its blinding daytime splendor but the condition that pervades when its interior and its surroundings are flushed by the chill and darkness of night. At night, the outside recedes into a tenebrous picture and darkness creeps into every corner of the house. In the loneliness of night, light becomes as threatening as the dark, and the house no longer hides its ghosts. The only things missing (expurgated by enlightened modernism) are the coiling snake on the ground and the nocturnal owl in the sky, which Giambattista Tiepolo, Francisco Goya, or Caspar David Friedrich would not have failed to include.[52] A lover of German art and architecture, Johnson may have seen one or another of Friedrich's watercolors of owls guarding sites of ruin and death (fig. 22). Friedrich's *Owl in a Gothic Window* of 1836 (Hermitage, St. Petersburg), or one of the ominous birds perching on coffins and shovels in graveyards or flying across the pale disk of the moon, cause the emblem of wisdom to slip into ominous darkness and become the harbinger of destruction and death.[53] Mark Wigley has drawn a portrait of Johnson as an owlish figure in a dark suit, invariably wearing those huge glasses that perpetually endowed him with an air of great expectation against all odds (fig. 23).[54]

fig. 20 Night view of the Glass House as reproduced in Johnson's article in *Architectural Review* (1950)

fig. 21 A "burnt village" such as Johnson observed during the German invasion of Poland, September 1939

fig. 22 Caspar David Friedrich, *Owl in a Gothic Window,* 1836. Sepia and pencil, 14 3/4 x 10 in. (37.8 x 25.6 cm). The State Hermitage Museum, St. Petersburg [OR-43908]

All who knew him remember, and numerous photographs preserve, an inscrutable yet personable expression of bemusement, alternating with wistful irony and caustic asides. The old bird did in fact resemble an owl, perhaps not the one perched on Athena's shoulder, but more likely the one on the roof of the hut in the dark forest where the witch kept feeding Hansel and Gretel in order to fatten her roast.

The photograph of Johnson's Glass House at night, it must be said to his credit, hints at an untold story: However avuncular, even Jesuit, his confession, it stirs from its dark nesting place like the bird of night. Few words can sound at once so innocent and so haunting as those recalling a "burnt wooden village [he] saw once." Yielding to the weight of these words, Johnson speaks first of the "cylinder" and the "platform" that form the "main motif of the house," and he concludes with another mention of the "chimney" that forms "its anchor." He makes it sound as if he had done nothing more than slip a "steel cage with glass skin" over the memory of a ruin. Elegantly conserving the image while eliding what caused it, he keeps visible what is gone. The vacant quality of the Glass House carries more than a hint of modern lightness and transparency, because its lightness is burdened and its transparency obscured by its own past.

In an essay that deliberately challenges the limits of reading the Glass House, Jeff Wall posited the complementary contradictions of day- and nighttime conditions as the crux of the house: "At night, [. . .] the landscape disappears in blackness. Even the floodlighting used by Johnson does not mitigate the profound disappearance of natural spectacle which the occupant depends upon for the process of suppressing anxiety. The interior artificial lighting necessary at night transforms interior surfaces of the glass walls into gigantic mirrors."[55] Multiple reflections render both the occupant and the surrounding nature spectral, as if sapped by an anxiety about their relationship. Exposed to full view from outside while unable to perceive the surroundings as anything but a dark maze of reflections, the occupant is vexed by "anxiety in the familiar form of fear of the dark."[56] But this anxiety springs from a precise physical condition, not only from the psychological state induced by the play of shadows and mirror images: "Privacy is instituted at the boundary line of the property, not at the surface of the window. At night, when nature withdraws, leaving only blankness and absence behind, it becomes an eye in its invisibility and emptiness."[57] Without following Jeff Wall's arguments to their conclusions, we may nonetheless recognize the solitary masculinity in the breach between the natural fold of the house and its anti-natural construct coming to the fore in anxious domination.

An incongruous but insoluble relationship preserves the charred in the pristine, conserving in a crystalline case what belongs to the darkness of the times. Karl Werckmeister's study of the Casa Malaparte recalls the idea of the house as a crystal that locks the ego in its all-embracing aspirations into the harsh reality with which it has to cope.[58] No better image could be evoked to capture the nature of this incongruity than that of a lonely person sitting quietly, perhaps at night, inside a glass house recalling shattering events in the world beyond. Just a year after World War I, Massimo Bontempelli penned a soliloquy to his cat during a power failure. In his *Nocturnal Discoveries* he said: "I alone will remain. Although I change thoughts, feelings and habits from year to year, from the trials of youth to the tribulations of adolescence and the lucid intelligence that reigns at maturity, I alone am always myself, while everything I see and feel changes its effect and its substance."[59]

The old image of a cracked mirror may still hold when we look at the various photographs of Johnson in his own Glass House. The first of them was taken by Arnold Newman for the article Johnson published in 1950 (fig. 24). It superimposes a series of receding planes, all but the first belonging to reflections in the plate glass. The photograph blends the silhouettes of trees with the shadowy outlines of the house's frame and furniture and the diminutive figure of Johnson seated dead center at a table. Peering past a drawn curtain, the viewer plunges into a mirage that continues to dissolve in multiple reflections of reflections, forever eluding his grasp.

You cannot, try as you might, bail out of your own past, but are fated to live with it, even if you have outlived it. Johnson tried for nearly a decade, between 1929 and 1939, to find something that would focus his energies and give purpose to his life. His moves proved erratic; they broke friendships and alienated people. His failures and disappointments, the wild jumps from one field of interest to another, from profound attachments to passing enthusiasms, led him, in late 1939, all the way back to school.[60] Belatedly he thus returned to an earlier phase of life, and moreover, to the site of his trials as an undergraduate at Harvard, where it took him seven years

fig. 23 Luca Vignelli, portrait of Philip Johnson

fig. 24 Johnson in his Glass
House, 1950

to obtain a bachelor's degree. This time he tried to attach himself to architecture as a
professional. He knew he was as late coming back to Harvard as he had been getting
out of it. The stunt of building himself a house in Cambridge, or should we say the
"display of a house," was followed, after the war, by the purchase of a plot of land in
chic New Canaan. If Johnson set out to build something to show off and to create a
place to receive friends and "influence people," to borrow those now hollow words, he
also made a purchase on his own future. The estate at New Canaan moved him closer
to clients he wished for, or at least into the milieu of a class of clients who might
be motivated by a desire to emulate the architect's own dwelling, as some did.[61] One
might say that Johnson moved into the ambit of his ideal milieu before he had fully
entered it himself.

Marcel Proust touched on a similar point when he observed in the "side of
Guermantes" that "we labor at all times to shape our life, but, as in a drawing, we
willy-nilly copy the traits of the person we are, not those of the person it would
please us to be."[62] Johnson drew and redrew the shape of his professional life, as
anyone would, but he was able to do so in a special way within the confines of his
estate. Here, the memorials and shadowy after-images of friends and experiences
stake out a theater of memory on the grounds of his estate. Among them, rather than
in the public eye, he yielded to what Proust considered to be involuntary mechanisms,
emotions that work *malgré nous*. Here, he allowed his ego to affirm itself in its
autonomy even when it acted according to a rationale of its own, shattering his life
more than once, but never more profoundly than in the 1930s. There was no lack
of other ruptures in Johnson's life. On the contrary, we need to recognize them as

the mark of personal paradox: just as he was able to reconcile the role of a modern gentleman architect with his oft-cited "I'm a whore," he could rest his own house—his most intimate work and the very image of crystal purity—upon the memory of one of the most clamorous mistakes he made among his life's allegiances. To create the pristine object of his house, he said he "slipped a steel cage with glass skin" over its chimney, and voilà! The glass cage, resting on an incongruous brick foundation and framed by the equivalent of charred beams, precipitates a memory that could not but rend his life. We won't need to look far to detect similar cleavages in Johnson's professional life, which seems fatally divided between "work for hire" and "labors of love," between public appropriation (of the work of others) and the occasional projection of a "*je m'en foutisme*" only the rich or the cynical can afford, and none better than those who are both.

Notes

1. Philip Johnson, "House at New Canaan, Connecticut," *Architectural Review* 108, no. 645 (September 1950): 152–159. See also Franz Schulze, *Philip Johnson, Life and Work* (New York: Knopf, 1994), 186–198; Schulze quotes Johnson's fellow student and occasional Harvard companion Landis Gores: "By the following spring [1949], every architecture editor in New York had been brought out to visit" (198).

2. This gives rise to the curious phenomenon of commemorative plaques affixed to new houses that have taken the place of the artist's original dwelling.

3. Eduard Huettinger, ed., *Kuenstlerhaeuser von der Renaissance bis zur Gegenwart* (Zurich: Waser, 1985); Hans-Peter Schwarz, Heike Lauer, and Joerg Stabenow, eds., *Kuenstlerhaeuser, Eine Architekturgeschichte des Privaten* (Braunschweig: Vieweg, 1989); Christine Hoh-Slodczyk, *Das Haus des Kuenstlers im 19. Jahrhundert* (Munich: Prestel, 1985); Kurt W. Forster and Richard J. Tuttle, "The Casa Pippi: Giulio Romano's House in Mantua," *architectura* 1 (1974): 1–12; and *Giulio Romano,* exh. cat. (Milan: Electa, 1989), 480–485. For the Zuccari, see esp. Detlef Heikamp, "Federico Zuccari a Firenze (1575–1579),"in *Paragone,* n.s., 27, no. 18, 207 (1967): 3–34; and Kristina Herrmann-Fiore, "Die Fresken Federico Zuccaris in seinem roemischen Kuenstlerhaus," *Roemisches Jahrbuch fuer Kunstgeschichte* 18 (1979): 35–112.

4. Peter Thornton and Helen Dorey, *Sir John Soane: The Architect as Collector, 1753–1837* (New York: Abrams, 1992). See also Gillian Darley, *John Soane: An Accidental Romantic* (New Haven: Yale University Press, 1999), 97–116.

5. See the essays in the *Giulio Romano* exh. cat., esp. Amedeo Belluzzi and Kurt W. Forster, "Giulio Romano architetto alla corte dei Gonzaga" (177–221). See also Kurt W. Forster, "Giulio Romano: Fondato, fiero, sicuro, capriccioso, vario, abondante ed universale," *Annali di architettura* 1 (1989): 9–28.

6. The theme of the "union of the visual arts," already central to Giorgio Vasari's vision of the artist's universality and the common root of the visual arts according to the doctrine of *disegno,* is echoed in Soane's chosen title for the publication of his house in 1827: "*Union of architecture, sculpture & painting.*" Though Soane was deeply dissatisfied with John Britton's handling of this publication project, the title stands as a reminder of his intentions. It isn't farfetched to suggest that Johnson's estate, while recognizing the differences among architecture, sculpture, and painting by housing the respective collections in separate buildings, nonetheless implies a unifying concept within the ambit of their common ownership.

7. Forster, "Fondato, fiero," 10 passim.

8. Forster and Tuttle, "Casa Pippi," 104–130. As he had with the transformation of his parents' residence in Rome, Giulio applied what was to become a signature feature of his entire career, an aedicula framed by paradoxical columns composed of alternating cubes and drums; see Kurt W. Forster and Richard Tuttle, "Giulio Romano e le prime opere vicentine del Palladio," *Bollettino CISA, A. Palladio* 15 (1973): 107–119.

9. See John Shearman, "Titian's Portrait of Giulio Romano," *Burlington Magazine* 107 (1966): 172–177.

10. Giorgio Vasari-Milanesi, *Le vite de' piu eccellenti pittori scultori ed architettori,* ed. G. Milanesi (Florence, 1906), 5: 524–556.

11. Perhaps Giulio Romano's greatest accomplishment in mounting ancient fragments within a work of his own invention was to be found in the so-called *Sala dei mesi* of the Regia gonzaghesca in Mantua (though his work was severely truncated by the removal of ancient fragments in a misguided modern attempt to separate originals from later additions). See Jacqueline Burckhardt, *Giulio Romano, Regisseur einer verlebendigten Antike. Die Loggia dei marmi im Palazzo Ducale von Mantua* (Zurich: N.p., 1994).

12. See Forster and Tuttle, "Casa Pippi," 124.

13. Mario Praz, *La casa della vita* (Milan: Adelphi, 1979). See also Mario Praz, *La filosofia dell'arredamento* (Milan: Editori Associati, 1993), 25: "La casa essendo un'espressione, un'espansione dell'io, essendo non soltanto un articolato sistema di convenienze, ma quel mondo intimo in cui piace all'io di rispecchiarsi cotidianamente, ne consegue come primo corollario il possesso."

14. Michael Donough, *Malaparte: A House Like Me* (New York: Potter, 1999), and Gianni Pettena, *Casa Malaparte* (Florence: Le lettere, 1999).

15. Malaparte departed from Adalberto Libera's plans as soon as he had secured a building permit. The variances of the actual building are such as to prompt Libera to exclude the work from the register of his autograph projects; see Marida Talamona, *Casa Malaparte* (Milan: Clup, 1990), 29: "Malaparte, infatti, per la fortissima valenza di autorappresentazione che sin dall'inizio ha assegnato alla casa, la sua casa 'definitiva', non puo certo limitarsi a un ruolo secondario."

16. For the Casa Malaparte, see the remarkable essay by O. Karl Werckmeister, "Casa Malaparte: Eine Topographie maennlicher Kreativitaet,"

Merkur 598 (January 1999): 28–39.

17. Jack McLaughlin, *Jefferson and Monticello: The Biography of a Builder* (New York: Holt, 1988). For Jefferson's relationship with France and his adoption of French cartographic technology, see also André Corboz, *Deux capitales françaises: Saint-Pétersbourg et Washington* (Gollion: Infolio Éditions, 2003).

18. For Jefferson's collection of architectural books, see William Bainter O'Neal, ed., *Jefferson's Fine Arts Library: His Selections for the University of Virginia Together with His Own Architectural Books* (Charlottesville: University Press of Virginia, 1976). Of special interest with regard to autobiographical houses is Jefferson's so-called second Monticello, where he formed a nexus of adjacent and interrelated spaces, such as the bedroom, study, library, and greenhouse on the south side; see William Howard Adams, *Jefferson's Monticello* (New York: Abbeville, 1983).

19. Regarding the scope of Jefferson's knowledge of European urban culture, see George Green Shackelford, *Thomas Jefferson's Travels in Europe, 1784–1789* (Baltimore: John Hopkins University Press, 1995), esp. 157–167. Among the most remarkable demonstrations of the power of print culture is the fact that Jefferson never laid eyes on a building by Palladio but that he felt, as the poet Goethe did before him, the ethical claim underlying Palladio's architecture.

20. See David C. Huntington, *The Landscapes of Frederic Edwin Church: Vision of an American Era* (New York, 1966) and "Frederic Church's 'Niagara': Nature and the Nation's Type," *Texas Studies in Literature and Language* 25, no. 1 (Spring 1983): 100. For Church's estate, see David C. Huntington, "Olana: The Center of the Center of the World," *World Art. Themes of Unity and Diversity,* 3: 767–774.

21. Angela Miller, *Empire of the Eye: Landscape Representation and American Cultural Politics* (Ithaca: Cornell University Press, 1993).

22. Stanislaus von Moos, *Venturi, Rauch & Scott Brown: Buildings and Projects* (New York: Rizzoli, 1987), 244–246.

23. Some allowances must obviously be made with regard to the duration of occupancy and the further evolution of the dwelling. Monticello was a never-ending project, whereas the Vanna Venturi House underwent only minor modifications. But even the latter's lack of evolution may cast a trait of Venturi's entire work into relief.

24. See Talamona, *Casa Malaparte* .

25. Curzio Malaparte, *Febo cane metafisico,* ed. Luigi Martellini (Pistoia: Via del vento, 1998).

26. Adalberto Libera's project, as submitted for permit, consisted of a starkly symmetrical prism whose lower story was to be faced in stone. The terrace above the landward ground floor had no external access, and the fenestration was extremely regular; see Talamona, *Casa Malaparte,* figs. 8–10.

27. See the documents published by Talamona, *Casa Malaparte,* 20–27, 74–77. The decision to exempt Malaparte's project from the recently enacted *piano regolatore paesistico* that was to preserve unique landscape features had already been taken by the minister Giuseppe Bottai. The local building committee had little choice but to ratify approval, citing the project's alleged "invisibility" as the basis for granting an exemption.

28. See Werckmeister, "Casa Malaparte," 28–39. It embraces the circles of at least four lives—Malaparte, the Italian writer Alberto Moravia, the Swiss-French filmmaker Luc Godard, and the German-American filmmaker Fritz Lang—and discovers their intersection in their ideals of masculinity and misogynistic obsession with their own creativity. Political agendas and Surrealist ideas, chiefly André Breton's, clash in the conflicts Godard introduces among man and woman, producer, directors, and actors in the film *Le mépris,* which he shot in Malaparte's house. In Werckmeister's view, it is precisely the political dimension of autobiography that ultimately undermines any attempt at self-stylization, securing for the Casa Malaparte, perhaps against the owner's intentions, a place among key sites of modern culture.

29. In his introduction to Talamona, *Casa Malaparte,* Giorgio Ciucci wrote "la casa e stata il luogo privato di Malaparte, memoria del confine di Lipari, 'immagine della mia nostalgia' per la prigione; ed e stata, al tempo stesso tante case, a secondo del momento e della poetica: alla vuota, surreale stanza di soggiorno si affianca la decadente 'stanza della favorita'; a un ambiente che mima la Stube di una baita alpina, con la grande stufa tirolese in maiolica, si contrappone l'immergersi nell'assoluto degli elementi naturali, da tragedia classica." As an inveterate traveler and war correspondent, Malaparte knew the Russian front, France (where he lived and published in the early 1930s), as well as Greece, Germany, and Poland. See Gianni Grana, *Malaparte* (Florence: La Nuova Italia, 1968).

30. Darley, *John Soane,* 255.

31. Joseph Gandy's representations of built and unbuilt projects seen as ruins from an imaginary moment in time future suggest the true measure of Soane's ambition and despair; see Darley, *Soane,* 242–245.

32. Soane's wish to educate his sons in his

profession prompted the design of his first house in Ealing, and motivated him, long after being forced to abandon his hopes for his sons, to deed the house at Lincoln's Inn Fields to the nation, so that young architects may find worthy models of every genre to study; Darley, *Soane,* 150–168.

33. Francesco Dal Co and Kurt W. Forster, *Frank O. Gehry: The Complete Works* (New York: Monacelli, 1998), 20ff, 150–161.

34. Josef Haeusler, *Profil Pierre Boulez* (Salzburg: Ritter Klagenfurt, 1995), 27–31. Boulez developed the piece from an idea dedicated to the memory of Igor Stravinsky. In fact, the score carries the autograph inscription "afin d'évoquer Igor Stravinsky—de conjurer son absence."

35. Although in planning for more than two years, the project of Gehry's new house in Venice has been temporarily suspended, apparently over hesitations on the architect's part. Interview with Frank Gehry, March 17, 2008.

36. The estate is now a site administered by the National Trust for Historic Preservation.

37. David Whitney and Jeffrey Kipnis, eds., *Philip Johnson: The Glass House* (New York: Pantheon, 1993).

38. Jeffrey Kipnis claimed as much in his introduction to *Glass House,* xxx.

39. "Tutto da me creato e trasfigurato." See Annamaria Andreoli, *Il Vittoriale* (Milan: Electa, 1993).

40. The choice of monastic terminology is of course familiar from Soane's designation of spaces at Lincoln's Inn Fields as a "crypt" and as a "monk's parlor."

41. In Whitney and Kipnis, *Glass House,* Francesco Dal Co stated categorically, if too exclusively, that "New Canaan does not admit basic explanations apart from the autobiographical purpose which Johnson has poured so liberally into these buildings" (121). As a matter of fact, Dal Co detailed at length his thesis that the "New Canaan complex has all the features appropriate to the dwelling of a collector," hence incorporating properties of a "museum" (115).

42. See Craig Owens, "Philip Johnson: History, Genealogy, Historicism," reprinted in Whitney and Kipnis, *Glass House,* 81–90.

43. Reprinted in Whitney and Kipnis, *Glass House,* 79.

44. Philip Johnson, "House at New Canaan, Connecticut," *Architectural Record* (1950), segments 9 and 10.

45. Perhaps the best example of Johnson's technique of distinguished "influences" is to be found in segment 11: "Except for the cylinder, the plan of the house is Miesian. The use of 6 foot closets to divide yet unite space is his. The grouping of the furniture asymmetrically around a coffee table is his. The relation of cabinets to the cylinder, however, is more 'painterly' than Mies would sanction."

46. Quoted after the English translation by Frederick Etchells of Le Corbusier, *Towards a New Architecture* (New York: Payson & Clarke, 1926), 43. Choisy chose to regularize and simplify the geometry of the Acropolis, while half a century later Costantinos A. Doxiadis laid the groundwork for an exceedingly complex and optically sophisticated interpretation of the site in his German dissertation of 1937, published in English translation as *Architectural Space in Ancient Greece* (Cambridge: Harvard University Press, 1972).

47. Peter D. Eisenman, introduction to *Philip Johnson: Writings,* foreword by Vincent Scully, introduction by Peter Eisenman, commentary by Robert A. M. Stern (New York: Oxford University Press, 1979).

48. Kenneth Frampton, "The Glass House Revisited," *Catalogue* 9 (September–October 1978), reprinted in *Glass House,* 92–113.

49. Cf. Nancy Curtis, ed., *Gropius House* (N.p.: Society for the Preservation of New England Antiquities, n.d.), and Winfried Nerdinger, ed., *Walter Gropius* (Cambridge: Busch-Reisinger Museum, and Berlin: Mann, 1986), 269.

50. Schulze, *Philip Johnson,* 139: "I was lucky enough to get to be a correspondent so that I could go to the front when I wanted to go and so it was that I came again to the country that we [Frau Bodenschatz and Philip Johnson] had motored through, the towns north of Warsaw. . . . We saw Warsaw burn and Modlin being bombed. It was a stirring spectacle." From a letter to Frau Bodenschatz.

51. Curzio Malaparte, *Benedetti Italiani* (Florence, 1961), as cited in Talamona, *Casa Malaparte,* 63: "Apro la finestra, ed e la notte di Capri sul mare, chiudo la finestra, ed e la notte di Capri nella mia casa solitaria a picco sul mare, la notte italiana sui libri e sui quadri della mia biblioteca. " Malaparte goes on to enumerate the paintings dear to him—the Delaunay, Kokoschka, Pascin, Chagall, and Morandi—clearly revealing a vision that converts the house into a chamber of transit between the views it offers and the paintings it harbors.

52. See Giambattista Tiepolo's *Capriccios,* Goya's *Proverbios,* and Friedrich's numerous watercolors of owls; cf. H. D. Russell, *Rare Etchings by Giovanni Battista and Giovanni Domenico Tiepolo,* exh. cat. (Washington, D.C.: National Gallery, 1972), and Roberto Calasso, *Il rosa del Tiepolo* (Milan: Adelphi, 2006), 180–192. For

Friedrich's watercolors of owls, see Hubertus Gassner, ed., *Caspar David Friedrich. Die Erfindung der Romantik,* exh. cat. (Essen: Museum Folkwang and Hamburg: Kunsthalle, 2006), 132–137.

53. These watercolors dating from the mid-1830s were united for the first time in the exhibition *Caspar David Friedrich* (2006), figs. 133–137. The exhibition also attempted to re-create transparent images that were artificially backlit and extremely popular in the early nineteenth century (350). In these images the contrast between trees (representing the life of nature) and ruins (descriptive of the inevitable corruption of all human handiwork) under moonlight form something of a cliché, but they resonate strongly with the same ambiguous meaning that strikes one in the night view of the Johnson estate.

54. Argument presented at the symposium "Philip Johnson and the Constancy of Change," at the Yale School of Architecture, New Haven, February 16–18, 2006.

55. Jeff Wall, *Dan Graham's Kammerspiel* (Toronto: Art Metropole, 1991), 57. I'm grateful to Detlef Mertins for suggesting that I consider this probing text in the specific context of my analysis.

56. Ibid., 57.

57. Ibid.

58. Werckmeister, "Casa Malaparte," 28–39.

59. Massimo Bontempelli, *"Scoperte notturne,"* in *Viaggi e scoperte* (Florence: Vallecchi, 1922), 148.

60. Schulze, *Philip Johnson,* 147ff.

61. Several of his early clients were collectors or were closely connected with the Museum of Modern Art, from the De Menils to Mrs. John D. Rockefeller III, from Burton Tremaine to Richard C. Davis. See also Schulze, *Philip Johnson,* 199–227.

62. Marcel Proust, *Le Côté de Guermantes* (1920), 1: 168: "Nous travaillons à tout moment à donner sa forme à notre vie, mais en copiant malgré nous comme un dessin les traits de la personne que nous sommes et non de celle qu'il nous serait agréable d'être."

Philip Johnson:
Act One, Scene One—
The Museum of Modern Art?

Terence Riley with Joshua Sacks

At once a rabble-rouser and a relative unknown, Philip Johnson was a zealous advocate of all things modern in the early stages of his career. His work at the Museum of Modern Art from 1930–34 can be seen as act one in a varied and long career. It was there that Johnson debuted as a twenty-four-year-old critic, organizing a series of important exhibitions that would inject a new design aesthetic into contemporary American culture.

Johnson discovered and then converted to modern architecture late in his undergraduate studies at Harvard. Until then he had been a directionless philosophy major who was so antsy that he installed a lectern in his room so he could study standing up. He left school a number of times for medical reasons, which he later described as a series of psychological crises. His senior year was a turning point. That year he met both Henry-Russell Hitchcock, who introduced him to the work of J. J. P. Oud, and the soon-to-be director of the new Museum of Modern Art, Alfred Barr, who was teaching at Wellesley College when Johnson's sister Theodate was finishing her studies there.

Like the conversion of St. Paul, Johnson's was sudden, life-changing, and accompanied by visions. While later in his life many saw Philip as a cynic, there is little evidence of that in the young college graduate. Consider excerpts taken from personal letters written in Europe during the summer of 1930, after he and Hitchcock had decided to write a new book on modern architecture. In a letter to his mother, Johnson writes on a new direction in his life: "I am having a thrilling time, perhaps the most thrilling of my life, but I guess you know me well enough to know that whatever time I am having is the most thrilling of my life. But just to have a real scholar like Russell want to work out a book with me is most thrilling."[1]

Architecture affected all phases of his life. "Last night I hardly dreamt of buildings at all. It is a strange fact that not one night has gone by but that I have had some dream on architecture. So has it got into my blood."[2] These visions were sparked by new discoveries. Johnson notes, "I wish I could communicate the feeling of seeing [Mies' Tugendhat House]. I have only had similar architectural experience[s] before [Oud's work] and in old things [like] the Parthenon."[3]

In Hitchcock he found someone who was both a colleague and a teacher (fig. 1). He spent the summer of 1930 with Hitchcock passionately discussing the new architecture that they were seeing in France, Belgium, the Netherlands, Sweden, Germany, and Switzerland, where they parted company, Hitchcock returning to the United States and Johnson traveling to Austria and Czechoslovakia. With regard to things architectural, Johnson learned to be critical with Hitchcock. "My relation to Russell in the business is somewhat that of an apprentice, but I struggle hard and with some success to keep my judgment independent. I find that if I contradict loudly and positively enough that he begins to think something is wrong with his ideas after all and then we come to some agreement."[4]

As he assumed a new persona, Johnson took pleasure in being perceived as tedious: "My business is to see that he actually gets on paper the results of our talks. Of course, to me it does not seem as if we talk and think shop all the time, but Cary [Ross] assures me that we talk nothing else and that it is if anything rather boring. But this is the first time I have known enough about anything . . . to be boring to people."[5]

Neophyte that he was, Johnson had a keen intellect and was worldly beyond his years, qualities that are equally evident in his letters from the period. "[Rubens's] Descent from the Cross struck me with renewed vigor. It is a tremendously religious picture, and I feel more at home with Rubens because of this masterpiece. [But] we couldn't stand [Antwerp] any longer and drove along in the late but light evening to a charming hotel on the mouth of the Rhine. . . . We had a real Dutch breakfast, which took us three hours to eat, since we combined it with a discussion of Proust. Russell is a wonderful traveling companion. [Theodate] knows all his bad sides and will tell you about [them] *con amore,* but he is very tender hearted, enthusiastic and brilliant intellectually. His mind works like mine in discontinuous jumps, but he really knows a lot and can synthesize his knowledge."[6]

Though Barr, Hitchcock, and Johnson were unabashed aesthetes, Barr, the son of a Presbyterian minister, had no patience for Proustian languor (fig. 2). In deputizing Hitchcock and Johnson to search out the new architecture, he also expected them to be activists in its cause. When Johnson missed an opportunity to cultivate a potential supporter, Barr dressed him down. Johnson responded, "I did not resent your sermon in the slightest. After all what I want most to do is be influential and if there is method why not learn it."[7]

While this ambition seems nothing less than adult-rated, in other letters Johnson is still clearly subject to parental guidance. He asks his mother, "And then there is one other matter, which I must talk over with you. There is this very great architect here who does the best interiors in the world. Do you think it would be too much expense to let him do my apartment? The furniture plus duty would not cost as much as [Donald] Deskey, [no]where near, I have found that out, and it would be the first room entirely in my latest style in America. Wire me if you think it out of the question."[8] (She didn't. Thus, the "very great architect"—who happened to be Mies van der Rohe—got his first commission in the United States; fig. 3.) In another instance, Philip speaks of his lawyer father, with whom he maintained a cool relationship: "I [got] father's letter on the boat and the other copy in Paris, and am very glad to have a [permanent] copy. He may rest assured I have no more intention of doing any building at this my youthful age. There are too many problems I should like to work out first. The strategic time is later, though if I had all the money in the world I would just build continuously, and keep on experimenting."[9]

While building would have to wait, at the end of 1930 Johnson was named director of MoMA's first exhibition on architecture, a parallel effort to Hitchcock's book, both of which would appear in February 1932. Hitchcock and Johnson

fig. 1 Henry-Russell Hitchcock, codirector of the exhibition *Modern Architecture: International Exhibition.* Photograph, 1938

fig. 2 Alfred H. Barr, Jr., Philip Johnson, Margaret Scolari Barr, Cortona, Italy, 1932. Museum of Modern Art Archives, New York, Margaret S. Barr Papers (MA2)

fig. 3 Turtle Bay apartment of Philip Johnson with furniture by Ludwig Mies van der Rohe, 1930, from the exhibition catalogue for *Modern Architecture: International Exhibition,* Museum of Modern Art, New York, February 9, 1932–March 23, 1932 (EX15.1.79)

preferred their life experiences to the formal training of their peers. "Russell and I find that we have a tremendous advantage over everyone else in that we have seen much more than anybody."[10] Beginning in the spring of 1931, Johnson—virtually unknown outside of the interlocking circles of Harvard and the recently opened Museum of Modern Art—began letting people know about this advantage. Johnson, Hitchcock, and Barr developed an entire lexicon for disparaging the architecture that strayed from the emerging International Style: Half-modern, modernistic, pseudo-modern, modernique. Johnson writes in an article in *Creative Art,* "The trips of Norman Bel Geddes and Joseph Urban to Europe have made ribbon windows the mode, even if these men have never fully understood the new architecture."[11]

When the then fifty-year-old Architectural League staged its annual exhibition in the spring of 1931, Johnson mounted a hugely successful campaign to support the young architects whose work had been excluded. Hired men paced in front of the League show wearing sandwich boards that urged people to go to a rented storefront to see "real modern architecture" at the *Rejected Architects* exhibition, which had been organized and funded by Johnson.

Though the architectural establishment was clearly flummoxed by the now twenty-five-year-old critic and activist, it would have been easy to ask, "What does he really know?" Well traveled as he was, Johnson had never studied architecture or architectural history. Yet his words belie an innate rapport with the aesthetic potential of modern architecture that transcended academic study (fig. 4). Johnson speaks of Mies's Tugendhat house: "The main room, which serves as dining room, living room, and library, is twenty seven meters long and the wall is completely of glass, as is one of the side walls, at least ten meters long. The steel posts are clad in chrome, an onyx wall separates the library from the main living room, and a curving wall of some exotic wood makes the dining niche. The room is very low. The proportions are exquisite."[12]

If Johnson identified Mies as a critical innovator, more so than did either Barr or Hitchcock, he shared their antipathy to functionalism. He derided Swiss architects and their handling of technology: "They sacrifice their ideas of beauty, which they regard as wrong, in order to have windows that, god knows, only the Swiss would find practical. . . . These people study technical things [too much]. They can't really understand it as well as an engineer, but if they know a little they think they know it all, and then instead of consulting an engineer they do their own work along that line and the result is anything but happy."[13]

Even as he was organizing the International Style show, Johnson not only injected himself into the League brouhaha, he also found time to obtain for Oud a visiting professorship at Columbia (which he declined), organize the short-lived American Union for New Architecture, and try to get commissions for various architects through his father's business contacts, resulting in Clauss & Daub's filling station for Standard Oil and a Richard Neutra design for an aluminum-bodied bus (fig. 5). He also floated the improbable idea that Mies might be a good candidate to design an airplane and persuaded his parents to commission Oud to design them a country house, which went unbuilt. Clauss & Daub subsequently produced a second design, featured on the cover of the *Rejected Architects* pamphlet, and William Priestley, a young American architect who had studied at the Bauhaus, produced a third. Whether his parents knew anything of the later designs is not clear.

His duties in organizing the International Style show were varied and not all glamorous. While he is rightly remembered for its content, Johnson also acted as registrar and installer, unpacking crates, hanging photos, producing drawings, and repairing damaged models on a shoe-string Depression budget (fig. 6). Exhausted, he spent the opening night of the show in a clinic, missing the festivities.

While the importance of the International Style show is now unquestioned, an impatient Johnson was disappointed in the immediate results: "For the most part, the critics either make excerpts from the catalog, or if they are constitutionally opposed to modern architecture, they merely remark that the exhibition displeases them."[14] Nonetheless, he and Hitchcock plunged themselves into their next project, *Early Modern Architecture: Chicago, 1870–1910,* which opened the next year. This more modest effort—there was no catalogue, only a mimeographed handout—was both a historical view as well as an implicit criticism of the New York skyscraper school.

Despite Johnson's disappointment in the reviews of the previous show, Henry McBride, writing for the *New York Sun,* exemplified the growing rapport between Johnson and the media: "Philip Johnson, I very much fear, is destined to die young. Some New Yorkers will probably massacre him—and shortly. Do you know what his latest is? He has arranged an exhibition in the Museum of Modern Art that tends to prove that Chicago invented skyscrapers. He snatches the one aesthetic glory we have left, snatches it in broad daylight with everyone looking—and takes it to Chicago" (fig. 7).[15]

Johnson makes the implicit criticism of New York's skyscraper architects explicit in various articles published at the same time, taking to task—among others—C. H. Edgell, dean of the Harvard School of Architecture, Ralph Walker, Thomas Talmadge, a writer and proponent of the influence of art deco, and Hugh Ferriss. In an article in *The Arts,* kettle-Johnson rather blithely points out that pot-Ferriss is "not an architect" but a producer of "falsely lighted renderings that picture fantastic crags rising high above dark caverns."[16] In a letter to Raymond Hood, the preeminent skyscraper

fig. 6 Installation view of the exhibition *Modern Architecture: International Exhibition,* Museum of Modern Art, New York, February 10, 1932–March 23, 1932 (IN15.1)

FROM MASONRY TO STEEL

fig. 7 Stages in the Evolution of the Skyscraper: Philip Johnson ... ," *Midweek Pict'l* (New York), January 23, 1933. Department of Public Information Records, I.2 (1; 802). Museum of Modern Art Archives, New York (MA551)

architect in New York, Johnson delivers the sort of passive-aggressive compliment/ critique for which he was becoming well known: "I am convinced that you have built by far the most successful [skyscrapers in New York] and may I tell you how much I like the McGraw-Hill Building? It is much better than any picture of it. Only the motif at the top strikes me as unnecessarily decorative."[17]

Johnson's first solo effort was to be a "big" show on industrial design. Depression-era economics demanded a more modest production entitled *Objects: 1900 and Today*, which opened the same year as the skyscraper show (fig. 8). Johnson described it thus: "This exhibition of decorative and useful objects is arranged with the purpose of contrasting the design, and the attitude toward design, of two modern periods. One is not necessarily better than the other."[18] The uncharacteristic evenhandedness was, undoubtedly, due to two factors. Johnson could have presumed that the then unfashionable art nouveau was no threat to his vision of contemporary design, not as great a threat as art deco, anyway. Furthermore, most of the turn-of-the-century objects on display had been borrowed from either his mother or members of the Rockefeller family, neither of whom he could afford to offend.

In one of the pairings, a decorative bibelot was contrasted with nothing but a card inscribed with the deadpan message: "Ornamental *objets d'art* are avoided in modern interior architectural schemes."[19] This sort of un-museum-like attitude further enticed the media. Writing in the *Post*, Aaron Marc Stein commented, "This contrast of an exhibit with no exhibit ... is rather more significant than a simply amusing stunt."[20] Others noted Johnson's "latest adventure in smart installation," which makes the rest of the museum look rather stodgy and forlorn."[21]

Yet another show opened that same year, *Young Architects from the Midwest*, again without a catalogue and with little visual documentation. Even so, it stands out as one of Johnson's great contributions to contemporary architectural criticism. While the Museum of Modern Art declared itself committed to the "conscientious, continuous, resolute distinction of quality from mediocrity," this show, the predecessor of all *Young Architect* shows, books, and lectures, was clearly speculative.[22] Johnson justified the effort: "The younger generation, now beginning their independent practice, have broken away from academic design. They have not had as much opportunity to build as their predecessors, but more to observe and study."[23] Conceiving an exhibition on the basis of the collective promise of George Fred Keck, Hans Oberhammer, Hamilton Beatty, Wallace Teare, and Howard Fisher, among others, rather than performance, was an unprecedented move by Johnson.

The media responded, in this case rather unconvinced, as if in dialogue with him: "The artists are modernists because—Mr. Johnson explains this with the utmost tact—they have not had as many opportunities to build as their predecessors and consequently have had more time to observe....This, which has heretofore been their misfortune, may ultimately prove to be their good luck."[24]

The "big" industrial design show, *Machine Art*, finally opened in 1934, showcasing not only objects by designers enamored of the machine aesthetic, such as Le Corbusier, but also objects designed by anonymous engineers, machine parts, and even whole machines (fig. 9). The promiscuous intermingling of art and machine within the walls of a museum provoked both outrage and delight.

Henry McBride, citing Henri Stendahl, Friedrich von Schiller, and Samuel Butler, thundered in the *New York Sun:* "I refuse to pretend that a machine is a human and that its children can be works of art."[25] A more supportive Helen Appleton Read, citing William Morris, the Bauhaus, and Thorsten Veblen, countered in the *Brooklyn Eagle:* "The exhibition has many sound reasons for being shown in a museum of modern art, although it is necessary to analyze them lest it be regarded as a somewhat precious and ultra stunt."[26] Critics even cited other critics' reviews in a highly unusual media dialogue. The *New Yorker* contributed a cartoon. The installation design, produced in collaboration with Jan Ruhtenberg, was also noted by the press. The *New York Times* review opened with the observation: "First of all, the exhibition is splendidly installed."[27] In just four years Johnson had emerged from the obscurity of gilded

fig. 8 Installation view of the exhibition *Objects: 1900 and Today,* Museum of Modern Art, New York, April 10, 1933–April 25, 1933. Photographic Archive, Museum of Modern Art Archives, New York (IN27.1)

fig. 9 Installation view of the exhibition *Machine Art,* Museum of Modern Art, New York, March 5, 1934–April 29, 1934. Museum of Modern Art, New York (IN34.2)

youth to become the talk of the town. He was widely appreciated for his wit, his energy, and his style in an age that valued all of them highly. Like a meteor, he suddenly appeared, caused a great burst of energy for all to see, and then, just as quickly, disappeared.

After *Machine Art* closed, Johnson left the museum to pursue a career in the extreme right of American and European politics. His initial proposal to forge a cultural alliance with the populist demagogue Huey "Kingfish" Long, then a senator from Louisiana, would have remained a historical farce had it not been for his subsequent associations with much less risible figures, including the anti-Semitic radio priest Father Coughlin. His presence at some of the twentieth century's most awful moments, including a Nuremberg rally and the Wehrmacht's invasion of Poland, was equally unconscionable.

Johnson broke off his political associations before America joined the war effort, served in the Army under the watchful eyes of suspicious superiors, returned to Harvard to study architecture, and then, after an absence of almost sixteen years, returned to the Museum of Modern Art as the director of the Department of Architecture and Design in the early 1950s. For the rest of his life his reputation would be stained by his activities in the mid- to late-1930s, causing some to see an inherently dark side to him, others to see a fatal flaw in his understanding of modernism, and others to dismiss him as unhinged by an obsession with Germans and things German.

Nonetheless, his contemporaries found his about-face inexplicable. One reporter referred to his sudden departure from the museum and its circle as surreal. I found occasions in the last years of his life to quietly discuss those years, and, to his credit, he never tried to insinuate a seed of justification for his actions, never adopted a position that was less contrite than that he had taken in public. But still, I asked, how he could have left the museum, an institution that had given his life so much direction and offered him so much accomplishment? He responded, after reflection, "My father thought I was a mama's boy, which I was. I never got a paycheck from the museum, so he thought of it as volunteer work, something women did. I felt I had to do something else."[28]

Poring over Philip Johnson's letters of the period leaves one feeling present at the birth of not only a new moment in modern architecture but of a self-realized individual as well. The names, dates, and places are a fascinating record of an amazing period in architecture and in Johnson's life. Invariably typewritten, with alternating Berlin and New York addresses on his self-designed sans serif stationery, the letters conjure an image of a young man happily away from home, furiously typing away well into the night to dispatch architectural reports from the front.

Characteristic of his letters is his notably parsimonious use of commas and even spaces between words, as if they were hindrances to his, literally, getting the word out, rat a tat tat tat. The same impatience was evident sixty-five years later. I recall one day when I was walking with him from his office on Third Avenue to his home in Museum Tower. As we talked, the light turned green, at which point the eighty-eight-year-old Philip began to sort of jog, all the while speaking. I asked him why we were running, if that was what you would call it, and he replied, "Well, if you walk you hit a red light at Park Avenue."[29]

Notes

1. Philip Johnson (The Hague), letter to Mrs. H. Johnson, June 20, 1930; Philip Johnson Papers, Museum of Modern Art Archives, New York (hereafter PJ, MoMA Archives).

2. Philip Johnson (Berlin), letter to Mrs. Homer H. Johnson, August 6, 1930: PJ, MoMA Archives.

3. Philip Johnson, letter to J. J. P. Oud, August 30, 1931; PJ, MoMA Archives.

4. Philip Johnson (Hamburg), letter to Mrs. Homer H. Johnson, July 7, 1930; PJ, MoMA Archives.

5. Ibid. Ross was a wealthy young graduate of Yale and served as Barr's unpaid assistant at MoMA. He was in Europe in the summer of 1930 to act as witness to Barr's marriage to Margaret Scolari-Fitzmaurice in Paris.

6. Philip Johnson (The Hague), letter to Mrs. H. Johnson, Junes 20, 1930; PJ, MoMA Archives.

7. Philip Johnson (Berlin), letter to Alfred H. Barr, Jr. (Paris), undated [August 1931]; PJ, MoMA Archives.

8. Philip Johnson, letter to Mrs. H. Johnson, July 21, 1930; PJ, MoMA Archives.

9. Philip Johnson (The Hague), letter to Mrs. H. Johnson, Junes 20, 1930; PJ, MoMA Archives.

10. Philip Johnson (Berlin), letter to Mrs. H. Johnson, August 6, 1930; PJ, MoMA Archives.

11. Philip Johnson, "Rejected Architects," *Creative Art* 8, no. 6 (June 1931): 435.

12. Philip Johnson (on board the *Bremen*), letter to J. J. P. Oud, September 17, 1930 (apparently this letter was never mailed); PJ, MoMA Archives.

13. Ibid.

14. Philip Johnson, letter to J. J. P. Oud, March 17, 1932; PJ, MoMA Archives.

15. Henry McBride, "Philip Johnson's Architectural Show Presents the Case Fully," New York *Sun*, January 21, 1933; Public Information Scrapbooks, no. 2, Museum of Modern Art Archives, New York (hereafter PIS, MoMA Archives).

16. Philip Johnson, "The Skyscraper School of Modern Architecture," *Arts* 17, no. 8 (May 1931): 569.

17. Philip Johnson, letter to Raymond Hood, May 27, 1931; PJ, MoMA Archives.

18. Philip Johnson, *Objects: 1900 and Today. An Exhibition of Decorative and Useful Objects Contrasting Two Periods of Design* (New York: Museum of Modern Art, 1933), [1].

19. Ibid., [14].

20. Aaron Marc Stein, "Art Nouveau: Museum of Modern Art Presents Design of 1900 and That of Today for Comparison," *New York Post,* April 8, 1933; PIS, no. 2, MoMA Archives.

21. Quoted in "Exhibitions in New York— Objects: 1900 and Today, unidentified newspaper, April 8, 1933; PIS no. 2, MoMA Archives.

22. Quoted in *A Memorial Tribute: Alfred H. Barr* (New York: Museum of Modern Art, 1982), [32].

23. Philip Johnson, *Work of Young Architects in the Middle West* (New York: Museum of Modern Art, 1933), [1].

24. "Attractions in the Galleries," unidentified journal, undated; PIS, no. 2, MoMA Archives.

25. Henry McBride, "Museum Shows Machine Art in a Most Unusual Display," *New York Sun,* March 5, 1934; PIS, no. 13, MoMA Archives

26. Helen Appleton Read, "Machine Art: Modern Museum Provides Long-Awaited Last Chapter in Machine Aesthetics—Social and Economic Aspects Convincingly Set Forth," *Brooklyn Eagle,* March 11, 1934; PIS no. 13, MoMA Archives.

27. Edward Alden Jewell, "Machine Art Seen in Unique Exhibit," *New York Times,* March 6, 1934; PIS, no. 13, MoMA Archives.

28. In conversation with Philip Johnson, December 1992.

29. In conversation with Philip Johnson, May 1993.

Johnson on TV

Beatriz Colomina

fig. 1 Mies van der Rohe, Farnsworth House, Plano, Illinois, 1945–50. *Blueprints for Modern Living*

fig. 2 Glass House, New Canaan, Connecticut, 1949. From John M. Jacobus, Jr., *Philip Johnson* (1962)

Two persistent dreams of the twentieth century, that of the all-glass house and that of television, were finally realized at about the same time and in the same place: the suburbs of America. If experiments with glass and glass fantasies had played a dominant role in science fiction and in modern architecture since the mid-nineteenth century, only by the mid-twentieth century was the dream inhabited, in Mies van der Rohe's Farnsworth House in Plano, Illinois, and Philip Johnson's Glass House in New Canaan, Connecticut (figs. 1, 2). Two spacecraft had landed: the Farnsworth, floating just above the ground, as though coming in to land, and the Glass House, finally resting on the ground, down on its solid pad, anchored in place and yet somewhat a "raft," in Johnson's words, or, one could even say, a flying carpet. What had been experimented with in drawings, models, writings, and pavilions in fairs had become useful (figs. 3, 4). As Louis Kahn put it in a television program with Philip Johnson: "The Glass House is a marvelous building because it stated very elegantly what was in the secret recesses of everybody's mind at the time of its conception. It brought out the picture of what modern architecture wanted to be."[1] The house as an image, then, a photograph of what everybody had in mind, a dream in physical form. The dream of transparency finally inhabited (fig. 5).

The Glass House represented the realization of the century-old dream of a transparent house that extended from the science fiction–like quality of Paul Scheerbart's images of glass buildings in an ideal future in his novels and in his 1914 collection of aphorisms *Glasarchitektur*, dedicated to Bruno Taut, to Taut's own Glashaus (the pavilion for the glass industry in the Werkbund exhibition of Cologne of 1914) (fig. 6), to Mies van der Rohe and Lilly Reich's Glass Room in Stuttgart (1927), his German Pavilion at the International Exhibition of Barcelona of 1929, and his project for a Glass House on a Hillside (1934); to George Fred Keck's House of Tomorrow and the Crystal House (photographed with Buckminster Fuller's Dymaxion car parked in the garage), both built at the 1933–34 Century of Progress International Exhibition in Chicago, and so on.

By 1949 this dream of a house defined only by glass walls—or, we could even say, the absence of walls—was fully realized in Mies's and Johnson's houses. But the absence of traditional walls does mean that the inhabitants of glass houses are exposed. As a Danish reporter seeing American houses with big picture windows in the postwar years put it: "A glass house bespeaks more security than a stone house because the owner can afford to dispense with the safety of the stone."[2] Or as Johnson said of his house in the 1965 CBS program *This Is Philip Johnson,* it was

fig. 3 Glass House, New Canaan, Connecticut, 1949. From John M. Jacobus, Jr., *Philip Johnson* (1962)

fig. 4 Farnsworth House, Plano, Illinois, 1945–50. From Werner Blaser, *Mies van der Rohe: The Art of Structure* (1965)

GLASS HOUSE

It consists of just one big room completely surrounded by scenery

As director of the Museum of Modern Art's architectural department, Philip C. Johnson likes to build extremely modern houses and try them out on himself. His latest experiment, amid the hilly scenery near New Canaan, Conn., is the current conversation piece of U.S. architecture. It consists of two striking structures, one almost entirely transparent, the other almost completely opaque (p. 96). The first is a 32x56-foot building of only one room completely walled by glass. Kitchen, dining, sleeping and living areas are separated merely by cabinets which stop short of the 10½-foot ceiling or by such subtle demarcations as furniture placement or a rug. Only the bath, in a 10-foot-wide brick cylinder, is enclosed. The second building, 100 feet away and virtually windowless, has two guest bedrooms, a picture gallery and a study where Johnson can enjoy the contrast of feeling thoroughly walled in.

After living transparently for nine months, Johnson regards his experiment as a success. On 11 acres he has privacy. Heat loss through the plate glass is compensated for by solar heat. Johnson claims the weather's "feel" is spine-tingling: from his fireside a storm is exciting, new snow a lovely miracle. For friends who joke about the perils of stone-throwing, he has an answer: "People don't throw stones at shop windows. Why should they throw them at mine?"

BY DAY anyone can see right through the house. Vertical fiber screens, like those at left and right, shield the interior from the sun's heat. At left: Johnson.

BY NIGHT floodlights illuminate trees outside. Low kitchen cabinets are at left, bath cylinder in center, "bedroom" at right. Dining area is beyond kitchen.

94

CONTINUED ON NEXT PAGE 95

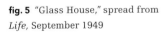

fig. 5 "Glass House," spread from *Life*, September 1949

fig. 6 Bruno Taut, Glashaus under construction, late March–early April, 1914

fig. 7 Glass House, New Canaan, Connecticut, 1949. *Architectural Review*, September 1950

an "opportunity to live in the woods."[3] He insisted that "a wall is only an idea in your mind. If you have a sense of enclosure you are in a room." And to the repeated question of whether his house was a fishbowl that exposed his body to the eyes of others, he answered that in the sixteen years that he had lived in the house, nobody had come up to glue their faces on the glass: "I think it is because people are afraid that you are looking at them."[4] The glass house operates both ways, as artists like Dan Graham have been exploring since the 1970s. But Johnson didn't even experience the glass as transparent but as wallpaper (fig. 7). In another TV program, he says the Glass House "works very well for the simple reason that the wallpaper is so handsome. It is perhaps a very expensive wallpaper but you have wallpaper that changes every five minutes throughout the day and surrounds you with the beautiful nature that sometimes—not this year—Connecticut gives us."[5] The glass provides enclosure, containment rather than openness:

> I built this glass house shortly after Mies van der Rohe gave us all the model with his famous glass house near Chicago [fig. 8]. This one came first, so people think I'm the original. I'm not. I knew the plans of the Farnsworth House very well.... But of course, there are differences.... I wanted to live on the ground. I wanted to be contained. I don't believe in indoor-outdoor architecture. What you want is a contained house to cuddle you, to hold you, to hold you near the hearth. You want to get your back up to a fireplace—any Anglo-Saxon does. Maybe the Italians don't care about that, but we do.... So this house is contained. I must admit the containment is a rather small feature—a black band that runs around the house—but it keeps the landscape away. It turns the landscape into a kind of wallpaper—expensive wallpaper to be sure—but wallpaper, where the sun and the moon and the stars make different patterns.[6]

It is this sense of complete envelopment that makes the minimalist statement architecture: "If you are in a good piece of architecture you have the feeling that you are surrounded."[7] Rather than dematerialize architecture, the glass reinforces its traditional role. "Architecture is how you enclose space. That's why I hate photographs, TV, and motion pictures," Johnson says during the same interview (fig. 9).[8]

fig. 8 Farnsworth House, model, 1947. *Architectural Review,* September 1950

fig. 9 Glass House, scheme XII, 1947, model

A NEW 3-BEDROOM HOUSE FOR $25 DOWN

WALTER AND AMY PRICE STAND IN BROADHURST OUTLINE AT SHOWING, SURROUNDED BY ALUMINUM WINDOWS AND OTHER EQUIPMENT THEY WILL GET

fig. 10 "A New 3-Bedroom House for $25 Down." *Life,* October 29, 1951

fig. 11 Mies van der Rohe with Herbert Greenwald. *Life,* March 18, 1957

Television, too, arrived in the United States at midcentury. Long part of science-fiction fantasies of the future, television was first publicly featured in 1927, prompting Fuller to state that his Dymaxion House, designed the same year, was organized around a TV communication center. The Dymaxion House, he claimed, was equipped with the latest media technology (telephone, radio, television, phonograph, Dictaphone, loudspeakers, microphone, and so on), but some of these technologies barely existed in 1927. Only in the late 1940s and 1950s was TV widely introduced to the American public. DuMont and RCA offered their first sets to the public in 1946, and between 1948 and 1955 nearly two-thirds of American families purchased a television set.[9] In 1950 the most famous of mass-produced suburbs, Levittown in Long Island, offered a television set built into the wall of its prefabricated Cape Cod house (fig. 10). Television had become part of the architecture of the American house.

Nothing could seem to be farther from the high-art world of Mies. And yet his former students and associates Edward Duckett and Joseph Fujikawa said of him, "He liked boxing, or at least he enjoyed watching it on television. . . . He had the largest television screen of anybody I knew. I think Herb Greenwald picked it out for him."[10]

Greenwald was a rabbinical scholar turned real-estate developer whom Mies met in 1946 (fig. 11).[11] The two built, among other projects, the 860–880 Lake Shore Drive apartments in Chicago, twin twenty-five-story glass-and-steel structures on the shores of Lake Michigan containing 275 glass apartments each (fig. 12). The project represented, according to one reporter, the fulfillment of Mies's thirty-year dream of a "skin and bone construction. . . . [Mies] wanted to give city apartment dwellers the feeling of living close to the out of doors, as people in suburbs do who have floor-to-ceiling picture windows in their houses."[12] Lake Shore Drive brings the suburbs to the city, as if stacking suburban houses on top of one another. The apartments are glass houses suspended in the air, their walls allowing "breathtaking" views of the lake from every apartment and at the same time turning each apartment into a display.

At night, the towers become multiplex theaters providing an audience for each other (fig. 13). Each looks on its identical twin as in a mirror image. Inhabitants seemed to feel perfectly at ease. As one of the first tenants put it: "I feel quite tucked in, and not nearly as exposed as I thought I'd feel, now the furniture is in place."[13]

Johnson's Glass House, built at a time when most Americans owned a television, avoided all media technology. There was not a TV set in sight in any of Johnson's houses, including the Hodgson House of 1951, whose client was a CBS executive. In one TV interview, Johnson insisted that the Glass House has "no television, no telephone, no gramophone . . . no noise of any kind."[14] No media in a house designed for the media (fig. 14).

And yet the Glass House itself was operating as a TV set, but not in the obvious sense of the views that the house makes possible. If one can argue that the postwar suburban house operated as a television set, broadcasting family life through the picture window, then Johnson's Glass House closed itself to the outside, much more radically than a stone house could, to become a TV broadcasting studio.

The model was picked up later by authorities on the American house—like

fig. 12 Mies van der Rohe, Lake Shore Drive Apartments, Chicago, 1948–51. From Werner Blaser, *Mies van der Rohe* (1965)

fig. 13 "At night, every apartment turns into a TV set." Mies van der Rohe, Lake Shore Drive Apartments. *Life* [18.03.57]

fig. 14 Glass House, interior view. *Architectural Forum,* November 1949

fig. 15 Johnson in the Guest House. *Life,* September 1949

Martha Stewart, who not only used her own house as a broadcast studio but also owned an estate in Westport, Connecticut, with a series of model houses, in the same way that Johnson had his estate with a series of model structures built over the years, each of which became an opportunity for broadcast. Each time the Glass House seemed to run out of steam, Johnson built a new pavilion, one that renewed the discussion both of the earlier house and of himself. "I keep building around the place because I get itchy," he said. "Nobody asks me to build funny things, so I do them myself as sort of tests. Clients always want something definite with toilets and other unnecessary gadgets, but I can always build what I like for myself. So about every five or six years I build another funny thing."[15]

The Glass House was built first, in 1949; the brick Guest House, also of 1949, was remodeled in 1953 (figs. 15, 16), the pavilion in the lake added in 1962, and the "swimming pool, which is an essential part of the composition, wasn't built until 1963. In 1965, I had some pictures I wanted to hang, so I thought, 'good opportunity, we'll try something funny for a gallery.' Since I didn't want to build it too close to the Glass House, I put it in a bunker. People think it is an underground gallery, but it's not underground at all.... 1970 was the sculpture gallery. I had nothing to build for a long time, and about 1978 I was itchy again, the land next door came up for sale, so I kept expanding."[16] The studio was built in 1980, the Lincoln Kirstein Tower and the Ghost House in 1985, and a visitors' pavilion, Da Monsta, in 1995.

The official story, passed on in architectural scholarship, is that the Glass House is Johnson's laboratory. As Johnson himself put it: "I consider my own house not so much as a home (though it is that to me) as a clearing house of ideas which can filter down later, through my own work or that of others."[17] What he doesn't tell you is that the house is a platform for him on the media—and not only the professional media of the architectural journals, but also the popular media of *Vogue, Look, House Beautiful, Ladies Home Journal,* the *New York Times Magazine, Newsweek, Business Week, House & Garden, Show Magazine,* and so on. Johnson also appeared with astonishing regularity on TV programs, from the 1951 Car Style Show for CBS to his last interview, with Charlie Rose for PBS. The house is almost always at the center of these programs, every new construction an opportunity for reviving the fire.

So what is this house?

The best descriptions are still those of Johnson, who likens his house to a "celestial elevator in which when it snows, you seem to be going up because everything is coming down."[18] The house levitates. As with the common experience of sitting on a train stopped at a station and feeling that it is moving only to realize that it is only the train across the platform that moves, one gets the same feeling in the stomach, the same sense of displacement, except that in the house the movement is vertical rather than horizontal as in a train or in a Mies or Le Corbusier house, where the framing is relentlessly horizontal. And this is precisely the point at which the Glass House, described by Michael Graves as more Miesian than Mies, departs from that lineage.

What is curious about the idea of an elevator is that Johnson also repeatedly noted how much he disliked elevators, how elevators represented the end of architecture, the end of the experience of space in movement. Of the Seagram Building, for example, he wrote: "Unfortunately, the entire experience of Seagram's leads but to the elevator. . . . That claustrophobic box brings visual, processional beauty to a complete dead stop. The visitor can only be restored, if at all, by looking out of a high window. Elevators are here to stay, but one is not forced to love them."[19] But then in "This Is Philip Johnson" he theatrically and proudly crosses the lobby of the Seagram Building and goes where? Into the elevator, where he repeatedly presses the button frenetically while the camera follows him all the way up to his office.

It seems as if the claustrophobia of the elevator goes away when there is only the elevator in the landscape. The Glass House. A free box. A glass elevator with four doors? Stay clear. The containing gesture is now exactly what allows the box to move. Even the black band going around the glass makes sense now, as if it is something to hold on to when the box moves.

Already in 1947, in his book on Mies accompanying the exhibition at the Museum of Modern Art, Johnson had described the Farnsworth House as a "floating

fig. 16 Guest House, New Canaan, Connecticut. *Life,* September 1949

self contained cage" (fig. 17).[20] And Henry-Russell Hitchcock described it as a "beached
yacht" with no provisions for outer living beyond the very confined space of the fly-
screened "deck" and the small travertine "dock" below it.[21] The idea of floating can
already be found in early articles in the popular press, as when *House & Garden* calls
the house a "glass shell that 'floats' in the air" (fig. 18).[22] Johnson happily picked up the
same metaphor for his house, describing it as floating on the sea, even if he disliked
the sea as much as he disliked elevators: "That's why I don't like the seaside. There's
nothing there, unless it's a boat. If there's a boat, it's O.K. In the East River wonderful
barges go by. But God keep me from the Atlantic Ocean. There are a lot of glass houses
that face the ocean, and people like them. But I say there's nothing there."[23]

fig. 19 Glass House, interior view. From *Processes: The Glass House, 1949, and the AT&T Corporate Headquarters, 1978*, September 12–October 31, 1978

fig. 20 Glass House. *Architectural Forum*, November 1949

If Mies's house is a beached yacht, Johnson would rather have his own house be at sea. The Glass House, Johnson says, was designed like a "Chinese box":

You have a box, then you take the lid off and there's another one, there's another one, there's another one. So what we do, we start with a room—but it's a rather large room. It is the landscape from the forest on the road to the forest in the forest. And from the north to the south it's the same way. That's the room. Within that room we create a raft of space—the green lawn around you. On the green lawn we make another raft, which is the house, separate entirely from the green lawn. On this brown lawn, as it where, of the brick floor, we make another lawn: the white rug.... So the living room is just this raft in the brown sea, or the brown lawn (let's mix metaphors) of the paving. That again is on a green lawn, which again is on a forest lawn around. So here [inside] we have the microcosm, and that's [outside] the macrocosm.[24]

To experience the house is to move from floating raft to floating raft, each providing a sense of containment. Space is defined by the outer lines of these rafts, the lawn, the pavement, the rug (figs. 19, 20). The Glass House is not a glass box but a horizontal surface, a raft, drifting among other rafts and having rafts drifting within it.

Is this horizontal movement contradictory to the idea of the vertical elevator or to Johnson's distaste for glass houses by the seaside? Not at all. Johnson accumulates metaphors and repeats them in different combinations. The raft lacks direction; it is floating in the sea, not looking at it from an anchored position as does the modern house. If the raft is an enclosure, if it provides shelter from the sea, which it does, it is in the vertical volume defined by the surface of the raft. "The intimacy of the raft is as great as the intimacy of a closed room. That's what's hard for older architects, who didn't have glass, to understand. On the ocean, on a raft, boy, you are enclosed. You can't step out. Well, you can't step off this white carpet either. And it brings you emotionally together so you can have a conversation."[25]

This evocative idea of the house as a raft had already been launched by Arthur Drexler within a month of the house's completion. In an article in *Interiors* he describes the site of the house as itself a room with carpets laid out within it, the brick platform with the herringbone pattern, and within the platform the "sand-colored carpet, like a raft in the ocean, provides safe passage for a low couch."[26] Was Drexler listening to Johnson, or was Johnson listening to Drexler? Did Johnson do the same thing with his words as he did with the design of the house, picking up ideas from all his critics? Probably. He was a sponge, soaking up things and refining them, simplifying them, like a TV personality, a journalist reporting on his own life in an easily understood language. There is no difference between the reporter and the thing being reported on. Johnson was simply a TV program, a reality-TV show that ran longer than anybody could have imagined.

Notes

1. Louis Kahn, "The Architect (Philip Johnson and Louis Kahn)," *Accent,* CBS, May 14, 1961.

2. Quoted in "Glass House Permits Its Owner to Live in a Room in Nature," *Architectural Forum,* November 1949.

3. *This Is Philip Johnson,* documentary, directed by Merrill Brockway, 1965.

4. Ibid.

5. Philip Johnson, "The Architect (Philip Johnson and Louis Kahn)."

6. Philip Johnson, three-part interview by Rosamond Bernier, *Camera 3,* CBS, 1976, partially transcribed in Rosamond Bernier, "Fons et Origo: The Glass House and What Came of It," working draft, 13–15. A shorter version was later made for the Museum of Television and Radio seminar series "The Artist at Work: Philip Johnson," September 26, 1991.

7. Ibid.

8. Ibid.

9. Lynn Spigel, *Make Room for TV: Television and the Family Ideal in Postwar America* (Chicago: University of Chicago Press, 1992).

10. William S. Shell, "Impressions of Mies: An Interview on Mies van der Rohe, His Early Chicago Years, 1938–1958," with Former Students and Associates Edward A. Duckett and Joseph Y. Fujikawa, pamphlet (Knoxville: University of Tennessee, 1988), 30.

11. Franz Schulze, *Mies van der Rohe: A Critical Biography* (Chicago: University of Chicago Press, 1985), 239.

12. Grace Miller, "People Who Live in Glass Apartments Throw Verbal Stones at Scoffers: Chicago Tenants Praise Lake Shore Drive Cooperatives," clipping from an unidentified newspaper, n.d., Mies van der Rohe Archive, Museum of Modern Art, New York.

13. Ibid.

14. In fact, there was a telephone in the Glass House and a television set in the Guest House, many people recalled.

15. Bernier, "Fons et Origo," 23.

16. Ibid., 24, 41–42.

17. "Philip Johnson (I)" and "Philip Johnson (II)," in Selden Rodamn, *Conversations with Artists* (New York: Devin-Adair, 1957), 52–56, 60–70. Quoted in Peter Eisenman, introduction to *Philip Johnson: Writings* (New York: Oxford University Press, 1979), 21.

18. Quoted in Kenneth Frampton, "The Glass House Revisited," *Catalogue* 9 (September–October 1978), reprinted in David Whitney and Jeffrey Kipnis, eds., *Philip Johnson: The Glass House* (New York: Pantheon, 1993), 99.

19. Philip Johnson, "Whence and Whither: The Processional Element in Architecture," *Perspecta* 9/10 (1965).

20. Philip Johnson, *Mies van der Rohe* (New York: Museum of Modern Art, 1947).

21. Henry-Russell Hitchcock, "The Current Work of Philip Johnson," *Zodiac* 8 (1961): 66.

22. "A Glass Shell That 'Floats' in the Air," *House & Garden,* February 1952.

23. Rosamond Bernier, "Improving His View," *House & Garden,* June 1986, reprinted in Whitney and Kipnis, *Philip Johnson,* 149.

24. "Philip Johnson Interviewed by Rosamond Bernier," 16–17.

25. Ibid.

26. Arthur Drexler, "Architecture Opaque and Transparent: Philip Johnson's Glass and Brick Houses in Connecticut," *Interiors,* October 1949.

SOCIETY, POWER, AND POLITICS.

The Figurehead:
On Monumentality and Nihilism
in Philip Johnson's Life and Work

Joan Ockman

Of Fountainheads and Figureheads

To which history of twentieth-century architecture does Philip Johnson belong (fig. 1)? The canonical histories center on "form-givers," regarded as geniuses and world-historical individuals; on epochal ideas, regarded as engines of historical change; and on the architectural objects themselves—the great buildings, the masterworks—taken as emblems of modernity. All three of these, which tend to overlap, may be called fountainhead histories; they are narratives of greatness and innovation, triumphal testaments to the wellsprings of architectural creativity. They are part of the heroic mythography of modern architecture. We may refer to them as histories of masters, manifestoes, and monuments, or simply, following Nietzsche in the second of his *Untimely Meditations,* as *monumental* history.[1]

In this second *Meditation,* written in 1874 and entitled "On the Uses and Disadvantages of History for Life," Nietzsche's aim is a practical one: to weigh the relative merits of various types of history for the purposes of thinking and living one's life. In invoking Nietzsche's essay here, my own aim is twofold: to reflect on the ways Johnson used history, and to highlight the problems posed to the architectural historian in writing about him. Johnson and his work do not belong to the monumental history of architecture, even if a handful of buildings among his sizable output—most notably the Glass House—have attained iconic status. But as Nietzsche makes clear, greatness isn't a club you can buy your way into. While Johnson would have given much to stake a place among the immortals, he had, to his credit, little illusion about his own artistic talents. As such, he might have heeded Nietzsche's warning against "the man who recognizes greatness but cannot himself do great things." "Much mischief is caused," Nietzsche notes, by "weakly endowed" artists who nonetheless act as arbiters of taste. In imitating and idolizing great monuments, "art can be slain by art."[2]

The second type of history that Nietzsche distinguishes in his *Meditation* is antiquarian. The antiquarian spirit is characterized by reverence for the past. It wants to discover where it has come from and to conserve this patrimony for the future. Like Goethe, who sensed the "strong, rough German soul" while standing in front of a monument to the master builder of Strasbourg Cathedral, the antiquarian seeks to solve the riddle of his own identity through his relationship with the past. "The history of his city becomes for him the history of himself. He reads its walls, its towered gate, its rules and regulations, its holidays, like an illuminated diary of his youth, and in all this he finds again himself, his force, his industry, his joy, his judgment, his folly and vices."[3]

But Nietzsche cautions against abusing this type of history too. For less pious souls, antiquarian history "knows only how to *preserve* life, not how to engender it." The antiquarian sensibility begins to give off a "stench of must and mould" when "it is no longer animated and inspired by the fresh life of the present." "Then there appears the repulsive spectacle of a blind rage for collecting," Nietzsche writes, "a restless raking together of everything that ever existed" and an "insatiable thirst for novelty."[4] For Johnson, the pursuit of a relationship with history impels the trying out and discarding of past styles like a succession of ill-fitting costumes. Yet such a relationship proves elusive. The effort to ascribe any meaning to Johnson's iconographic repertory is thus a mostly meaningless exercise, except as an index of the increasing availability of history itself in the twentieth century as an object to be ransacked and consumed.

The most elaborated manifestation of Johnson's obsessive historicism is, of course, his compound at New Canaan, where monumental longing and antiquarian effeteness converge and are pushed to the point of producing an original but thoroughly narcissistic synthesis. Here Johnson's eclectic and literally farfetched list of "sources" for his Glass House—a list extenuated by the allusions that inform his subsequent, equally *recherché* additions to the estate—is more than a mere conceit.[5] In this personal park, where the sophistication of the connoisseur underwrites the collector's passion for novelty, the architect-owner seeks to arrest time in its tracks, to possess history once and for all by sheer will and wealth. "Every grown-up child should have his version of a playhouse," Johnson declares, like some Bachelardian seigneur, of the dwarf-scale garden folly he constructed on the grounds in 1962, with references to Chinese, Moorish, and Palladian precedents.[6] At New Canaan, the monument becomes the miniature; the sublime, the picturesque. History's tragic passage is transcended through the prerogatives of private property,

fig. 1 David Diao, *Figure/Ground*, 2005

a rich man's solipsism. The sparsity of the main house is thus more a matter of style than substance—of the glass being half full, one might say, rather than, as with Mies van der Rohe's Farnsworth, its principal model, half empty in both a physical and a metaphysical sense.

But if monumental and antiquarian motifs intermingle in Johnson's use of the past, Johnson also mobilizes Nietzsche's third and last type of history, and with more radical and contradictory implications. "If he is to live, man must possess and from time to time employ the strength to break up and dissolve a part of the past," writes Nietzsche. "He does this by bringing it before the tribunal, scrupulously examining it and finally condemning it."[7] Nietzsche calls this type of history *critical;* Michel Foucault, in a postmodern reading of Nietzsche, has connected this concept of critical history to what Nietzsche elsewhere calls genealogy.[8] The critical-genealogical perspective shatters the illusions of totality and continuity, of teleology and evolutionary development, which the monumental and antiquarian approaches, respectively, labor to construct. It approaches history with a lower-case *h,* as a "profusion of entangled events." "If it chances upon lofty epochs," writes Foucault, "it is with the suspicion—not vindictive but joyous—of finding a barbarous and shameful confusion."[9] From such a vantage, history is seen as an "endlessly repeated play of dominations." Its rules are empty in themselves and capable of being bent to multiple purposes. "The successes of history belong to those who are capable of seizing these rules," writes Foucault, "to replace those who had used them, to disguise themselves so as to pervert them, invert their meaning, and redirect them against those who had initially imposed them."[10]

So understood, the history of architecture includes everything from power relations, public relations, business practices, and the caprices of personality and patronage to pure chance. It encompasses both the flow of the mainstream and the rivulets of the avant-garde. And it is within such a history of twentieth-century architecture that Philip Johnson's career may be written large. But critical history too comes with its caveats. In Johnson's case, it reproduces, in a kind of tautology, its subject's own "Nietzschean" self-construction. To dwell on the ironies and mockeries, the perversities and transgressions of the "wicked architect" thus not only seems predictable—they have been rehearsed many times over by Johnson's biographers, critics, journalists, friends, and enemies, and not least flaunted by Johnson himself— but further burnishes the historiographic myth that threatens, now that he is dead, to become hagiography: Nietzsche raised to the second degree—that is, to a style, an aesthetic. Indeed (as with Andy Warhol, whose affinities with Johnson have frequently been noted), Johnson's personal style may be his principal legacy. Philip Johnson's greatest claim to fame may be his claim to fame.

Yet as far as Nietzsche is truly concerned, if the German philosopher's signal contributions to contemporary thought were his revelation of Enlightenment reason as a delusion, of Judeo-Christian morality as a pathology, and of individual will as sovereign in human history, it is important to emphasize that the ultimate purpose of his critique was not simply destructive. In laying bear the "aberrations, passions, and errors" in which the history of human actions is rooted, Nietzsche aimed to implant "a new habit, a new instinct, a second nature, so that our first nature withers away."[11] Read properly, Nietzsche's critical history may, in fact, serve to expose the more cynical misapprehensions of Nietzscheanism.

It was, initially, inherited wealth that gave Philip Johnson the means and independence to achieve a privileged position in the world of architecture. The size of his fortune, derived from holdings in aluminum stock, was a matter of good luck, having appreciated far in excess of his father's expectations when Homer Johnson divvied up his investments among his son and two daughters. Yet if by his own description Philip was a spoiled brat with no reason to subscribe to the work ethic of less privileged individuals, he was still insecure enough to need to prove his worth to himself and others. Nor did he lack the sense of obligation or guilt possessed by certain representatives of his class that it was his duty to contribute something to society. "I'd wasted my life," Johnson explains of the sense of emptiness and despair he felt around 1940 after his failed foray into politics and prior to his decision to pursue a professional career in architecture. "I have a great Puritan sense, that rich people especially should do something. I didn't want to make money, but there has to be something of interest. I realized that I wasn't writing, I wasn't contributing to any cause, black, white, indifferent. So I realized that there was something terribly, terribly lacking."[12]

The series of "misadventures" that commenced a half dozen years earlier, in December 1934, with a road trip to Baton Rouge to throw in his lot with the Louisiana senator Huey P. Long combined a young man's fatal attraction to power with his embrace of a political agenda that was, in fact, not altogether unaltruistic. Earlier that year, Long, a Democrat and an electrifying populist with a weakness for machine guns and graft, had launched his Share Our Wealth campaign with the slogan "Every Man a King" as a response to the poverty and crime unleashed by the Depression. Initially a supporter of Roosevelt's New Deal, he had become frustrated with the American president's initiatives, believing them too superficial to root out the nation's underlying economic problems. Long called for more radical redistribution of wealth and even greater government intervention. The centerpiece of his program was a tax on private fortunes, inheritances, and personal incomes above a certain level, the revenue from which he proposed to give back to every family—"enough for a home, an automobile, a radio, and the ordinary conveniences."[13] Share Our Wealth also included benefits such as federal financing of college education on a merit basis, old-age pensions, bonuses for war veterans, shortened work hours, subsidies for agriculture, and an array of public works programs. While these populist ideas were denounced by those on the right as socialist, by those on the left as resembling the promises Hitler was making in Germany, and by others as so much demagoguery, Long insisted on his belief in private ownership and the profit motive, and argued that by reducing the concentration of vastly disproportionate wealth in the hands of the very few, his program would actually increase the number of American millionaires.

In March 1934 Long accepted an invitation to debate Norman Thomas, the leader of the American Socialist Party, at the grandiose Mecca Temple on West 55th Street in New York City. The resolution on the table was that "capitalism is doomed and cannot now be saved by redistribution of wealth." The Louisiana politician took the negative, arguing that capitalism should not be rejected but rather reformed. The debate's subject was prompted by a book that had been published two years earlier by a maverick political economist named Lawrence Dennis. The mulatto son of a wealthy Georgia lawyer and his mistress, Dennis was a prodigy who had acquired fame as a child evangelist and written his autobiography at the age of ten. Thirteen years older than Johnson, he had attended Exeter and then Harvard, graduating in 1920. After spending a decade in Latin America as a diplomat and subsequently as a consultant to the Seligman Trust—one of the largest international banking firms in New York, established by German-Jewish immigrants—he became thoroughly disillusioned with the American political and financial system and quit his career to concentrate on writing philosophy, publishing *Is Capitalism Doomed?* in 1932. Dennis predicted in this book that the current debt-ridden and decrepit American system of government would find itself hard-pressed to compete with the rising tide of totalitarianism in Europe, whose vitalist popular appeal he compared to a living religion.[14]

Johnson had likewise come to feel Roosevelt was a "weasler" after initially backing him.[15] Upon reading *Is Capitalism Doomed?* shortly after it was published, he sought Dennis out and became his acolyte. Johnson may well have been in the packed audience of twenty-five hundred New Yorkers who turned out to hear Thomas and Long debate. He may also have been present two days later when Dennis himself debated the editor of the *Daily Worker,* Clarence A. Hathaway, in the same venue on the question of whether fascism or communism could more effectively supplant capitalism. The following month, in April 1934, Johnson and Alan Blackburn, a colleague at the Museum of Modern Art and another Harvard alumnus, began holding planning meetings in Johnson's Manhattan apartment with the intent of founding a national political party. Johnson's abrupt departure from the rarefied aesthetic milieu of MoMA later the same year to follow Long, and his embrace of an economic program that would have put his own fortune on the line, thus must be understood not just as the headstrong act of an overprivileged rich boy but as a symptomatic response to the Depression's darkest years. While the stock market had bottomed out under Roosevelt's incentives and unemployment had begun to rebound slightly from its high of one-quarter of the population the year before, banking empires and personal fortunes were still crumbling and bread lines remained ubiquitous in 1934. If some of Johnson's associates at MoMA and in the press viewed his decision with incomprehension or as an escapade, it is not insignificant that A. Conger Goodyear, then president of the museum and the scion of a Louisiana lumber fortune, gave Johnson his blessing.[16]

Johnson has repeatedly been described as chameleonlike in terms of both his politics and aesthetics. I would argue the contrary. Once he had been socially and intellectually formed by his patrician family background, by his years at Harvard and in the New York cultural milieu of the late 1920s and early 1930s, and by his experience of the Depression, his worldview remained entirely consistent, philosophically speaking, throughout his career. He held two beliefs as deeply and unwaveringly as any religious creed. The first of these—epitomized by his well-known quip that he would rather sleep in the nave of Chartres Cathedral with the closest toilet two blocks away than in a Harvard house with back-to-back bathrooms[17]—was in the primacy of art and beauty. The second was in the superiority of will and instinct over reason. This latter belief, underpinned by the Heraclitean conviction that the only constant in human history was change, and confirmed by the philosophy of Nietzsche and the tutelage of Dennis, shaped his instrumental and unsentimental view of power. It resonated with the overarching idea that Dennis was to put forward in his next book, *The Coming American Fascism* (1936), in which the theorist affirmatively answered the question he had posed in *Is Capitalism Doomed?* "The fascist scheme of things is an expression of human will," stated Dennis, "which creates its own truths and values from day to day to suit its changing purposes." In contrast to a defeatist liberalism resting on vague moral absolutes like "equality" and "reason," fascism is essentially "the human will reacting to the changing situations of life in the eternal struggle for existence."[18]

Johnson's veneration of beauty and his belief in this *Lebensphilosophie* were the fundamental values by which he set his compass until his death in 2005. Although undoubtedly a political dilettante in the 1930s, he was also more than an overexcited homosexual with a taste for leather and jackboots when he accompanied the Wehrmacht into Poland in September 1939 as a correspondent for Father Coughlin's far–right-wing *Social Justice*. The earnestness of his ideological commitment is attested to by a project he completed only two months earlier, a studious translation into English of an essay by Werner Sombart, *Weltanschauung, Science and Economy* (Weltanschauung, Wissenschaft und Wirtschaft) (fig. 2). Dedicated by Sombart upon its original German publication the previous year to Hitler's erstwhile economic minister and head of the Reichsbank, Hjalmar Schacht, the essay is a relatively minor work in Sombart's oeuvre. But it is founded on his belief or wish that a new "worldview" was coming into being that would supersede the era of free-market economy with one of centralized planning and would displace the "liberalistic-pacifistic-individualistic standpoint" with the binding force of "national community."[19]

Sombart had begun his career around the turn of the century as an economic historian and social thinker in the lineage of Marx and Engels, and his trajectory exemplifies the shared roots of Marxism and National Socialism as critiques of capitalism. But in distancing himself from the perspective of Marx's historical protagonist, the proletariat, in favor of an organic, neo-medievalist conception of nationhood, Sombart upheld a hierarchical and aristocratic model of society, a stance that undoubtedly appealed to Johnson's own predispositions. In an earlier book, *Händler und Helden* (Merchants and Heroes, 1915), Sombart had hailed World War I as the inevitable clash between the noble *Kultur* of Germany and the base commercial *Zivilisation* of a nation like Britain. He counterposed the "trader spirit" of the latter, contemptibly preoccupied with little more than individual happiness, to the heroic Germanic warrior ethos, predicated on values of sacrifice, loyalty, virility, and obedience. In other writings, Sombart increasingly associated the rise of capitalism with the spread of Jewish mercantilism and finance, portraying the Jew as the archfigure of usurious business dealings, rootlessness, and abstract rationalism. This line of thought culminated in *Deutscher Sozialismus* (German Socialism, 1934), his magnum opus, in which Sombart displayed his true colors as an anti-Semite and Nazi fellow traveler.

Johnson's attentive reading of Dennis, Sombart, Oswald Spengler, and other right-wing thinkers whose philosophies lent themselves increasingly to the hate-mongering demagogues of the day is further displayed in his article "*Mein Kampf* and the Business Man," published in the *Examiner* in the summer of 1939.[20] A laudatory review of Hitler's autobiography, Johnson's article on the eve of World

WERNER SOMBART

WELTANSCHAUUNG SCIENCE AND ECONOMY

Translated by
PHILIP JOHNSON

NEW YORK
VERITAS PRESS
1939

fig. 2 Title page of *Werner Sombart, Weltanschauung, Science and Economy,* translated by Philip Johnson, 1939

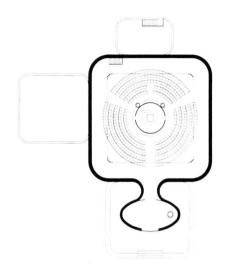

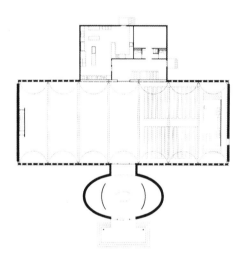

War II hails the barbarism and heroism of war as "true freedom" while denouncing liberal democracy as a form of plutocracy and the American business community's politics of pacifism as self-serving. If just over a year later, and under suspicion of being a spy, Johnson backed away from this ideology, it is not altogether self-evident what he jettisoned and what he retained. Shortly after the war he offered a formal apology for his activities in the 1930s to the Anti-Defamation League of B'nai Brith, although this was apparently prompted by a further investigation of his political involvements instigated by Edgar Kaufmann, Jr. Later on, on various occasions, he would refer to his behavior as "stupid," particularly with regard to the racist side of the causes he had embraced.[21] Nonetheless, in a letter of 1964, he would still note archly that Hitler's regime had produced better architecture than Roosevelt's, and in an interview of 1992, he would credit Mussolini's "social fascism" as having had some virtue.[22] As Susan Sontag was famously to suggest in her essay "Fascinating Fascism," concerning Leni Riefenstahl's career as a photographer and filmmaker after the Nazi period: "It is generally thought that National Socialism stands only for brutishness and terror. But this is not true. National Socialism—more broadly, fascism—also stands for an idea or rather ideals that are persistent today under the other banners: the ideal of life as art, the cult of beauty, the fetishism of courage, the dissolution of alienation in ecstatic feelings of community, the repudiation of the intellect."[23]

Yet if Johnson continued to harbor some of these ideals in covert—and, indeed, less idealistic—form, what overtly changed after World War II was his new focus on business rather than politics. This spurred him to pursue a professional career as an architect, and it also entailed a different set of metaphors. Instead of earnest endorsements of war as social-economic hygiene, he now advertised his easy availability as an architect for hire, someone not above doing a job for the money, boasting "I am a whore." While Johnson is usually credited as making this bad-boy remark, with its (homo)sexual scandalism and apparent self-mockery, on the occasion of a conference in Charlottesville, Virginia, in 1982, he actually said the same thing in an interview a decade earlier, and most likely on plenty of other occasions as well.[24] More mildly—but also as a retort to the deplorable moralism of modernist orthodoxy—he liked to characterize himself as a "business functionalist." Such statements presumably helped him rationalize a lot of bad buildings. At the same time, on a more philosophical level, they also reflected his abiding belief in will and opportunism over ethical scruples.

Strange Bedfellows: Johnson and the Jews

I've always been a violent philo-Semite.
—Philip Johnson

Johnson also made the above statement, with its ambiguous and disturbing use of the word "violent," more than once.[25] What exactly is to be made of it? In the mid-1950s, he designed a synagogue for a Conservative Jewish congregation in Port Chester, New York. The commission, for which he took no fee, was widely publicized as a gesture of atonement for his behavior in the 1930s. Some, most recently including Robert A. M. Stern in a staunch defense of his friend against the obituary writers who felt compelled to dwell on Johnson's activities during those years, have had little trouble pardoning him for what Stern calls a "social anti-Semitism" that was "a fact of American life until well after World War II," especially among the upper classes.[26] Nor does Stern fail to repeat the argument that some of Johnson's best friends were Jewish—Edward Warburg and Lincoln Kirstein, to take two of his earliest and closest; later Peter Eisenman, Frank Gehry, and Stern himself would fall into this category. Stern further argues that the fact that many in this country and elsewhere failed to recognize Hitler's true intentions until it was too late was no different from others turning a blind eye on the brutalities of Stalin. In his article, Stern lauds the "limpid, light-filled, Soane-inspired space" of the synagogue at Port Chester as evidence of the authenticity of Johnson's contrition.

In fact, Johnson offered the congregation of Temple Kneses Tifereth Israel his plan for the synagogue only after his commission for a church in Greenwich, Connecticut, for which it was originally conceived, fell through (fig. 3). Characterized by an elliptical domed vestibule and a centralized plan, the scheme also derived from a project for an unbuilt office that Johnson had designed for himself in New Canaan. A Jewish friend and neighbor of Johnson's, the theater magnate Albert A. List, husband of the art patron Vera List, reputedly brokered the deal with the synagogue, and Johnson agreed to it on condition that his original plan not be altered much. Ultimately, the need for expandable seating space to accommodate large crowds on the high holidays necessitated its modification into a rectangle entered at the midpoint of the longitudinal axis (fig. 4). In any case, the synagogue project represented, in 1956, not just a deviation from strict Miesian aesthetics but also Johnson's largest commission for a public building to that date, and at a moment when he was striving to establish his professional practice. Questions of conscience aside, it was a desirably "monumental" building type with good publicity value.[27]

Apropos of architectural patronage, what seems more remarkable about the synagogue commission than Johnson's magnanimity in taking it on is the fact that the client was willing to accept such an unkosher gift. It is true that the 1950s was the high tide of suburban synagogue building in the United States, and the commissioning of an architect like Frank Lloyd Wright to design Beth Sholom in Elkins Park, Pennsylvania, for example, challenged other Jewish congregations to keep up with the Joneses (or Cohens) by hiring big-name architects.[28] But if the real explanation for the congregation in Port Chester receiving Johnson's beneficence like manna from heaven is that it had little idea of the extent of his Nazi associations, one can only wonder how much pause it gave to members of the building committee years later when the record became widely known.

But genealogy, as we have suggested, revels in strange bedfellows. In 1995, in an article published in the neoconservative Jewish journal *Commentary,* the art critic Hilton Kramer expressed his disgust that Johnson should have placed a sculpture by Ibram Lassaw on the altar at Kneses Tifereth Israel very similar to the one that he had commissioned a few years earlier from the same Egyptian-Jewish artist for his Guest House bedroom at New Canaan, the "scene of rituals of a very different sort" (figs. 5, 6).[29] In the boudoir at New Canaan, Lassaw's welded-metal *Clouds of Magellan* hangs directly over the bed. Kramer's comment seems above all to be a reflection of his own homophobia, yet more to the point is the fact that Jewish sculptors and painters were among those whose work Johnson collected most assiduously

fig. 5 Philip Johnson, Temple Kneses Tifereth Israel, Port Chester, New York, 1956

fig. 6 Philip Johnson, Guest House bedroom, New Canaan, with wall sculpture by Ibram Lassaw

fig. 7 Philip Johnson, Glass House, New Canaan, Connecticut, 1949, with Elie Nadelman's *Two Circus Women* in foreground

during his career and to which he gave pride of place in his buildings. There is also, notably, Elie Nadelman's *Two Circus Women* inside the Glass House (fig. 7). A Polish-born artist, Nadelman became so depressed after his family members were killed in the Holocaust that he committed suicide in 1946. Johnson not only placed his larger-than-life-size papier-mâché sculpture, of two standing nudes joined from the shoulder down, on a pedestal in his sparsely furnished interior, but later had it reproduced in marble at a monumental scale for the lobby of the New York State Theater at Lincoln Center. He also carefully situated a bronze figure by Jacques Lipchitz on the lawn at New Canaan between the Glass House and the Guest House, where it stood for many years like an inverted exclamation mark, and commissioned another Lipchitz to hang over the fireplace at the Rockefeller Guest House, later moving it to the theater at Lincoln Center along with the Nadelman (figs. 8, 9). A third Lipchitz occupies the epicenter of Johnson's interdenominational Roofless Church in New Harmony, Indiana, completed in 1960 (fig. 10).[30] Johnson also commissioned a large wood construction by Frederick Kiesler in 1952, one of the artist's *Galaxy* series, for his New Canaan lawn (fig. 11).

Johnson's habit of collecting Jewish art over many years may be primarily attributable to the taste and advice he was receiving from his trusted friends Kirstein and Alfred Barr, or from gallerists like Julien Levy and Sam Kootz, or perhaps simply to the prevalence of Jewish artists on the interwar and postwar American art scene. Certainly Johnson must be credited as one of the first architects to collect abstract expressionist painting and sculpture, patronizing Mark Rothko, Barnett Newman, Adolph Gottlieb, and Philip Guston, among others. Slightly later Frank Stella would also become a favorite. In contrast, Henry-Russell Hitchcock, in his book *Painting Towards Architecture* (1948), remained inclined to the more European and "architectural" aesthetic of geometric abstraction.

Yet in light of Johnson's activities in the 1930s, what are we to make of his inviting Jewish art into the bosom of his home? To reverse Hilton Kramer's question, was his decision to sleep underneath the Lassaw, with its subtle evocation of barbed-wire fencing, another act of atonement? Might it be seen as analogous to his placement of a circular brick fireplace in the interior of the Glass House?[31] Was Johnson's embrace of the Jew-as-artist a tacit disavowal of the stereotype of the Jew-as-crafty-capitalist? Or, wading further into psychological territory, aided this time by Julia Kristeva, might we instead interpret the Lassaw above the bed as an act of abjection—a gesture of self-defilement and transgression by Johnson, presumably aimed at some ultimate catharsis? For the architect who worshiped on the altar of art but called himself a whore, was the Jew, indeed, a kind of ineluctable alter ego, a dialectical Other? As Kristeva writes in *Powers of Horror*: "The sense of abjection . . . is anchored in the superego. The abject is perverse because it neither gives up nor assumes a prohibition, a rule, or a law; but turns them aside, misleads, corrupts; uses them, takes advantage of them, the better to deny them. It . . . establishes narcissistic power while pretending to reveal the abyss—an artist who practices his art as a 'business.'"[32] She continues: "The various means of *purifying* the abject—the various catharses—make up the history of religions, and end up with that catharsis par excellence called art. . . . The artistic experience, which is

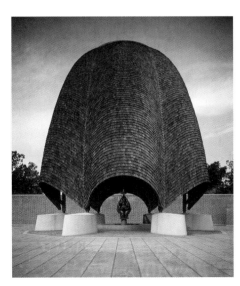

fig. 11 Frederick Kiesler, *Galaxy* (1952), on the lawn at Johnson's residence in New Canaan, Connecticut, next to the Glass House

rooted in the abject it utters and by the same token purifies, appears as the essential component of religiosity. That is perhaps why it is destined to survive the collapse of the historical forms of religions."[33]

Art, then, as surrogate religion for Johnson, as transcendence attained through debasement? Not by chance does Kristeva's study of abjection center on the French novelist Louis-Ferdinand Céline, a fascist and Nazi sympathizer. "The Jew, he's afraid of nothing," Céline rants. "He's mimetic, he's a whore."[34] In a series of pamphlets written between 1936 and 1941 that reveal what Kristeva calls the "phantasmatic substratum" of his work, Céline's ravings on Jews and fascism oscillate between pornographic disgust and nihilistic laughter, between apocalypse and carnival.[35] As Céline writes in *L'Ecole des cadavres* (1938): "Christianic religion? Judeo-Talmudo-communism? A gang! The apostles? Jews. All of them! Gangsters all! The first gang? The Church! The first racket? The first people's commissariat? The Church! Peter? Al Capone of the Canticles! A Trotsky for Roman muzhiks! The Gospel? A code for racketeers ... "[36] In the Célinian literary economy, the Jew functions as the traumatic symbol of both the Law and a corrupt morality. Against this phantasmatic figure anti-Semitism becomes an element of what Kristeva calls "parareligious" secularism, an affirmation of everything Judeo-Christian civilization has repressed: nation, race, body, sex drives, pantheistic totality. To be sure, Céline's vitriol exceeds Johnson's closet connoisseurship in both its rabidness and its art. But might not a similar mechanism be at work?

Between Mies and Michelangelo

To return to the subject of patronage and the dangerous miscegenation of art and business, Johnson's relationship with the painter Mark Rothko was destined, all too predictably, to have explosive consequences in the 1950s and 1960s. Associated with Mies van der Rohe on the design of the Seagram Building, Johnson was given primary responsibility for planning the Four Seasons Restaurant on the building's ground floor. In 1958, he and Phyllis Lambert, the daughter of the building's client and owner, Samuel Bronfman, commissioned Rothko to create 550 square feet of mural painting for the restaurant. The total fee for the commission was to have been $35,000, payable in installments over four years.

An artist with a volatile temperament and an outsize ego, hypersensitive to associations between his high-serious, quasi-sacral paintings and corporate "lobby art," and a self-described anarchist, Rothko claimed to have been ignorant of where his canvases were going to hang in the building. Johnson roundly denied misleading Rothko on this score. Nonetheless, when the artist realized that the role of his work was to serve as decoration for one of the most elite and opulent watering holes in the city—"a place where the richest bastards in New York will come to feed and show off"—he became incensed.[37] Resolving to spite his patrons by painting something that would "ruin the appetite of every son of a bitch who eats in that room," he found a source of inspiration in Michelangelo's Laurentian Library, which, with its mannerist compression of space, had a powerfully oppressive and claustrophobic atmosphere. "[Michelangelo] achieved just the kind of feeling I'm after," Rothko declared. "He makes the viewers feel that they are trapped in a room where all the doors and windows

are bricked up, so that all they can do is butt their heads forever against the wall."[38] Rothko—who also, ironically, was deeply influenced by Nietzsche's philosophy— thus maliciously conceived his series of somber, blood-colored paintings with the intent that they should have an indigestible effect (fig. 12). In 1959, after working intensively on the mural cycle for eight months, he decided to take a break and left for Europe with his family. Upon returning to dine at the newly opened Four Seasons, he immediately realized that his intended subversion would be ineffectual in such a setting: "Anybody who will eat that kind of food for those kind of prices will never look at a painting of mine."[39] With this he repudiated his contract and returned the $14,000 he had been paid thus far.

Rothko eventually gave most of the paintings intended for the Seagram Building to the Tate Gallery in London, together with detailed instructions on how to install them. They arrived in 1970, on the same day that news was received of his suicide. Prior to this, however, the bad chemistry between the artist and architect repeated itself. Soon after Rothko pulled out of the Seagram commission he was approached by the Texas arts patrons Dominique and John de Menil, who had visited Rothko's studio in 1960 and been deeply impressed by the murals intended for Seagram hanging there, to execute a series of new paintings for a nondenominational chapel to be built on the campus of St. Thomas University in Houston, a Catholic institution of which they were the major benefactors. The de Menils also asked Johnson, whom they had previously engaged to design their home as well as the master plan and architecture for St. Thomas, to design the chapel. Inspired by the example of Matisse's Chapel of the Rosary at Vence in southern France, the project counts, in the words of one historian, as one of the twentieth century's most serious attempts to reintegrate art and religion and to produce a synthesis of art and architecture.[40] Rothko accepted the commission on the condition that the interior should contain no works other than his. Johnson envisaged the building as a monumental climax to the long axis of the campus mall. The initially square plan was to be topped by an 80-foot-high pyramidal or polyhedral dome culminating

fig. 12 Mark Rothko, *Untitled (Seagram Mural),* 1959. Painting intended for the Four Seasons Restaurant in the Seagram Building. Oil on canvas, 104 1/2 x 180 in. (265.4 x 457.2 cm), National Gallery of Art, Washington, D.C., Gift of The Mark Rothko Foundation [1985.38.6]

in a skylight (fig. 13). Rothko, however, disliked the classicizing grandiosity of Johnson's scheme. Impressed by Frederick Kiesler's contemporaneous Shrine of the Book in Jerusalem (1959–65), as well as other work by Kiesler, including an environmental sculpture entitled *Last Judgment* exhibited at the Guggenheim in 1964, he insisted on a more intimately scaled octagon with canted walls, reminiscent in both plan and spirit of early Christian baptisteries. After such a space was painstakingly mocked up in his carriage-house studio in Manhattan, he insisted that it be replicated in Texas (fig. 14). This time it was Johnson who, after making numerous revisions to the design, bowed out of the project. Citing irreconcilable differences, he acknowledged diplomatically that Rothko was a "great painter" but "not an architect."[41]

With respect to the Seagram Building, Johnson's relationship with Bronfman was yet another classic encounter between opposites, although with happier results. In deciding to build his company's flagship on Park Avenue in midtown Manhattan, the Canadian millionaire was not initially looking to make a major civic statement, or to underwrite an iconic work of architecture. He did, however, wish to compete with Lever Brothers, whose headquarters stood diagonally across the street, and more importantly, to give a patina of respectability to the fortune he had made selling liquor in the United States during Prohibition. While Bronfman's relationship with Johnson was mediated by Lambert, who had a degree in art history from Vassar, Bronfman's immigrant roots and his reputation as an aggressive tycoon inevitably evoked the stereotype of the Jewish businessman. Nor were the ironies of bringing a man like Bronfman into the orbit of Mies's refined aesthetics lost on Johnson, who was initially responsible for recommending the German architect to Lambert.

But in another caprice of history—quite literally a case of Nietzsche's iron hand of necessity shaking the dice-box of chance—Johnson received a commission to design a casino-hotel in Havana at the very same time he was working on the Seagram Building. The client for this project, known as the Monaco, was a consortium of businessmen led by Meyer Lansky, one of the *machers* of American organized crime and, in the waning Batista era of the mid-1950s, a central figure in Cuban gambling rackets. Lansky was also an associate of Bronfman's from "old bootlegging days," when Canadian whiskey found its way across Lake Erie (thus nicknamed the "Jewish lake") into New York, Detroit, and Johnson's hometown of Cleveland. Johnson, who found the Jewish mobster affable and witty, related that Lansky would come

fig. 13 Philip Johnson, drawing of front elevation of Rothko Chapel, Houston, prior to October 1964, with sketches by Rothko. Menil Collection, Houston

fig. 14 Philip Johnson, plan of Rothko Chapel, Houston, prior to October 1964

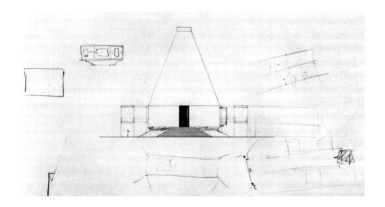

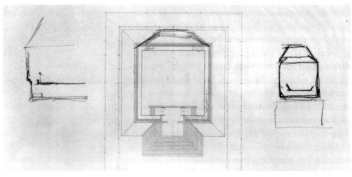

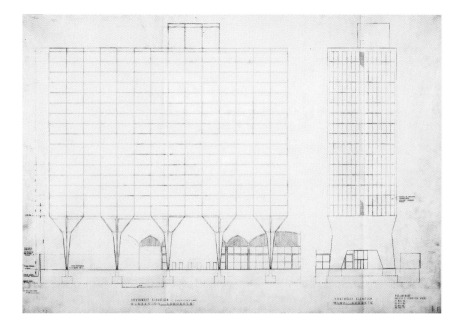

fig. 15 Philip Johnson, project for
Monaco Hotel, Havana, 1956

into his office and ask after his Seagram client, "How's old Sam?"[42] The Havana hotel,
a twenty-story building on *pilotis* vaguely reminiscent of Oscar Niemeyer's high-
rise buildings in Brazil (fig. 15), was ultimately renamed the Riviera and completed
by another architect before Castro nationalized it in 1960 and outlawed gambling.

Finally, on the subject of Johnson's Jewish clientele, it is still difficult to
fathom a commission that the architect received in 1960 from the state of Israel
for a nuclear reactor at Rehovot near Tel Aviv. In this case, too, the commission was
a direct result of the prestige Johnson commanded in the American architecture
world, the powerful network of movers and shakers in which he circulated, and the
elite level of schmoozing that the Glass House facilitated. It reputedly came about
in the course of a visit to the New Canaan estate by Shimon Peres, then deputy
Israeli minister of defense and loyalist to Prime Minister David Ben-Gurion. Peres
asked Johnson why he had never built anything in Israel, and Johnson professed
himself eager to do so. It was as simple as that.[43] Or perhaps not quite. Together with
Ben-Gurion, Peres had been one of the original promoters of Israel's atomic energy
program over the opposition of many of his countrymen, who felt it would lead the
new nation down the path of nuclear proliferation. The Israeli hawks prevailed
by the early 1950s, and when, in 1953, Dwight D. Eisenhower inaugurated his "Atoms
for Peace" program, making American nuclear expertise and matériel available to
foreign states that agreed to use them for peaceful purposes, Israel was among the
first countries to benefit. An agreement was reached in 1955 for the United States to
finance and supply Israel with a small "bathtub" reactor to be used for research and
for medical and industrial purposes. This facility, known as Nahal Soreq, was the one
Johnson would design. Soon after the agreement was reached with the Atomic Energy
Commission, however, the Israelis sought to persuade the United States to allow them
to expand and upgrade the reactor for plutonium production. This the United States
strictly forbade. The result was that while the Nahal Soreq reactor was built subject
to American inspections in the early 1960s, Israel clandestinely (and with the help of
France, the other major nuclear power of the day, which owed a debt to Israel for its

fig. 16 Philip Johnson, Nahal Soreq nuclear reactor, Rehovot, Israel, 1960. Rendering of complex in landscape

fig. 17 Philip Johnson, Nahal Soreq nuclear reactor, view of interior courtyard, Rehovot, Israel, 1960

support during the Suez crisis) undertook the development of a second, much larger reactor at Dimona that was capable of producing nuclear weapons. Once the Nahal Soreq reactor opened, American scientists unwittingly became involved in training the Israeli technicians who would subsequently be employed at Dimona. Thus the American reactor served to facilitate and provide cover for the secret Dimona project.

With respect to the architectural commission, two things may readily be conjectured: that it was desirable from both an American and an Israeli standpoint (if for different reasons) that the reactor be designed by a prestigious American architect; and that it project more a cultural than a military image so as to disarm Israel's nuclear critics. Indeed, what is most striking architecturally about this award-winning technical facility located in a barren stretch of the Israeli landscape is its resemblance to a fortified temple precinct (fig. 16). Reminiscent of Johnson's contemporaneous Roofless Church in New Harmony, the faceted form of the reactor is set behind heavy battered concrete walls. The nuclear "holy of holies" culminates the axis of an ascetic grass courtyard ringed by a colonnade of bayonet-shaped columns (fig. 17).[44]

From the Little Flower to the *Hour of Power*

If Nietzsche's annunciation of the death of God opened a path as liberating as it was nihilistic for Johnson, it also led him, as already suggested, to seek secular substitutes for religion, in fascist politics during the 1930s and ultimately in the art of architecture. Paradoxically, however, given his self-proclaimed status as a nonbeliever, Johnson also seems to have had a kind of magnetic attraction for religious clients, and he was commissioned by them to execute numerous buildings and projects throughout his career. In fact, Johnson realized his first commission from such a client even before he was a trained architect. This was a speaker's stand for Father Charles E. Coughlin.

Father Coughlin's ministry was located at the Shrine of the Little Flower in Royal Oak, Michigan, which also served as the headquarters of his right-wing political party, the National Union for Social Justice. Casting about after Huey Long's assassination in 1935 for another cause to embrace, Johnson sought out the Catholic radio priest. Long may have been a more sympathetic figure to Johnson both personally and ideologically, but Coughlin gave him a warmer welcome in the

Midwest than Long's lieutenants had in Louisiana. In September 1936, the priest held his largest rally to date, in Riverview Park in Chicago before a crowd estimated at between eighty thousand and one hundred thousand people, and Johnson availed himself of the opportunity to design an open-air stage and speaker's platform for it (fig. 18). It is likely that Johnson also funded its construction. According to newspaper reports, the structure, "bordering on the moderne," provided a "glaring white background 50 feet wide and 20 feet high for the solitary figure of the priest, who stood on a platform slightly above the center of the white expanse."[45] Prior to Coughlin's speech, party members and well-wishers filed up to and down from the dais on a symmetrical double ramp, their progress punctuated by an array of

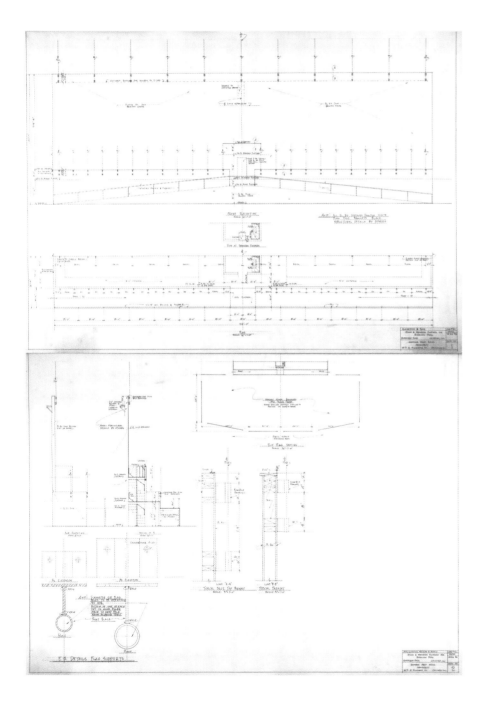

fig. 18 George Fred Keck, working drawings for stage and speaker's platform for Father Charles E. Coughlin designed by Philip Johnson, Riverview Park, Chicago, 1936

fig. 19 Philip Johnson (Johnson/
Burgee), Crystal Cathedral, Garden
Grove, California, 1980

American flags waving in the wind. Coughlin used Johnson's monumental backdrop
to full effect, his voice carried to the huge crowd by an innovative amplification
device hanging on his chest. Gesticulating rhetorically, he assailed Roosevelt's
economic policies, calling for the money changers to be driven from the temple and
branding the Federal Reserve Bank "one of the ulcers of modern capitalism."

While Johnson's departure from MoMA has usually been viewed as an
interruption of his mission on behalf of the new architecture, the "moderne" platform
for Coughlin's rally provides evidence to the contrary. Johnson claimed that the
design was inspired by a speaker's stand he had seen at a Hitler Jugend rally in
Potsdam in 1932.[46] More intriguing is the fact that this very pure example of what
can only be described as Fascist International Style was drawn up and carried out

under Johnson's supervision in the office of the modernist architect George Fred Keck. Johnson was familiar with the Chicago architect's work, having included a model of a prefabricated housing project by Keck and Robert Paul Schweikher in an exhibition at MoMA in the spring of 1933 entitled *Work of Young Architects in the Middle West*, which Keck helped to organize. He had also visited Keck's experimental House of Tomorrow at the Century of Progress exhibition and been impressed by its technical aesthetic. Keck, for his part, had seen and appreciated the International Style show when it traveled to Chicago. A liberal Democrat and Roosevelt supporter with a wife who was Jewish, Keck was, according to an associate in his office, not happy about collaborating on the stand for Coughlin. However, Johnson was already enough of a power in the architecture world that he felt compelled to oblige.[47]

fig. 20 Philip Johnson, model for Cathedral of Hope, Dallas, 1996

fig. 21 Walter Gropius, *Monument to the March Dead,* Weimar, Germany, 1921, as reconstructed in 1945

Forty years later, in the age of television, Johnson would again demonstrate his talent for the mediagenic mass spectacle. The client was another maverick churchman, the televangelist Robert Schuller. Schuller likes to describe himself as in the business of retailing religion. Having begun his career in the mid-1950s preaching in a drive-in movie theater in Orange County, California, he was by the 1970s the shepherd of a ten thousand–strong local congregation and its televised *Hour of Power,* broadcast to millions around the world. Johnson's star-shaped Crystal Cathedral for Schuller's extended flock appears to fuse the utopian expressionism of Bruno Taut's Glass Chain fantasies with the secular sublime of Joseph Paxton's Crystal Palace to produce an iconic pop-culture mega-church (fig. 19). Once again, it was both chance and charisma that brought the architect and client together. Having outgrown his previous church on the same site in Garden Grove—designed by Richard Neutra in 1961—Schuller happened to encounter Johnson's name while looking through a copy of *Vogue* magazine with his wife on an airplane flight and decided to approach him. The two forged a bond in an initial phone conversation when Johnson confided his admiration for the *Hour of Power.* While Johnson at first favored a building with solid walls, it was Schuller's inspired idea, by all accounts, to build the church entirely of glass looking out on a gigantic parking lot.[48] Johnson's status as both an atheist and a homosexual apparently posed no obstacle for Schuller despite his family-values mission. Indeed, Schuller has characterized his association with Johnson as a "spiritual relationship."[49]

Offering a final twist on this theme of spirituality in Johnson's career is one of his very last projects, a two thousand–seat church in Dallas called the Cathedral of Hope (fig. 20). Commissioned by a branch of the Universal Fellowship

THE KANSAS CITY WAR MEMORIAL IS DESIGNED FOR NIGHT AND DAY

The creation of H. Van Buren Magonigle, executed by the architectural firm of Wight & Wight, this 207-foot high monument of World War I combines scale and setting with the possibilities of illumination, proving especially impressive to those approaching the city by air. The sculptured frieze is work of Edmond Amateis.

WAR MEMORIALS
What Aesthetic Price Glory?

by Philip C. Johnson

TODAY the climate of opinion in this country is unfavorable to the concept of the traditional war memorial. One college president has suggested that we endow hospital beds instead. The Dean of Architecture at Harvard urges that we build playgrounds, schoolhouses, parks, anything rather than "to increase the dreadful population" of our monuments "by so much as a single increment." Even returning GI's are quoted as taking a stand against cast iron soldiers.

This negative attitude toward monuments is something quite new in the Western world. Ever since the mound builders of Ohio and the artisans of the grand monoliths of Stonehenge monuments have been considered the highest form of architecture. Of the Seven Wonders of the Ancient World, all monumental structures, only two could be called even slightly useful: the Lighthouse at Alexandria, the huge size of which precludes the idea that it was built solely for use, and the Hanging Gardens of Babylon. The other five—the Colossus of Rhodes, the Pyramids, the Mausoleum at Halicarnassus, the statue of Zeus at Olympia, and the Temple of Artemis at Ephesus—are religious statues, or temples or memorials to the dead.

The monumental buildings and sculpture on the Acropolis, which the Athenians erected during the Periclean Age, are for the most part memorials to the Persian Wars. The Parthenon itself was built as a shrine for the chryselephantine Athene, who held in her hand a statuette of Nike, the Goddess of Victory; while nearby another temple, the temple of Nike Apteros, was dedicated solely to the latter goddess. But the most impressive structure of all was Pheidias' colossal statue of Athene Promachos (Athene the Warrior) made from the bronze booty of Marathon. According to Demosthenes, this statue dominated the water approaches to Athens, just as the Statue of Liberty dominates New York Harbor, and with much the same effect on the homecoming traveler.

We have, however, only to look at the monuments in this country built in the last hundred years to understand one of the causes of their unpopularity. They are very ugly.

But there is a deeper cause, rooted in our current philosophy of life. We are spiritual descendants of John Calvin and the English seventeenth century Puritans, and though we are no longer religious we still have some of Cromwell's iconoclasm in our blood. When we see monuments of marble and bronze, we see Veblen's "conspicuous waste." We consider monumental statuary semi-idolatrous and, remembering our eighteenth century New England fear of the bogey of Popery, we frown upon any ceremonial ritual that is likely to arouse our emotions.

Besides being spiritual heirs of the Puritans, we are utilitarians; and utilitarianism is but a later outgrowth of the same seventeenth century morality, plus French rationalism and English materialism. The utilitarians' moral valuations were based on the criterion that what is useful is good. They believed in the efficacy of knowledge and reason, as opposed to inspiration and faith. Hence memorials, the main function of which is to inspire, received a low place in their esteem.

The functionalists of our day have applied the philosophy of utilitarianism to the field of design; according to them what is useful is beautiful. The logic of this position creates the anomalous situation whereby many functional designers hesitate to accept commissions for churches and monuments because without "usefulness" as a guide they would have no basis for a design. Sullivan's famous precept "Form follows function" has no application to the design of a *baldacchino*.

Hence, we may expect a large crop of useful, or what are called "living" memorials after this war. But the conquest of utilitarianism

Photos, above and top opposite: Ewing Galloway

THE FORMAL architectural setting of St. Gaudens' "General Sherman" lends dignity, insures viewing at proper distance; semi-circular screen of trees discourages approach from rear.

MEMORIAL from last war in Pennsylvania town, typical of dozens across the country, constitutes traffic hazard, presents realistic rear view of sculpture to at least half its beholders.

9

fig. 22 Opening spread of "War Memorials: What Aesthetic Price Glory?" by Philip Johnson, *Art News,* September 1945

of Metropolitan Community Churches, the world's largest gay and lesbian ministry, and incomplete at his death, the neo-expressionist design is suggestive of "icebergs, ships, mountains, fortifications, and crystals," according to the church's website. More ironically, its expressionistic, folded form also recalls the small *Monument to the March Dead* built by Walter Gropius in a cemetery in Weimar shortly after World War I, though with a more digital look and at a giant scale (fig. 21). The Cathedral of Hope, currently planned to be realized posthumously, was described by Johnson, how sincerely we cannot know, as the crowning achievement of his life.[50]

Is *Nothing* Sacred?

It seems rather audacious, given that he had only recently been disinfected of his unsavory wartime associations, that Johnson should have published an article in *Art News* in September 1945 on so "German" a topic as war memorials (fig. 22). Titled "What Aesthetic Price Glory?" the article advocates the erection of more war memorials in the United States, and attributes the widespread negative attitude toward them to the fact that most tended to be "very ugly" and, more important, to an ingrained American Calvinism or Puritanism preferring the "efficacy of knowledge and reason" to "inspiration and faith." Citing a lineage extending from the pyramids to Germany's "monumental and dignified" World War I memorials to an unbuilt design for a giant totemic sculpture by Picasso, Johnson stresses that this "highest form of architecture" need have no relationship to "usefulness." "Imagine," he romantically concludes, "the effect of a lonely, man-made mountain in the shape of a perfect cone, rising from an endless plain; or a row of megaliths, each a tower of rough-hewn granite, curving up a treeless hill."[51]

It is noteworthy that Johnson's article coincides in date with the famous wartime call by Sigfried Giedion, Fernand Léger, and José Luis Sert for a "new monumentality."[52] Yet while Giedion and his coauthors specifically insist on the need to infuse postwar monuments with a new civic symbolism, Johnson is interested primarily in aesthetic effects and "glory." Empty of content, his Ozymandian vision brings to mind the overwrought "Nietzschean" atmosphere of another artifact of the day, Ayn Rand's novel *The Fountainhead,* whose rival protagonists Roark and Keating might in a sense be seen as pulp avatars of Johnson's schizoid combination of sublime aesthetics and cynical commercialism.

To return to our initial reflections on the uses of history, we may understand Johnson's life and work in terms of two different conceptions of monumentality, fatefully entangled in his career. On the one hand, he regarded monuments as supreme and timeless works of art. A largely unattainable ideal in his own architectural practice, the artistic monument was nonetheless bound up for him with what appears to have been a deep psychic need for redemption and transcendence. This quasi-religious belief in architecture as art contributed, at best, to making him a generous and loyal patron. On the other hand, as Nietzsche's critical history illuminates and as Johnson understood, monuments are also markers of wealth, privilege, and the triumph of will. Staring out from the famous cover of *Time* magazine in 1979, wearing the signature glasses that exaggerate his eye sockets and skull like a death's-head, holding aloft a model of the AT&T building that could be his own granite tombstone, Johnson's image is a memento mori, a reminder that monuments are never merely empty forms. They are effigies of power, often built to confer respectability on dirty deeds. Spectacles, by the same token, are forms of distraction. They serve, at least temporarily, to ward off boredom and nihilism (fig. 23).

"Wars I Have Seen": An Epilogue on Viola Bodenschatz

In completing my research for this essay, I made a discovery in Columbia University's Rare Book and Manuscript Library. Housed there as part of the archive of one Ned Edward Hoopes, an author and English professor at Pace University who died in 1984, are notes, documents, and correspondence related to the life of Viola Bodenschatz together with Hoopes's manuscript for a biography of her. The latter bears the working title "Viola Bodenschatz: America and Germany."[53] Born in Louisville, Kentucky, Viola Heise Bodenschatz (1899–1967) married a German alien, George K. Bodenschatz, during World War I. George was the brother of Karl Bodenschatz, Hermann Goering's future chief of staff. In the 1920s and '30s Viola Bodenschatz spent her summers in Germany

fig. 23 "Is nothing sacred?"
Cartoon by Gahan Wilson,
early 1960s

and had privileged access through her brother-in-law to the highest officers in the Nazi command, including Adolf Hitler, as well as their sympathizers in the German aristocracy. Between 1934 and 1938 she also made pro-Germany speeches in Europe and the United States and published half a dozen propagandistic pamphlets.

In the summer of 1939, on the eve of World War II, Viola was Philip Johnson's traveling companion on the first of his two excursions into Poland. Three years later she and her husband were incarcerated in the United States for forty-four months as unregistered Nazi agents. Upon their release from prison she separated from her husband and befriended a theatrical designer named Bertram Heckel, to whom she eventually bequeathed her journals, letters, photographs, newspaper clippings, and other documents. Heckel in turn gave a portion of this material to Hoopes for the purpose of writing her life story. Hoopes's unpublished manuscript—rejected by several publishers as either credulous or lacking in interest—contains a ten-page account of the road trip with Johnson. The Columbia archive also contains the originals of a pair of letters written by Johnson to Bodenschatz in the spring and fall of 1939 (figs. 24, 25).[54] Copies of these two letters subsequently found their way into Johnson's FBI file, where Franz Schulze discovered them with Bodenschatz's name redacted. When Schulze questioned Johnson about the letters, he recalled having written them to Bodenschatz. Beyond her name, however, Johnson's information was sketchy, and Schulze's account of their relationship is inaccurate in several particulars.[55]

Hoopes's narrative of Bodenschatz's and Johnson's five- or six-day trip into Poland during the first half of August 1939 details their experiences and conversations while driving in Johnson's American car through the Polish Corridor and the free zone of Danzig to the German border and then into Warsaw and the towns of Lodz and Alexandrof. Poland was on edge at this moment with near certainty of German invasion. Military preparations were in evidence, and Bodenschatz and Johnson encountered suspicion and hostility from the residents in some of the towns they passed through. As they prepared to return to Germany by way of the border at Kepno, they were stopped by Polish guards and arrested. Bodenschatz's camera was confiscated and Johnson was strip-searched. After what was apparently a somewhat harrowing interrogation in the local police station, Bodenschatz succeeded, according to Hoopes, in "charming" the official in charge. Their American passports and camera were then handed back and they were escorted to the border.

Hoopes describes the trip as motivated by journalistic curiosity and perhaps also thrill-seeking on Johnson's part. It is revealing not just by virtue of the picture it paints of Johnson's access to the most elite ranks of the German political and social hierarchy, but also for its account of the brazenness of two well-to-do American citizens pursuing personal agendas in extremely dangerous territory armed with Nazi safe-conduct passes. More broadly, Hoopes's biography, which uncritically portrays the lavish parties and rest cures, teas with the Kaiser, and first-class travel and luxury hotels enjoyed by Bodenschatz, offers a picture of the relations between a privileged class of Germans and Americans who were able to overlook, or who tacitly approved, the mounting evidence of Nazi brutalities.

Hoopes notes that Viola Bodenschatz's collection of photographs was extensive. Unfortunately, this material was retained by Heckel and is not part of the Hoopes archive. Heckel died in 1987 in Puerto Rico, and efforts to trace his collection have been unsuccessful. Nor does Hoopes's manuscript explain under what circumstances Bodenschatz and Johnson met. They seem to have had no contact after the war.

It is clear, however, that Bodenschatz shielded Johnson from what she calls the "Nazi witch hunt" while she was in prison. The following is an excerpt from her notes in which she recounts an interview that the FBI conducted with her:

> "'Do you know _____ Johnson?'
> "Well, I knew a spoiled rich man's son, a Harvard graduate who had been
>   interested in Huey Long, then in Father Coughlin, worked there without pay,
>   and came to Europe representing Social Justice. But I said briefly:
> "'I know he wrote a book of architecture.'"

Next spread:

fig. 24 Letter from Philip Johnson to Viola Bodenschatz, April 23, 1939

fig. 25 Letter from Philip Johnson to Viola Bodenschatz, undated [fall 1939]

194 East End Ave
New York, N. Y.
April 23, 1030
                                              193

Dear Mrs. Bodenschatz,

        I was glad to get your booklet. It is a very
goodjob indeed. What interests me especially is, how
do you get distribution? Do you just send it around
to friends or is there some organized way of seeing
that they get into many hands? That seems to me the
key question of those of us who would like to get
some daylight into the every darkening atmosphere
of contemporary America.

        This winter has been a long series of lectures
for me and I have enjoyed the experience immensely.
Talking is always so flattering the the ego, don't
you think? My plan to do something about the American
Mercury fell through. The Jews bought the magazine
and are ruining it, naturally. And now I am planning
to go to Europe and cover the whole continent this
time, Russia Turkey, Spain as well of course as
Germany.

        What are your plans? Are you going over soon?
I hope we are going to meet. I was so sorry not to
get West this winter so I could visit you, but things
have kept me here.

        Your brother was certainly right about everything,
what? And now what on the German horizon? Do you
look for war? I do not, but that may only be because
I am ignorant. I feel that England won't fight and
that Hitler can take what he wants when he wants to.
But I would give a good deal to hear from you before
I jump into the cauldron maybe. What think?

        Maybe we can go over on the boat together. I
leave about the first of June? Does that coincide
with you? We had such fun that I should like to pro-
long the pleasure. Please give my very best to the
mister.

        Here's hoping to see you soon.

                              As ever,

                                   Philip Johnson

Philip Cortelyou Johnson
1906   1939
American Architect   1906
                       33

TOWNSEND FARMS

New London, Ohio   *Owners: Homer H. Johnson*   *Manager: C. C. Sengstock*
                    Philip Johnson

Dear Mrs. Bodenschatz,

    You are a very mysterious woman. Where are
you and how are you?? I called Berlin when I thought
war was coming but you had just sailed for America and
then I knew there was going to be war so I stayed and
watched it. We certainly had the Polish part of it
prognosticated, nest-ce pas? I was back in Danzig for
Hitler's speech on the 18 of September and had a talk
with Loebsack. He was believing the Nazi propaganda
that the war would stop but I told him England couldn't
stop now. And she can't - at least not this year.

    Everything was fine and dandy in Berlin when
I left about October 6. They were just putting in food
rationing with cards and the Bristol had no more coffee
so you see you got out in time. Everyone was taking
the war very well indeed. I was lucky enough to get to
be a correspondent so that I could go to the front when
I wanted to and so it was that I came again to the
country that we had motored through , the towns north
of Warsaw. Do you remember Markow? I went through that
same square where we got gas and it was unrecognizable.
The German green uniforms made the place look gay and
happy. There were not many Jews to be seen. We saw
Warsaw burn and Modlin being bombed. It was a stirring
spectacle.

    But I can't tell you everything in such a
hurried note. I am going to Cleveland for the holidays.
Where will you be? We must get together and compare
notes. I actually got an article in a good magazine
and I have lectured before the Foreign Policy Assocation
and kindred places. Not in concentration camp yet.

    Do drop me a line, 2171 Overlook Rd. Cleveland
if you are going to be up our way. If you come to
New York, my addresssis 751 Third Ave. I have a little
house.
    I Hope to see you very soon. I sent you my
translation of Sombart. Hope you got it.

        Yours, as ever,

        Philip

Notes

1. Friedrich Nietzsche, "On the Uses and Disadvantages of History for Life," in *Untimely Meditations,* trans. R. J. Hollingdale (Cambridge: Cambridge University Press, 1997), 67–72.

2. Ibid., 71–72.

3. Ibid., 73.

4. Ibid., 75.

5. See Philip Johnson, "House at New Canaan, Connecticut," *Architectural Review* 108, no. 645 (September 1950): 152–159. The list ranges from Mies's Farnsworth House to Le Corbusier's Radiant Farm, Schinkel's Casino at Glienicke to Ledoux's House at Maupertuis, English picturesque landscape to Choisy's view of the Acropolis, a painting by Malevich to one by Van Doesburg, and more. On the use of history at New Canaan, cf. Craig Owens, "Philip Johnson: History, Genealogy, Historicism," in *Philip Johnson: Processes. The Glass House, 1949, and the AT&T Corporate Headquarters, 1978, Institute for Architecture and Urban Studies Catalogue* 9 (1978): 2–11; Owens also offers a Foucauldian reading of Johnson's use of history, although his argument differs from mine.

6. "Full Scale False Scale," *Philip Johnson: Writings,* foreword by Vincent Scully, introduction by Peter Eisenman, commentary by Robert A. M. Stern (New York: Oxford University Press, 1979), 251–252. For a thoughtful exploration of themes of scale in relation to desire, the body, and the world of objects, see Susan Stewart, *On Longing: Narratives of the Miniature, the Gigantic, the Souvenir, the Collection* (Durham, N.C.: Duke University Press, 1993), esp. chapters 2 and 3.

7. Nietzsche, "On the Uses and Disadvantages of History for Life," 75–76.

8. "Nietzsche, Genealogy, History," in Michel Foucault, *Language, Counter-Memory, Practice,* trans. Donald F. Bouchard and Sherry Simon (Ithaca, N.Y.: Cornell University Press, 1977), 139–164.

9. Ibid., 155.

10. Ibid., 150–151.

11. Nietzsche, "On the Use and Disadvantages of History for Life," 76. On the question of ethics in Nietzsche's philosophy, see Peter Berkowitz, *Nietzsche: The Ethics of an Immoralist* (Cambridge, Mass.: Harvard University Press, 1995). For a revealing comment by Johnson himself on morality, mortality, and monumentality, see an interview published in 1973: "The reason I use [the word] 'monumental' instead of 'aesthetic' is because I refer to scale and dignity. From the point of view of eternity, *sub specie aeternitatem,* it's everything you do. I design *sub specie aeternitatem.* If you leave out that desire for immortality, you just get cheap design, or the diagonal line that is 'in' this year, rather than a sense of monument—you see, I use the word all the time! Because if you think it's going to live on, if you think it's part of your desire for immortality, everything you do should . . . I am a moralist, of course, like all myth-makers and people who tell people what to do. Although I don't believe in morals, I use them myself. *I am a moralist; I can't help it.* To me, every artist should be conscious of his place in history. He's destroying a piece of the landscape when he builds. Therefore, he'd better be monumental." John W. Cooke and Heinrich Klotz, *Conversations with Architects* (New York: Praeger, 1973), 44.

12. Interview with Robert A. M. Stern, February 27, 1985, Temple Hoyne Buell Center for the Study of American Architecture Oral History Project, Columbia University, 2: 54.

13. See T. Harry Williams, *Huey Long* (New York: Vintage, 1981), 693.

14. Lawrence Dennis, *Is Capitalism Doomed?* (New York: Harper and Bros., 1932), 85.

15. Interview with Robert A. M. Stern, February 27, 1985, 2: 36.

16. Ibid., 2: 38.

17. Johnson first said this in a lecture at Yale in 1949, according to Vincent Scully, "Doldrums in the Suburbs," *Journal of the Society of Architectural Historians* 24, no. 1 (March 1965): 46–47.

18. Lawrence Dennis, *The Coming American Fascism: The Crisis of Capitalism* (New York: Harper and Bros., 1936), 105–106.

19. *Weltanschauung, Science and Economy* (New York: Veritas, 1939), 11. In a preface to this booklet, Johnson thanks Lawrence Dennis for assistance in preparing the translation. According to Kazys Varnelis, Veritas Press was a publishing house funded through the German Library of Information for propaganda purposes; see Varnelis, "'We Cannot Not Know History': Philip Johnson's Politics and Cynical Survival," *Journal of Architectural Education,* November 1994, pp. 93–94 and 103n25. Varnelis also states that the translation appeared first in the *Examiner.* Concerning the *Examiner,* see the next note.

20. "*Mein Kampf* and the Business Man," *Examiner,* Summer 1939, pp. 291–296. The *Examiner,* in which at least two of Johnson's articles appeared, was a quarterly journal that began publishing in 1938 under the editorship of Geoffrey Stone. It was a successor to the recently defunct *American Review,* for which Stone served as managing editor during its final period. A piece published in *New International*

in 1938 offers background: "In February of this year there appeared the first open expression by some of the respectable people of this country that they are getting ready for American fascism. *The Examiner*, a quarterly of more than a hundred pages, was issued by Geoffrey Stone from Rye Beach, New York. The Spring issue has followed in due course. During the past year or two, the *American Review* and the *American Mercury* [a magazine that Johnson attempted unsuccessfully to buy in 1938 or 1939] have come to be known as more or less fascist magazines. Neither of these, however, would admit the charge. And though they publish articles sympathetic to fascism on occasion, the bulk of their material is little or not at all fascist in character. *The Examiner* is altogether another matter. Its policy is frankly and avowedly fascist; it seeks, more particularly, an American form of fascism.... Let us put out of mind at once associations drawn from a knowledge of fascist mass journals and broadsides. Here is no wild invective, no ultra-violent Jew-baiting (a few carefully introduced anti-Semitic phrases, that is all), no flaming scare-heads, no shattering bombast. That is not at all the job of *The Examiner*. Here all, or almost all, is suave, calm, measured, more 'reasonable.' This, we must not forget, is the voice of the respectable people.... *The Examiner* could not have appeared unless the social soil had been ripening for it (Geoffrey Stone has been for years a fascist, but it was not until now that he was able to issue a magazine). Many of the respectable people have sensitive noses. They can smell corruption ahead; and they aim to get going while there are still pickings left. This is why *The Examiner* is important. *The Examiner* is a barometer, marking the drop in the social atmosphere toward the storm of crisis." James Burnham, "Fascism's Dress Clothes," *New International* 4, no. 7 (July 1938): 207–208. What seems important to grasp apropos of American fascism in the 1930s is the fairly diverse spectrum of views it encompassed, with its common denominator being a "final disenchantment" with liberal democracy as having ushered in the economic chaos of the Depression. On the "gentleman intellectual" as fascist, see Albert E. Stone, Jr., "Seward Collins and *The American Review:* Experiment in Pro-Fascism, 1933–37," *American Quarterly* 12, no. 1 (Spring 1960): 3–19. In many cases, American right-wing ideology escalated from fairly benign forms of cultural traditionalism and elitism in the first half of the 1930s (at times contradictorily mixed with populist sentiments) to a more fanatical embrace of authoritarian politics and eugenic social policy by the end of the decade.

21. On the apology to the Anti-Defamation League, see Franz Schulze, *Philip Johnson: Life and Work* (New York: Knopf, 1994), 238. On stupidity, see, for example, Academy of Achievement, "Interview: Philip Johnson, Dean of American Architects," February 28, 1992, http://www.achievement.org/autodoc/page/joh0int-3, p. 11; and Kurt Andersen, "Philip the Great," *Vanity Fair*, June 1993, p. 151.

22. Modern Architecture Symposium Archives, Avery Architectural and Fine Arts Library, Box 5, Folder 18, letter from Philip Johnson to George Collins, January 16, 1964; Academy of Achievement, "Interview: Philip Johnson," 11.

23. Susan Sontag, "Fascinating Fascism" (1975), in *Under the Sign of Saturn* (New York: Farrar Straus and Giroux, 1980), 96.

24. See Cooke and Klotz, *Conversations with Architects*, 37: "Whoever commissions buildings buys me. I'm for sale. I am a whore. I'm an artist." Cf. *The Charlottesville Tapes* (New York: Rizzoli, 1985), 19. *The Charlottesville Tapes* are a recording of the so-called P3 conference at the University of Virginia; the "P" stood for Philip and Peter (Eisenman), the two impresario-godfathers of this exclusive gathering of powerful male architects. It is not clear whether there was also a third P, or the name was simply an in-joke referring to Propaganda Due, the right-wing ultra-secret society in Italy with close ties to the Vatican, involved at this time in a $2 billion banking scandal that brought down the Italian government.

25. Tom Buckley, "Philip Johnson: The Man in the Glass House," *Esquire*, December 1983; interview with Robert A. M. Stern, February 27, 1985, 2: 47.

26. Robert A. M. Stern, contribution to "Philip Johnson: American Idol," *Architectural Record*, May 2005.

27. Philip Riesman, "Philip Johnson's Synagogue Design Blends Beauty, Apology," *Journal News* (Westchester, N.Y.), January 30, 2005. Johnson somewhat snidely expressed displeasure that functional considerations threatened to compromise the monumentality of his plan; see his statement in Richard Meier, *Recent American Synagogue Architecture* (New York: Jewish Museum, 1963), 22: "The problem of designing the contemporary synagogue is a nearly impossible one. It would not be so if only the sanctuary were the problem.... The difficulty comes from the habits of the High Holy Days, when the attendance, shall we say, swells. Now a space is either great small or great large, but it can hardly act like an accordion and be great small

and large. How to design a room that will be great both ways? Our solution at Port Chester was a great room, with a small screen divider, because it seemed to us that most of the congregation comes only on High Holy Days and we wanted the community to enjoy the temple. Once this hurdle is crossed, the design of a synagogue is the finest problem in architecture."

28. Other significant American synagogues were commissioned in the first half of the 1950s from leading Jewish architects like Eric Mendelsohn and Percival Goodman.

29. Hilton Kramer, "Philip Johnson's Brilliant Career," *Commentary* 100, no. 3 (September 1995): 44. For a vivid account of a night—not a very hedonistic one—spent in the Guest House bedroom, see Selden Rodman, *Conversations with Artists* (New York: Capricorn, 1961 [1957]), 60–70.

30. The Lipchitz sculpture at New Harmony is inscribed "Jacques Lipchitz, Jew, faithful to the religion of his ancestors, made this virgin for the better understanding of human beings on the earth so that the spirit may prevail."

31. Johnson associated this element with his memory of seeing the remains of a "burnt wooden village . . . where nothing was left but foundations and chimneys of brick." Johnson, "House at New Canaan, Connecticut," 58. Peter Eisenman was among the first to pick up on this veiled reference by Johnson to his trip into Poland in the fall of 1939; see Eisenman's introduction to *Philip Johnson: Writings,* 22–23.

32. Julia Kristeva, *Powers of Horror: An Essay on Abjection,* trans. Leon S. Roudiez (New York: Columbia University Press, 1982), 15–16.

33. Ibid., 17.

34. Ibid., 181.

35. Ibid., 174–187.

36. Ibid., 176.

37. See John Fischer, "The Easy Chair: Mark Rothko. Portrait of the Artist as an Angry Man," *Harper's Magazine,* July 1970, p. 16. See also Jonathan Jones, "Feeding Fury," *Guardian* (London), December 7, 2002, http://arts.guardian. co.uk/critic/feature/0,1169,931796,00.html.

38. Fischer, "Easy Chair," 16.

39. Jones, "Feeding Fury."

40. See Sheldon Nodelman, *The Rothko Chapel Paintings: Origins, Structure, Meaning* (Austin: University of Texas Press, 1997), 43.

41. After Johnson's departure, Howard Barnstone and Eugene Aubry were brought in to complete the chapel. For a detailed history of the project and the conflicted relationship between Johnson and Rothko, see Nodelman, *Rothko Chapel Paintings,* 62. Johnson did

realize a rectangular reflecting pool in front of the chapel, which was designed to display Barnett Newman's *Broken Obelisk.* Three decades later, in 1995, he would also complete another religious building at St. Thomas, the "deconstructivist" Chapel of St. Basil.

42. Schulze, *Philip Johnson,* 266.

43. Ibid., 283–284. Schulze relates that Johnson's old friend Edward Warburg, a major philanthropist on Israel's behalf, probably also played a role in gaining him the job.

44. Johnson won an AIA honor award for his design in 1961. On Israel's nuclear program and the Nahal Soreq reactor, see Michael Karpin, *The Bomb in the Basement: How Israel Went Nuclear* (New York: Simon and Schuster, 2006). I wish to thank Deborah Natsios for assistance with research on this project.

45. Parke Browne, "Coughlin Slams President; Vast Crowd Cheers," *Chicago Daily Tribune,* September 7, 1936, p. 1. A nearly identical report, including the description of the platform, appeared the same day on the front page of the *New York Times.* Film excerpts of the speech are in the Hearst Collection of the UCLA Film and Television Archive, Hollywood: "Father Coughlin Addresses Large Crowd," Hearst Vault Material, can 575, roll 1.

46. Schulze, *Philip Johnson,* 126.

47. On Keck's collaboration with Johnson, see Betty J. Blum, *Interview with Robert Bruce Tague,* Chicago Architects Oral History Project (Chicago: Art Institute of Chicago, 1995; revised 2005), http://www.artic.edu/aic/libraries/caohp/ tague.pdf, 14–15. The project drawings are in the Keck & Keck archive at the Wisconsin Historical Society. The project also appears in the client list in Robert Boyce, *Keck & Keck* (New York: Princeton Architectural Press, 1993), 154. I am indebted to Salomon Frausto and Lara Allison for research assistance in tracking down this project.

48. See Calvin Tomkins's profile of Johnson, "Forms Under Light," *New Yorker,* May 23, 1977, pp. 47–48; and Robert Schuller, *My Journey: From an Iowa Farm to a Cathedral of Dreams* (New York: HarperCollins, 2001), 344–347.

49. Tomkins, "Forms Under Light," 48. See also Manfredo Tafuri, "Subaqueous Cathedral," *Domus* 608 (July–August 1980): 8–12: "An exceptional effort aimed at emphasizing the communicative capacities of the building ends up in an astonished celebration of banality. . . . The 'great theatre' of the 'Crystal Cathedral' does not offer itself to violent desecrations, but only to 'unpleasant' considerations on the vanity of forms and the enigma of their existence" (12).

50. On this project, see the YouTube video on the Cathedral of Hope website, http://www. cathedralofhope.com/NetCommunity/Page. aspx?pid=544&srcid=305. The resemblance between Johnson's Cathedral of Hope and Gropius's World War I memorial is ironic inasmuch as Johnson and Gropius held antipodal positions on architecture and philosophy. The well-known antipathy between the two, which came to fruition when Johnson was a student at Harvard in the 1940s, was wholly mutual. Johnson had little use for Gropius's ethos of "teamwork," his attempt to banish history from the architect's education, and the sanctimonious humanism he preached throughout his career, succinctly summed up in the title of his last book, *Apollo in the Democracy: The Cultural Obligation of the Architect* (1968). From the standpoint of the former Bauhaus director, the cynical and Dionysian Johnson was the veritable antichrist.

51. Philip C. Johnson, "What Aesthetic Price Glory?" *Art News,* September 1945, pp. 8–9, 24–25.

52. "Nine Points on Monumentality" was drafted by Giedion, Léger, and Sert in 1943 for an unpublished volume planned by the American Abstract Artists. Giedion further elaborated the argument in "The Need for a New Monumentality," which appeared the following year in a book edited by Paul Zucker, *New Architecture and City Planning;* in it he cites Picasso's painting and sculpture as models for the new monumentality in architecture. Johnson's references to Picasso in his article suggest that he was familiar with Giedion's argument.

53. Ned Edward Hoopes Papers, Rare Book and Manuscript Collection, Columbia University, box 3.

54. Apropos of credulity, Hoopes's biography is largely sympathetic to Viola Bodenschatz and does not fault her for being anything more than naive. Following Viola, he gives credence to Karl Bodenschatz's characterization of Goering as a "Falstaffian character [with] a certain magnetism, impeccable manners, and excellent taste." Hitler, on the other hand, apparently regarded Karl Bodenschatz himself as a "cold cynic"; see *The Goebbels Diaries, 1942–1943,* ed. Louis P. Lochner (Garden City, N.Y.: Doubleday, 1948), 281.

55. See Schulze, *Philip Johnson,* 135–136, 138–140.

Liquidity:
Architecture and Oil

Reinhold Martin

Two dark, crystalline solids are poised corner-to-corner on a diagonal and separated by a tense, narrow gap (fig. 1). For twenty-eight stories, each of these consists of an extruded trapezoid, in the form of a rectangle with one of its corners cut off. From floors twenty-nine through thirty-six, each volume has another corner cut off in section, at an angle that slices forty-five degrees in opposite directions. Seen frontally (and at some distance), the resulting figure resembles an elongated, archaic house form with a slit down the middle. Seen from other angles (and closer in), the figure breaks up and the two solids vie for dominance, as right angles and diagonals bounce off one another in what their tinted, reflective surfaces capture as an overlay of lines and planes. At the base, these reflections become literal on the exterior and virtual on the interior, as two mirrored-glass planes stretch up from the sidewalk on opposite sides of the site, and into the ten-foot-wide crevice that separates the two volumes. Inside, this atrium roof is supported by a latticework of triangulated trusses that match up with the gridded curtain walls in which the two volumes are wrapped.

The object (if, indeed, a composition of two elements can still be called an "object") has many corners. There are inside corners and outside corners (fig. 2); there are corners that turn at right angles, at acute angles, and at obtuse angles, in both plan and section. At each turn of each corner, something happens. The figure either asserts itself by aligning certain corners while setting others in counterpoint or it disintegrates, its contours falling away as corners compete in three dimensions, one turning this way, the other that—an effect that is particularly evident as one looks up from the base at the vertiginous play of one chamfer against another at the top. These competing effects pose a series of difficult questions with remarkable efficiency: Is this a symbol, or is it simply a form? Is it representational or abstract? Or is it both? Neither? Regardless of how such questions are answered, however, their very posing secures one indisputable fact about the object: It is a work of architecture.

Or is it? In 1992, the novelist and cultural critic Amitav Ghosh asked why the transnational oil economy, unlike the spice trade in earlier days, had yet to produce great literature.[1] The same might be asked about its architecture, though the oil economy has produced, directly or indirectly, a great number of buildings. Among these are several designed and built by the firm of Johnson/Burgee in Houston, including the object described above, Pennzoil Place. These are not necessarily works executed on behalf of oil companies but, rather, works executed in and by a milieu fueled by the petrodollars that flowed freely into the U.S. economy during the 1970s.

Philip Johnson belonged to this milieu and profited from it. But again, both Johnson's activities and the commissions that his firm received were only indirectly linked to the oil industry. For example, his long friendship with members of the de Menil family, whose wealth derived from the Schlumberger Oil equipment company, translated mainly into art institutions such as the Amon Carter Museum in Forth Worth (1961). Frank Welch has written a detailed account of Johnson's personal ties to the Houston cultural scene and the commissions his firm accumulated as a result.[2] Rather than repeat such details, I want to take up a particularly vexing aspect of this long chapter in Johnson's professional career, as it bears on certain more abstract realities.

fig. 1 Philip Johnson (Johnson/Burgee), Pennzoil Towers, Houston, 1976

fig. 2 Pennzoil executive office at point of tower with diagonal sloping roof. *Progressive Architecture*, August 1977

However commercial it may seem, so-called developer architecture is never entirely reducible to the economic interests behind it. It is still, in some sense, architecture. And so in Johnson's collaborations with developers in Houston and elsewhere, his longstanding commitment to architecture as an art form—we can call it architecture with a capital A, or [A]rchitecture—was both tested and affirmed. The context for this was an increasingly global marketplace that, during the 1970s, generated new combinations of finance capital, cultural capital, and real estate speculation. Despite his increasing celebrity, Philip Johnson did not exactly become a "brand" during this period. Nor was he reduced to a mere commodity (or "whore," to use his own terminology). Instead, he and his work were, in a technical sense, media. That is to say: Johnson was not only a media figure, he was also a medium, in the sense of a figure who channels ostensibly spiritual or—more to the point— otherworldly forces (fig. 3). And in Houston, he and his architecture specifically channeled the force called *oil*.

Circulating as it does in the mass media but also in various semi-scholarly contexts, oil is what we can call a fetish.[3] A fetish is something that both reveals and conceals at once. That is why we can be told that Americans are addicted to oil by

George W. Bush, the man who started an oil company with the comical name Arbusto Energy in 1977.[4] Simply put, oil is a thing that we name, desire, and sometimes go to war over whose spectacular nature or *aura* actually works to conceal the complex and often violent social and historical processes that make it possible in the first place. In that sense, buildings like Johnson/Burgee's Pennzoil Place, designed and built for the developer Gerald D. Hines in Houston between 1973 and 1976, do not really represent oil; rather, the buildings *produce* it, in the form of a fetish—an object with special powers.

In other words, these buildings do not merely symbolize the power of oil companies. This is partly because what we call oil is really a hybrid plurality of actual objects, including the chemical called petroleum in its various states of refinement, as well as the various mechanisms via which it is extracted, and those via which it is processed, and those via which it is transported, and those via which it is sold and burned, and the gases thereby emitted, and the human bodies thereby propelled in machines, and those (perhaps in Nigeria) whose land is expropriated that these machines may receive more fuel, and the various organizations that do the expropriating, refining, selling, burning, and so on. All of these actualities are, in a sense, forced together into the phantasm called oil, which in turn exists only by virtue of its capacity to keep the inherent contradictions and conflicts of interest that it harbors at bay—to say nothing of its periodic, outright savagery. In helping to channel these various objects and the forces flowing from and through them— amplifying some, screening out others—architecture helps quite literally to build this phantasm, the existence and effects of which are inescapably real.

But all of this occurs indirectly, through varying degrees of mediation. In fact, despite its name, Pennzoil Place was not built directly for an oil company. It was built for a real estate developer who had been approached by an oil company to build an office building in downtown Houston. As it turned out, the building involved two oil companies. In 1954 Pennzoil's chairman and Hines's client Hugh Liedtke

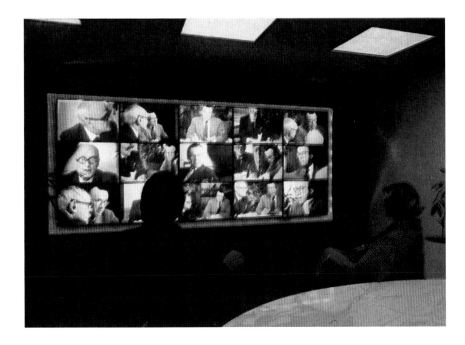

fig. 3 A fifteen-screen, multi-image slide show on the creative collaboration between Philip Johnson and developer Gerald D. Hines. Slide show created by Motiva. *Progressive Architecture*, August 1977

fig. 4 Atrium inside Pennzoil Place,
Houston, 1976

had formed a partnership with the elder George Bush in an entity called Zapata Petroleum (named after the film *Viva! Zapata*). In 1959, Bush sold his interests in Zapata Petroleum to Liedtke's Pennzoil conglomerate while spinning off the Zapata Offshore Oil Company for himself.[5] During the planning phase of Johnson's building, Hines and Liedtke brought in Zapata Petroleum as an additional major tenant and, with it, the criterion that both companies be recognized in the building's architecture.[6] The result was a kind of twinned Seagram Building skewed along the diagonal that runs from one corner of the site to the other. Each tower has a distinct but counterposed diagonal roof. At the base, the atrium joins the two together as it presents another, lower diagonal volume to the street (fig. 4). Other major tenants of the complex included the Pennzoil-owned United Gas Pipeline Company and the Houston office of the accounting firm Arthur Andersen, which later became involved in the collapse of Enron.

Stylistically, Pennzoil Place was among Johnson's last recognizably "modern" buildings. In 1954, Johnson had already theorized the various forms of fetishism characteristic of modern architecture, calling them "crutches" even as he admitted relying on them himself on occasion. But according to Johnson, architects who rely too heavily on these crutches obscure the aesthetic essence of architecture—its true, unfettered status as an art object.[7] Crutch-free architecture is autonomous architecture, architecture standing on its own, a position with which Johnson's name has long been associated. So it seems only fair to test out his theory by applying it to his building.

First crutch: The crutch of history. Though in 1954 Johnson could declare this crutch relatively inoperative, by 1973 it was certainly an issue and included, in this case, the history of modernism itself. That history is captured here in the form of a mannered quotation of Seagram's four-foot, seven-inch module, squashed into two-foot, six-inch units and spread in what Johnson called an "all over pattern" that stretches over Pennzoil's canted "roofs."[8]

Second crutch: The crutch of pretty drawing, or the "pretty plan." Johnson once compared the plan of Pennzoil to the then-new NBC logo, turned backward with a gap in the middle. Still, it is true that presentation drawings were not very important at Pennzoil. In their place was a twelve-foot-square model of Houston, a five-foot-tall model of the building, two interior models of the atrium, and a fifteen-screen slide show starring Johnson himself, in which he explained to potential tenants the oceanic swell of emotion they would experience upon entering the building each morning.[9]

Third crutch: The crutch of utility. Here is Johnson in 1954: "They say a building is good architecture if it works. Of course, this is poppycock. All buildings work."[10] Pennzoil certainly works, and by most accounts works well. What does it do? Among other things, it helps to produce the phantasm called oil.

Fourth crutch: The crutch of comfort, in which "environmental control starts to replace architecture." In an echo of Johnson/Burgee's earlier, environmentally controlled atrium space in the IDS Center that defended against cold winters in Minneapolis, the air-conditioned atrium at Pennzoil is among its most distinct architectural features. Given the cost-pressures of a speculative office building, it would probably not exist but for its capacity to defend oil industry workers against the extreme heat of a Houston summer.

Fifth crutch: The crutch of cheapness, or what Johnson called the "economic motive." As speculative office buildings go, Pennzoil was relatively expensive. Still, its economics were never far from the surface, and as Gerald Hines suggested at the time, its high level of design—its proximity to [A]rchitecture (and, we must assume, to the name of Philip Johnson)—made it attractive to tenants willing to pay a dollar or so more per square foot.[11]

Sixth crutch: The crutch of serving the client. As Johnson put it, "Serving the client is one thing and the art of architecture another."[12] True. But at Pennzoil, among the various services offered by Johnson's firm to their client Hines was a work of [A]rchitecture, an artwork. Why? Because it would fetch higher rents.[13]

Finally, there is the seventh crutch: The crutch of structure, of which Johnson happily admitted, "I use it all the time myself."[14] And indeed it is there at Pennzoil, in the regular column grid and in the trusses carrying the atrium roof, one precedent for which is the atrium-like roof covering the multilevel space of the sculpture galley at Johnson's New Canaan estate, completed in 1970. But in a perfect reversal, the actual structure at Pennzoil was built by oil itself: in this case, by Zapata Petroleum's affiliate, Zapata Warrior Constructors.[15]

Does this mean that architecture, having become dependent on—or addicted to—these seven crutches, is unable to stand on its own at Pennzoil? Well, yes and no, because [A]rchitecture also helps to prop up all the crutches. To demonstrate, I would like to add an eighth crutch—or really, a counter-crutch—to Johnson's list. Call it the "crutch of the corner," since it is often said that the real test of any [A]rchitect (capital A) is how she turns the corner (consider, for example, Ludwig Mies van der Rohe at the Illinois Institute of Technology). Johnson himself was fond of this criterion, as when he suggested that Mies had achieved at the Seagram Building a corner of sufficient nuance to merit comparison with the pilastered turn executed by Karl Friedrich Schinkel at the Altes Museum in Berlin. According to Johnson, such a comparison offered a salutary demonstration of the degree to which "architecture can be judged by corner treatment."[16]

As we have already seen, Pennzoil is, in a sense, all corners, inside and out. It is therefore potentially all [A]rchitecture, inside and out, at least to the degree that the turning of various corners is aesthetically pleasing, if not at times sublime. But the building's evident reliance on crutches one through seven seems to contradict this possibility, or at least to reduce it to an honorable compromise between the architect and a developer-patron who knew good architecture when he saw it. Since Pennzoil's corners also sublimely serve the client with some of the most dramatic corner offices around, to say nothing of the relative ease with which they accommodated Hines's budget, or the relative comfort of the multicornered atrium, or the elegance of the plan, or the structural resonance of the module, or the economy with which the program is accommodated or, subliminally, history is invoked.

But there is still hope. Johnson's former mentor-collaborator Mies rather notoriously used to say that God (read here: [A]rchitecture) is in the details. Bearing in mind that the various theories of commodity fetishism to which I have been alluding with respect to oil begin with a definition of the fetish as a religious object most often found in so-called pagan religions, and given the possibility that for the quasi-Miesian Johnson, [A]rchitecture was one such religion, it is only logical that

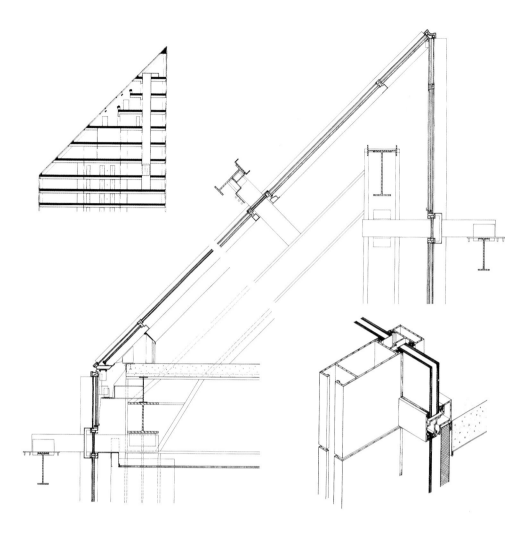

we seek out its gods in Pennzoil's details. Among these, one stands out. This is the turning of the corner at the peak of each tower, as the curtain wall folds diagonally across the building's volume to produce the double-canted profile that gives the building its distinctive identity. Johnson called the resulting effect "pure shape" and celebrated the economy of means by which it was achieved. Apparently, this architectural bonus added only eighty cents per square foot to the building's bottom line.[17] In return, Hines got what some (including Johnson) saw as the ghost of Minimal art—or again, in Johnson's words, "basic prismatic shape."[18]

The detail by which this was achieved is not particularly elegant. In fact, one member of the Houston firm that actually worked it out, S. I. Morris Associates, called it a "real dude" (fig. 5).[19] Still, the corner detail did what it had to do. It even contributed a little crypto-classicism to Johnson's still-evolving aesthetic grab-bag, in the form of the barely perceptible split pediment at the scale of the entire building that Frank Gehry later (and rather perceptively) identified as a possible predecessor to the Chippendale roof atop Johnson/Burgee's AT&T building of 1984.[20] So, as Pennzoil's temple form comes into view, and with it the god called [A]rchitecture, it seems difficult to say that it also worships the god called oil. But again, this is not necessarily a question of representation, or even a question of a so-called iconic building paying symbolic homage to the powers that be. It is a question of what you do not see as much as what you do see when you watch [A]rchitecture appear and disappear on the skyline of history.

Juan Pablo Pérez Alfonzo, the former Venezuelan oil minister and founder of OPEC, once called oil the "devil's excrement."[21] Its corrupting promise of instantaneous wealth, in the form of a "black gold" worthy of El Dorado, operates on a mythic level. It works in a way that is comparable to the holy grail that currency traders call arbitrage, which is in effect a nearly risk-free exploitation of a momentary imbalance in the financial markets. Perhaps no place in the world exemplifies this better than Nigeria, where the brutalities of what Michael Watts has called "petro-violence" have included a civil war, a succession of military coups, and other internecine conflicts that are in large part wars over the control of oil sold to major transnational corporations. Watts has shown how this economy finds its phantasmagoric expression in Lagos, where periodic mob violence erupts over (false) rumors of the organized theft of male genitalia, the spoils of which are thought (like oil) magically to produce instant wealth.[22] That Nigeria is sometimes called the Texas of Africa should give pause in this respect. Since (though there may not yet have been any cases of genital theft reported in Houston) that city too harbors a dreamlike, specular economy in which fetishes like oil with their promises of magical powers circulate.

Referring to the various financial interests that it served, one critic favorably described Pennzoil Place as a "monument to liquidity." It was designed for the purpose of making money and was 60 percent leased by the time of groundbreaking and 97 percent leased—at about 5 percent higher than market rates—by the time of occupancy. The risk-reduction strategy of "preleasing," common today, unleashed what the same critic called a "river of revenue" that in turn made possible a $60 million mortgage based on 75 percent of the building's presumed value, backed up by the leases that were in turn made possible, as Hines himself claimed, by the building's distinguished [A]rchitecture.[23]

In Houston in the mid-1970s, the liquid called oil was at the base of all of this liquidity. Rather uncannily, the basement level of Pennzoil Place feeds a series of air-conditioned subterranean tunnels that crisscross the city. Distant relatives of the nineteenth-century Parisian arcades in which Walter Benjamin discerned a dreamworld of wish images, these cool, dark interiors connect Pennzoil's street-level lobby (which was first inhabited by a bank) and its below-grade shopping arcade with its Houston neighbors. Among these is Number One Shell Plaza, the office building designed for Hines by Bruce Graham of Skidmore, Owings & Merrill and leased to Shell Oil that set a precedent for Hines's hiring of well-known architects like Johnson. In the years that followed, Johnson/Burgee would add a number of nodes to this network—a network that is both virtual (in the sense of a space through which the fetish called oil circulates) and real, in the sense of the financial, technological, political, and cultural infrastructures linking oil companies, banks, and governments in Houston and across the world, infrastructures that are visible, we can say, in the circuitry of the tunnels but also in the buildings above.

fig. 6 Philip Johnson (Johnson/Burgee), Transco Tower, Houston, 1985

fig. 7 Philip Johnson (Johnson/Burgee), RepublicBank and Pennzoil Towers, Houston, 1984

Among other nodes in this network are Johnson/Burgee's stand-alone Transco Tower of 1983 located ten miles to the west, and, just next door to Pennzoil (and linked to that building by a tunnel), their RepublicBank Center of 1984 (figs. 6, 7). When seen in series with Pennzoil, these buildings tell a different story from the one usually told about architecture's historical transition from modern to postmodern and Johnson's much-debated role therein. It is a story about liquidity and about circulation. It is about the air-conditioned air that fills these buildings and the so-called oil money that flows through them. But most important for us, this story is about the [A]rchitecture that both reveals and conceals such flows and the violence they frequently entail, as it helps literally to produce that magical, dangerous thing called oil.

Notes

1. Amitav Ghosh, "Petrofiction," first published in *New Republic* (March 2, 1992) and reprinted in Ghosh, *Incendiary Circumstances: A Chronicle of the Turmoil of Our Times* (New York: Houghton Mifflin, 2005), 138–151.

2. Frank D. Welch, *Philip Johnson & Texas* (Austin: University of Texas Press, 2000).

3. An example of the treatment of oil as a mythic cultural object, or fetish, is in Daniel Yergin, *The Prize: The Epic Quest for Oil, Money, and Power* (New York: Free Press, 1991). The principle of commodity fetishism to which I am alluding here is explicated by Marx in *Capital,* vol. 1. See Karl Marx, "The Fetishism of the Commodity and Its Secret," *Capital,* trans. Ben Fowkes (New York: Vintage, 1977), 1: 163–177. On semischolarly, epic histories of commodities, see Bruce Robbins, "Commodity Histories," *PMLA* 120, no. 2 (March 2005): 454–463.

4. Arbusto means bush in Spanish. On George W. Bush's early career in the energy business, see George Lardner, Jr., and Lois Romano, "Bush Name Helps Fuel Oil Dealings," *Washington Post,* July 30, 1999, p. A1. In his 2006 State of the Union speech, Bush declared that "America is addicted to oil, which is often imported from unstable parts of the world." George W. Bush, "State of the Union Address by the President," January 31, 2006.

5. Herbert S. Parmet, *George Bush: The Life of a Lone Star Yankee* (New York: Scribner, 1977), 82–86.

6. Peter Papademetriou, "Is 'Wow!' Enough?" *Progressive Architecture* 58, no. 8 (August 1977): 66, and William Marlin, "Pennzoil Place," *Architectural Record* 160, no. 7 (November 1976): 106–107.

7. Philip Johnson, "The Seven Crutches of Modern Architecture," *Perspecta* 3 (1954): 40–44.

8. Philip Johnson, quoted in John Pastier, "Evaluation: Pennzoil as Sculpture and Symbol," *American Institute of Architects Journal* 71, no. 7 (June 1982): 42.

9. Papademetriou, "Is 'Wow!' Enough?" 68.

10. Johnson, "Seven Crutches of Modern Architecture," 42.

11. With reference to Pennzoil Place and other commercial developments, Hines said of his firm that "we are in the business of building not only successful buildings but also *exciting* ones. The two go together, as I have come to see it" (quoted in Marlin, "Pennzoil Place," 110). For more general comments on the relationship between developers and architects in this context, see "Interview: Gerald D. Hines and Peter Eisenman," *Skyline,* October 1982, pp. 18–21.

12. Johnson, "Seven Crutches of Modern Architecture," 43.

13. Papademetriou, "Is 'Wow!' Enough?" 66–68.

14. Johnson, "Seven Crutches of Modern Architecture," 43.

15. Marlin, "Pennzoil Place," 106. Papademetriou, "Is 'Wow!' Enough?" 66.

16. Philip Johnson, "Schinkel and Mies" [1961], in *Philip Johnson: Writings,* foreword by Vincent Scully, introduction by Peter Eisenman, commentary by Robert A. M. Stern (New York: Oxford University Press, 1979), 171.

17. Marlin, "Pennzoil Place," 109.

18. Ibid., 110.

19. Hal Weatherford of S. I. Morris Associates quoted in Marlin, "Pennzoil Place," 110.

20. Frank Gehry's observations are noted in Pastier, "Evaluation: Pennzoil as Sculpture and Symbol," 42.

21. Juan Pablo Pérez Alfonzo cited in Terry Lynn Karl, *The Paradox of Plenty: Oil Booms and Petro-States* (Berkeley: University of California Press, 1997). This quotation is the basis for Watts's title, below.

22. Michael J. Watts, "Oil as Money: The Devil's Excrement and the Spectacle of Black Gold," in Stuart Corbridge, Nigel Thrift, and Ron Martin, eds., *Money, Power, and Space* (Oxford: Blackwell, 1994), 406–445. I am grateful to Brian Larkin for bringing this work to my attention.

23. Marlin, "Pennzoil Place," 110.

Philip Johnson's Empire:
Network Power and the AT&T Building

Kazys Varnelis

If Philip Johnson was indisputably good at anything, it was networking. While it will be up to history to judge the merits of his architecture as well as his influence on the field, there is no question about Johnson's native ability to capitalize on his connections in business and finance, art and architecture. In the words of Paul Goldberger, Johnson "was the man who *invented* networking."[1]

He took up the role early and eagerly as he traveled through Europe with Henry-Russell Hitchcock, collecting material that they would eventually develop into their landmark 1932 show, *Modern Architecture: International Exhibition* at the Museum of Modern Art in New York. In doing so, Johnson helped put together a seminal show while accumulating contacts among key figures of the day. But more than that, the show reframed the reception of architecture. Throughout the 1920s, modern architects exhibited their work to a broad section of the public, primarily through commercial venues such as expositions and trade fairs.[2] In bringing the show to a museum of art, Johnson removed architecture from the domain of building and technology and installed it in the context of connoisseurship, a move signaled by the label he and Hitchcock appropriated for the work from art-historical scholarship, "the International Style." Architecture became less a matter of performance and more a question of taste, with Johnson, the curator, as arbiter.

After his reprehensible foray into right-wing politics in the 1930s, followed by his time in the military and his return to architecture as a student at the Harvard Graduate School of Design in the early 1940s, Johnson set about designing his Glass House as the principal base for his networking operations.[3] The Four Seasons Restaurant in the Seagram Building would become equally important in this regard a decade later. Arguably his best works, these two spaces were venues in which Johnson played out his role as networker par excellence in spectacular fashion, deploying as instruments of power not only the spaces themselves, but also the power of the gaze: as the setting where he staged his social interactions, the Glass House became the vanishing point of his own field of view, while the Four Seasons—the most important table in the most important power-lunch venue in the most important city in the world—served as the focal point for his public appearances.[4]

But Johnson's past haunted him, and he was not able to return to MoMA in any official capacity until 1948, as acting director and consultant on architecture to the department of architecture and design. He told Peter Blake, who worked as a curator under Johnson, "Some of my trustees can't forget my Nazi past and would resign if I become the official director of the department." Johnson's activism on the behalf of the radical Right was a sore point for Edgar Kaufmann, director of the industrial design department until 1948 and an active foil to Johnson at the museum.[5] To counter Johnson's opponents, Blake later explained, "we maintained the fiction—I was the head of the department of Architecture and Industrial Design, and Philip was a sort of unofficial consultant. Nobody, needless to say, was fooled."[6] Having consolidated his position behind the scenes, Johnson officially rejoined the staff as director of the architecture and design department in 1949. He remained there, making his mark on the museum not only through the exhibitions he staged but also quite literally with his design for the annex building. This continued until 1954, when Johnson handpicked Arthur Drexler (who had been ensconced as curator of the department since 1951) as his successor.[7]

After the construction of the Glass House, Johnson also began to actively cultivate his network of patrons and artists, holding elaborate lunches at the Glass House for the cosmopolitan vanguard and high society, entertaining the likes of Jasper Johns, Merce Cunningham, George Balanchine, Lincoln Kirstein, Mrs. Bliss Parkinson, Edward M. M. Warburg, and Jacqueline Kennedy Onassis. As he expanded his connections and MoMA became the world's most important showplace of contemporary art, Johnson became one of the art world's biggest power brokers. By the late 1950s, being liked by Johnson meant that an artist had achieved a significant coup. Being bought by Johnson, in turn, meant that the artist had established himself. Johnson's unique position can be gauged from a remark by a dealer—nameless, of course—to the effect that Johnson was the only collector to whom he would give a 50 percent discount as long as it meant placing an artist in his collection.[8]

But it was in architecture that Johnson's power was virtually unrivaled. Even as a student at Harvard he had established his house at 9 Ash Street as a salon, but the Sunday pilgrimages to the Glass House, his directorship at MoMA, and later his power lunches at the Four Seasons allowed Johnson to consolidate his position. As the attention paid to his dramatic shift away from Mies in the 1950s showed, Johnson would be a leader of architectural fashion. If Johnson showed little modesty in reviewing his own book on his own work, *Philip Johnson: Architecture, 1949–1966*, for *Architectural Forum*, it wasn't a mere matter of narcissism, but rather a frank acknowledgment that as trendsetter and tastemaker in the field he had no equal.[9]

Virtually from that point on, however, Johnson came under attack and quickly found himself marginalized within the architectural vanguard. After a series of disparaging comments about Johnson's work appeared in *Architectural Design*, Robin Middleton responded with an open letter to the architect that quickly turned into a withering attack of the sort that only the British can muster. I offer only an excerpt:

You appear infinitely more intelligent and articulate than most American spokesmen for architecture, . . . not only are you impassioned and wise on the subject of architecture, but distinguished amateur that you are (and I mean this in the best possible sense of the term), you have been able to influence not only a wealthy and cultured minority in New Canaan and New York, but a far greater range of art conscious hangers-on than you realize. In America you are an authority on architecture—whether you or other architects like it or not. You are an architectural power. You have to be taken seriously. It would be much easier of course, not to take you seriously. A busy, eclectic architect, a master of techniques, a detail-at-a-time genius, a scholarly romantic, a demolisher of all over-earnest beliefs, a scandalmonger, you raise delicious questions—are you in fact in earnest? a charlatan? a mountebank? a juggler?—that are the very stuff of which architectural magazines are made. You are good copy, even in Fortune. But this won't do. You are a devil's advocate. Even if you had built nothing, your ideals would have to be denounced as heresy.... However, you have built, prolifically and diffusely, houses, churches, universities and museums—all in a span of seventeen years, and these works speak for themselves.

Your early buildings are beautiful contrivances, your Glass House, I am sure, is an object still of pilgrimage. But then there are post-Miesian designs, most of which I imagine, are unvisited by architects from abroad. What went wrong?[10]

What went wrong, in Middleton's view, was that Johnson was trapped in an "exercice de style," poaching at will from historical sources but turning them into "meaningless fictions and fantasies." Middleton pulled no punches, concluding that "each of [Johnson's] buildings is imbued with the dull complacency of great wealth." The public buildings that Johnson built in the 1960s were "conceived in the tradition of the great palace museums of Europe: they are remote repositories of great treasure, designed to emphasize as firmly as possible the distinction between those who can afford to buy and endow such collections and those who are graciously permitted to view them."[11]

If Middleton's critique was intense, he wasn't off the mark when it came to Johnson's intents. In 1964, an article in the *New York Times* noted that Johnson "has been called a rebel and a reactionary—perhaps rebelling and reacting against the same thing: the architectural establishment. But as one observer has said, he now is the establishment."[12] During an interview with Ada Louise Huxtable that year, Johnson confirmed that observation: "I'd like to be *l'architecte du roi*.... I mean the country's official architect for its great public buildings.... I want to take the dirty connotations out of the words 'official' and 'academic.'"[13] But Johnson's timing couldn't have been worse. Middleton concluded that Johnson failed to grasp the "real problem of 20th-century architecture—to build an adequate living environment for an ever-increasing mass of people."[14] In this critique, Middleton anticipated the rising complaints of a new, activist choir, the first generation to grow up under modernism, which called for architecture to be socially responsible but had little love for the forms of either the International Style or classicizing modernism.

As social critics decried Fordist hegemony and the top-down plan, architecture students turned against the modernist faith with Oedipal fury. Johnson became increasingly unpopular at universities and even found an enemy in Louis Kahn, one of the few modernists widely admired by younger architects.[15] To be sure, Johnson was among the first to understand that high modernism's days were numbered. His experimentation with classicism and with form-making as an end in itself is clear evidence of this. But Johnson's rejection of modernism was far from the radical rethinking of the field being proposed by the generation coming of age in architects such as Robert Venturi and Denise Scott Brown, Archigram, Archizoom, or Arata Isozaki. Nor did his elder statesman persona convince them. Harvard charm and cultivated wit held little appeal for the generation to whom activist Jerry Rubin was speaking when he said, "Don't trust anyone over thirty." Johnson was already twice that age at the time.

Instead, Johnson plunged headlong into corporate architecture, making John Burgee a partner in 1967 to undertake massive commissions for commercial real estate developers such as the 1968–73 IDS Center in Minneapolis and the 1972–76 Pennzoil Place in Houston.[16] These were precisely the kind of "big" architecture that the rebellious youth of the day detested, and the classicizing modernism of his public works reeked of authoritarianism to counterculture critics. With university students radicalized by the New Left, Robert A. M. Stern observed, "Johnson became persona non grata at most campuses."[17]

But a decade later Johnson reinvented himself—with some help from Stern and Peter Eisenman—as mentor and supporter of a generation of cutting-edge architects, his "Kids," as he called them, a group that would eventually included an entire generation of leading architects—both Stern and Eisenman, but also Frank Gehry, Richard Meier, Michael Graves, and Rem Koolhaas. In the process, Johnson would become a cultural superstar, an operator par excellence, at the center of a network that was stronger than ever. Like Johnson, his Kids shared a love for architecture as form. Johnson applauded this in the text that marked his reemergence, the postscript to the second edition of *Five Architects*.[18] Four of them—Eisenman, Graves, Meier, and to some extent even Gwathmey—could count themselves among the Kids. But so could the Five's opponents, the Grays, who came together around the 1973 "Five on Five" issue of *Architectural Forum* and were led by Stern.[19]

The opposition between the Whites and the Grays was not a paradox. Rather it was strategic: a Kuhnian paradigm-shift in which social activism, post-Archigram high tech, and media-driven practice in the vein of Superstudio or Ant Farm were not so much argued against as marginalized by a new debate on the nature of architectural form. The leaders of the two opposing groups, Stern and Eisenman, were longtime friends. As Stern described it, his friendship with Peter Eisenman was based on "the very oppositeness of his nature from mine ... [he] is my perfect alter-ego: 'If I didn't invent Peter Eisenman who would have?'"[20] Eisenman, for his part, once stated that, "If Stern had not existed, I would have had to invent him, and vice versa."[21]

Nor were Stern and Eisenman really poles apart, as Stern would later explain in reflecting on the conditions that brought the two together:

We were concerned with the break-up of the seemingly monolithic modern movement; and we were both contemptuous of the kind of stylish appliqué Modernism that we saw around us as well as the anti-architectural philistinism that was the unfortunate by-product of the student movements of the late 1960s. I was only too familiar with the latter, as much from teaching experiences at Columbia as from my own student days at Yale where its earliest manifestations could be seen in the back-to-the-woods, architecture-as-act movements of the 60s. Though Eisenman and I approached the situation from quite opposite points of view, we each saw the so-called revolutionary conditions of architecture of the 60s as ideologically confused, artistically debilitated, nihilistic, and anti-intellectual. Although these student movements supplied a necessary criticism of the then current scene and made it obvious

*the hypocrisy that afflicted our national political attitudes toward the war
in Vietnam and the situation of minorities at home, it hadn't led to anything
positive in terms of architectural production. What had begun as a useful
critique of a situation proved unable to develop a positive direction of its own;
it had no firm commitment to form-making or even a coherent political or
social program. It was against things but not for things.*[22]

Johnson was a natural as the ideological sponsor of this debate. Not only was the
enemy that united Stern and Eisenman the same enemy that had brought Johnson
low, but the movements these two protagonists advocated were united by their
reference to Johnson. For if the New York Five returned to the architecture of
Johnson's International Style, the Grays did as well. Eisenman's original title for
Five Architects—a book that in fact remained untitled—was "Cardboard Architecture,"
a term rejected by other members of the group for being too closely linked to
Eisenman's own theories. But it was Stern who first deployed the term—originally
coined by Frank Lloyd Wright to disparage the International Style—with its valence
flipped to describe the work included in his 1966 catalogue for the "40 Under 40"
exhibition at the Architectural League in New York, for which Johnson was the
patron and which included not only the majority of the Whites but also the Grays.[23]
Stern had counted Johnson as a supporter since his days at Yale editing *Perspecta*,
and Eisenman would soon see the benefit of working with Johnson as well, later
observing that "Philip was always troubled by how people of the intellectual
establishment viewed him. And [in the early seventies] I was somebody who clearly
did not regard him that way. I reinvented Philip. In a sense, we were inventions
of each other." Johnson, in turn, introduced Eisenman to patrons who helped
fund Eisenman's projects, such as *Oppositions* and the Institute for Architecture
and Urban Studies.[24] Sitting between Stern, whose architecture might anticipate
Johnson's future turn to postmodernism, and Eisenman, whose architecture might
recall the International Style, Johnson served as what Kenneth Frampton once
called an "ambivalent patron."[25]

The rise to prominence of the Whites and the Grays must have been a delight
for Johnson, both a final defeat of the modernist functionalism he had fought since
the 1930s and a repudiation of the more recent social critique that had marginalized
him. In a lecture at Columbia University in 1975, he exclaimed: "The day of ideology
is thankfully over. Let us celebrate the death of the *idée fixe*. There are no rules,
only facts. There is no order, only preference. There are no imperatives, only choice;
or to use a nineteenth-century word, 'taste'; or a modern word, 'take': 'What is your
"take" on this or that?'"[26]

Johnson's use of the terms taste and take is worth remarking on. For as
sociologist Pierre Bourdieu pointed out, taste is by no means innocent. On the contrary,
it is a marker of distinction, an indirect indicator of class. Proper understanding
of taste, Bourdieu explains, is based on a lifelong process of acculturation begun
in childhood. The child of upper-class parents (Johnson being an ideal example)
encounters art objects frequently and comes to understand that the most perfect
art object is disinterested, entering into discourse only with other art objects.[27] In
contrast, the lower classes are deprived of such experiences and therefore unable
to understand the class value of discussing art as art for art's sake, and thus justify

works by appealing to extrinsic, nonformal values such as age, the labor involved in their production, and subject matter.[28]

Bourdieu's explanation of taste explains Johnson's dislike of functionalism during the 1930s and after. Since the eighteenth century, architecture's tie to functional use relegated it to the lowest rank in the classification of the arts, far from the apex occupied by the more disinterested and abstract arts of poetry and painting.[29] The product of an upbringing conditioned by late nineteenth-century values, Johnson would have been a classic product of the kind of cultured bourgeois elite that Bourdieu describes.

But Bourdieu is also clear that the turn to *art pour l'art* is a compensatory measure for artists and academics who are, by nature, not members of the upper class but rather spectacles for the elite to observe. Especially after Johnson became a practicing architect, his social equals would—if anything—have viewed his new career as a step down, perhaps explainable only as a distraction from his political activities of the 1930s. Unlike philosophy, in which he had taken his undergraduate degree, architecture would not, in general, have been an acceptable object of study for a child of old money who would be expected above all to keep his fingernails clean. Johnson's strident advocacy of architecture as a matter of taste, not of function or social engineering, together with his repeated denial of his own seriousness as an architect, allowed him to occupy the only position within the field that would have been socially acceptable for his class: gentleman architect, dabbling in architecture occasionally (and often unsuccessfully, as if on purpose), but really nothing more than an esthete whose primary role was that of a patron and tastemaker.

Likewise, cardboard architecture could be read, in Bourdieu's terms, as a strategic replay of the International Style. Writing about art of the 1960s, Hal Foster describes the neo-avant-garde's turn to the past as a way "to reconnect with a lost practice in order to disconnect from a present way felt to be outmoded, misguided, or otherwise oppressive."[30] But if cardboard architecture understood the late modernist present to be obsolete, the return to the "heroic" period of the 1920s and 1930s took place under the trope of irony. For his dissertation, written under the supervision of Colin Rowe at the University of Cambridge, Eisenman produced the first thorough analysis of how modernist form of the heroic period was generated, but by the time he struck out on his own as an architect, Eisenman willingly deformed the language and rules he had previously identified.[31] As the two key members of the Grays, Stern and Charles Moore followed the project outlined in Venturi's *Complexity and Contradiction,* deploying the cardboard language of the International Style while introducing elements from popular culture and the history of premodern architecture. Bourdieu describes such recourse to pastiche or parody as a "heretical break," a strategic means by which cultural producers demonstrate their mastery of the past and thereby objectify it as a way of definitively breaking with it.[32] In doing so, then, the Whites and the Grays could join with Johnson to leave behind the modernist legacy, not only dismissing its claims to function and social engineering, but also paving the way for the more radical departures of the postmodernist and "deconstructivist" movements.

In return for Johnson's patronage, Eisenman and Stern launched a barrage of positive publicity about him. In 1977 both wrote essays on the Glass House in *Oppositions.*[33] These were followed in 1978 by the ninth in the Institute of

Architecture and Urban Studies' series of catalogues, *Philip Johnson: Processes. The Glass House, 1949, and The AT&T Corporate Headquarters, 1978,* and in 1979 by *Writings,* a collection of Johnson's essays on architecture edited by Stern with an introduction by Eisenman and a foreword by Vincent Scully. The latter was published in an elegant edition by Oxford University Press, a name that telegraphed academic respectability (not coincidentally, it was the press that published the second edition of *Five Architects*).[34]

His status as leader of the avant-garde restored, and with large projects under way in Texas, Johnson was back in the public eye and the stage was set for a period of immense power and fame. By 1979 he could boast that, "When Neimee gives you the Cartee Blanchee [*sic*], by God you know you've arrived."[35] Indeed, by the end of that year Johnson had received not only the Cartee Blanchee from Neimee, he had graced the cover of *Time* magazine and been awarded the first Pritzker Prize—the architectural equivalent of the Nobel Prize, an honor which Philip himself had long advocated be established for the field.[36] Above all, however, he was delighted by what he considered the commission of his lifetime, the headquarters for the American Telephone & Telegraph Company in Manhattan.[37]

Given the turn against postmodernism in the academy during the 1990s, AT&T has been singularly undervalued in Johnson's oeuvre, a mistake not only because it is Johnson's best postmodern work, but because it is also essential for a broader understanding of networks and Johnson's role in them. For if the Glass House has been better received among architects, the AT&T building—bigger, bolder, and one of the most lavish structures ever constructed—sited on Madison Avenue between 55th and 56th streets looms over the pilgrim who travels from the Seagram Building to the Museum of Modern Art. And yet, if the building is symbolic both of Johnson's role as networker and the largest corporate enterprise in history, by the time it was complete, AT&T itself had been undone.

In the fall of 1975, AT&T contacted twenty-five leading architectural offices, Johnson/Burgee among them, to announce it was constructing a new corporate headquarters building and to solicit their responses to four pages of questions regarding a possible approach. According to Johnson, "It got here, but we threw it away. We don't like questionnaires."[38] Later he elaborated that firms have to spend vast sums to compete for such projects, and that Johnson/Burgee not only didn't have the money, they also didn't believe they stood a chance.[39] Burgee, on the other hand, has suggested that they confused the request with an old "order" for an AT&T branch office in Chicago.[40]

Regardless of what happened, Johnson/Burgee found itself on a short list of three firms charged with making a presentation to John D. deButts, chairman of AT&T. In the trademark fashion of the office, Burgee and Johnson played on the former's cool expertise and the latter's wit, presenting only two photographs, one of the Seagram Building and one of Pennzoil Place, modernist projects that in retrospect seem unlikely precedents, considering the AT&T building's turn to historical eclecticism. This bluff of a presentation played well to deButts, a strong believer in the force of personality. As Michael Graves later observed, "Bernini persuaded the Pope to be his patron, and Johnson did the same with AT&T."[41] Company officials privy to the decision-making process suggest that "there was no close second."[42]

DeButts knew that a new corporate headquarters would provide a symbolic center for a firm that had seen better days. When he took over AT&T in 1972, deButts was immediately confronted with a corporation in crisis. Bad management decisions during the previous decade had resulted in severe service problems in New York and other cities. Private line providers, most notably a small firm called MCI, were nibbling at the edges of AT&T's profitable Long Lines network and initiating legal skirmishes. The corporation's shares had been flat for two years, and AT&T was failing to make money for its investors. DeButts set out to reaffirm the culture of the Bell System, a finely tuned Fordist hierarchy of loyal employees working in high technology, while reorganizing the company to make it conform better to market needs. After he pledged to set a firm course for the company during his first speech at a meeting of high-level AT&T managers, deButts became known throughout the Bell System for his "decision to decide," and he was widely regarded as a strong leader for the company.[43]

But the new building was not merely a symbolic gesture. By the mid-1970s, AT&T was straining the limits of its aging corporate headquarters at 195 Broadway, and the world's largest company anticipated further growth (fig. 1). Still, many in the organizational structure of Ma Bell subscribed to midwestern humility, Gray Suit anonymity, and an engineer's disregard for symbolism. This contingent wanted a practical building. L. K. O'Leary, one AT&T executive, wrote:

> *If we had our portrait painted, it should be by Norman Rockwell.*
> *If we were ancient builders, we would have built the Roman aqueducts*
> *instead of the Cathedral of Notre Dame....*
> *If we were a state, we would be Midwestern, probably Iowa....*
> *If we were a tree, we would be a huge and utilitarian Douglas fir—not a*
> *sequoia, and certainly not a dogwood.*
> *If we could choose an epitaph (never believing such a thing would be needed)*
> *we would choose, "Millions of customers, but it served them well, and one*
> *at a time."*[44]

DeButts was no typical AT&T Gray Suit. Johnson described him as a "strong man. There were some on the board who didn't like the design, but deButts could outvote the entire board."[45] He wanted a "monument for the biggest company in the world," a structure on the level of the Seagram Building, but not a glass box.[46]

The CEO who had earlier made the decision to decide swiftly approved Johnson/Burgee's now-familiar tripartite proposal for the structure: a 60-foot-high loggia loosely derived from the Pazzi Chapel, surmounted by a 37-story, 648-foot-high structure capped by the familiar broken Chippendale pediment, distinctly recognizable from across the city like a skyscraper from the 1920s. Johnson/Burgee proposed to sheath the building in granite, much like AT&T's other recently completed New York skyscraper, John Carl Warnecke's windowless 1974 Long Lines building in lower Manhattan (fig. 2). But if Warnecke's monolithic structure took function to an unprecedented level of abstraction and late-modern starkness (only possible, perhaps, because the structure houses telephone equipment and not people, and is designed to function autonomously for up to two weeks in the event of a nuclear holocaust), Johnson/Burgee's structure revels in its historicist monumentality. Whereas Warnecke's skyscraper was an early example of the use of a traditional material like granite for curtain wall construction, Johnson/Burgee's

fig. 1 AT&T headquarters at 195 Broadway from 1916–83, built by Welles Bosworth from 1912–23

fig. 2 Long Lines building by John Carl Warnecke, 1974

fig. 3 Philip Johnson (Johnson/ Burgee), AT&T Corporate Headquarters, New York, 1979–84

AT&T building revived the premodern era's lavish use of stone (some thirteen thousand tons of Stony Creek granite like that used to build Grand Central Station) for a facade consisting of panels up to ten inches thick, and thus three times what was typical for the time, creating an impression of solidity and relief instead of cardboard thinness and surface effect, a gesture that required six thousand additional tons of steel to support (figs. 3, 4). In this respect, AT&T is an echo of Seagram, Johnson/Burgee's thick granite a response to Mies's regal bronze. Although the granite facade was billed as an "innovative" response to the energy crisis, the building's lavish budget surprised some observers. "Well, it's no standard office building," deButts retorted.[47] The headquarters' entrance loggia is a sendup of Seagram as well; instead of the generous open square of the earlier structure, at

AT&T Johnson/Burgee reinterpreted the city's demands for a public amenity with an open forest of columns that created a public space under the structure. Johnson later explained that the "space was basically tailored to AT&T—it is an imperial space. AT&T didn't want lingerie stores in the lobby. They said 'Make it the front door into our empire. Let's make it so you'll be impressed when you go by.'"[48]

Johnson said of AT&T that "they were an imperial company and they thought of themselves that way. Chairman deButts was a one-man democracy. He wanted to build. Nobody on the board wanted to build a building."[49] On March 30, 1978, AT&T officially announced plans for its new headquarters, then estimated to cost $110 million (in the end the building would cost a good deal more, with some estimates ranging to double that amount). For New York, a city still struggling to recover

fig. 4 AT&T Corporate Headquarters foyer with Evelyn Beatrice Longman's *Genius of Electricity* from 1916

fig. 5 Cover of *Time*, January 8, 1979

from fiscal troubles in the midst of an era when corporations were fleeing cities for suburban headquarters, AT&T's return to Manhattan from its offices in Basking Ridge, New Jersey, would be a great boon. According to Johnson, deButts was a New Yorker and hoped to relocate the firm to the city.[50] He stated his intentions to the press: "We would like the building to say loud and clear, 'We love New York,'" referring to the Milton Glaser ad campaign promoting the metropolis. Mayor Koch was enthusiastic, responding that the project was "of great importance to New York City's economic growth and stability, as well as to our prestige as the undisputed communications capital of the world."[51]

The controversial structure was an attention-getter: *Time* featured Johnson on its January 7, 1979, cover in a pose evoking the image of Moses holding the tablets of the Law (fig. 5). Johnson, as the cover suggested, was the master architect of the day, and AT&T the new face of Big Business. If the decade had started with the radical high tech of the Centre Pompidou, it was drawing to a close with the postmodernism of AT&T. Whereas Warnecke's Long Lines recalled the monolith from *2001: A Space Odyssey*, Johnson's AT&T was the even more technologically sophisticated Baroque space in which the astronaut Dave Bowman awakens at the end of the film. No longer wearing technology on its sleeve, but rather absorbing it, the AT&T building suggested that the new American corporation would be based on the solidity of cultural precedent, technology to be replaced by "family values." The videophones promised in the 1960s were nowhere to be seen, and in their stead was a return to Ma Bell tradition, a concept AT&T soon marketed with "retro" telephones. Above all, this folksy American skyscraper communicated AT&T's role as a "natural" feature of the country, specifically suggesting that AT&T was entitled to maintain a "natural monopoly," the principle behind the company's belief that it was exempt from antitrust law.

But AT&T itself was far from solid, and the stone cladding of its new headquarters only thinly disguised an entity starting to crumble. In November 1974, Attorney General William Saxbe declared that AT&T was abusing its status as a "natural monopoly" regulated by the FCC, and announced the federal government's intent to dismantle the communications giant under Section 2 of the Sherman Antitrust Act. This was a piece of nineteenth-century legislation aimed at breaking up the imperial holdings of the robber barons into more fluid entities, thereby releasing monopoly capital into the economy, a statute used to challenge the monopolistic practices of Standard Oil and American Tobacco, which were dismantled in 1911, and subsequently (albeit unsuccessfully), in the 1980s and 1990s, against IBM and Microsoft.

Saxbe's was only the latest in a series of efforts to split up Ma Bell dating back to the days of banker J. P. Morgan's involvement with the corporation, but the renewed effort on the part of the federal government, triggered by AT&T's resistance to the inroads being made by MCI to carry specialized private-line traffic, was serious. DeButts wasn't fazed. He believed the lawsuit to be baseless and characterized the government's stance as a national catastrophe, declaring, "AT&T would fight to the death."[52] But for the first time since the Progressive era, the climate was distinctly anti–big business. AT&T would not escape this time.

In February 1979, just one month after Johnson made the cover of *Time*, Charles E. Brown succeeded deButts at AT&T. Whereas deButts was outspoken, Brown was restrained. Whereas deButts detested competition, Brown considered it a fact of life but hoped to move the company into the information age. At one point, referring to the common conception of AT&T as "Ma Bell," Brown declared, "I would appreciate your passing the word that Mother doesn't live here anymore."[53] Reportedly, Brown initially hoped that construction on the tower could be stopped, but he backed off when he realized that such a move would have generated too much negative publicity.[54]

As construction proceeded, Brown had greater worries than the cost of his headquarters building. The corporation came under more fire from William F. Baxter, new head of the Antitrust Division under the Reagan administration. Adamant that competition is the basis for economic growth, Baxter saw AT&T's natural monopoly as an example of big government meddling and moved forward, making his intention clear during his first press conference: he would litigate this case "to the eyeballs."[55]

The building was not yet completed when, on January 8, 1982, AT&T agreed to divest itself of its monopoly over local telephone services. Although the corporation was allowed to keep its long-distance service, it would face increasing competition from other carriers. In return, AT&T hoped to capitalize on the ubiquity of its brand to sell personal computers, a plan that soon failed in the face of the rampant cloning of the IBM PC by cut-rate hardware manufacturers. AT&T's failure proved that Ma Bell's brand might be readily identifiable, but it was far from loved.

By the fall of that year, AT&T had decided that it would not use all of the office space in the new building, and it sought a tenant to occupy at least half.[56] Failing to find a suitable skyscraper-mate, however, AT&T remained the principal tenant. Five years later, struggling to establish itself in the new post-divestment world, the company's imperial ambitions having been thwarted by more flexible, lower-cost networks, AT&T announced that it would vacate its offices, leasing up to 75 percent of the building.[57] Finally in 1992, in the wake of the failure of its post-divestment strategies, AT&T sold the building to the Sony Corporation, which closed off Johnson's imperial arcade.

The story ends in November 2005, when, having spectacularly failed to rebuild its position during the broadband boom, AT&T ceased to exist as an independent company and was bought by SBC, a "Baby Bell" that had been spun off during the divestment. The fact that SBC immediately renamed itself AT&T and has imperialistic ambitions of its own does little to ameliorate the fact that the old empire is gone, having lasted only a few months longer than the architect of its corporate headquarters.

Nor is AT&T's failure unique. To the contrary, in *Empire*, Michael Hardt and Antonio Negri contend that the old world of imperial expansion, composed of centered hierarchies in accord and strife with one another, is giving way to the limitless field of Empire, a universal order without boundaries or limits, as flexible, all-pervasive networks replace the hierarchical systems of the previous order. This is not so much a matter of revolution as capital adapting to its ever-increasing size and complexity. As recent research in network theory suggests, well-connected hubs— whether one is talking about the twentieth-century imperialist state, AT&T, or Philip Johnson the power broker—emerge naturally and work efficiently for networks up to a certain size, allowing information to be transmitted rapidly. For a time these hubs grow exponentially and in the process can become extremely powerful, as Johnson did. But these studies also suggest that such hubs also inevitably break down once the network reaches a certain threshold, at which point they become overloaded by the possibilities for making connections and begin to evolve into more distributed, or at least decentralized, topographies in which either individual agents or smaller, more nimble hubs establish connections to one another. The clearest example of this is the failure of the hub-and-spoke system used by airlines in the United States. At a certain point, flights became so numerous that hubs were overloaded, causing slowdowns for travelers and mounting costs for airlines, and it was at precisely this point that more nimble rival carriers could introduce point-to-point services that bypassed the ailing hubs and allowed them to flourish as the old airlines collapsed.[58]

This, too, is the legacy of AT&T: its iconic skyscraper rendered obsolete before its completion, the company nevertheless refused to abandon its equally obsolescent imperial networks and was twice annihilated, first in 1982 and then in 2005. The federal government's antitrust action was necessary to allow American telecommunications to grow. The antiquated, centralized system of AT&T simply couldn't compete with the more opportunistically organized rival carriers.

Johnson was a pioneer, the first to admit that networking was more important than the buildings he created. But Johnson's network was hierarchical, based on

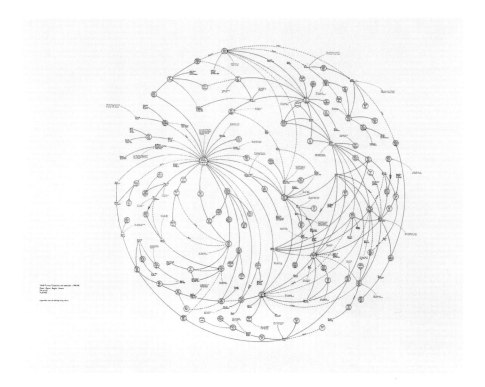

the model of sovereignty, with Johnson as the singular power broker at the apex.

Just as there was only one Louis XIV, there can be only one Philip Johnson. Just as Ma Bell's monopoly is gone, the architecture network that Johnson built—imperial, sovereign, singular—is also a thing of the past. Under Empire, the global system of architecture culture is simply too large, too complex, and too dispersed to accommodate another Philip Johnson. To be sure, there will always be individuals with greater and lesser degrees of connectedness, but contemporary networks of power are distributed, as Mark Lombardi's flow chart diagrams demonstrate (fig. 6). The post-Johnson model of power is characterized by unprecedented scandals involving innumerable players, so that culpability is distributed through the network to the individual agents themselves. Even if it was still possible to map the flows of power operative in the imperial model, in the network culture that makes up Empire, it is now moot, a fact that Lombardi eloquently captures in the paranoiac connections of his drawings. In Lombardi's diagrams, a chance acquaintance leads to implication in a scandal. Power emerges not from a center, but from the network itself, not just from the top, but from below too, from the innumerable bit players in global capital.

But network culture is not revolutionary. If Hardt and Negri explain that we, as the multitude, collectively hold the reins that collectively bind us, then we have to ask, why do we continue to do so? Some may have more power than others, but regardless, today we are all implicated in its construction, we are all players. The distributed power of the society of control ensures that we maintain order over ourselves far more effectively than we ever would have under disciplinary power. Far beyond what Peter Sloterdijk called cynical reason, today we are all heroes and villains.[59] Today we are all Philip Johnson.

fig. 6 Mark Lombardi, *World Finance Corporation and Associates, c. 1970–84: Miami, Ajman, and Bogotá-Caracas (Brigada 2506: Cuban Anti-Castro Bay of Pigs Veteran) (7th Version),* 1999

Notes

1. Paul Goldberger, quoted in Kurt Andersen, "Philip the Great," *Vanity Fair,* June 1993, 138.

2. In this light, the decision to let the 1932 exhibition travel to department stores such as Carson, Pirie, Scott and Company in Chicago and Bullocks in Los Angeles was not the anomaly, but rather the norm.

3. On Johnson's political activities in the 1930s, a part of his life that we must consider in any accounting of his contributions, see my "'We Cannot Not Know History': Philip Johnson's Politics and Cynical Survival," *Journal of Architectural Education,* November 1995, 92–104.

4. "To be invited to visit the Glass House might seem like a sign that one had been admitted to a fairly exclusive club. Actually the club had a very exclusive membership: sooner or later, everyone of any standing in the arts, in the U.S. or abroad, would show up at the house if he or she happened to be within a hundred miles or so of New Canaan." Peter Blake, *No Place Like Utopia: Modern Architecture and the Company We Kept* (New York: Knopf, 1993), 151.

5. Kaufmann was director of the industrial design department from 1946 to 1948, when the industrial design and architecture departments were merged under Johnson's directorship. Subsequently, Kaufmann would remain as a consultant to the museum.

6. Blake, *No Place Like Utopia,* 108 and 128–133. On Kaufmann's opposition to Johnson, see also Franz Schulze, *Philip Johnson: Life and Work* (New York: Knopf, 1994), 181.

7. The dates for who worked at MoMA and when often conflict in the literature. According to the MoMA archives, however, they are as follows: Edgar Kaufmann, Jr., was curator (1940–46) and then director (1946–48) of the Department of Industrial Design. From 1948 to 1950, he was research associate and consultant in industrial design. Philip Johnson was acting director and consultant on architecture (1948–49), then director (1949–54). Peter Blake was curator (1948–50).

8. Sophy Burnham, *The Art Crowd* (New York: David McKay, 1973), 38–39.

9. See "Review of Philip Johnson: Architecture, 1949–1965," *Architectural Forum* (October 1966), 52–53, reprinted in Philip Johnson, *Philip Johnson: Writings,* foreword by Vincent Scully, introduction by Peter Eisenman, commentary by Robert A. M. Stern (New York: Oxford University Press, 1979), 254–256. In the introduction to the piece, Robert Stern remarks, "How much like a lunch with Johnson at his 'corner table' at the Four Seasons this magnificent piece of *chutzpah* seems! At top speed, running with the hare and hunting with the hounds, thinking and proclaiming, Johnson reviews his own books, and frankly bares his own intentions to make as certain as possible that history recognizes his achievement, that it looks at his oeuvre in the context of contemporary practice as well as in the context of the grand tradition of Modern architectural history taken as whole," 254.

10. Robin Middleton, open letter, "Dear Philip," "Cosmorama," *Architectural Design,* March 1967, 107.

11. Middleton, "Dear Philip," 107.

12. "Architect of Elegance: Philip Cortelyou Johnson," *New York Times,* November 16, 1964, 33.

13. Ada Louise Huxtable, "He Adds Elegance to Modern Architecture," *New York Times Sunday Magazine,* May 24, 1964, 100.

14. Middleton, "Dear Philip," 107.

15. Blake, *No Place Like Utopia,* 308.

16. Schulze, *Philip Johnson,* 305–310.

17. Johnson, *Writings,* 258. On this time in Johnson's life, see also the chapter titled "The Sixties: Laurels and Ass's Ears" in Schulze, *Philip Johnson,* 273–286.

18. Philip Johnson, "Postscript," *Five Architects* (New York: Oxford University Press, 1975), 138.

19. "Five on Five," *Architectural Forum,* May 1973, 46–57.

20. Charles Jencks, "Dialogue with Robert A. M. Stern," *Robert A. M. Stern: Selected Works,* Architectural Monographs 17 (London: Academy Editions and St. Martin's Press, 1991), 131.

21. Thomas S. Hines, "Citizen Stern: A Portrait of the Architect as Entrepreneur," in *Architecture and Urbanism Extra Edition: The Residential Work of Robert A. M. Stern,* July 1982, 229.

22. Stern, "Notes on Post-Modernism," in *Robert A. M. Stern: Selected Works,* 113.

23. Robert A. M. Stern, ed., *40 Under 40: An Exhibition of Young Talent in Architecture* (New York: Architectural League of New York, 1966).

24. Peter Eisenman, quoted in Andersen, "Philip the Great," 152.

25. Kenneth Frampton, "Zabriskie Point: la traietorria di un somnambulo," *Casabella* 586–587 (January–February 1992), 9.

26. Philip Johnson, "What Makes Me Tick," in Johnson, *Writings,* 260–261.

27. Pierre Bourdieu and Alain Darbel, *The Love of Art: European Art Museums and Their Public* (Cambridge, England: Polity, 1991), 37–39; originally published as *L'amour de l'art: les musées d'art européens et leur public* (Paris: Editions de Minuit, 1969).

28. Bourdieu and Darbel, *Love of Art,* 39–44.

29. For a more historical and consequently in some ways more serviceable account of taste than Bourdieu's, see M. H. Abrams, "Art-As-Such: The Sociology of Modern Aesthetics" and "From Addison to Kant: Modern Aesthetics and the Exemplary Art," in *Doing Things with Texts: Essays in Criticism and Critical Theory* (New York:Norton, 1989), 135–187.

30. Hal Foster, "What's Neo About the Neo-Avant-Garde?," *October* 70 (Autumn 1994): 7.

31. Peter D. Eisenman, "The Formal Basis of Modern Architecture," Ph.D. diss., Trinity College, University of Cambridge, 1963.

32. Pierre Bourdieu, *The Field of Cultural Production: Essays on Art and Literature* (New York: Columbia University Press, 1993), 11.

33. Robert A. M. Stern, "The Evolution of Philip Johnson's Glass House, 1947–1948," *Oppositions* 10 (Fall 1977): 56–67, and Peter Eisenman, "Behind the Mirror: On the Writings of Philip Johnson," *Oppositions* 10 (Fall 1977): 1–13.

34. Kenneth Frampton, ed., *Philip Johnson: Processes. The Glass House, 1949, and The AT&T Corporate Headquarters, 1978* (New York: Institute for Architecture and Urban Studies, 1978), and Johnson, *Writings.*

35. Johnson, quoted by Vincent Scully in his foreword to Johnson, *Writings,* 6.

36. Johnson was on the cover of *Time* on January 8, 1979. On the Pritzker Prize, see "Oral History of Carter Manny as Interviewed by Franz Schulze," Chicago Architects Oral History Project (Chicago: Art Institute of Chicago, 2001), available at http://www.artic.edu/aic/libraries/caohp/manny.pdf (source accessed March 20, 2006).

37. For Johnson on AT&T, see Andersen, "Philip the Great," 155.

38. Craig Unger, "Tower of Power: The Extraordinary Saga of the AT&T Building," *New York Times,* November 15, 1982, 45.

39. Hilary Lewis and John O'Connor, *Philip Johnson: The Architect in His Own Words* (New York: Rizzoli, 1994), 104.

40. Schulze, *Philip Johnson,* 345.

41. Unger, "Tower of Power," 47.

42. Ibid.

43. Peter Temin, with Louis Galambos, *The Fall of the Bell System: A Study in Prices and Politics* (Cambridge: Cambridge University Press, 1987), 74.

44. Unger, "Tower of Power," 51.

45. Ibid.

46. Schulze, *Philip Johnson,* 346.

47. Maurice Carroll, "AT&T to Build New Head-quarters Tower at Madison and 55th Street,"

New York Times, March 31, 1978, B4.

48. Johnson, quoted in Lewis and O'Connor, *Philip Johnson,* 106.

49. Ibid., 109.

50. Ibid..

51. Carroll, "AT&T to Build New Headquarters," B4.

52. James B. Stewart, "Whales & Sharks: The Unexpected Fates of AT&T and IBM May Offer a Lesson to the Clinton Justice Department," *New Yorker,* February 15, 1993, 37.

53. Temin, *Fall of the Bell System,* 161.

54. Unger, "Tower of Power," 51.

55. Ibid., 53.

56. Diane Henry, "Real Estate: AT&T in Role of Landlord," *New York Times,* September 29, 1982, D24.

57. Albert Scardino, "AT&T Is Vacating Much of Its Tower," *New York Times,* March 27, 1987, A1.

58. See Michael Hardt and Antonio Negri, *Empire* (Cambridge: Harvard University Press, 2000), and Mark Buchanan, *Nexus: Small Worlds and the Groundbreaking Theory of Networks* (New York: Norton, 2002).

59. Peter Sloterdijk, *Critique of Cynical Reason* (Minneapolis: University of Minnesota Press, 1987).

Philip Johnson and the Smile of Medusa

Charles Jencks

Immortality

The constancy of change? The television film *Philip Johnson, Godfather of American Architecture,* produced by the BBC in 1993, opens with the architect's profession of faith in the primary drive of mankind, immortality. There he appears as the wise elder, a wizened eighty-six years old, set off by those young friends he calls the "Kids"—Peter, Bob, Jack, and Frank—wistfully meditating on the fleeting compulsions of life. The Godfather can feel the end may be nigh, and in his melancholically thin voice he whispers like Don Corleone: "The desire for immortality is the driving force. Sex—sex is very temporary. The Chinese were right, it's sort of a disease, but you get over that ... and, uh, the desire for immortality, how can you get over that? ... It gives you a goal that is totally unattainable, that comes from the inside, the way hunger and sex do. For me the desire for immortality is best expressed in buildings, because they last beyond cultures even."[1] *Vita brevis est, ars longa.* Life is short, art is long, architecture even longer.

By the end of the film, Philip is not so sure that his buildings will last a thousand years. It's a touching scene of self-doubt and self-recognition, King Lear without the words, the Godfather without machine guns. Will Philip's buildings last to the year 3000, or will they fall to the necessities of fashion, erosion, capitalism, war, entropy—or, final defeat, judgment? Change, the constancy of change, might get them in the end, as it did the thousand-year Reich—all is vanity.

A Personal Aside

Having now read Franz Schulze's biography of Johnson (1994), in which I am called "one of the most determined tormentors of Johnson," I should clarify some personal points. Like so many, I enjoyed Philip's company, his wit and generosity, especially when it came to supporting the outré and the overlooked, architects such as Frank Gehry and Eric Moss. While few of his buildings may have had depth, I found his gardens excitingly planned for what he called the "processional element in architecture"—that is, a leisurely walk in a peaceful and surprising space (fig. 1). His influence on American architecture and his cavalier disdain for social and political values, especially his lying, were appalling and deserved to be censured; it is worth saying, though, that on occasion he could be more truthful about his own failings than

his critics. From 1973 through 1989 I had four long interviews with Johnson, and he inscribed several books with praise even after the torment that Schulze mentions.

Inevitably this anguish circled around the connections between his Nazi past and his present position in American architecture, a subject that was taboo at the time and had been successfully repressed. In the 1973 interview Johnson said Albert Speer, whose biography he had just read, would make a great American skyscraper architect. This was a shocking throwaway, and a parallel worth pursuing. But it had not been pursued, in the press at least. Why? As Schulze suggests, Johnson had made his peace with the FBI, and, in spite of his anti-Semitism of the 1930s, made his peace with the Jewish community. He had designed a synagogue and a nuclear reactor in Israel, and was friends with Shimon Peres and Teddy Kollek, the powerful mayor of Jerusalem.

To underline the strength of the taboo, it is worth recounting the way information can be suppressed by the threat of lawsuits, especially in the United Kingdom. In 1972, I had been commissioned to write a book on Johnson by the mainstream English publisher Thames and Hudson. James Stirling, returning from a teaching stint at Yale, brought up Johnson's flirtations with the Nazis, saying that a comment on this episode could be found in William Shirer's *Berlin Diary* (1941). But surprise, there was no mention of this in British editions of the book. Yet Stirling insisted that he could not have dreamed up the reference: he had certainly read about Johnson being in Danzig with Hitler at the outbreak of World War II. Only U.S. editions of the book carried the facts.

Johnson and Shirer had indeed spent the night together, as two American reporters covering the war, and Shirer was convinced that Philip was a secret Nazi sympathizer because of his previous writings for Father Coughlin. Shirer writes only of his distaste and suspicions, nothing we would find particularly censorious or libelous today. But the British publishers had excised this passage, just one paragraph out of a book hundreds of pages long. Indeed, when I included the interview with Johnson for the book, Thames and Hudson turned down the

fig. 1 Philip Johnson's compound landscape, New Canaan, Connecticut, 1949 manuscript as too risky. In America, publishing law is more respectful of the truth; in Britain, when it might be thought to damage a reputation, the truth comes very much second (or at least did, before the era of the Rupert Murdoch press). Fear and self-censorship, as always, are the best of gags.

In the event, part of the interview was finally published in the U.K., in 1973, in the small academic journal *Architectural Association Quarterly*.[2] The article, "The Candid King Midas of New York Camp," was written in the prevailing neo-hysterical style fashioned by Tom Wolfe, a mode well suited for exploring the underbelly of hyperreality. In the interview Johnson admitted many "mistakes" and fascist leanings, especially when prompted by other examples: Le Corbusier's advances to Mussolini and Petain, Gropius's overtures with Goebbels, and Mies's with the Nazis. At this point Johnson came to the unlikely idea that Speer would make a "good" American architect, a "really great skyscraper architect," because he was an "extremely sensitive man and really a businessman architect . . . an organizer."

Speer a "sensitive man"! That insight unsettled me more than Philip's revelations about his past, because it sounded plausible. Just as John Kenneth Galbraith predicted, after he debriefed the captured leader in 1945, Speer managed to pull the wool over Americans' eyes. His suave self-deprecation, owning up to being bad in general while denying accusations in particular, made him the good-bad Nazi, and a best seller in America. My article quoted the spectre that was being raised in those troubled post-Vietnam times, by Noam Chomsky among others, that what was needed in American society at large was "a kind of denazification." The crypto-fascist work of Johnson and others at Lincoln Center and elsewhere showed the point. Now Johnson was suggesting there were deeper reasons for the similar styles.

About ten years previously Nikolaus Pevsner had recommended the stripped classicism of Mussolini and showed its positive parallels with recent corporate work. There *are* corporate affinities and psychologies in architecture, which Johnson was pointing out in Speer, even if not a single classical style. At all events, such issues and taboos were to haunt the obituaries of Johnson in 2005. As Schulze's book makes clear, Johnson was himself troubled by this past and his anti-Semitism. Yet there is a problem. Though he felt badly, and said in the 1973 interview, "I was wrong. . . . I hoped something good would come out of it. No, this was *before* concentration camps were started . . . ," he did not, as far as I know, apologize publicly for his anti-Semitic writings. Why not, especially since he admitted to so many other failings? There may be no answer; but perhaps, despite all the change, at a deeper level Johnson remained the same.

Change/No Change

In many ways Philip Johnson kept zigzagging down the hill as he slalomed through life. He shifted his stylistic loyalties at least four times; he restructured his office four times; he changed friends throughout his life and moved house and apartments to suit his varying lifestyle. His epigrams on the necessity of change and his constant quote from Heraclitus—"Everything flows and nothing abides"—would seem to confirm this incessant incessancy. Fashionable change became his demon, and therefore trying to preempt the zeitgeist his method of action. But, like Cedric

Price, the British architect who spoke so continuously of change, the paradox is that Johnson did not modify the inner core. Like a character in a drama who has grown up completely in act 1, scene 1, the trajectory of his personality seems to have been set in white marble: an easy and icy beauty. It always has this classical cool, like Canova's *Three Graces,* a manner Mario Praz deftly called the Erotic Frigidaire.[3] That is the paradox: How could a man who is associated so much with the constancy of change turn the multifarious experiments in different styles and fashions into one sensual icebox? Here is a case for speculation and a little psychohistory.

The Unreasonable Power of the List

Like many successful Americans, Johnson ordered his life by sequential hero worship. He loved to fall in love with one Great Man after another, and like so many rich Americans with a superabundance of choice, the object of his affections constantly changed. Sometimes he was a serial monogamist, as with his love life, counting by his own reckoning "four Mrs. Johnsons"; other times it was architectural group sex as, with the New York Five in the early 1970s, or the American Eight soon afterward (on the occasion of his AIA Gold Medal).

In 1929, at twenty-three years of age, he pronounced J. J. P. Oud the world's greatest architect, and, in the same year, determined that Walter Gropius "may be the greatest of them all." British understatement was not his style. He called the architectural historian Henry-Russell Hitchcock, his traveling companion in 1930, a "genius," and by that summer the two of them had found a new hero: "Mies is the greatest man we or I have met. Oud I like better ... but Mies is a great man. He keeps his distance ... only letting down graciously once in a while, thus honouring you as the nod of a god would.... He is a pure architect."[4]

Falling in love with gods who graciously nod from a careful distance became a method of negotiating dangerous territory, and Johnson loved to live dangerously, like Nietzsche's superman. When you are losing direction, when you have suffered two nervous breakdowns, as he had in the late 1920s, the hero comes to your rescue and leads you, if not into a promised land, at least down a new route, past some pitfalls.

When people lose direction they may start navigating by composing lists of great men. Perhaps Philip's two breakdowns, associated with the loss of faith in the Platonic world and the rise of his Nietzschean nihilism, signal a psychic confusion, a world turned upside-down, one in which there are no fixed standards. That is certainly how he describes his incipient disorientation in the flux of values. If the only constant is change, then the only fixed markers are heroes that litter the field, and they can be graded into a list of great men. In Britain today the media augment their power by putting these roll calls up to a national vote. The BBC narrows the field of the "Greatest Brit" to Shakespeare, Churchill, and (happily for the design profession) I. K. Brunel. *Time Out,* the London weekly, has as its front cover story "100 Movers, Shakers & Opinion Makers 2005." The British intellectual magazine *Prospect* runs features and polls on the world's one hundred greatest intellectuals (Noam Chomsky wins), while the Scottish architectural magazine, with the same name, *Prospect,* votes Lord Fraser the "most powerful" force in the north (because he investigated the cost overruns of the Scottish Parliament). Meanwhile, *Building Design,* which goes out to all forty thousand British architects, also comes up *not* with the expected architect (such as Lord Foster, or Lord Rogers), but with a politician (the head of China).

Every year end the major newspapers carry a feature on the one hundred best wines, and such selections as "the forty best writers choose the one hundred best books of the year" (so people know what to give at Christmas). A veritable listomania breaks out, obviously driven by the imperatives of capitalism, the necessity of clearing stocks for the new year, and making sure that everyone keeps up with baseline culture. Whereas pluralism creates over-choice, a surfeit of consumer freedom, the list comes to the rescue and culls the variety. The list, in a disoriented society, takes on an unreasonable amount of power. As the internet search engine Google has shown, being at the top of its list, if you are, for instance, selling shoes for outsize feet, can make you a sudden fortune. Dropping to the middle of their Big Shoe list means extinction. Although it sounds ludicrous, in an information society where word of mouth has been replaced by mechanized inventories, it has become the Dictatorship of the List.

In this situation, Nietzsche's "will to power" can become an organizing principle of the professions. *Time* magazine summarizes a list of these lists for its "man of the year," and a circular Darwinian process begins to operate—survival of the most noteworthy. Media notoriety becomes important, and being famous for being famous becomes the cliché—all of this Philip learns in his twenties and passes on to his later friend Andy Warhol.

Le Corbusier, equally infected by the Nietzschean virus with the cult of the Great Man, was attracted to Moses, Orpheus, Plato and, above all, by the example of Pythagoras and Jesus. He read Edouard Schuré's *Les grands initiés* in 1908, at the tender age of twenty-one, just as he was swallowing the Nietzschean doctrine of the superman. As opposed to Johnson, however, the necessity for the "transvaluation of values" led Le Corbusier in an idealist and spiritual direction, to futurism and utopia. For Philip the death of God and rise of nihilism led in a pragmatic direction. It liberated him from conventional morality, allowed him to lampoon customary hypocrisy and admit, candidly, to failings that normal mortals would deny. Typically he would disarm critics who were attacking him by a tongue-in-cheek self-deprecation that was more radical than their barbs.

He shut up students who accused him of being "facile" by replying, "That is because I am a bad architect."[5] To accusations of superficiality, he answered that it was a consequence of having no beliefs; when the Miesian epigram was leveled at him—"I don't want to be interesting; I want to be good"—he replied, "I wouldn't know how to be good." Being "bad" or being wicked was a part of Philip's upper-class charm, his studied nonchalance and *sprezzatura,* his aristocratic disdain for political correctness, for the morality of the herd. On Mies's so-called collaboration with the Nazis he would also escalate—"Mies would work for anyone, even the devil"— implying that his own attempts at prostitution were equally amoral, beyond good and evil. Indeed, his epigram "I am a whore," to which Johnson returned several times in the 1980s (and I will follow suit), was the supreme form of aristocratic self-abuse— one that had another meaning. Like irony and parody, these cynical remarks carried an implicit, opposite charge—"*You* would work for the devil: but *I* admit it."

Throughout his controversial life, Johnson aired his lists of the great, and these became the strength of his power brokering. They were always limited to a few paragons. Following Nietzsche's attacks on the masses and Christian compassion, they were meant to be elitist and purged of values other than good form. Nobility, good looks, sexuality, glamour, artifice—these were the values of Nietzsche's warrior class (and, with less glamour, that of corporate culture)—not truth, complexity, commonality, morality. High society, not general society. That the majority envied him his money, power, and class only added to his delight in exposing their hypocrisy, or their lack of self-awareness. But the pursuit of the great leader had its pitfalls; first Huey Long in the early thirties, then, as he described it, "all the right wing fringes," including such anti-Semites as Father Coughlin, whose radio programs were heard by as many as 30 million Americans.[6]

Of course, the German Führer was his "one large mistake," as Abby Aldrich Rockefeller called it, one "that every young man should be allowed to make."[7] Philip was attracted to the great leader for the reasons so many others were, and because of his Nietzschean views, and for special reasons of his own. As he told his biographer Franz Schulze, it was the excitement of the Nazi rallies, especially the "crescendo and climax of the whole thing, as Hitler came on to harangue the crowd." Moreover, he felt a sexual thrill, in his own words, at the sight of "all those blond boys in black leather."[8] Philip told me much the same thing when I interviewed him in the early 1970s. On certain aesthetic matters he could be carefully candid, and to the right question provocatively frank.

On other points, such as his 1930s anti-Semitism, he could be in denial with the worst equivocators. For instance, he said to an *Esquire* reporter in 1983: "You know, far from being an anti-Semite, I've always been a violent philo-Semite."[9] Schulze quotes from enough letters of the thirties to leave us in no doubt that Johnson was being more than economical with the truth when he made this remark; perhaps he was being hopeful that his later views had made up for the earlier ones. Again, the point with Johnson is not the truth of a statement but its effect and affect. After all, his favorite quote from Nietzsche, which he came up with in 1953 at Smith College, became his mantra: "Truth is ugly. Art is with us in order that we may not perish through truth."[10]

He repeated this on one occasion, when Peter Eisenman, Jeffrey Kipnis, and I were on the way to debate the role of history and he wished to assert the priority of power over truth. About four years later, in 1988, I asked, "Are you still reading Nietzsche?"

"I don't get the time to read anything," he answered with typical self-mockery, "but what did he mean by 'Art is more important than truth'—or my favourite sentence, 'art is with us so we don't perish from the truth.' What the hell is he talking about?"
"—Art as a kind of religion."
"All right."
"And that is the quintessential Modernist position."
"All right, if you want to say one has a philosophy I got it straight out of Nietzsche. My position is straight from the Nietzsche-Heidegger-Derrida line."[11]

This returns us to the priority of great men over the herd, art over truth, culture over civilization, and the primacy of heroism. These antitheses are taken up in his 1939 article for the *Examiner,* titled "*Mein Kampf* and the Business Man"—he might have written "versus" the businessman and his economic liberalism.

> *Hitler, it hardly needs saying, is not a doctrinal pacifist; the name of his book, after all, is* Mein Kampf. *But his point of view is not a novel, Hitler-invented barbarism, but it is part of the stream of German thought....German thinkers, since Nietzsche, have not denied their "barbarism," if civilization as the opposite of barbarism is to be equated with Liberal democracy. They have thought of themselves as standing for "culture" against civilization, to use Spengler's terminology. To such Germans, Liberal ideals are centered on comfort, not on heroism. The comfort pursued in the name of "freedom" cancels out true freedom, which is not a matter of happiness but of effort, and effort is, in the nature of things, quite likely to include war.* [12]

And Philip followed Hitler into the war, into Poland. So, if "culture" and heroism are to be Johnson's momentary beacons for navigation through the maelstrom of life, he selects his heroes to the extent they embody "art," any art that is powerful and of the moment. Hence "The List," his canon of greats, zigzags from Oud, Le Corbusier, Gropius, and Mies in the early thirties to the American formalists in the fifties—Marcel Breuer, Gordon Bunshaft, Wallace Harrison, John Johansen, Louis Kahn, Matthew Nowicki, Paul Rudolph, Eero Saarinen—and to one populist architect, Edward Durell Stone, and two individual creative designers, Frederick Kiesler and Bruce Goff.[13] These were architects, as he saw it in the title to his talk, who were in "Retreat from the International Style." Compared to most of his lists, this one is messy, mid-cult, and without much influence.

More to his elitist point was the 1972 list of the Five, those committed to art and idea in architecture: Peter Eisenman, Charles Gwathmey, John Hejduk, Richard Meier, and Michael Graves. Or his later chosen few, the eight deconstructivists of 1988: Frank Gehry, Bernard Tschumi, Peter Eisenman (again), Zaha Hadid, Rem Koolhaas, Daniel Libeskind, Wolf Prix, and Helmut Swiczinsky. He didn't put either team together, the Five or the Eight, but relied for help on Eisenman and, in the *Deconstructivist Architecture* show, playing several critics against each other until he could see the virtues and vices of each hero.

Another group of eight was assembled in 1980 (fig. 2). Now Cesar Pelli, Charles Moore, Stanley Tigerman, and Robert Stern join the select few (that is, Graves, Gwathmey, and Eisenman), adding the postmodernists to the late modernists, as if Philip were having it both ways and in charge of a hedge fund. Eisenman told me that Philip wanted to surround himself with his peers as an insurance policy, and when the PM fashion waned, several of these high-fliers were dropped from the First Team. In any case, Philip dominates the center of the photograph, raising the golden apple of judgment for postmodernism in his right hand (or is he, rather, an American president, about to toss the first pitch on opening day?).

To mix another metaphor, there was not a bandwagon on which Philip could jump without sinking it. Speaking at Yale on the emergent postmodern movement, in 1978, I outlined the major reasons modernism had died—the ten basic causes

of its death. This list was headed by the chief villain, the incredible size of present-day commissions, the $200 million headquarters, the imperatives of late-capitalist competition that led to one-liners. The next morning, the zealous young burst into my hotel bedroom brandishing the *New York Times.* There was Philip's AT&T Building on page one, as it was to appear on the cover of *Time* magazine and on the front page of the *London Times* and in media across the globe—the building shot heard round the world. AT&T, the world's largest corporation with the largest number of stockholders, was building a postmodern monument (in Paul Goldberger's phrase) in the center of New York. "Is postmodernism dead?" the attentive students quite logically demanded. The AT&T design was clearly pastiche, *and* the largest, most powerful corporate example of the incipient movement—the "Tower of Power," as it was called in another story, this one in the *New York Times.* Postmodernism was not so much dead as suddenly middle-aged. Commercial appropriation, which had picked up every architectural movement since 1800, was now doing its work on PM— soon to become pomo.

Should Johnson be blamed for this? After all, his excuse was that he was the bellwether of change, the cock who first crows; and he admitted that his song lacked depth. He said this all the time, and on TV for the BBC film *The Godfather.* Since Johnson was so candid the blame rather should go to society. Is it their fault for *not* commissioning the originators of a movement, its exemplars rather than the followers? Is he not implying, again, "If I'm a whore, then clients are pimps and misogynists"? Furthermore, he justifies his trend spotting opportunism *because* it links up with power. His eagle eye opens the door for the masses to follow, or at least

fig. 2 Philip Johnson and the First Eight, 1978. Back row, from left: Michael Graves, Cesar Pelli, Charles Gwathmey, Peter Eisenman; front row: Frank Gehry, Charles Moore, Philip Johnson, Stanley Tigerman, Robert A. M. Stern

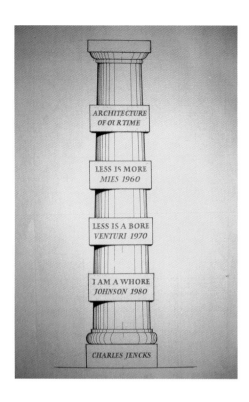

fig. 3 Ian Hamilton Finlay,
Architecture of Our Time, 1984

for the large practices—SOM, KPF—who were just behind him. That's the American way of architecture, now the International Style. Connoisseurship and power brokering are complex and critical activities, even if not very deep ones, and Johnson always developed his "eye," his gaze, his journalistic ability to size one up for the media.

In this he was helped a great deal by Eisenman, who was constantly putting together, in his mind, virtual teams of architects, like clubs of football players, to see who would come out on top. Eisenman's great game of critical opposition, called after the Vatican Lodge "P2," was labeled to give it mafia-style overtones, "P3" (a pun on Peter's initials, backward, and wordploys of no great consequence). That particular conspiratorial list consisted of The 25, obviously too great a number to identify a single style and consistent idea, which in any case was not Eisenman's point. The point was, rather, to set off a series of discussions that would be amplified by others, to create a media event. In this courting of controversy and debate he was highly successful.

The conclave of P3 was in 1983, at Charlottesville, Virginia, where Johnson first uttered his infamous self-defense to counter Robert Krier's attack on his large skyscrapers. "I have read your book" on urban form, Philip said, countering Krier, "and I agree with it completely, but I am a whore and I am paid very well for building high-rise buildings."[14] The phrase was picked up immediately by the *Boston Globe* and *New York Times,* among many newspapers. It was Anthony Lewis's blistering attack in the latter that probably led to Philip losing the job to construct yet another Boston skyscraper. Curiously, given his otherwise coy relationship to the media, Johnson repeated this self-deprecation in many different ways, a fact not lost on the British press, especially in their obituaries.

"I am a whore" means many things. For the second-oldest profession—corporate highfliers such as SOM and KPF or anyone with a large office—it clearly means—"So are you, you hypocrites." He clarifies this point: "We can turn down some projects like they can turn down some client, but finally we've both got to say yes to someone if we want to stay in business."[15] Here is Johnson, the candid and wicked joker in a room full of po-faced professionals on the make. This constant quote of his, in the early 1980s, gave me a nightmare, which I then recounted to Scotland's concrete poet, Ian Hamilton Finlay. He quickly turned it into one of his ironic and classical columns, with embossed quoins (fig. 3): "Architecture of Our Time ... Less Is More— Mies 1960 ... Less Is a Bore—Venturi 1970 ... I Am a Whore—Johnson 1980."

Reductivism, slogans that lead architecture, one-liners, rhymes. If not the golden-hearted whore, at least Johnson was a chiming one, and charming one. If you appeared on his dining lists you could be sure of a very amusing lunch at the Four Seasons, a résumé of New York architectural gossip, a lot of flattery and a little philosophy, the encounter with a glamorous table-hopper, and perhaps, if you passed muster with Peter, an invitation to an evening's debate at the Century Club. These presentations and critiques were black-tie affairs composed usually of men on The List who would meet to sharpen The List.

The idea of a cultured elite meeting at a club to decide who was in and what topic was out, was very eighteenth century, very Freemasonry, and much too much for the local egalitarians from Columbia University, who secretly filmed the paragons as they arrived and departed. In a way, these meetings culminated Johnson's recurrent idea of a brain trust, a type of clerisy, an American intellectual elite that could drive evolution forward. If not a club of Nietzschean supermen, at least they were a collection of powerful architects—who might be donated a Johnson client (he had over $2 billion of work in the 1980s)—designers who had taste, style, and architectural ideas. Just the kind of dinner companion one might want to debate the big questions, and "whither architecture?"

Here several of Philip's Lists of the Great & the Good might support each other. The Blue Blood Yanks and Oil Yanks, the Rockefellers, Goodyears, Blisses, Burdens, Schlumbergers, and above all the Museum of Modern Art elite might be hooked up with the architectural elite.

Contribution

Here Johnson the power broker comes into his own metier. This is perhaps his greatest and most lasting contribution: to marry American money with good architects, to throw jobs to the New York Five, to raise cash for institutions such as MoMA and the Institute of Architecture and Urban Studies to cross-pollinate class and architecture, to glamorize (suitably ugly word) the avant-garde such as Zaha Hadid and Rem Koolhaas, to make middle-class professionals rise above their limited horizons, to be an impresario of the new, to publicize and amplify any architectural movement he could see move. Organizing support for the IAUS, its magazine *Oppositions,* and its Forum was important; he gave $100,000 to the IAUS for several years and got the developer Gerald Hines to contribute $1.5 million. He gave support to this institute to help Rem Koolhaas write *Delirious New York.*

As Robert Stern put it in *The Godfather,* "Philip has been the most generous to younger architects. He's certainly helped me, he's been critical for my career. He brought me to New York to be the head of the programming at the Architectural League. . . . I've been on countless lists that Philip has been asked to supply to clients about who would be good to do a building." There's The List, again. Frank Gehry continued the thanks: "Did Philip Johnson invent Frank Gehry? Possible. . . . He certainly put a spotlight on me, when I didn't have a spotlight. So in the public sense, he said several times, occasionally on public TV and in the press, that he thought my work was something to look at." Eisenman adds: "For me he's a father figure, no question . . . the most powerful architect since Bernini. . . . I have been a protégé" (fig. 4). So many architects of note owed him something or other that his ninetieth birthday photograph looks like—what?—a heavenly choir of black-tied angels (with Rem naturally tieless), or is it Aged Whiffenpoofs, or is it the architectural mafia at payback time?

He often gave a lift up to underrated architects such as Eric Moss. He supported Richard Rogers in 1971 for the Pompidou Competition, and Michael Graves in 1980 for the one in Portland: both were crucial jury roles. More positive power brokering? In 1991, he smoothed the way for Eisenman and Gehry as the American entrants for the Venice Biennale.[16] He gave constant and long-term support for the institution of architecture at MoMA and elsewhere—all of this was unparalleled in America at the time. As Gehry insisted, Philip put architecture on the national map, and kept doing it over his long life, nothing less.

You may say Philip dispensed largesse while taking the best jobs for himself,

fig. 4 Johnson's ninetieth birthday
at the Four Seasons Restaurant,
New York, July 9, 1996

you may argue his altruism and gifts always furthered his own career, you may
believe that while he touted the bandwagons of modernism, postmodernism, and
deconstructivism he also prostituted them—and you would be right.

Still, one shouldn't underrate his generosity, or benevolence, just because it had
a mixed motive. After all, he *did* call himself a whore, he told us what he was up to,
he was often more radically self-critical than the critics—and who *hypocrite lecteur,
mon semblable, mon frère,* is a pure altruist? As the Christian saying goes, let him
cast the first foundation stone.

Foundations

Johnson's slippery foundations were built, I'm arguing, on a fascination for the
Greats. These provided him with the basic references for design, the method
for thinking and working his way through architectural creativity. In order to design
his own Glass House, he cast about in a veritable snake pit of historical references.
He worked up seventy-nine different schemes, at first derived from a mixture
of Miesian and modernist sources, and then classical and nineteenth-century ones,
from Breuer to Richardson and then back through Ledoux and Persius to Greece.
Seventy-nine hybrids! The final Glass House, a minimalist box of "almost nothing,"
was so stuffed full of almost nothings that its seventeen program notes listed
references to six Greats: Le Corbusier, Theo van Doesberg, Choisy, Schinkel, Ledoux,
Malevich, and then mostly Mies—the other eleven. That's why Philip was called

Mies van der Johnson. The American critics and public loved his roll call of almost nothing—it reminded them of Parnassus—where the architect had seemingly disappeared behind a perfection of paragons.

At about the same time, in the 1950s, American academia was founding its core courses on the Fifty Great Books, American publishers were successfully marketing the Hundred Great Ideas and Thousand Great Authors, a new synthetic culture was in formation—the ten thousand Peak Moments, the one hundred thousand Perfect Orgasms. Yankee attainment could be measured, like the motto of the Olympics, "faster, higher, stronger," in yards and microseconds. It produced a generic culture, compiling the best that has been thought and felt and built, smoothed out and edited like the *Reader's Digest.* Johnson was quite right to insist that one cannot *not* know history, and he turned his erudite knowledge into an eclectic machine for churning out references to the Greats.

By 1966, in a letter to Patwant Singh, he finally had settled on the Ultimate List, the "ten greatest architectural works of all time" ("*all* time!"—very American where there's not much time, so the list expands to fourteen). Most are the predictable greats—Imhotep's stepped pyramid, the Parthenon, the Pantheon, Chartres Cathedral, Brunelleschi's Santo Spirito, Borromini's San Carlo, Mies's Barcelona Pavilion, Wright's Johnson Wax, and Le Corbusier's Ronchamp. Some are gardens rather than architecture—the Zen Ryoanji in Japan and Le Nôtre's geometrical topiary at Vaux-le-Vicomte. And three are not the usual choices—Fatehpur Sikri, the ruined Mughal palace, Schinkel's work in Potsdam, and Antonio Gaudí's marvelously naturalistic public garden, Park Güell.[17]

The folly of this list, like all the others from *Time* and *Prospect,* is that it is an ellipsis—opinionated, with the context for judging the opinions absent, missing. *Ten greatest?*—what about the Taj Mahal, Katsura Palace, and Stonehenge? There must be at least five hundred existing contenders for the mantle of the ten greatest, and because most of them will be based on widely differing assumptions, opposite values, and contrary ways of life—the context for judging—the whole enterprise is mad. Where, to point up the silliness of the ten greatest, is Lascaux? The roll call makes sense only for a person touring the world in a great hurry, one who has to have answers when the bags are packed, right now.

Evolution versus Lists

There are profound implications in his architecture of The List. Besides its operational power for the tastemaker and connoisseur (or tourist board), there is the question it raises of historical value and how the great building always relates to a tradition and context of valuation. As theme parks demonstrate, take the latter away and you drain the forms of significance. Second, the evolutionary chains of meaning, which give value to a building, are essential to appreciate in the very act of architectural perception. Of course, one can go to Stonehenge and be impressed at the abstract circle of heavy boulders, but it is to miss their point.

Once when I had lunch with Philip in the Four Seasons, about 1984, I mentioned casually that I always carried in my pocket the list of the twenty greatest architects in the world. I could tell he was excited about seeing this inventory, but I was reluctant

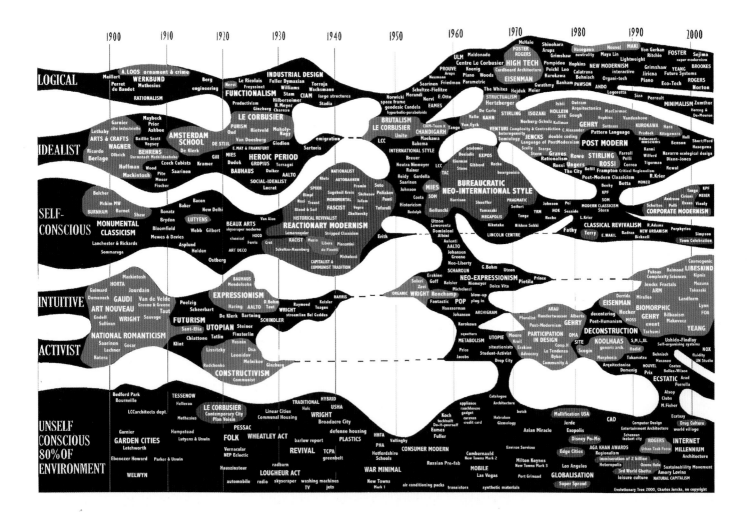

fig. 5 Charles Jencks, *Evolutionary Tree*, 2000

to show it to anyone (knowing that the value of a list of the best stocks lies in its secrecy). Besides, I explained, from his point of view it had one drawback. The greatest architect in the world was a position permanently unoccupied, because no mortal was good enough to fill its shoes. When he finally prevailed, and I pulled out a version of two evolutionary trees—one for late and one for postmodern architecture—the difference between his kind of list and a historical diagram became apparent (fig. 5). If the value of any architecture is partly in its relative position, and oppositions, an abstract list of greats loses meaning to the extent it is decontextualized. At that time, Frank Gehry, Leon Krier, and Richard Rogers—to name three architects involved in countertraditions—were all important, but for entirely different reasons. Evolutionary trees of discontinuous movements brought this out; abstract lists obscured the point. The former were also more inclusive and closer to historical truth.

Philip and I touched on this point when we debated who was in and out of the decon show that he and Mark Wigley had put on at MoMA in 1988. I objected to his excluding John Johansen's Mummer's Theatre—"by the 1970s, the most cogently built Deconstructionist building at that time in the US"—and also excluding the work of Peter Cook, the Architectural Association, James Wines, and the Japanese (such as Hiromi Fujii). Some of this architecture had been influenced by Derrida. Wines had even written on deconstruction, and all the above had important historical connections to the trend. But, I said to Philip, you have excluded Wines because he is too Low Church and you have an intention to be High Church. He answered:

> PJ: I think you may be right there too—my preciosity, or desire for it, comes out.
> CJ: Couldn't Hiromi Fujii [have] gotten in your church?
> PJ: Fujii could not—but he was close. I remember discussing Archigram and the whole Japanese thing. It didn't really add up. And to make it High Church you have to have dogmas, or forms in my case that were close together. But leaving out [Charles Rennie] Mackintosh in the story of Art Nouveau—although he doesn't use a whiplash—would narrow it down terribly.
> CJ: Exactly. That's why I want a broader Church.
> PJ: All right, but I wanted a narrower one.[18]

Contradiction Produces a Constant Style

Here one touches the heart of Philip's great contradiction: the opposition between his romantic nihilism and narrow dogmatism, the desire to change but the stronger passion to be a tastemaker. Look at the same contradiction in terms of philosophy. Johnson was a Nietzschean who profoundly believed in a meaningless world driven by power and fashion, a world in which God was dead and anything goes. Yet at the same time one of his best buildings, the Crystal Cathedral, could be designed for a fundamentalist TV sect, for the Reverend Robert Schuller's *Hour of Power,* which, like Father Coughlin's broadcasts, had a large national following (fig. 6). Johnson, at its televised opening, proclaimed to the world that he couldn't have done it without help from the divine. His incredulous biographer Franz Schulze asked him, "Philip, how *could* you?" And "Philip briefly buried his head in his hands in mock shame, then grinned and replied, 'Wasn't that *awful!*'"[19]

Yes, the lie was awful, and in Philip's mind justifiable for its inconsequentiality and pragmatic effect. But it is also awfully revealing of the contradiction at his heart. It is one that leads directly to his recurrent manner, the style of frozen perfection. Looking at all of Johnson's architecture, produced from 1945 to 2000, it is striking that although the literal skin is always changing, in a Nietzschean manner, the inner heart remains unchanged, in a Platonic manner—for effect. Because Johnson couldn't draw his way through architectural problems, nor develop consistent ideas or formal themes, his work always remained brittle, frozen at the first move. Except for his Glass House, and its seventy-nine variants, there is very little elaboration. His best work is always a simple gesture minimally made, such as his twin Pennzoil Place Towers (fig. 7). These are, in effect, one dark Miesian rectangle cut in two, rotated on the diagonal with the two vertical corners "almost kissing." Take a good idea of someone else's, make a minimal but deft change, and leave it alone. Minimal thought, minimal risk, minimal creativity—even Philip's maximally baroque work, such as his RepublicBank, is minimalist.

fig. 6 Philip Johnson (Johnson/Burgee), Crystal Cathedral, Garden Grove, California, 1980

fig. 7 Philip Johnson (Johnson/Burgee), Pennzoil Towers, Houston, 1976

The reason for this, aside from the fear of flying, is that Johnson actually preferred a constant, beautiful minimalism because it had media impact and iconicity, and was reducible on the cover of *Time.* That is, while he preached the constancy of change, he remained in temperament a neoclassicist—never changing. This taste was reinforced by the discovery that one-liners sell and make airwaves, column inches, controversy, notoriety, headlines. The Erotic Frigidaire is the natural style of the front page. As the curtain rings down on his starring role on TV, as the *Godfather of American Architecture,* he returns to his favorite themes of power and immortality. "Nietzsche said the will to power is more important than sex. . . . I can see that . . . power enables you to do wonderful buildings. . . . You have to think that what you are doing is of importance beyond your lifetime. That's why Plato was much more right than Freud, it's the desire for immortality that makes things go round." His voice goes quiet as he adds bitterly, "And that's what I hope will happen to me . . . but it won't. With 5 or 20 billion people on the planet, what kind of hopes get realized—*none* of them."[20]

His voice trails off as he half realizes the problem here. He assigns it, wrongly, to the population explosion, as if the number of people on the planet were a threat to genius, as if he had stood up heroically against the masses, when in fact he had always followed a preexisting taste, a ready-made model. But also, he realizes he is not going to make the final cut, the Last Judgment List, and this is right.

As mentioned, my first stab at Philip Johnson way back in 1973 was called "The Candid King Midas of New York Camp," the myth of a distraught king who had a reverse Midas touch. Every time he imagined a new building through others' eyes, he turned the design into gold leaf, fool's gold. But there is a more apt myth, the smile of Medusa, the look at the captivating other, one that ensnares. Medusa was a gorgon of absolute beauty who made others mad with jealousy, particularly Athena. Hence she was transformed into a frightening and destructive beauty, with a viperine hair of hissing serpents, a castrating woman whose cataclysmic attraction pulled in every man who regarded her. The sight of her ravishing beauty was too powerful, and any mortal who gazed at her face was quickly turned to stone. The Greats had the same effect on Philip. They attracted him so much that they froze his thought and stilled his pen. The more he stared at immortality, the more the Medusa stared back, exacting its revenge, robbing him of lastingness, just as he had borrowed their visage, turning him into an unchanging monument to the power of fashion, and its melancholic transience.

Notes

Conversations with Peter Eisenman and Frank Gehry helped with this article.

1. Quotes from Frank Gehry, Peter Eisenman, Robert A. M. Stern, and Philip Johnson on immortality are from *Philip Johnson, Godfather of American Architecture,* BBC-TV, August 1993, produced by Sharon Maguire, Janice Hadlow, The Late Show.

2. Charles Jencks, "The Candid King Midas of New York Camp," *Architectural Association Quarterly* 5, no. 4 (Winter 1973): 26–42.

3. Mario Praz's phrase Erotic Frigidaire is quoted in Robert Rosenblum, *Transformations in Late Eighteenth-Century Art* (Princeton: Princeton University Press, 1967).

4. Franz Schulze, *Philip Johnson: Life and Work* (New York: Knopf, 1994), 52, 53, 62, 69.

5. Ibid., 376.

6. Ibid., 123.

7. Ibid., 143.

8. Ibid., 89–90.

9. Ibid., 283.

10. Ibid., 232.

11. Charles Jencks, "Dialogues with Philip Johnson," in Jencks, *The New Moderns* (New York: Rizzoli, 1990), 157.

12. Schulze, *Philip Johnson,* 140.

13. Ibid., 270.

14. Ibid., 376.

15. *Daily Telegraph,* London, Obituaries, Philip Johnson, January 28, 2005.

16. Schulze, *Philip Johnson,* 400.

17. Ibid., 438, note 300.

18. Jencks, "Dialogues with Philip Johnson," 164.

19. Schulze, *Philip Johnson,* 342.

20. *Philip Johnson, Godfather of American Architecture.*

The Plot Against Architecture

Michael Sorkin

With apologies to Philip Roth

After the election of Charles Lindbergh to the presidency in 1940, the anxiety in the business community about doing business with Germany, which had reached such a pitch in Roosevelt's second term, relaxed considerably. Of course there remained a certain sense of reserve in some quarters, but the profit to be made supplying the military needs of the Reich were so substantial that any political restraint was swept away. In particular, Henry Ford—who became Lindbergh's Secretary of the Interior—was quick to supply the Reich with trucks and other vehicles.

Indeed, much of Ford's advertising came to feature heavily images of its two-ton trucks doing service on the eastern front, and the slogan "Keeping the Red Tide at Bay" appeared over lurid images of Ford convoys rolling east, filled with chiseled storm troopers ready to do battle with the Soviet enemy. In a number of these ads, a tide of prisoners could be seen marching west to captivity. Although there were sporadic protests, many of these prisoners were marked by what were clearly meant to be "Jewish" features, and Ford himself continued to be forthcoming about the dangers of "World Jewry" and the importance of the war in curbing its invidious influence. This continued the jeremiad he had begun in the 1920s with his "investigation of the Jewish question" in his newspaper, the *Dearborn Independent,* subsequently published as the *International Jew.* Here Ford urged that in the cleansing of America from the various scourges that afflicted it, "the International Jew and his satellites, as the conscious enemies of all that Anglo Saxons mean by civilization, are not spared."

In the early years of the war, Germany also became a considerable tourist attraction, despite the sporadic and largely ineffective British bombing of its cities. Indeed, for the groups being shepherded by their energetic *Hitler Jugend* guides, a trip to a well-appointed shelter became an almost obligatory part of the tour. Many returned home in disappointment that no raid had interrupted their journeys through the New Germany, and travel agents were eventually obliged to include a simulated air raid on their itineraries if the real thing proved unavailable.

The groups that made these visits included many branches of the German-American Bund, worker groups from the factories that were supplying armaments and materials, a constant stream of contractors bidding orders big and small, as well as interested citizens from many walks of life. Visits became de rigueur for many architects and planners as well. As the war provided more and more resources to the Reich, and as its sense of its own destiny grew more and more firm, Hitler's massive program for Germany's reconstruction became an ever higher priority, and the highways, housing projects, civic buildings, and urban developments proliferated in astonishing numbers.

Under the indefatigable direction of Albert Speer, this reached a truly enormous level, and there was much derisive comparison with the efforts of Roosevelt's WPA, much of which was abandoned following his defeat in 1940. *The New German Architecture*—the title of a glossy publication issued by Goebbels with an introduction by Philip Johnson entitled "A New International Style" in which he renounced the austere modernism he had previously advocated—found a wide audience in the United States. Enthusiasm for the "German model" reached such a level that Lindbergh responded with his own program of superhighways and with the short-lived New American Village project. America's emergence from the Great Depression via these public projects was materially assisted by the rapid and profitable growth of an arms industry that was able to sell to Germany, Britain, and the Soviet Union; Lindbergh and his economic advisors—among whom Ford was the most prominent—pursued their "guns and butter" policy with some success.

The New American Villages, of course, were both a public works program and a critical component of Lindbergh's efforts at ethnic and population redistribution, part of his *Life with Your Neighbors, Life with Your Kind* initiative—the so-called Coughlin Plan—that had begun in 1941, shortly after Lindbergh took office. Eager to court the vast audience of the celebrated radio priest Father Coughlin, Lindbergh appointed Coughlin his special advisor for community affairs and quickly agreed to the massive effort that he hoped would refigure much of the American landscape under the banner of "One Nation, Divided," a slogan with special resonance in many southern states. This project was administered by Lindbergh's Office of American Absorption, which quickly began its work "encouraging America's religious and national minorities to become further incorporated into the larger society."

Philip Johnson's involvement with the project was partly serendipitous. Because of his long involvement with fascist and proto-fascist causes, including his frequent trips to Germany as a reporter for Coughlin's newspaper *Social Justice* (for which he had written enthusiastically about Nazi policies and about the war, deriding, in equal measure, the French, British, and Jews), and because of his spirited public embrace of Nazi architecture, he was invited to the controversial dinner at the White House that President Lindbergh gave to celebrate the first state visit of Foreign Minister Von Ribbentrop to Washington. Thanks to his close relationship with Coughlin, he was seated at the president's table. His place fell opposite the first lady Anne Morrow Lindbergh, herself seated to the right of Von Ribbentrop. Coughlin was on Johnson's immediate left, next to Henry Ford.

Coughlin found the opportunity to discuss his redistributive project and launched into what was, by then, a well-rehearsed argument—drawing variously on biblical and eugenic sources—about the necessity for the "harmonious sequestration" of incompatible components of the population, particularly Negroes and Jews. That particular evening he dilated on the ideal of small-town America, suggesting that the corruptions of "big city cosmopolitanism" might be addressed both via the concentration and "protection" of racial groups and through the benign influences of "traditional villages with traditional houses and traditional ways." This formulation found enthusiastic support from Von Ribbentrop, who not simply urged Coughlin on but turned to Ford and said (as Johnson later reported), "*Lieber Heinrich,* just imagine: one thousand Greenfield Villages for America!"

Ford—with whom Coughlin had long discussed the matter—agreed to press Lindbergh on the initiative and proposed, on the spot, to prime the pump for the project by financing the design and construction of ten model villages on the assembly-line model. "Works for cars and tanks, don't see why it shouldn't work for houses," Ford offered. Johnson sensed an opportunity in the making and joined the conversation with enthusiasm. Recognizing that something well beyond style was at stake, he spun out the argument he had begun to make in *The New International Style* in a way that he thought would have special appeal for Henry Ford. Turning to the automaker, Johnson made his point with vigor. "Modern architecture is about *process,* about a way of doing things, about harnessing the logic and might of industrial production for the masses, the people, the *volk.* The way a building—or a town or a city—looks should be an expression of a nation's will to form, a will that must grow from its rootedness in history. You cannot not know history, of course."

Warming to the subject, Johnson proposed the homology between the *klein Dorf* and the small town, arguing the alignment of the purity of their architectures—half-timbered Gothic and white-painted "classical"—with the purity of their inhabitants. "The danger is not from the wisdom of tradition, it is rather from its corruption, from the mingling of disparate streams, which is as sure a formula for degeneracy in building as it is for degeneracy in the population." Johnson, who now had the ear of the table, including Lindbergh, went on to extol the virtues of having a Führer devoted to architecture as a means of channeling and vitalizing "the people's sacred blood and soil" and compared him to Thomas Jefferson, another leader who understood the national project as the conjunction of philosophy, building, and the organization of the "space of the nation." He ended his impassioned oration with a seething dismissal of "Franklin Delano Rosenfeld" and his "bad dealers," and a highly unfavorable comparison of "puny new towns laid out by and for socialists" with "the bright order and social power" of Theresienstadt, to which he had recently paid a visit. In the glowing article he had published about it in *Social Justice,* he'd written that this "handsomely gilded ghetto represents a fine and final solution to the Jewish problem that so taxes the nations of the civilized world."

By the time dinner was over Ford had engaged Johnson to direct a project for the creation of ten New American Villages, and Johnson soon established offices in Dearborn and Washington to undertake the work. His first initiatives were to establish the Congress for the New American Town to propagandize for the initiative and offer a neutral harbor and conduit for architects and planners eager to participate in what was envisioned as a huge gravy train, and to hire Walt Disney as the primary design consultant. This latter move was variously regarded as scandalous (mainly by architects) and brilliant (by almost everyone else). Johnson—who was, at this point, untrained as an architect—had a deep appreciation for Disney's artistry, his mass appeal, and his politics (Disney had been generous in his support of the Lindbergh campaign, and his racial views were in constellation with those of Coughlin, Ford, and Johnson). In addition, Hitler's own enthusiasm for Disney was well known: not simply were Disney cartoons a regular feature of evening entertainment in the Chancellery, "When You Wish Upon a Star" was—along with the "Horst Wessel Lied" and the overture to *Tannhäuser*— a favorite tune. Speer reported that Hitler had begun whistling it as they stood at the Palais de Chaillot, overlooking conquered Paris.

Johnson was also inspired by the great popularity of the Rockefeller-financed reconstruction of colonial Williamsburg and, of course, Ford's Greenfield Village, an imaginative re-creation of his boyhood home, understanding them as "architectural distillates of the nation." As Johnson put it in his charter of the Congress for the New American Town, "Architecture must have a *theme,* a cultural portrait that at once gives it meaning and simplifies its expressive component in such a way that the people can easily identify it. As with any other product of mass manufacture, the underlying armature will be usefully and efficiently repetitive. However, by precisely locating those suggestive inflections that will right away evoke the Rabbi or the Minstrel, those people they represent can be, as it were, put in their place."

The construction of New Plantation, Alabama, and New Warsaw, Arizona (privately referred to as Coontown and Kikeville by Johnson), began within three months of the launch of the New American Village initiative. Sensitive to the fact that the earlier program to disperse minority populations to "unprepared" areas of the country had resulted in numerous "disturbances," including dozens of murders and lynchings, New Plantation and New Warsaw were sited in what were held to be more hospitable climes. New Plantation, in fact, returned blacks from cities in the Northeast and Midwest to an area of the country from which many had fled just a generation or two before. The Arizona site was tucked in a corner of a Navajo reservation established during a prior concentration regime. In fact, after Roosevelt returned to office in 1942, New Warsaw became an internment camp for Japanese Americans, a hat trick of ethnic separation.

Formally, the towns were virtually identical. Each had an axial main street lined with two-story row houses and culminating, in the case of New Plantation, at the portico of the Uncle Remus Baptist Church and, in that of New Warsaw, at the very similar portico of Temple Jolson. Behind this main street lay a neat grid of roads along which small wooden houses were carefully aligned. The architecture, however, was scrupulously inflected by the Disney scenographers, right down to what appeared to be long-faded (but actually freshly produced) signage and advertising in Yiddish in New Warsaw and an ancient-looking locomotive at the siding of the New Plantation Station, periodically fired up to take residents in a similarly old-fashioned looking coach on a short loop around the town, its public address system blaring the specially composed "Zip-A-Dee-

Doo-Dah" (a tune which, after the war, became a hit number in Disney's 1946 *Song of the South*). In fact, traffic to and from both towns was highly restricted, largely confined to new arrivals periodically dropped off by bus, and the sporadic supply of goods.

This latter was one of the initial difficulties the OAA had with the towns. Although the planners had kitted them out with shops, schools, civic and religious buildings, and extensive landscape buffering, they had neglected to provide any economic basis for their survival. In the case of New Plantation, the assumption had been that the sharecropping economy would provide appropriate subsistence. In fact, this was the only employment locally available, but given the size of the town, it obliged residents to seek work many miles away. As a result, the town was largely and rapidly hollowed out and—despite the meting out of sometimes draconian punishments—the houses were covertly dismantled to provide timber for shacks built on the distant fields its population tilled. Johnson's own direct architectural contribution to New Plantation seems to have been limited to the much publicized Tar Baby Caryatids, which held up the front porch of "De Gen'ral Sto" on Main Street.

At New Warsaw, Johnson and his planners assumed that the relocated Jews would be able to survive on, as he put it, "those ducats they've all squirreled away," or on the largesse of their wealthy coreligionists. In fact, there was much disagreement within the Jewish community about how to respond to the situation. At one extreme were collaborationists like Rabbi Lionel Bengelsdorf of Newark, who made common cause with the program—actually serving as titular head of the OAA—in the hopes that appeasement would spare the Jews further trouble. At another were the "New Zionists" who saw the Arizona town as a possible bridgehead to a Jewish state, and a group of them attempted unsuccessfully to start agricultural enterprises on the unyielding sands of the Arizona desert. Most of the community was simply divided between outrage and fear, especially as the scope of the Nazi atrocities in Europe came to be known. In the end, the economy of New Warsaw depended on covert gifts from the free Jewish community—still the major portion of American Jewry—and from piecework for the garment industry, goods driven back and forth from Los Angeles in dilapidated cars by the so-called cloakies. Indeed, many of the neat clapboard houses grew to resemble the sweatshops of New York whose workers had been the parents of so many of those resettled in New Warsaw.

In October 7, 1942, following the assassination of Walter Winchell, the Lone Eagle took off on a solo flight in the *Spirit of St. Louis* to rally his constituency for his social programs and his ongoing insistence that the United States stay out of "Europe's war." His disappearance—many alleged he had ditched his plane in the Atlantic to be picked up by a German U-boat—resulted in the return of Roosevelt to office and with it the unraveling of the New American Village project and the return home of its internees. New Plantation and New Warsaw were the only towns completed before the end of the Lindbergh presidency, and there are no physical remains today, although they survive in numerous publications from the time, including issues of Johnson's glossy—if short-lived—monthly, *America Builds.* His editorial in the first issue might serve as an epitaph for his career.

"Architecture serves power and every architect must do its bidding. In this he has no choice. Lucky the architect with the opportunity to work for power that wields the truth. In this, today's America—and today's Germany—have a near monopoly. I glory in the opportunity to bend to this hurricane of national will and to direct its power to blowing out the reeking miasma of impurity that holds America back by my unquestioning obedience to my masters."

RECKONING WITH MODERNISM.

The Delicacy of Modern Tastes

Detlef Mertins

In 1932, Henry-Russell Hitchcock and Philip Johnson redefined modern architecture as style—International Style—to correct a fallacy they perceived in the rhetoric of modernism. For, as they pointed out, the "doctrine of anti-aesthetic functionalism" had rejected the artistic conception of architecture, favoring instead function, material, technology, and society as its generative sources and authorities.[1] Functionalists generally also eschewed the term "style," with its associations of eclecticism and the codification of forms and motifs. One notable exception to this was the organicist functionalist Walter Curt Behrendt, whose *Victory of the New Building Style* (Der Sieg des neuen Baustils) of 1927 had retooled the notion of style as building style precisely to avoid any hint of representation.[2] Like other functionalists, Behrendt favored a scientific conception of formative process in which the results were not to be predetermined. Hitchcock and Johnson, however, insisted that, "consciously or unconsciously the architect must make free choices before his design is completed.... Whether they admit it or not is beside the point."[3] Their recuperation of the idea of style and aesthetic choice echoed the historian Geoffrey Scott, who, in *The Architecture of Humanism* of 1914, had criticized what he called the mechanical, ethical, and biological fallacies of contemporary thought, external factors that he claimed distorted any direct assessment of architecture as a sensuously given artifact and as a work of art.[4]

Throughout his career Johnson would reiterate his belief in architecture as an artistic practice based on aesthetic choices. Yet he rarely used the word "taste." Of course, functionalist doctrine had also rejected the term, along with "style" and "aesthetic choice." But does that mean that Johnson shared something with functionalism, whether he admitted it or not? What might have been at stake in embracing aesthetics but forgetting taste?

Although Johnson often spoke of what he liked and how his likes related to those around him and to general preferences that were in the air, there are, for instance, only two places in Johnson's published writings where he used the word "taste." The first was in 1955, in a speech given at Barnard College, titled "Style and International Style." Johnson explained, "I do not want to wander alone among the arbitrary wilds of 'taste,' as I would have had to in the last century. In that jungle, only a Richardson or a Sullivan could survive. Now I rejoice, I can lean on my elders, then hope to stand on their shoulders, reaching toward an architecture which will perfectly express my time."[5]

At the age of forty-nine, having established himself as a force in modern architecture—first as curator, then as architect, teaching at Yale and collaborating with Mies on the Seagram Building—Johnson saw the International Style as a protection against wandering alone among the arbitrary wilds of taste. Put another way, he declared that, "The onus of designing a new style any time one designs a new building is hardly freedom; it is too heavy a load except for the greatest of Michelangelos or Wrights."[6] Yet he was quick to point out that style was not a rigid set of rules or shackles but a "climate in which to operate, a springboard to leap further into the air."[7] As a category, style remained a bit vague and indeterminate, and it was this indeterminacy that assured its ongoing vitality. Style was something known, shared, and historically specific, but open to change and imagination; in fact, this tension helped stimulate originality and propel architecture into the unknown. In this, Johnson was still very much a modernist. Aesthetic formalists too, like functionalists and rationalists, sought the magic formula for combining commonality and difference in a living architecture whose hallmark would be creativity within givens, individuality within collectivity, and variety within unity. Functionalists conceived commonality in terms of a spatial-constructive system, but Johnson spoke of a climate. They saw function as the engine for generating form, but he looked to individual artists and their aesthetic preferences.

My second example is from Johnson's lecture "What Makes Me Tick," delivered at Columbia University in 1975, twenty years later. Now he declared, "There are no rules, only facts. There is no order, only preference. There are no imperatives, only choice; or, to use a nineteenth-century word, 'taste'; or a modern word, 'take': 'What is your "take" on this or that? ... we have no faiths. I have none. 'Free at last,' I say to myself.... We today are anarchistic, nihilistic, solipsistic, certainly relativist, humorous, cynical, reminiscent of tradition, myth-and-symbol minded rather than rationalistic or scientifically minded. What makes a building satisfactory—the word 'beautiful' is more than ever treacherous—to Stern or Venturi, for instance, is bound to be different from what is satisfactory to me. Vive la différence, we live in a pluralistic society."[8]

In both of these statements Johnson used the word "taste" to designate a mode of discernment that was wild, arbitrary, and individually determined, not to say cut off from others. In the earlier statement he seemed fearful of such isolation and rejected it in favor of a shared style; later he seemed to relish the independence and emancipation it appeared to offer.

It is tempting to interpret these differences as symptomatic of changing periods in Johnson's life and in the history of architecture—from modernism to postmodernism. But would that be right? Haven't nihilism, cynicism, relativism, and humor always been part of some modernist cultural practices? Think of Nietzsche and his influence in the arts. Think of Duchamp, whom Johnson admired as the greatest intellect of the twentieth century, of Dada, or of Warhol, whom he "loved." Wasn't Johnson's shift, more accurately, one within modernism, from a predominant craving for a new overarching order to the rise of counterculture radicality, which valued freedom over order?

The conception of taste as variable, unstable, and unreliable has been a staple of artistic discourse at least since David Hume, whose essay "Of the Standard of Taste" of 1747 began with the following description:

The great variety of Taste, as well as of opinion, which prevails in the world, is too obvious not to have fallen under every one's observation. Men of the most confined knowledge are able to remark a difference of taste in the narrow circle of their acquaintance, even where the persons have been educated under the same government, and have early imbibed the same prejudices. But those who can enlarge their view to contemplate distant nations and remote ages, are still more surprised at the great inconsistence and contrariety. We are apt to call barbarous whatever departs widely from our own taste and apprehension; but soon find the epithet of reproach retorted on us. And the highest arrogance and self-conceit is at last startled, on observing an equal assurance on all sides, and scruples, amidst such a contest of sentiment, to pronounce positively in its own favor.[9]

Notwithstanding his sensitivity to the inconstancy and relativity of taste, Hume went on to seek a Standard of Taste, which he defined as a "rule by which the various sentiments of men may be reconciled; at least a decision afforded confirming one sentiment, and condemning another."[10] Having recognized that discernment was contingent on the "natural equality of taste"—on each mind as well as each "bodily taste"—he argued that not all determinations of the understanding could be right, because they refer to something objective, to a matter of fact.[11] While some "creatures" possessed a greater delicacy of imagination that made them sensitive to every beauty and every blemish, cultivating improved taste in the liberal arts served to form "juster notions of life" and maintain social decorum.

In a second essay on the subject, "Of the Delicacy of Taste and Passion," Hume elaborated on the plight of those people "subject to a certain delicacy of passion" that heightens their sensitivity and intensifies their feelings of joy as well as grief. "People of this character have, no doubt, more lively enjoyments, as well as more pungent sorrows, than men of cool and sedate tempers ... [yet] men of such lively passions are apt to be transported beyond all bounds of prudence and discretion, and to take false steps in the conduct of life, which are often irretrievable."[12] For Hume, the delicacy of taste—cultivating higher and more refined standards—was the best "cure" for this delicacy of passion and the hallmark of the critic.

While modernist discourse refused to acknowledge any residual reliance on taste, Hume's call for standards that would control its vagaries and caprice may, in retrospect, be understood as a template for those countless reiterations of the drive for objective foundations, moral principles, and new style that followed, including the drive for universalities of subjectivity, which motivated the birth of modern aesthetics, Kant's turn to epistemology (and his critique of Hume), and the transformation of the humanities in the late nineteenth century into the social sciences. The cultivation of discernment was sublimated in modern psychology and sociology, in art history and art theory, as well as in the functionalist architecture that Johnson eschewed. Yet its character *as* taste—as *socialized* taste—was most often denied in these domains. While Hitchcock and Johnson brought this denial to light in the case of functionalist ideology, they left it unacknowledged in aesthetics.

As Pierre Bourdieu points out in his book *Distinction: A Social Critique of the Judgment of Taste* (1979), taste is not, in fact—or at least not solely—a "gift of nature," but the "product of upbringing and education," a vehicle of class distinction, an instrument of power and economic manipulation.[13] He suggested that the "enchanted experience of culture" as an autonomous field of pure vision or primary encounters, which was how aesthetic formalism conceived of art, implies "forgetting the acquisition of the codes" on which it depends. This is the case even when appreciation turns from beauty to the sublime or the ugly, or when it embraces populism, plurality, license, nihilism, and cynicism.

In his book *The Tastemakers* (1949), Russell Lynes provided a social history of American taste marked by the unresolved tension between the "natural equality of tastes" and disciplinary authorities seeking to maintain power and class distinctions. For Lynes, a graduate of Yale who wrote for *Harper's* and published a history of the Museum of Modern Art in 1973, the story of democratic taste began in the late 1820s, "when the long period of control over taste by a landed intellectual aristocracy came to an end. For a long time the gentlemanly classes had set the standards of society and from their comfortable mansions they handed down the precepts of taste in art and architecture and fashion. But when Andrew Jackson was elected to the presidency in 1828 on a "wave of cocksure Americanism" there came with him not only a new 'age of the common man'" but the beginning of what Lynes called the "'the Age of Public Taste.' Taste became everybody's business and not just the business of the cultured few."[14]

Nevertheless, the tastemakers of the day tried to "discipline" everyone to a higher appreciation of the arts and to a finer sensibility to their surroundings. They managed to stimulate public interest but found to their dismay that the Public Taste was not to be controlled. And so they turned to the Private Taste, to the rich who could be offered as models of behavior and to "housewives in whose hands local standards of refinement and culture were maintained."[15] The Age of Private Taste came to an end, according to Lynes, when "the tastemakers became exercised about what is now familiarly (but I think mistakenly) called 'mass culture.' It was then that the curtain went up on the Age of Corporate Taste, and the tastemakers took to working through mass communications media and vast corporations to reach millions upon millions of people."[16]

As Lynes describes it, the subsequent history of taste in America entailed a complex interplay of high brow, low brow, and an ever-expanding middle brow— combining control and pandering, stark beauty and crude bombast, peaks of frivolity and abysses of dinginess. It included the birth of museums in the 1860s and '70s by "art missionaries" eager to improve popular tastes, but also flamboyant hotels as palaces of the people. It included stately homes *and* tacky suburbs, societies for truth and beauty *and* Hollywood films. And it included the missionaries of modernism, along with its detractors.

Lynes describes modernism as a "new wind" that "began to blow quietly at first and then with increasing velocity until it reached the full cry of a hurricane."[17] He recounted that it had begun in America with Richardson and Sullivan, reformulating the quest for honesty and sincerity that had earlier propelled the Gothic revival and the Queen Anne style (fig. 1). It was transplanted to Europe and then brought back to the United States in the 1920s as a European idea, but it became a movement in America only during the Depression of the 1930s. Notwithstanding the broader history of modernization in construction and especially in housing, to which the account alludes, Lynes singled out the Museum of Modern Art as a "prime factor in

A Taste for Honesty

The moral arguments for architectural styles persist but the looks change. Each of the buildings on this page is an example of the "honest" architecture of its day—the Gothic Revival house, above left, was said to be more honest than Greek Revival. The Queen Anne house, above right, displaced the Gothic for the same reason. Below is today's honest architecture—the entrance hall of Lever House, New York City.

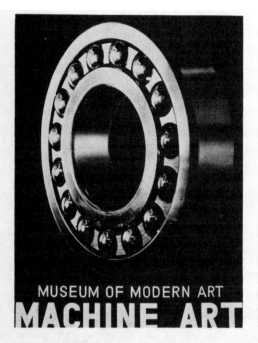

fig. 2 From Russell Lynes, *The Tastemakers* (1949), showing the exhibition *Machine Art,* curated by Johnson at the Museum of Modern Art in 1934, as emblematic of the "marriage of art and industry"

INDUSTRIAL ART.

MUSEUM OF MODERN ART
MACHINE ART

The Marriage of Art and Industry

When the Museum of Modern Art staged its first Machine Art exhibition in 1934, it gave industry the aesthetic nod. An earlier nod was made at the Centennial Exposition in 1876, which produced the chandelier above. By the 1930's the marriage of art and industry had a new best man—the industrial designer. Below is a bathroom by Crane before and after one of them, Henry Dreyfuss, had at it.

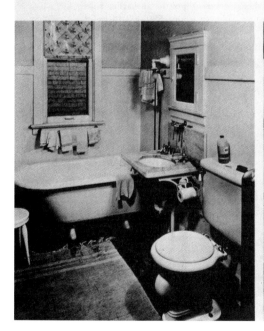

fig. 3 From Russell Lynes, *The Tastemakers* (1949), showing Johnson's House in Cambridge of 1941 as a potential model for improving the suburbs

Trying to Outguess the Public

The post-World War II building boom looked to the tastemakers like a golden opportunity. Buckminster Fuller's "Dymaxion" house, top left, was going to be mass-produced by Beech Aircraft; it never was. The *Ladies' Home Journal* put its bets on such houses as the one by Philip Johnson, center above. But *Good Housekeeping* picked the "Western Style" house. If there is any question who was right, look at a portion of Levittown, Pennsylvania (16,000 ranch houses), below.

spreading the gospel of the new architecture." He retold the story of its founding, of Alfred Barr, Jr.'s desire to include architecture and industrial design along with the fine arts and then turning to two friends to do so: Henry-Russell Hitchcock and Philip Johnson.

Johnson's own aesthetic education, first through his family and later through Barr, Hitchcock, Lincoln Kirstein, and others, was enmeshed in this history. It is telling that he appears several times in Lynes's account—first as a founding figure of the International Style, then as the curator who broadened modern taste into industrial design and objects of everyday life, and again as the architect of an exemplary modern home, his own house in Cambridge of 1941 presented as a prototype for the suburbs (figs. 2, 3). Let us recall that Philip Johnson was the son of a prosperous Cleveland lawyer and a mother from a well-to-do industrial family (fig. 4). He grew up in a solid Tudor house and was raised with Puritan yet progressive and artistic values (fig. 5). His mother seems to have been one of those housewives cited by Lynes as instrumental in the movement to improve local standards of taste (fig. 6). When Johnson was five years old his mother remodeled several rooms in the house in what Franz Schulze has called a "crisply simplified geometric décor, not just in tune with contemporary modes but prophetic of the modern architecture Philip would one day make the central issue of his life."[18]

Johnson developed into a young man of cultivated good manners and charm, bristling intelligence and wit—able to befriend the likes of Alfred North Whitehead as an undergraduate at Harvard, but not able to convince the great man that his mental quickness could sustain him through doctoral studies in philosophy (fig. 7). He delighted in learning but was impatient, mercurial, and even superficial, as well as prone to depression.[19] Perhaps he struggled with disciplining what Hume would have recognized as his delicacy of passion. So he turned to the arts and ultimately architecture, finding support for this through his discovery of Friedrich Nietzsche.[20] And he turned to cars and fast driving. Johnson's choice of a new Packard convertible to take over to Europe for his first excursions in modern architecture certainly speaks volumes about his taste at that time (fig. 8). Manufactured in his native Ohio, the Packard had a reputation for speed *and* dependability. Having reclaimed the land speed record for America in 1919, its manufacturers gave it a big square body with solid elegance, and it became one of the finest prestige cars in the country. Futurist dynamism harnessed, and safe enough for delicate aristocrats. An American fusion of Apollonian and Dionysian impulses.

It was through Hitchcock, no doubt, that Johnson discovered Scott's *Architecture of Humanism: A Study in the History of Taste.* Later, in the 1940s, Johnson said that it was his "favorite theory of architecture," though it was barely a theory at all, given Scott's anti-academicism.[21] While Scott's subject was the Italian Renaissance, Hitchcock had already in 1929 pointed to the continuity of modernism from the Renaissance into the twentieth century, and he praised Scott's critique of the mechanical, ethical, and biological fallacies of contemporary thought.[22]

By aesthetic, Scott meant the taste for form, or perhaps more precisely the feeling for form.[23] While he proffered aesthetic taste as a general principle for judging architecture, he considered it especially important for understanding the architecture of the Renaissance, which was, he declared, "pre-eminently an architecture of taste."[24] He meant this, first, as a general preference for being "surrounded by forms of a

fig. 4 Portrait of Philip Johnson, c. 1917

fig. 5 Homer and Louise Johnson Residence, 2171 Overlook Road, Cleveland, Ohio, c. 1915

fig. 6 Louise Pope Johnson with (from left) Theodate, Philip, and Jeanette, c. 1917

fig. 7 Philip and Jeannette Johnson, Nice, 1928

fig. 8 Packard convertible automobile, 1929

certain kind," taking delight in "certain combinations of mass and void, of light and shade," but, more specifically, as the preferences of *individual* artists.[25] For Scott the Renaissance was "at once daring and pedantic, a succession of masters the orthodoxy of whose professions is often equaled only by the license of their practice."[26] Notwithstanding a consistent allegiance to antiquity and the authority of Vitruvius, its creative output was inconsistent, "guided on no sure or general course." The differences in form between Brunelleschi, Bramante, Michelangelo, and Palladio led him to conclude that the Renaissance "passed in a continuous succession through phases of extraordinary diversity, brevity and force."[27] He characterized it in terms of "liberty of thought" and "keen individualism"—as an "age when creative vigor was still, beyond measure, turbulent."[28] The pace of this turbulence demanded an art that was "rapid and pictorial in its appeal." "Shaped by a desire as powerful as it is undefined, its inventive impulse remains unexhausted, and style succeeds to style in the effort to satisfy the workings of an imagination too swift and restless to abide the fulfillment of its own creations. In this," he concluded, "the Renaissance stands alone."[29] Or did it? As we have already seen, Hitchcock understood twentieth-century modernism to be continuous with the Renaissance, and the terms Johnson later used to describe first the International Style and later postmodern pluralism each suggestively resonate with Scott's portrait of Renaissance humanism.

To ears retuned to the social construction of taste, Scott's focus on taste suggests that he, like Bourdieu and Lynes, understood it to be a social and political practice involving codes that define classes and maintain relations of power. Yet Scott's history of taste was not in fact a social history and did not concern itself with these problems. Rather it was a psychological one, focused on feelings for beauty. It is written in a language of vivid evocations and indebted to the nineteenth-century theory of empathy, to the notion that through their creative activity artists and architects projected personal and collective desires into the environment for their own enjoyment and the enjoyment of others.

Vincent Scully, in 1961, declared that, "Johnson at his best ... [possesses] the most ruthlessly aristocratic, highly studied taste of anyone practicing in America today."[30] But as both a tastemaker and an architect Johnson displayed more than studied taste implies; he displayed that extraordinary wit that so many have remarked upon—irreverent, ironic, surprising, biting yet disarming, always funny. And he did not shy from making fun of himself as well as others, or from baring the devices of his own stagecraft. He was intensely self-reflexive and unlikely to have ever forgotten his upbringing or the social construction of aristocratic taste. In fact, it seems he understood that it had a role to play in a country heading ever more, as Lynes observed, toward the democratization of taste, first by attempting to improve the standard through modernism, then by embracing the popular desire for decadence, seduction, kitsch, and low-brow vulgarity. It will remain for others to explore in detail the politics of Johnson's contribution to this "democratization of aristocratic tastes." Perhaps one measure of its irresolution, however, may be found in his unending oscillation between the delicacy of passion and the delicacy of taste, between the quest for natural freedoms and the desire for social authorities. In this oscillation Johnson was certainly not alone, and he may turn out to be a delicate and telling barometer of the twentieth century.

Notes

The author would like to thank Keller Easterling for her thoughts on this essay during its preparations and for pointing to the writings of Russell Lynes and Pierre Bourdieu.

1. Henry-Russell Hitchcock and Philip Johnson, *The International Style* (New York: Norton, 1960), 36.

2. Walter Curt Behrendt, *Der Sieg des neuen Baustils* (Stuttgart: Fritz Wedekind, 1927), trans. Harry Francis Mallgrave, edited and introduced by Detlef Mertins, *The Victory of the New Building Style* (Los Angeles: Getty Research Institute, 2000).

3. Hitchcock and Johnson, *International Style,* 37.

4. Geoffrey Scott, *The Architecture of Humanism: A Study in the History of Taste* (1914; London: Methuen, 1961).

5. Philip Johnson, "Style and International Style, 1955," in *Philip Johnson: Writings,* foreword by Vincent Scully, introduction by Peter Eisenman, commentary by Robert A. M. Stern (New York: Oxford University Press, 1979), 76.

6. Ibid.

7. Ibid.

8. Philip Johnson, "What Makes Me Tick," 1975, *Writings,* 260–261.

9. David Hume, "Of the Standard of Taste," in *Of the Standard of Taste and Other Essays,* ed. John W. Lenz (Indianapolis: Bobbs-Merrill, 1965), 3.

10. Ibid., 5.

11. Ibid., 6.

12. David Hume, "Of the Delicacy of Taste and Passion," in *Of the Standard of Taste and Other Essays,* 25.

13. Pierre Bourdieu, *Distinction: A Social Critique of the Judgment of Taste,* trans. Richard Nice (Cambridge: Harvard University Press, 1984), 1.

14. Russell Lynes, *The Tastemakers* (New York: Grosset and Dunlap, 1954), 7.

15. Ibid., 6.

16. Ibid., 6–7.

17. Ibid., 242.

18. Franz Schulze, *Philip Johnson: Life and Work* (New York: Knopf, 1994), 16.

19. Ibid., 43.

20. Ibid., 44.

21. Philip Johnson, "Afterword," *Writings,* 270.

22. Scott, *Architecture of Humanism,* 10–11. See also Henry-Russell Hitchcock, *Modern Architecture: Romanticism and Reintegration* (New York: Hacker, 1970), 236. "The architecture of the New Pioneers, if not at all an architecture of humanism, is nevertheless the more comprehensible critically to those who are familiar with, if not altogether won to, Geoffrey Scott's theories." In a footnote, Hitchcock pointed out that Scott had died as *Modern Architecture* was going to press. "It is more than sad to think," he wrote, "that there may now be no further work on architecture from a pen that set forth the subject more brilliantly than has been done since Ruskin. But the *Architecture of Humanism* will continue to hold its place, reminding us of a time when Humanism had a brighter meaning than it does today."

23. Scott, *Architecture of Humanism,* 19.

24. Ibid., 32.

25. Ibid., 33.

26. Ibid., 16.

27. Ibid., 15.

28. Ibid., 16.

29. Ibid., 17–18.

30. Quotation by Vincent Scully in 1961, in Schulze, *Philip Johnson,* 368.

Playboy Architecture Then and Now

Stanislaus von Moos

The term Playboy Architecture was used by Sigfried Giedion in the 1962 edition of his *Space, Time and Architecture*. "Confusion and boredom," he writes in the introduction to the book, have become the mark of the times. "A kind of playboy-architecture became *en vogue:* an architecture treated as playboys treat life, jumping from one sensation to another and quickly bored with everything."[1] As he explicitly referred to a small symposium titled "Modern Architecture: Death or Metamorphosis?" we may assume that he primarily had in mind the New York scene, of which Philip Johnson was a protagonist.[2] And Giedion goes on with characteristic contempt for the International Style and for everything that went wrong with architecture since the style's proclamation. "Many designers who had adopted the fashionable aspects of the 'International Style,' now found that the fashion had worn thin and were engaged in a romantic orgy. This fashion, with its historical fragments picked at random, unfortunately infected many gifted architects" (fig. 1).[3]

And he continues: "By the sixties its results could be seen everywhere: in smallbreasted, gothic-styled colleges, in a lacework of glittering details inside and outside, in the toothpick stilts and assembly of isolated buildings of the largest cultural center."[4] Only in the foreign-language editions of *Space, Time and Architecture is* the mysterious cultural center with its "toothpick stilts" identified as New York's Lincoln Center (fig. 2). As to such descriptions as "smallbreasted" and "gothic-styled," as well as the "lacework of glittering details inside and outside"—these seem to have been chosen to evoke the recently opened and much publicized Jewett Arts Center at Wellesley College by Paul Rudolph (fig. 3). Buildings by Minoru Yamasaki or an embassy by Edward Durell Stone also may come to mind.

By the time of the fifth edition of *Space, Time and Architecture* (and with CIAM, the Congrès Internationaux d'Architecture Moderne, already buried), Giedion's diatribe was all the more bitter, as he may have been feeling increasingly abandoned on the bridge of the ship of high modernism.[5] In fact, a few months before these lines appeared in print, Philip Johnson had expressed his own decidedly less moralizing point of view on the issue. In a talk at the Architectural Association in London he had welcomed the "really nice juicy chaos" of the present architectural scene, leaving no doubt that he had chosen to jump onto the lifeboat of "functional eclecticism" instead of lamenting the demise of the modernist canon.[6]

"Playboy"? The nature of Giedion's diatribe suggests that the reference to the homonymous American magazine first published in 1953 is only indirect.[7] Also, sexuality was at stake only by implication in his antilibertarian exhortation. Yet

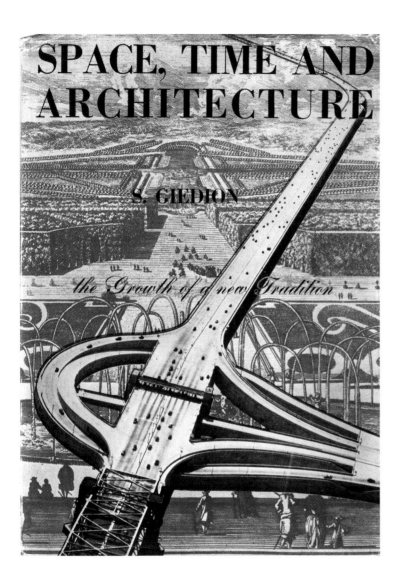

Giedeon does pinpoint boredom as a characteristic Playboy reflex: the word appears in the title of the section quoted above, as well as in the text itself. Being bored, one remembers, was a topical condition in the culture of the 1960s: Andy Warhol's laconic "I like boring things" (which he later spelled out by adding: "But that doesn't mean I'm not bored by them") serves as the backdrop for Johnson's confession that he was "bored" with Mies.[8] And seen in this context, Venturi's proverbial transformation of Mies's "Less is More" is merely a variation on a theme.

Could Johnson be seen as a Playboy? The formula of the "really nice juicy chaos" at least illustrates what Schulze may have had in mind when he referred to Johnson's posture as a "garden variety upper middle-class snob."[9] And Schulze's description of this particular moment in Johnson's career reads almost like a reflection of Giedion's earlier comments. Regarding the 1960s, Schulze writes: "With the passing of time, more and more American architects seemed bent on inventing an assortment of forms and shapes demonstrably modernist but consciously alternative to what they perceived as the aging and constricting canon of the International Style. None of his colleagues, however, tried on as many costumes as Philip, who looked elegant in some, considerably less so in others."[10]

In this essay I intend to shed light on the relationship between Johnson and Giedion, two rather exposed tastemakers and ideologues, even though their actual contact was hardly more than occasional. For many years their interests ran parallel. Paradoxically, their most serious disagreement was probably a question of style rather than of ideology—apart from the fact that the notion of "style" was central to the argument.

The International Style

In the copy of *The International Style* that is now preserved with the Giedion papers at the ETH in Zurich there is a handwritten note by Philip Johnson that credits Giedion, "with great respect," as the "leading architectural critic in Europe."[11] One may note that the dedication is in German, as is Johnson's entire correspondence with Giedion at that time, and that Johnson's coauthor, Henry-Russell Hitchcock, signs somewhat at a distance, at the bottom of the page (fig. 4).[12] In fact, in 1930, when

fig. 2 Lincoln Center for the Performing Arts, New York

fig. 3 Paul Rudolph, Jewett Arts Center at Wellesley College, Wellesley, Massachusetts, c. 1958. Color slide by Bernhard Hoeslir, c. 1965. Courtesy gta-Institut, ETH, Zurich

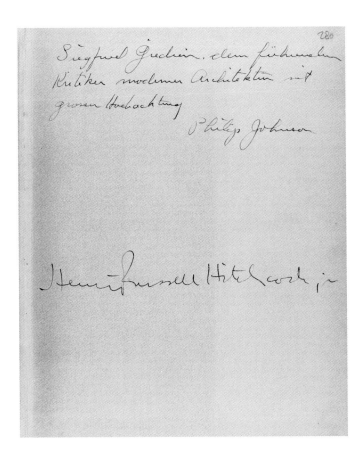

Alfred H. Barr, Hitchcock, and Johnson began working on their International Style project for the Museum of Modern Art (not knowing whether it would become a book or an exhibition, or both), Giedion had just published *Bauen in Frankreich,* the book that made him, a Swiss pupil of Heinrich Wölfflin, known as a leading historian and ideologue of the new architecture.[13] As secretary general of CIAM, founded in 1928, Giedion was also at the hub of the European network. Nothing appeared more obvious to the MoMA team than to turn to Giedion for advice in the context of their fieldwork.

Johnson apparently saw his project as a desperately needed counter to what writings like Giedion's *Bauen in Frankreich* stood for. In his eyes, Giedion was a "functionalist" and, as such, not primarily interested in the aesthetic components of the new architecture. Johnson probably had Giedion in mind when, in a letter to J. J. P. Oud, he referred to that scene of "German critics" who are only "too apt to claim that the style has other than aesthetic foundations." This is why, in his view, it was so important to "show just what this aesthetic foundation is and how it came about."[14] The misunderstanding is not entirely implausible. The adventurous historiographic shortcuts, which render dynamic Giedion's *dimostrazioni,* do little to correct such an impression (for example, the "montage" of Mart Stam's 1926 office building for Amsterdam with the Eiffel Tower, fig. 5). Not to mention the outspoken anticlassicist bias of his text—for example, when Giedion criticizes Le Corbusier, the architect he admires most, for using *tracés régulateurs* (regulating lines) in his designs.[15]

Yet, seen in the light of Giedion's own art-historical agenda and his friendship with the Bauhaus master Moholy-Nagy, what appears as forced structural determinism is rather meant as a visual technique in the service of revealing not

fig. 4 Henry-Russell Hitchcock and Philip Johnson, *The International Style* (1932). First page with authors' dedication to Sigfried Giedion, 1932

a genealogy but the aesthetic principles at work in the modern movement. Among these principles are both "transparency" and "simultaneity"—as evoked by the juxtaposition, side by side, of an upward and a downward view of one of the Eiffel Tower's legs.[16] If "style" means the constancy of form or of expression in the art and life of an individual, a group of individuals, or an entire epoch, then Giedion's project, as illustrated here, is obviously involved in this notion, no less than Hitchcock's and Johnson's. Granted that, since Giedion's visit to the Bauhaus, in 1923, *Stilwille* (idealism) is intrinsically linked with the materiality of things. In fact, even the title of Giedion's book (*Bauen in Frankreich, Bauen in Eisen, Bauen in Eisenbeton* [Building in France, Building in Iron, Building in Ferro-Concrete]) insists on material determinism—not unlike Hilberseimer's *Beton als Gestalter* (Concrete as Form Giver) (1928)—while in the text, the term "style" is abandoned altogether.[17]

Space, Time and Architecture follows the same agenda. Its declared ambition is to define a "New Tradition" in the handling of architectural space, and to identify the roots of this phenomenon in leading trends of modern science and art. However, though Giedion continues to draw on the visual rhetoric of techno-determinism, especially in the sections that are taken from *Bauen in Frankreich*—and certainly in Herbert Bayer's beautiful Lissitzky-esque cover design (see fig. 1)—the language of "technology" is no longer at the center of the argument. Or rather, it is redefined (and mystified) in terms of form and space. Thus, with the help of "constituent" works of art, such as Delaunay's *Eiffel Tower* (1910) or Picasso's *L'Arlésienne* (1911), Giedion places the narrative of modern architecture into a Wölfflinian mold of formalist art history.

fig. 5 Sigfried Giedion, *Bauen in Frankreich, Bauen in Eisen, Bauen in Eisenbeton* (1928). Spread juxtaposing the Eiffel Tower and Mart Stam's office building project for Amsterdam from 1926

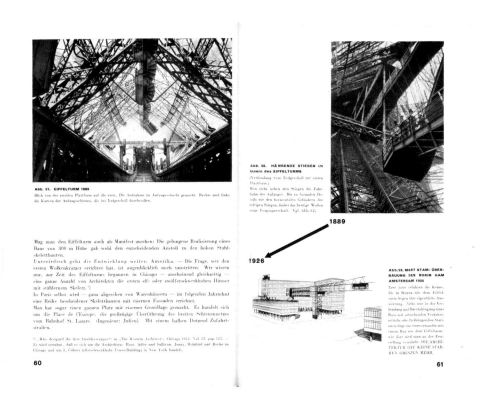

By the 1950s, the more radically architecture became defined in terms of form and space, the more emphatically the notion of style was dismissed as inoperative— even though the 1950s was a time of considerable interest in style, both as an art-historical and as an anthropological category. When the anthropologist Alfred L. Kroeber, for example, uses the term "style" in his attempt to unravel the "essence of civilization," it could be said that the ambition is profoundly analogous to Giedion's despite the difference in terminology.[18] As to the latter's discussion of the mostly anonymous artifacts of medieval and modern techno-culture as a reflection of psychic and aesthetic attitudes of Western man (in *Mechanization Takes Command*, of 1947, Giedion's most important book), it could be defined as an even more immediate precedent to anthropological notions of style.[19]

But then, Giedion turned out to be one of the most vocal critics of the term "style" in general, and "International Style" in particular. The very graphic pulse of some of his lecture manuscripts illustrates how much the term as such made him nervous (fig. 6). And of course the rejection is not put forward in terms of "functionalism," much less of "revolution," as Hitchcock and Johnson would have suspected at the time they defined their posture as aesthetes of modernity. (As early as the 1940s, to turn away from the "Illusion of progress" had become Giedion's own motto.[20]) What sense is to be made of this terminological blind spot? Is it a mere question of modernist esprit de corps? It is well known that Gropius had refused the notion of style in the context of the Bauhaus as thoroughly as he distrusted De Stijl (or at least van Doesburg as the group's ideologue). Le Corbusier, after all, flatly

fig. 6 Sigfried Giedion, notes for a lecture given in Boston in 1958, with references to the notion of "style"

fig. 7 Le Corbusier, "L'architecture n'a rien à faire avec les styles." From *Précisions sur un état présent de l'architecture et de l'urbanisme* (1930)

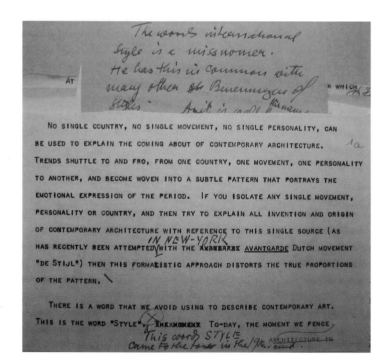

declared that "architecture has nothing to do with styles" (fig. 7).[21] No coincidence, thus, that the term was banned from the CIAM vocabulary.

Revisions 1: Toward the "Flimsy-Effeminate"

By circumscribing modern architecture as a style, Hitchcock and Johnson managed to depoliticize the phenomenon and make it acceptable for American patronage. Reyner Banham summarized this view, widely shared by American critics, as follows: "The case really was that the New Architecture would be presented without the Socialist fire in its belly, or it might not be presented at all"—the implication being that "style" and "Socialist fire" are mutually exclusive.[22] And so they were in the doctrinaire understanding of the architectural left. As to Giedion, he was convinced that the pursuit of a "new style" presupposed the rejection of "styles" as well as, by implication, "ornament"—that is, what he called "decorative slime."[23] Yet clearly his commitment to modernity was no less determined by an aesthetic choice than was Hitchcock's and Johnson's—albeit rationalized as a tribute to the zeitgeist.

In the long run, the real dividing line in his "battle of style" was a question of taste. Taste in the guise of zeitgeist is at stake in Giedion's contempt for the "toothpick stilts," for the "lacework of glittering details," for a cultural center formed as an "assembly of isolated buildings" as well as for "smallbreasted" and "gothic-styled colleges." Though the tapering pillars of Max Abramowitz's Philharmonic Hall can doubtless be compared to this instrument of dental hygiene, who knows if the toothpick metaphor had not been coined in other circumstances, possibly as early as in 1939, at the Swiss National Fair in Zurich (fig. 8). Seen in the context of the present argument, some of the pavilions of this fair, which were mostly built as light structures in wood, appear to foreshadow nothing so much as the decorative modernism of the 1950s. Seen in retrospect, the "lacework" of the pavilions of Hans

fig. 8 Max Abramowitz, Philharmonic Hall, Lincoln Center for the Performing Arts, New York, 1962

fig. 9 Swiss National Fair in Zurich. "Theatre Square" (Hans Hofmann, architect, 1939)

Les éléments de la construction en bois combinés avec des effets de lumière offrent des possibilités illimitées à la phantaisie décorative.
Gli elementi della costruzione in legno combinati con effetti di luce offrono delle possibilità decorative senza fine.

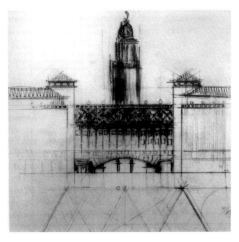

fig. 11 Haefeli, Moser, Steiger, *Kongresshaus,* window blinds, Zurich, 1938–39

fig. 12 Johannes Jacobus Pieter Oud, project for Amsterdam Town Hall, 1936–37

Hofmann, the architect in chief of the exhibition (whose soap factory in Zurich only a few years previously had been sampled by Hitchcock and Johnson among the Swiss examples of the International Style) appears like a prelude to the 1950s (figs. 9, 10).[24] Not to mention the "glittering details" of the Zurich Kongresshaus, built in 1939 by the CIAM cofounders Max Haefeli, Werner M. Moser, and Rudolf Steiger.[25]

These Swiss revisions of the modernist code around 1940 are part of an international scenario. The stock market crisis of 1929 had compromised the dreams of rapid industrialization, and architects were quick in reacting to this new situation with a heightened sensibility for the vernacular, for issues of regional "identity," and the organic. More specifically "Swiss," however, is the monumentalization that this classicizing and ornamental modernism found at the National Fair (*Landesausstellung*) of 1939 with its mandate to express the national ideal. Needless to say, the outbreak of World War II in 1939 gave mythic dimensions to this predicament.

The ideologue of this "nationalization" of the modern was Peter Meyer, an architect and critic who was then editor-in-chief of the Swiss journal *Das Werk.* Meyer had been impressed with the recent architecture of Sweden, which he documented lavishly in *Das Werk,* knowing only too well that even the *parti* of the Zurich fair and the playful grouping of its pavilions along the lake shore had been directly inspired by Gunnar Asplund's master plan for the Stockholm Exhibition of 1930. Meyer saw the National Fair as a fulfillment of his own vision of architectural modernity (which involved a firm commitment to the notion of "style" in art and architecture).[26] He went so far as to claim that its refusal of the overt neoclassical monumentalism that had been central to the axial planning of the Paris World's Fair of 1937 made the Swiss fair the most successful of the entire decade.

As to Giedion, the other protagonist in the small world of Swiss architectural theory and criticism,[27] he had lost interest in the project once he realized that his own rather ambitious proposal for the thematic organization of the fair had been filed.[28] Apart from this disappointment, he appears to have been increasingly irritated by the trend toward crafted details, often in wood, and the use of ornament in the work of some among his closest CIAM friends, though for the time being he decided to voice his frustration only indirectly or in private. As patron of the Doldertal flats, two elegant apartment buildings by Alfred Roth, Marcel Breuer, and Emil Roth, built from 1933–35, he had encouraged his architects to abandon the straitjacket of functionalism in favor of an emphatically "organic" approach (fig. 11). But he could not accept the next step on the ladder toward a postmodern revision. When, during a visit to Amsterdam in 1938, J. J. P. Oud showed him his Amsterdam City Hall project with its Venetian loggia and surface patterns, Giedion was horrified (fig. 12).[29] The result was a break with his closest ally within CIAM. As is well known, Hitchcock and Johnson too regarded Oud as the leading Dutch architect, though, interestingly, their reaction to his ornamental phase was no less skeptical than Giedion's.[30]

A few years later these frustrations finally broke into the open. In a broadside against the concept of New Empiricism that had been launched by the *Architectural Review* in 1947, in the context of a discussion of recent trends in Swedish architecture, Giedion argued: "There are sometimes women who can commit every sin and will yet be pardoned, because they do it so nicely that it would be almost bad taste to measure them with a common yardstick. When the Swedes are designing architecture, we are very much in the same dilemma. Whenever they are making the same faux pas as the others do, they do it so charmingly that it is difficult to object. But historians, by their trade, are unfortunately brutal and, even if they would like to, they must not be seduced by a smile."[31]

Giedion's patronizing way of gendering the trend toward the decorative may have been predictable in the context of the times, as the characterization of the style used at the Festival of Britain, in 1951, as "Flimsy-Effeminate," appears to suggest.[32] For Giedion the issue was whether the arts and crafts tradition continued to be relevant for current practice: "This pseudo-idyllic conception," he argued, "is a harkback to the art décoratif of about 1907 when it is true that the charming Dresden and Viennese *Werkstätte* had an important role to play in clearing the ground."[33]

Finally, Giedion proclaims: "What they propose as the 'New Empiricism' is a 'New Escapism' which is as much a *cul-de-sac* as the Stockholm Town Hall or as the 'New Classicism' of the twenties which was so charming, but had no constituent force."[34]

Giedion continued to castigate the "escapist" trends in an international perspective: "particularly astonishing," so he argues in *CIAM: A Decade of New Architecture,* has been the "retrogressive movement which occurred in Holland during the late '30s and the '40s," all the more so "as during the '20s Holland undoubtedly played a leading role both in art and architecture." That spirit, according to Giedion, has "vanished" from most Dutch rebuilding projects, "which exhibit unscientific city planning or pseudo-romantic tendencies." Like Sweden, Holland is "endangered by sentimental trends such as the 'new empiricism' which, under cover of 'humanizing' architecture leads it only into another *cul-de-sac.*" Switzerland, too, was "moving under a similar cloud of 'coziness' for its housing schemes, while sterile and desiccated business blocks are destroying the organic kernel of its largest city."[35] In the German version of the text Giedion refers to a politician who allegedly coined the term *Bastelstil* (handicraft-style) for the new trend in housing.[36]

Revisions 2: "New Monumentality"

Yet Giedion's contempt for the decorative and eclectic revisionisms of Playboy Architecture and its "toothpick stilts" and "lacework" does not imply a wholesale verdict against "history"—or, obviously, against the values of regionalism or the "organic." In fact, while he banned the "suave" Swedes and the "decorative" Dutch (in particular, Asplund and Oud) from the post-1945 editions of *Space, Time and Architecture,* he eventually canonized Aalto as a leader of world architecture.[37] Meanwhile, the frustration with the semantic deficits of prewar functionalism grew even within the CIAM. The side effect was a new interest in the historic cityscapes of Italy as models for the "Humanization of the city." Thus, in short, *Space, Time and Architecture* criticized Playboy Architecture yet it canonized the Piazza del Campidoglio in Rome as one of the references for the CIAM doctrine on the New Monumentality.[38] Lincoln Center is part of the same story.

Naturally, more than the toothpick stilts as such, it is the very neoclassicism of the center's layout and architectural orchestration that made it unacceptable for Giedion. Seen in a Swiss context one cannot but think of his antagonist Peter Meyer once again. In an article on the Musée d'Art Moderne in Paris, opened in 1937, Meyer had first addressed the issue of a modern classicism.[39] His basic assumption was

fig. 13 Jean-Claude Dondel, *Musée d'Art Moderne,* Paris, 1936–37

fig. 14 Auguste Perret, Navy Building Office in Paris, 1930, and figurative artworks by Georges Rouault and Aristide Maillol. Page from Peter Meyer, *Europäische Kunstgeschichte* (1947)

that in architecture, the "monumental" will inevitably in some way be defined by the classical tradition, which was why, in Meyer's view, the "stripped classicism" of the Musée d'Art Moderne had to be taken seriously as architecture of our times, and possibly even as an example for the future (fig. 13).[40]

Meyer wrote no fewer than five articles on monumentality between 1937 and 1941. It was thus not out of the blue that, in 1942, Giedion published his "Nine Points on Monumentality" (together with José Luis Sert and Fernand Léger).[41] Not surprisingly, they took a stand that was diametrically opposite to Meyer's. Whereas for the editor of *Das Werk* the time had come to learn the lessons of Auguste Perret properly, and to accept Maillol rather than Brancusi as the century's great sculptor (to which J. J. P. Oud, for one, would obviously have agreed), Giedion refused any classicist and ornamental compromise (fig. 14).[42] In his view, the survival of neoclassicism, or, more precisely, the stifling impact of Durand upon subsequent generations, had merely produced an architecture of pseudo-monumental corpses, fundamentally out of step with the spirit of the times.[43] As a result, arches, colonnades, cross vaults supported by huge pillars—the entire catalogue of what in his eyes was tantamount to "pseudo-monumentality"—was banned from the architectural menu, in favor of the spatial dynamism and organicist morphologies derived from engineering and abstract art (fig. 15). The roots of modernity, so he thought, were to be sought *not* in classicism, nor incidentally in the arts and crafts movement, but in engineering, in the artistic revolution of the years around 1910, and more particularly in cubism.

After 1945 the notion of the New Monumentality became an increasingly important factor of the architecture of the Pax Americana. As to the prejudices, which cautioned a subsequent generation's ravages in the architectural heritage of the early industrial age, they too were codified in this context.[44] For Giedion, with the devil of neoclassicism, only a "yes" or a "no" regarding colonnades seemed possible. What was dismissed with colonnades, however, was not just a set of forms that was doubly compromised, in his eyes, for its association with Nazism and with Stalinism. What was dismissed was the framework of a theoretical system that understood architecture in its symbolic relation to culturally determined functions (private, public, commercial, ceremonial), and that determined its handling according to the paradigms of "character" and "composition."[45]

Of course the *real* history of modern architecture did not follow the battle lines as uncompromisingly as CIAM's secretary general would have had it. Ultimately, even the architecture of Giedion's most celebrated heroes, Le Corbusier and Mies, can be described only in terms of their borrowings from both sides of the "divide."[46] By including Mies as well as Chandigarh *and* Brasília, *Space, Time and Architecture* cannot but acknowledge the survival of various classical traditions in the modern movement. But, unlike Meyer's early articles on monumentality—*and* some of Philip Johnson's canonic writings—the book fatally stops short of drawing any conclusions from that "paradox."[47]

From Playboy to Highboy

"It's all very well to say we admire Mies, and that some discipline is a good thing for young minds, but what if one is bored?"[48] Note that this was said in 1960, and by

fig. 15 Glass House. From Robert Venturi, *Complexity and Contradiction* (1966)

fig. 16 Venturi and Rauch, Guild House, Philadelphia, 1961–66

the architect who helped build the Seagram Building! Six years later Robert Venturi made a pun that quickly became famous: "Less is a bore."[49] Moreover, Johnson, again in 1960, claimed that "one should use the very chaos, the very nihilism, the relativism of our architectural world" to merely create "whimsies."[50]

The year Johnson began to be bored with Mies, Venturi began working on the Guild House, postmodernism's first large building, as Heinrich Klotz once claimed (fig. 15).[51] With the Guild House, built from 1961–66, a new sensibility for inclusiveness, complexity, broken codes, and irony in the use of historic reference came to the fore, a mix of gravity and artistic lightness unseen since Le Corbusier's Beistégui apartment. Johnson's work of the 1970s and 1980s appears curiously unwhimsical by comparison. As much as he knew how to be artfully informal in a school or conference situation, he inevitably turned classicist when it came to design. And whereas he was playfully enjoying his weakness for stylishness and opulence, others may have simply been better at transcending chaos with architectural whimsies.

From the 1970s onward, Philip Johnson and Robert Venturi probably form a far more critical constellation than the one examined in this essay.[52] Johnson in fact plays a decisive role in the argument of Venturi's *Complexity and Contradiction in Architecture* (1966). Whereas Giedion and Le Corbusier are referred to as part of the cultural baggage with which an architect could work with (in particular, Venturi likes to use Le Corbusier as a model for the formal strategies he advocates), Johnson figures prominently as a counterexample of what the book stands for.[53] In the very first chapter, entitled "Simplification and Picturesqueness," Johnson's Glass House is chosen as an illustration for the qualities of "simplicity" and "serenity," which an architecture that wants to be "connected with experience" should avoid (fig. 16).[54] Venturi begins by comparing it to the Wiley House, where, "in contrast to his Glass House, Johnson attempted to go beyond the simplicities of the elegant pavilion.... But even here the building becomes a diagram of an oversimplified program for living—an abstract theory of either-or. Where simplicity cannot work, simpleness results. Blatant simplification means bland architecture. Less is a bore."[55] (That it is

fig. 17 Spread from Robert Venturi, *Complexity and Contradiction in Architecture* (1966), with Philip Johnson's Port Chester synagogue, 1956 (bottom right)

the Glass House that inspired the famous parody of Mies's "Less is more" is ironic given Johnson's own generational conflict with Mies.)

Thus Johnson is forced into the role of "villain" in Venturi's plot—as he had been in Giedion's four years previously, albeit for different reasons. Though this does not make Venturi a follower of Giedion, it does cast some light on Johnson's status as a "negative authority" in the architectural world of the 1960s.

Yet with *Complexity and Contradiction* the author's polemical agenda stands in the way of its broader message. Looked at from a distance, *Complexity and Contradiction* probably owes more to Johnson than meets the eye. Venturi himself credits Johnson for having transcended the blandness of the Glass House in some of his more recent works. He has been "*almost unique* in emphasizing multiple enclosure in plan and section," Venturi states in his chapter titled "The Inside and the Outside," referring to the "canopy inside his guest house in New Canaan and the Soanian canopy within the synagogue in Port Chester."[56] The "almost unique" appears to suggest that Venturi in 1966 saw these works as decisive steps toward an architecture of complexity and contradiction (fig. 17).

Many among the Venturian themes—accepting Main Street as "almost all right," promoting irony as design strategy, the appreciation of mannerism—obviously evoke issues that are topical for Johnson. If an "epigrammatic, humorous, and metaphoric" discourse about architecture became part of the Venturi rhetoric—especially so in *Learning from Las Vegas* (1972)—one might add that Johnson had shown the way.[57] And referring to *Complexity and Contradiction in Architecture*: Does the formalist bias of the book not make it eminently comparable to *The International Style*? And does not the inclusion of contemporary American art from the Museum of Modern Art (a combine painting by Robert Rauschenberg, Jasper Johns's "Flags," and so on) represent yet another, implicit tribute to the museum—and moreover to Philip

Johnson as one of its patrons?[58] The very fact that *Complexity and Contradiction in Architecture* was published as the first of the Museum of Modern Art Papers on Architecture defines what might be called its pedigree. It makes it a part of a tradition of architectural theorizing that was, after all, inaugurated at the Museum by Barr, Hitchcock, and Johnson.[59]

As to Johnson himself, he probably had already come around to some of the criticism Venturi had formulated against him by the time of the book's publication, though he appears to have frequently been horrified by the looks of Venturi's projects.[60] And when he reemerged around 1970 from the shadow of the Lincoln Center as a mentor of the younger American avant-garde, he acknowledged the relevance of the book and later appropriated some of its argument as well as, in his architecture, some of the imagery (figs. 18, 19). In fact, it may be tempting to ask who was first to build a "decorated shed"—although the question as such is almost meaningless even in light of the Venturian definition of the term (it includes, among others, Amiens cathedral as well as the Palazzo Ruccellai). However, the issue of priority in formal invention apparently *does* intrigue the architects involved. In *Learning from Las Vegas,* Denise Scott Brown, Robert Venturi, and Steven Izenour described the Seagram Building as a "decorated shed" avant-la-lettre: "Less may have been more," they argue, "but the I-section on Mies van der Rohe's fire-resistant column, for instance, is as completely ornamental as the applied pilaster on a Renaissanced pier or the incised shaft in the Gothic column."[61] Yet while they pinpoint the theoretically intricate as well as (allegedly) unadmitted duality of structure and ornament in Mies, they fail to mention that Johnson had already made a programmatical issue of this conceptual duality with his Kline Biology Tower at Yale (fig. 20). And that before the term "decorated shed" was coined, he had played with the idea of defining the arched façade of the Asia House in New York as a decorative entity entirely detached from the structural system behind.[62]

Considering these premises within Johnson's work, the broken pediment at

fig. 18 Robert Venturi, "The Decorated Shed," from Robert Venturi, Denise Scott Brown, and Steven Izenour, *Learning from Las Vegas* (1972)

fig. 19 Cover of *Time*, January 1979. Philip Johnson with model of the AT&T Building

fig. 20 Kline Biology Tower,
New Haven, Connecticut, 1965.
Color slide by Bernhard Hoesli,
c. 1965. Courtesy gta-Institute,
ETH, Zurich

the top of Johnson's and John Burgee's AT&T Tower in New York, inspired by an American highboy, is not entirely unexpected—though the analogy with Venturi's sketch of a "decorated shed," published in *Learning from Las Vegas* ten years before the AT&T building was designed, *is* striking (see figs. 18, 19).

"Today the word style is discredited by all except critics attempting to reduce serious research by young architects through derogatory labels (decon, neomodernism), unfairly ignoring the social and programmatic concerns that often underlie contemporary experimentation."[63] Bernard Tschumi's somewhat belligerent foreword to Terence Riley's 1992 catalogue on *The International Style* seems to indicate that yesterday's avant-garde resistance to the notion of style and formalism in architecture has become the canon within the academy, at least in the United States.

What or whom did Tschumi have in mind? Perhaps Robert Venturi, whose essays, often peppered with "mal-mots" on the -isms blossoming within and around the architectural school culture, have become notorious in the 1990s?[64] Or Denise Scott Brown? In an article, "On Architectural Formalism and Social Concern" (1976), she argued that, indeed, "architects' concern with form and esthetics can be reconciled with social concern and social idealism."[65] And she does so primarily in defense of her own research and that by Venturi and Izenour on Las Vegas (which began in a Yale studio, in 1968). Scott Brown's essay begins as a critique of Johnson's and Hitchcock's tendency to aestheticize and thereby depoliticize the modern movement by recasting it as a style. It then continues to refer to the no less aesthetic bias of her own reading of Las Vegas, arguing that the study, notoriously criticized for its lack of sociopolitical analysis, is relevant in view of the architectural challenges of suburban sprawl and popular taste.[66]

Yet, if studying the phenomenology of the Strip can serve social goals, why should the formal analysis of "functionalist" schools, factories, and housing complexes built around 1930 not serve an analogous agenda? As to Venturi's *Complexity and Contradiction in Architecture,* the book was but marginally interested in style or styles—though part of its message *is* of course about style. Moreover, in its ambition to define aesthetic categories for an architecture that would be true to its time, the book can be said to connect both with *The International Style* and with *Space, Time and Architecture,* though it obviously presents a counterposition to these sacred texts.

The dynamics of modernization have made the word "style" almost inapplicable in its meaning as period style—at least for the past two centuries. At the same time it turned out to make it all the more unavoidable for group identification in the marketplace—which is why today the term enjoys such a success with the general public and such a mixed reception within the "school culture." Meanwhile, "style" is used in cultural studies or in anthropology for the description of everyday artifacts or for the analysis of technological systems.[67] Le Corbusier (and Giedion and Tschumi) claimed that "l'architecture n'a rien à faire avec les styles." Maybe it would be more appropriate to acknowledge that on the level of its popular reception, architecture is automatically perceived as being part of a "style," especially under the conditions of the "nice juicy chaos" of the late twentieth century.

The same holds true for architects as well as historians—which is why Giedion's confrontation with Johnson and Johnson's with Venturi and Scott Brown was also, and perhaps first of all, a conflict of *personal* and *professional* styles. Speaking of Giedion and Johnson, the paradox is that the professional roles appear to be switched: the architect plays the act of the disengaged observer, surfing on his erudite ironies, while the historian, in his ambition to unravel the roots of a modern era that perhaps never existed, falls back upon the archaic pose (and the messianic prose) of the seer.[68] Predictably, Johnson's intellectual agility, charm, and, after all, "style"—he was closer to Henry James and Tom Wolfe than to Heinrich Wölfflin— turned out to be incompatible with Giedion's. Nor did Giedion accept Venturi's view that Main Street is "almost all right" of a few years later, and much less Johnson's idea that "one should use the very chaos, the very nihilism, the relativism of our architectural world," to create "whimsies."[69]

By associating stylistic pluralism and eclecticism with sexual license and even lasciviousness, as he did in the opening chapter of the 1962 edition of *Space, Time and Architecture,* Giedion made modern architecture look more puritan than he might have intended. On the other hand, and granted the cyclic movement of action and reaction not only in the history of style by also in styles of writing about architecture, Johnson's *Baukunst* turns out to be considerably less whimsical than his own utterances suggest.

Notes

The idea for this essay originated with a brief encounter with Philip Johnson in Basel in the spring of 1997. I want to thank Victoria Newhouse for having made possible this encounter, and Emmanuel Petit and Thomas P. Hughes for their editorial advice.

1. Sigfried Giedion, "Architecture of the 1960s: Hopes and Fears," in *Space, Time and Architecture* (Cambridge: Harvard University Press, 1962), xxxl–lvi.

2. Giedion reported that the meeting was held at the Metropolitan Museum of Art. In fact it was held at the Grace Rainey Rogers Auditorium in New York's Metropolitan Museum but organized by the Architectural League of New York. I am grateful to Dean Robert A. M. Stern for clarifying this point.

3. Giedion, *Space, Time and Architecture,* xxxii.

4. Ibid.

5. Giedion had been the secretary general of the CIAM from 1928 to 1956.

6. Quoted by Nikolaus Pevsner in his "Wiederkehr des Historismus," in Pevsner, *Architektur und Design: Von der Romantik zur Sachlichkeit* (Munich: Prestel, 1971), 509. For excerpts from the lecture, see Franz Schulze, *Philip Johnson: Life and Work* (Chicago: University of Chicago Press, 1994), 270ff.

7. As has been brilliantly described by Beatriz Preciado, lifestyle and the ambition to define masculine domesticity are crucial themes in *Playboy* magazine. Ironically, in that they attempt to restore male authority in the domestic sphere, projects like Hugh Hefner's "Playboy Town House" of 1962 or the highly mechanized "Playboy Penthouse" directly relate to one of the key subjects of Giedion's *Mechanization Takes Command* (New York: Oxford University Press, 1947), 512 (chapter titled "Mechanization Encounters the Household: The Feminist Movement and the Rational Household").

8. See Andy Warhol and Pat Hackett, *POPism: The Warhol '60s* (New York: Harcourt Brace Jovanovich, 1980), 50.

9. Schulze, *Philip Johnson,* 108.

10. Ibid., 250.

11. Institut für Geschichte und Theorie der Architektur. I am grateful to Bruno Maurer, the head of the archive, and Daniel Weiss for their help and advice.

12. The correspondence is preserved at the Giedion archive at the gta-Institute, ETH Zurich. Johnson's use of German in his correspondence with Giedion is not to be attributed to a particular "Germanophilia." It is only around 1933–36 that English supplanted German as the "official" language of modern architecture, as was recently pointed out by Ed Taverne, Cor Wagenaar, and Martien de Vletter, *J. J. P. Oud: Poetic Functionalist, 1890–1963. The Complete Works* (Rotterdam: NAI, 2001), 365. Inevitably, there were other contacts between Giedion and Johnson in subsequent decades, but these are not at stake here. Most notable perhaps was their collaboration in view of an exhibition on the work of Robert Maillart at MoMA, planned for 1947 but held in 1948 (see Iris Bruderer, *Vision in Flux: Hugo Weber. Ein Pionier des abstrakten Expressionismus* (Bern: Benteli Verlag, 1999), 23ff).

13. Sigfried Giedion, *Bauen in Frankreich, Bauen in Eisen, Bauen in Eisenbeton* (Leipzig: Klinkhardt and Biermann, 928); English ed.: *Building in France, Building in Iron, Building in Ferro-Concrete*, introducted by Sokratis Georgiadis (Santa Monica, Calif.: Getty Center Publication Programs, 1995). On Giedion, see *Hommage à Giedion: Profile seiner Persönlichkeit* (Basel: Birkhäuser, 1971) and Sokratis Georgiadis, *Sigfried Giedion: Eine intellektuelle Biographie* (Zurich: Ammann/ Institut gta, 1989).

14. Letter to Johannes Jacobus Pieter Oud, 1930, quoted in Paolo Scrivano, *Storia di un'idea di architettura moderna: Henry-Russell Hitchcock e l'International Style* (Milan: Franco Angeli, 2001), 37. See also Taverne, Wagenaar, and de Vletter, *J. J. P. Oud,* 321ff. It is symptomatic that neither Adolf Behne nor Walter Curt Behrendt referred to in Schulze's biography of Johnson. Both authors had arrived at a much more differentiated view of the architectural discussions by 1930.

15. See Giedion, *Bauen in Frankreich,* 92.

16. On Giedion's notion of transparency and its later reconceptualization by Colin Rowe and Robert Slutzky, see Detlef Mertins, "Anything But Literal: Sigfried Giedion and the Reception of Cubism in Germany," in Eve Blau and Nancy Troy, eds., *Architecture and Cubism* (Montreal/ Cambridge: CCA/MIT Press, 1997), 219–251.

17. Rosemarie Haag-Bletter refers to Giedion's "curious combination of idealism (*Stilwille*) with materialism" in her introduction to Harry N. Mallgrave, ed., *Adolf Behne: The Modern Functional Building* (Santa Monica, Calif.: Getty Research Institute for the History of Art and the Humanities, 1996), 1–83.

Giedion's first book, *Spätbarocker und romantischer Klassizismus* (Munich: Bruckmann, 1922), which had established his reputation as an art historian in the tradition of Heinrich Wölfflin, was about defining a style while carefully avoiding the term or using it ambiguously and in contradictory ways. In this book the author at one time insists that "Klassizismus ist *kein* Stil. Klassizismus ist eine *Färbung!*"("classicism is *no* style. Classicism is a *tinge,*" 9). By denying neoclassicism the status of a style he leaves open whether the term needs to be used for such notions as romanticism instead, or abolished altogether in favor of a notion that could characterize the cultural whole. Elsewhere, he insists that style "doesn't know the obstacles that are part of any growth process" ("kennt die Hindernisse nicht, die im Entstehen liegen," 115).

18. See, in this context, Alfred L. Kroeber, *Style and Civilizations* (Ithaca, N.Y.: Cornell University Press, 1957), as well as the earlier study by Meyer Schapiro, "Style," in Alfred L. Kroeber, ed., *Anthropology Today* (Chicago: University of Chicago Press, 1953), 287–312. Though Schapiro refers to the issue of eclecticism, he does not focus on this issue that in turn was vividly discussed by architectural historians at that time. See, e.g., Carol Meeks, *The Railroad Station: An Architectural History* (New Haven: Yale University Press, 1956), or J. A. Schmoll gen. Eisenwerth, "Stilpluralismus statt Einheitszwang: Zur Kritik der Stilepochen-Kunstgeschichte," in Martin Gosebruch and Lorenz Dittmann, eds., *Argo: Festschrift für Kurt Badt zum 80. Geburtstag* (Cologne, 1970), 77–95.

19. Giedion, *Mechanization Takes Command.* See also my postscript to the German edition of the book, *Die Herrschaft der Mechanisierung* (Frankfurt: Europäische Verlagsanstalt, 1982), 816.

Looked at more closely, Giedion's own historiographic project is profoundly influenced by nineteenth-century theories of style, and in particular by those by Semper and Riegl. See Gottfried Semper, *Der Stil in den technischen und tektonischen Künsten oder Praktische Aesthetik,* 2 vols. (Frankfurt: Verlag für Kunst und Wissenschaft, 1860/63), and Alois Riegl, *Stilfragen: Grundlegungen zu einer Geschichte der Ornamentik* (Berlin: Georg Siemens, 1893). On Giedion's concept of style, see Joseph Rykwert, "Giedion e la nozione di stile," *Rassegna,* 1985 (1950), no. 25: 82–88. Characteristically, Giedion felt closer to Riegl than to Semper, given the latter's alleged "materialist" bias.

20. See "Man in Equipoise," in Giedion, *Mechanization Takes Command,* 713, 723.

21. See Le Corbusier, *Précisions sur un état présent de l'architecture et de l'urbanisme* (Paris: Vincent Fréal, 1930), 71.

22. Given the "network of the Rockefellers, Goodyears and other very rich persons with whom [Hitchcock and Johnson] were involved in getting the MoMA off the ground." Reyner Banham, "Actual Monuments," *Art in America,* October 1988, pp. 173–177, 213, 215; reprinted in Mary Banham, P. Barker, L. Sutherland, and C. Price, eds., *A Critic Writes: Essays by Reyner Banham* (Berkeley: University of California Press, 1996), 291.

23. See Giedion, *Bauen in Frankreich,* 49 ("den dekorativen Schleim zu überwinden").

24. Henry-Russell Hitchcock and Philip Johnson, *The International Style* (New York: Norton, 1960), 160.

25. The Zurich Kongresshaus is currently threatened with demolition for a cultural center designed by Rafael Moneo. For ample documentation on the building, see Arthur Rüegg and Reto Gadola, eds., *Kongresshaus Zürich, 1937–1939: Moderne Raumkultur* (Zurich: D'Arch/gta, 2007), as well as Sonja Hildebrand, Bruno Maurer, and Werner Oechslin eds., *Haefeli Moser Steiger: Die Architekten der Schweizer Moderne* (Zurich: gta Verlag, 2007), 289–296 and passim.

The ideas discussed here are developed in greater detailed elsewhere: Stanislaus von Moos, "'New Escapism'? Sigfried Giedion, das Kongresshaus und die Architektur um 1940," in Rüegg and Gadola, *Kongresshaus Zürich, 1937–1939,* 10–21.

26. In his *Schweizerische Stilkunde* (Zurich: Schweizer Spiegel, 1942), Meyer describes the antagonism of *Heimatstil* and *technischer Stil* as fundamental for the course of modern architecture. For a summary of Meyer's thoughts, see Katharina Medici-Mall, *Im Durcheinandertal der Stile: Architektur und Kunst im Urteil von Peter Meyer (1894–1984)* (Basel: Birkhäuser, 1998), 279–314.

27. As early as in 1929, H.-R. Hitchcock had noted the singularity of this duo of critics. That Switzerland has these "two excellent critics … bodes better for the immediate future than all the activity in Slavic lands so lacking balance and restraint," Hitchcock claimed; see *Modern Architecture: Romanticism and Reintegration* (1929; New York: Da Capo, 1993), 198. The library of the Kunsthistorisches Institut at the University of Zurich owns a copy of Hitchcock's book dedicated to Meyer, who taught there from 1956–64.

28. See Dorothee Huber, ed., *Sigfried Giedion: Wege in die Oeffentlichkeit. Aufsätze und unveröffentlichte Schriften aus den Jahren 1926–1956* (Zurich: Ammann/gta, 1987), 82–87.

29. In a letter to Laszlo Moholy-Nagy written

July 27, 1938, Giedion reports—after his visit to Holland—that Oud was on a dangerous path ("Er ist auf einem gefährlichen Weg der Reaktion") and that the public before which he spoke in Amsterdam was opposed to about everything considered important and valuable by CIAM: "Bis Maillol—und keinen Schritt weiter. Was nachher käme habe alles nur verschlechtert." Referring to Oud's recent projects for Amsterdam and The Hague Giedion quotes Oud: "'Fingerübungen,' sagt Oud. Das sind, so weit ich sehen kann, Müdigkeitserscheinungen und ausserdem die Rechnung an die Leute, die meinten, man käme mit der Funktion aus, ohne Malerei, ohne Gefühl!" (Giedion archive at the gta-Institute, ETH Zurich).

30. Johnson was by no means ready to accept Oud's move toward decorative eclecticism in 1944; see Schulze, *Philip Johnson,* 176.

31. Giedion, "S. Giedion. A talk given at a joint meeting of the MARS Group and the Institute of Contemporary Arts," *Architect's Journal,* 1947, August 26, 1948, pp. 206–207.

32. Banham, "The Style: Flimsy … Effeminate?" in Mary Banham and B. Hillier, eds., *A Tonic to the Nation: The Festival of Britain, 1951* (London: Thames and Hudson, 1976), 190–198.

33. Giedion, "A talk given," 206–207.

34. "S. Giedion. A talk given." Eric de Maré's definition of "New Empiricism" ("The antecedents and origins of Sweden's latest style," in *Architectural Review* January [1948], pp. 9–12, the text that triggered Giedion's critique), almost literally reflects ideas voiced by Peter Meyer, ten years earlier, in *Das Werk.* For more details, see von Moos, "'New Escapism'? Sigfried Giedion, Das Kongresshaus und die Architektur um 1940," 10–21.

35. Sigfried Giedion, ed., *A Decade of New Architecture* (Zurich: Girsberger, 1951).

36. German summary of the introduction, added to the book as a separate enclosure.

37. A chapter entitled "Alvar Aalto: Irrationality and Standardization" was added to the third edition of *Space, Time and Architecture* (1953).

38. This canonization had already occurred in an earlier edition of the book. The respective chapter is reprinted in *Space, Time and Architecture,* 55–71.

39. Peter Meyer, "Musée d'Art Moderne, Paris, 1937," in *Das Werk* 25, no. 1 (1938):4–8. For a listing of Meyer's subsequent writings on monumentality and of his respective ideas and their sources, see Katharina Medici-Mall, "Diskutieren über Monumentalität," in Medici-Mall, *Fünf Punkte in der Architekturgeschichte: Festschrift für Adolf Max Vogt* (Zurich: Birkhäuser/gta, 1985), 276ff., as well as—more

specifically focused on Meyer—Simone Rümmele, *Peter Meyer: Architekt und Theoretiker. Peter Meyers Beitrag zur Architekturdiskussion der Zwischenkriegszeit* (Zurich: Zentralstelle der Studentenschaft, 1999), 146–164.

40. It is interesting that Hans Schmidt, the most vocal representative of the political left within the Swiss CIAM group, who had just returned from the Soviet Union, where he had been converted to Socialist Realism, responded with a defense of Le Corbusier's much less classicizing proposal for the same site. See Schmidt, "Anmerkungen zum Musée de l'Art Moderne in Paris," *Das Werk,* no. 4 (April 1938): 120–123.

41. Written jointly with José Luis Sert and Fernand Léger and reprinted in Sigfried Giedion, *Architecture, You and Me: The Diary of a Development* (Cambridge: Harvard University Press, 1958), 48–51. See also Giedion's more general remarks on "The Need of a New Monumentality," ibid., 25–39. The best recent summary of the debates around this issue is by Eric Mumford, *The CIAM Discourse on Urbanism, 1928–1960* (Cambridge: MIT Press, 2000), 150–152 and passim.

42. See Giedion, *Architecture, You and Me,* n41.

43. See, in this context, Giedion's irresponsibly belligerent comments on nineteenth-century historicism in *Architecture, You and Me,* 25 and passim.

44. On the role of such prejudiced judgments on the practice of urban renewal, especially in the United States, see Vincent Scully, *American Architecture and Urbanism* (New York: Praeger/ Henry Holt, 1969), 165ff.

45. An excellent introduction to the "survival" of academic thought in modern architecture is given by Carlos Eduardo Diaz Comas, "'Corollaire brésilien': L'architecture moderne et la tradition académique," in Philippe Panerai, ed., *Brésil France: Architecture* (Paris: Editions du patrimoine, 2006), 47–66. On the role of "composition" in Le Corbusier's work see the important study by Mary McLeod, "'Order in the details,' 'Tumult in the whole'? Composition and Fragmentation in Le Corbusier's Architecture," in Barry Bergdoll, B. Oechslin, and W. Oechslin, eds., *Fragments: Architecture and the Unfinished. Essays Presented to Robin Middleton* (London: Thames and Hudson, 2007), 291–322.

46. See Colin Rowe, "Neo-'Classicism' and Modern Architecture I" and "Neo-'Classicism' and Modern Architecture II," in Rowe, *The Mathematics of the Ideal Villa and Other Essays* (Cambridge: MIT Press, 1976), 119–158. For a more general discussion, see Alan Colquhoun, *Modernity and the Classical Tradition*

(Cambridge: MIT Press, 1989).

47. Johnson, of course (unlike Hitchcock) did not know of Peter Meyer, and Meyer to my knowledge never commented on Johnson's work. Yet in her monograph on Meyer, Katharina Medici-Mall plausibly sees Johnson's position as architect prefigured in Meyer's thinking on classicism. See Medici-Mall, *Im Durcheinandertal der Stile,* 202.

48. Philip Johnson, quoted in Schulze, *Philip Johnson,* 270.

49. Robert Venturi, *Complexity and Contradiction in Architecture* (New York: Museum of Modern Art, 1966), 25.

50. Philip Johnson quoted in Schulze, *Philip Johnson,* 271.

51. For a more thorough reading of the Guild House, see my *Venturi, Rauch & Scott Brown: Buildings and Projects* (Fribourg/New York: Office du Livre/Rizzoli, 1987), 22 and passim. Most important among the several more recent studies on Venturi's work is David B. Brownlee, David G. de Long, and Kathryn B. Hiesinger, *Out of the Ordinary: Robert Venturi, Denise Scott Brown and Associates. Architecture, Urbanism, Design* (Philadelphia: Philadelphia Museum of Art, 2001).

52. See Denise Scott Brown, "On Architectural Formalism and Social Concern: A Discourse for Social Planners and Radical Chic Architects," in *Oppositions* 5 (1976): 100–112, as well as, more specifically on Johnson, her "High Boy: The Making of an Eclectic," *Saturday Review,* March 17, 1979, pp. 54–59.

53. Vincent Scully called *Complexity and Contradiction in Architecture* "probably the most important writing on the making of architecture since Le Corbusier's *Vers une architecture* ("Introduction," in Venturi, *Complexity and Contradiction,* 11.

54. Venturi, *Complexity and Contradiction,* 25.

55. Ibid. Note that Denise Scott Brown later offered a more balanced view of the Glass House. When visiting the house she was impressed by its "sturdiness," a quality she attributes to Johnson's fascination with the thinking of Geoffrey Scott (thereby referring to a mentor Venturi shares with Johnson). See Scott Brown, "High Boy."

56. Ibid., 78. Emphasis in original.

57. It was in fact Denise Scott Brown who had characterized Johnson's writing as "epigrammatic, humorous, and metaphoric" ("High Boy," 56).

58. It was Johnson who, with his donation of paintings by Warhol and Rauschenberg, had ended the museum's longtime indifference toward contemporary American art. It is intriguing that Venturi explicitly connects with the museum's new openness toward the present, whereas otherwise he remained silent on the role of modern painting and sculpture for architecture.

59. Note also that on the back of the book's title page, Johnson is listed as a trustee of the Museum of Modern Art (together with David Rockefeller, James Thrall Soby, Alfred H. Barr, and others).

60. Cf. Brownlee, De Long, and Hiesinger, *Out of the Ordinary,* 43 and passim.

61. Robert Venturi, Denise Scott Brown, and Steven Izenour, *Learning from Las Vegas* (Cambridge: MIT Press, 1972), 79.

62. Franz Schulze, *Philip Johnson,* 253ff. In fact, the solution appears to reflect nothing so much as Oscar Niemeyer's Alvorada Palace in Brasília (1958), perhaps the first monument of late modernism programmatically defined as a structure surrounded by an entirely "symbolic," i.e., basically "ornamental," arcade.

63. See Terence Riley, *The International Style: Exhibition 15 and the Museum of Modern Art* (New York: Rizzoli, 1992).

64. See Robert Venturi, *Iconography and Electronics upon a Generic Architecture: A View from the Drafting Room* (Cambridge: MIT Press, 1996).

65. Scott Brown, "On Architectural Formalism," 101.

66. Venturi, Scott Brown, and Izenour, *Learning from Las Vegas;* in the paperback edition Scott Brown appears as the first author.

67. Thomas P. Hughes, *Networks of Power: Electrification in Western Society, 1880–1930* (Baltimore: Johns Hopkins University Press, 1983), 40 and passim; George Kubler, *The Shape of Time: Remarks upon the History of Things* (New Haven: Yale University Press, 1962), 129.

68. Note that Johnson's and Venturi's interests in the American everyday and in the paraphernalia and the rhetoric of contemporary consumerism coincide in time with Giedion's studies in primeval art and the architecture of Babylon and Egypt. See Giedion, *The Eternal Present I: The Beginnings of Art* (New York: Bollingen Foundation, 1962) and *The Eternal Present II: The Beginnings of Architecture* (New York: Bollingen Foundation, 1964).

69. Venturi, *Complexity and Contradiction,* 102.

Philip Johnson:
Breaking with Modernism—
The "Whence & Whither" of It

Phyllis Lambert

Philip Johnson left an extraordinary legacy, unique in all architecture, explaining his work—not so much what he did and how he did it, but his personal motivations at various moments in time, essentially the whence and whither of his intent as an architect. Or as he put it, "what makes me tick."[1] I draw here largely upon Philip's published writings, informed by my close relationship with him, especially during the 1950s and 1960s. Occurring in this time frame were Philip's first avowals of a passion for history (while he was still an acolyte of Mies van der Rohe), and also his lectures to students (mostly at Yale), which I consider in relation to buildings completed as well as those in design. It is hard to fathom Philip's architecture without reading what he had to say. I will draw attention to some things he never spoke of directly in the documented record, to the sources he drew upon, and to the tremendous appeal that sensual and dramatic environments held for him. I also will point to some things he did talk about but never adhered to, at least in this period, such as the independence of form and structure. What I would like to show is his use of history as he directed his changing approaches to design.

Following his remarkable article for *Architectural Review* in 1950, in which he divulged the historical sources for his Glass House and its siting, by 1954, in

his celebrated talk to students at Harvard entitled "The Seven Crutches of Modern Architecture," Johnson made *history* his article of faith.[2] "I'm a traditionalist. I believe in history. I mean by tradition the carrying out, in freedom, the development of a certain basic approach to architecture which we find upon beginning our work here. I do not believe in perpetual revolution. I do not strive for originality."[3]

There was, however, to be no break with the immediate past. Johnson bombastically envisioned a brave new world viewed from the shoulders of his forebears. "We have very fortunately the work of our spiritual fathers to build on [Walter Gropius, Le Corbusier, Mies van der Rohe, Frank Lloyd Wright]. . . . Isn't it wonderful to have behind us the tradition, the work that those men have done? Can you imagine being alive at a more wonderful time? Never in history was the tradition so clearly demarked, never were the great men so great, never could we learn so much from them and go our own way, without feeling constricted by any style, and knowing that what we do is going to be the architecture of the future."[4]

Johnson's works from 1950 to 1954 were clearly Mies-inspired, among them the Museum of Modern Art's Annex, the Oneto house, Irvington, New York, and the MoMA Sculpture Garden of 1953 (figs. 1–3). However, in 1953 he inserted a vaulted ceiling into his 1949 Guest House at New Canaan, "my first break from the International Style," he later said (fig. 4).[5]

By 1957, Johnson's discourse had shifted. In an interview published that year, the International Style had become his whipping boy. "The duty of the artist is to strain against the bonds of existing style—in our case, the International Style—and only this procedure makes the development of architecture possible. . . . So now the flood gates are open to the delights of pure form, whatever its origin. Anything goes."[6]

In one of his experiments Johnson moved away from the steel skeleton to the brick-piered Schinkelesque-Hofgärtnerei-inspired Boissonnas House, New Canaan, completed in 1956 (fig. 5). Although critics at the time saw a new direction, it would have no follow-up. For Hitchcock, the house "looks forward not backward, or rather so far backward that it might have seemed altogether novel" had Johnson not

fig. 1 Museum of Modern Art, 53rd Street facade, New York

fig. 2 George C. Oneto House, Irvington-on-Hudson, New York, 1951

fig. 3 Museum of Modern Art Sculpture Garden, New York

revealed his interest in Schinkel's work in Potsdam.[7] Of the same year is Johnson's Kneses Tifereth Israel Synagogue in Port Chester, New York, with its ovoid "baroque" entrance, and, in continuity with the velarium of his Guest House in New Canaan, the "decorated ceiling dripping around the slots" of colored glass (figs. 6, 7).[8] As the synagogue was structured by an exposed steel frame, with "the *beat,* the rhythm of the steel uprights, inside as well as out," Johnson called his approach "a 'theme and variations' one rather than a complete break loose."[9] However, a year later, in a lecture at Yale to Vincent Scully's students, he claimed that the synagogue at Port Chester was "still pure International Style."[10] This was said in a lecture entitled "Retreat from the International Style to the Present Scene," in which he invoked Wallace Harrison's just completed fish-shaped First Presbyterian church in Stamford,

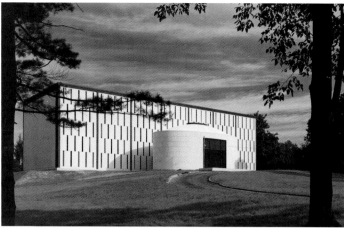

fig. 5 Eric Boissonas House, New Canaan, Connecticut, 1956. View from below terrace

fig. 6 Kneses Tifereth Israel Synagogue, Port Chester, New York, entrance facade, 1956

fig. 7 Kneses Tifereth Israel Synagogue, Port Chester, New York, interior view, 1956

fig. 8 Model of the Monaco Hotel, Havana

fig. 9 Pier Luigi Nervi, main hall of the Torino-Exposizioni, detail of Supports, Turin, Italy

fig. 10 Study model for column of the Monaco Hotel, Havana

Connecticut, remarking that "you can hardly go further than this [church] in a denial of the rigid structural simplicity that we have all been used to."[11]

In this lecture, despite inaccuracies of fact and self-contradictory remarks, structural form was the principal subject. "A good deal of [the revolt from the International Style] was instigated by engineering....We are fascinated—everyone ...in my generation—with Bucky Fuller's work, and with Nervi's, and with other engineers' works. Maillart was an early example. We got fascinated with the idea that you didn't have to use trabeated, that is, skeletal, up-and-down-and-straight-across forms. We got rather bored with the simplicity of the International Style....Now Nervi, of course, is our greatest inspiration right now....He is quite a man to inspire us with his shapes."[12]

In his 1956 project for the never-built Monaco Hotel in Havana, Johnson was clearly inspired by the shape of one of Nervi's layers of supports for the Turin Exhibition Hall of 1948–50 in devising his sculpturally shaped columns (figs. 8–10). He asked the engineers if his design would hold up, and when they replied that if he drew the outlines of what he wanted they would make it work, Johnson threw up his hands, as if loosening shackles on his wrists. I was struck by this, for he was essentially telling me that if structure did not matter, then in effect Mies didn't either.

In the same 1958 lecture Johnson roamed through the work of his contemporaries: the "wavy-roof boys," whom he considered (along with the neo-functionalist Louis Kahn) the "leading revolutionaries," whose work began with Nowicki's Livestock Judging Pavilion in Raleigh, North Carolina, Saarinen's skating rink for Yale, and buildings by Johansen and Kiesler. He contrasted Rudolph's 1952 Walker Guest House, on Sanibel Island in Florida, the work of a self-styled "poor man's Mies,"[13] with the lacework structure of Rudolph's Blue Cross–Blue Shield building in Boston (1956–60), "his structure entirely free to do with what he pleases—it is no longer the International Style."[14] He cited Saarinen's Milwaukee War Memorial of 1951, of which he said, "You see all the characteristics of the International Style: tension, cantilevering in the extreme....Well, now look at what he is doing now" at the TWA terminal being built at Idlewild (now Kennedy) airport.[15] Saarinen was doing flying shells that were cantilevered, but for Johnson, the shape, not the structural paradigm, mattered.[16] "We want to make shapes that please and arouse awe out of the shapes that the engineers are giving us on their drawing boards."[17]

Johnson's venture into built shapes would come later, but certainly his Munson-Williams-Proctor Arts Institute Museum of Art in Utica, New York, of 1960, still on the drawing board at the time with its Crown Hall undertones (functions below, exoskeletal girders above), would arouse awe in the severity of its blank facades (figs. 11, 12). As he described it, "With these great strap concrete members that hold the building up . . . it is again slightly International Style in the idea that the cube floats, but it's awfully heavy, and these enormous beams would never have been used in earlier times."[18] But the scales were weighted differently. From 1949 to 1959—from the Glass House in New Canaan to the Four Seasons Restaurant at the Seagram Building (figs. 13, 14)—Johnson's move away from Mies and the International Style was not related to tectonics. Rather, as I have argued previously, he wanted to invoke another sort of awe in the unleashing of his refined and dramatic use of light and

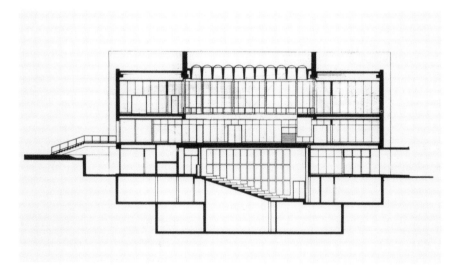

fig. 11 Munson-Williams-Proctor Arts Institute, Museum of Art, Utica, New York, 1960, section drawing

fig. 12 Munson-Williams-Proctor Arts Institute, Museum of Art, Utica, New York, 1960, exterior view.

fig. 13 Night view of the Glass House, New Canaan, Connecticut

fig. 14 Four Seasons Restaurant, Seagram Building, New York. Detail of Bar Room, 1959

materials.[19] To Mies's appreciation of Schinkel's "wonderful constructions, excellent proportions and good detailing" Johnson brought Schinkel's *other* genius for evoking drama and atmosphere, or *Stimmung*.[20] From 1960, with an ever-diminishing Miesian orientation, with history at his elbow, Johnson would follow still other directions.[21]

Early in 1959 Johnson pronounced that the International Style had "lasted ... from 1923 to 1959." He was speaking in the context of a talk entitled "Non-Miesian Directions," which he presented at the opening of an exhibition of his work organized by Yale students.[22] Johnson riposted, "I am just as Miesian as I ever was.... Mies stands out so far today that one must stand for him, against him, underneath him, on top of him, on his shoulders if you can get there. My stand today is violently *anti*-Miesian.... My direction is clear: traditionalism."[23]

Not revivalist, but eclectic. This lecture encapsulated Johnson's work of the late 1950s when he was moving distinctly away from Mies, and it seems clear that he was very much the originator rather than the promoter of the experiments he engaged. Johnson connected the International Style with "this idea that architecture had something to do with morals," the moral strength of structural expression that goes back to Viollet-le-Duc and Ruskin, their hatred of Renaissance architecture as "fakery" and their love for Gothic "truth." "I sometimes think Goethe was the founder of Modern architecture ... [with] his famous sentence, 'the pilaster is a lie.'"[24] In this way Johnson established the pivotal point of his lecture, the four tasks of architecture "in which I think the puritanical religious background of the International Style has failed me."[25] The first is the theater; second, the facade; third, the religious building; and last, the plaza. Johnson of course was concerned with concept, not building type. I present them in the order that he talked about them.

On the facade: The flattened vault inserted into Johnson's Brick House launched his obsession with the elliptical arch, which as he later put it, he "sort of got stuck with."[26] Thus, in 1959, his concept for the rejected facade for Asia House (fig. 15). No longer a transcription of the plan and structure, the facade, as Johnson asserted in the same lecture at Yale, was independent, detached from what went on inside: "This building to me is pure facade; there is nothing behind it. You could build it first and build something behind it some other time."[27] I was in architecture school at the time, and found this to be pure heresy—the idea of "facade" was simply anathema to those of the Miesian persuasion. Johnson considered the portico for the Amon Carter Museum at Forth Worth (not completed until 1961) mere "decoration in front of the building," but of the curved arches, which he described as being carved out of "real stone," he spoke of the "great satisfaction" derived from building in "solid stone" (fig. 16).[28] This was a huge event at the time. He talked about how he and George Howe, who was chairman of the School of Architecture at Yale from 1950 to 1954, "used to sit over a Scotch and dream of the days of stone, once again to be able to build in solid stone!"[29] Johnson would continue to design arcuated structures through 1963, including both his Lake Pavilion in New Canaan, constructed of precast concrete, and the Sheldon Memorial Art Gallery, built of stone (figs. 17–19). His design for Lincoln Center Plaza of 1958 was intended as a continuous arcade that would lend dignity to the open space and establish a sense of enclosure, with the two side buildings—his own State Theater and across from it, and the Philharmonic—tacked on at the sides (fig. 20). The idea of the "decorated front" surely led to the portico for his third, and finally built facade for the New York State Theater at Lincoln Center

fig. 15 Asia House, New York, study 1, 1959

fig. 16 Amon Carter Museum of
Western Art, Fort Worth, Texas.
Main facade, 1961

fig. 17 Model of Lake Pavilion,
Philip Johnson estate,
New Canaan, Connecticut

in 1964 (figs. 21, 22). And I suppose that it was also the impetus for the open portico
of his AT&T building before it was filled in by Sony.

On the theater: Johnson rejected the fan-shaped house, which he traced back
to Semper in the mid-nineteenth century, showing how it gave way in the twentieth
century to utilitarian acoustics and sight lines. As with religious buildings and
plazas, Johnson stressed the need for enclosure—the enclosed "court" theater from
the sixteenth to the eighteenth centuries—to achieve intimacy. The five-tier walls
of the New York State Theater were to be "paved, covered, wallpapered with people"
(fig. 23).[30] In a marvelous statement underlining the primacy of the art of architecture,
which he always espoused, and at the same time expressing his disdain for function,
Johnson remarked that in the State Theater, even where you can't see so well, "at
least you say, 'I'm in the midst of a wonderful place where something is going on.'"[31]

On the religious building: "There is no way for a perfectly straightforward
structural system to give us emotional satisfaction."[32] Again Johnson argued for
the need for enclosure: "There shouldn't be windows in religious buildings."[33] The
bedroom in his Guest House exemplifies this: "It does something to cradle the spirit
to be in a curved surface."[34] So does the Roofless Church in New Harmony, Indiana,
with its compound curved surfaces referencing the Indian *stupa* and mystical
meanings associated with the circular shape that he found in his readings of Jung,
albeit after the fact (figs. 24, 25). Of the nuclear reactor at Rehovot in Israel he said,
"We are still designing religion in a way.... You enter through a court like the narthex
at St. Ambroise, and as at St. Ambroise, the church (reactor building) looms over
the court" (figs. 26, 27).[35] Parenthetically, the folded wall of the reactor was surely
inspired by the great hall of Breuer and Nervi's UNESCO building in Paris.

On the plaza: Johnson considered this a problem "too difficult for the International Style to handle."[36] You couldn't enclose space as in St. Peter's Square,
or St. Mark's, he said.[37] Still smarting from the "ideological" rejection of his scheme
for Lincoln Center Plaza, Johnson remarked: "There are architects of the modern
persuasion ... who would never place buildings on the three sides of a plaza, and

fig. 18 Johnson standing in the Lake Pavilion, New Canaan, Connecticut

fig. 19 Model of Sheldon Art
Gallery, University of Nebraska,
Lincoln, 1963

fig. 20 Lincoln Center Plaza,
New York, preliminary drawing
for arcade

fig. 21 New York State Theater,
New York, facade model,
second version

fig. 22 New York State Theater,
New York, 1964, model photo

fig. 23 New York State Theater, New York, 1964, interior

then cement them into a single outdoor room, the way I would do."[38] In effect, he tacked the facade of the building onto the arcade. Likewise, at the University of St. Thomas in Houston, begun in 1957, where Miesian language was applied to a Jeffersonian plan, whatever buildings were needed could be tacked on (figs. 28, 29).

This was 1959, which marked the end of the International Style, according to Johnson. It was the year that the Four Seasons Restaurant opened in Mies's Seagram Building, and, with the exception of the East Wing and Garden Wing of the Museum of Modern Art (completed in 1964), the last time Johnson would use a Miesian vocabulary. These rooms, like the Glass House and the magical guest bedroom of his Guest House, exemplify the sense of intimacy and emotional satisfaction with which he wished to infuse his recent projects. Now he sought to activate this sense of Stimmung by means of *procession*.

In 1965, in an essay published in *Perspecta* entitled "Whence & Whither: The Processional Element in Architecture," parodying Le Corbusier, Johnson wrote that "architecture is surely *not* the design of space, certainly not the massing or organization of volumes. These," he said, "are auxiliary to the . . . organization of procession. Architecture exists only in *time*."[39] He continued with the concept of *temenos,* or sacred precinct, citing his Kline Biology Tower at Yale and the lobby of the New York State Theater, "designed as a procession,"[40] like the rearranged entrance to MoMA, carrying through vertically into the enlarged garden (fig. 30). He cites as well the rebuilt road leading to his New Canaan property, where the idea of procession incorporates the element of surprise on turning the corner and seeing his Glass House for the first time.[41] "The whence and whither is primary. Now almost secondary is all our ordinary work, our work on forms, our plans, our elevations. What we should do is to proceed on foot again and again through our imagined buildings. Then after months of approaching and reapproaching, and looking and turning, then only draw them up for the builder."[42]

Again there is a convergence between designs Johnson was working through and statements he made about architectural ideas, so that in the same year, 1965, he often spoke to his friends of procession at Frank Lloyd Wright's Taliesin West, one instance of which was captured by John Peter in a sound recording, "Conversations Regarding the Future of Architecture." I have transcribed the original 78 rpm recording.[43] It so brilliantly demonstrates the point that I would like to present the whole description:

> *Taliesin—The essence of the house is the human element, the procession through the building. I once counted the number of turns that you make when you approach the building until you get into what he called the cove. The number of turns, I think, is 45. Now, he is playing with you as you walk through that space. You park your car some two hundred feet away before you get to the entrance. Then you start down the steps, up the steps, to the right, to the left, then you go down the long—a very long—pergola, and you turn to the right to get out on to the famous prow, and you take the few steps down out to the magnificent view that has been concealed from you for two to three hundred feet of walking. Then you see Arizona stretched out as he meant*

fig. 24 Roofless Church, New Harmony, Indiana, 1960, view from precinct wall

fig. 25 Roofless Church, New Harmony, Indiana, 1960, view from entrance gate

you to. And then you go into the little tent room.... This tent light that trickles down, filters down into this private room.... You are bathed in the canvas light and when he opens the flap onto the little secret garden you say there are no more surprises, there cannot be any more unfolding of the spaces—but there are.... You finally get to the cove, and just when you are used to the six-foot ceiling, it has a fourteen-foot ceiling. The fireplace runs the length of the wall. No windows at all, no canvas, and all of a sudden you are entirely enclosed in the middle of this experience. By then you have been handled and twisted, much as a symphony will, until you get to the crisis.

In a lecture at Columbia University in 1975, after almost ten years' absence from teaching, Johnson described the sculpture gallery of 1970 at his New Canaan estate (and practically his only built work in five years), in similar terms, as *a play of changing directions, of procession*—surprise views, steps down, turn, down again, turn again (fig. 31).[44] A new intention is there—borrowing and overlapping four side bays with the focal space twelve feet down, around which the visitor was made to turn. "You carom off the entrance wall and settle down a turn and a quarter from the entrance door like a dog which has sniffed out a room and settles circularly into his place."[45] This is Johnson playing with the visitor, as he so often did with his audiences. The talk addresses three aspects of building that act as a measure, a hope, for his work and allow him "to brush away the cobwebs of infinite possibilities and try to find some way out."[46] These are: "Footprint," which is about procession and how space unfolds; the "Cave," or "space that contains, cuddles, exalts";[47] and the third aspect, which Johnson declared to be the most difficult, "Building as a Work of Sculpture."[48] Envisaging no structural limitation, Johnson states, "we can warp or carve or tilt our buildings the way we will."[49] The Pennzoil Building in Houston was for him his most successful sculpture: "John Burgee and I have had fun in the last few years with shapes and funnels, plazas, 'gozintas' [entrance to his gallery], indoor

fig. 26 Nuclear reactor, Rehovot, Israel, 1960, view from outside precinct wall

fig. 27 Nuclear reactor, Rehovot, Israel, 1960, view into court

streets, sloped sides and/or roofs, making processional, spaces and sculptures. . . . What a grand period for us to live in today! Contrariwise, what will all this sound like in ten years?"[50]

Now, thirty years later, we can assess his evolution across a longer trajectory. A new Johnson emerged in the 1970s from the chrysalis of the International Style, the great dramatic atmospheric works he conjured, the coziness and emotional satisfaction of enclosure he advocated, the impulsion of history at his elbow, the play of procession, and his teaching at Yale, where, above all, his message to students was that "we cannot not know history."[51] Although he was often accused of restlessly changing positions, from the 1950s to the 1970s there was a coherence to Johnson's design. The Miesian variants of the 1950s were followed by his relentless pursuit of the elliptical arch between 1959 and 1964, when he embraced experiments in diverse materials (from plaster to precast concrete and hand-carved stone) and equally diverse forms, moving with gathering courage from vault to portico and arcade, free-standing structure, and in its final transformation, a reticulated porch at the New York State Theater in 1964.

fig. 28 University of St. Thomas, Houston, auditorium and classroom buildings, view of interior court

fig. 29 University of St. Thomas, Houston, master plan drawing 1957–59

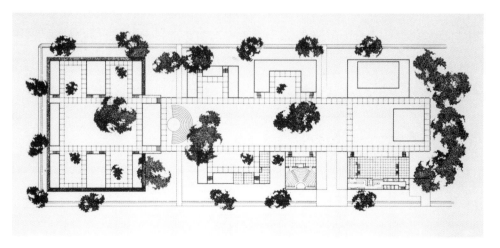

While contemporary American critics considered Johnson's work of the 1960s to be on a par with that of his peers, in England it was "rudely dismissed."[52] Only in the 1970s did Johnson manifest in his design work an assertion he made in 1960, namely, "We are going through a foggy chaos. Let us enjoy the multiplicity of it all."[53] Johnson's skyscrapers of these years were, as he put it, "all over the place" by design, because he wanted them to look different.[54] Some stand out and can be studied as models of public private space. On the other hand, in the 1980s, he was responsible for some regrettable, even pompous, retrospective pastiches. Arthur Drexler and I used to secretly guess what period would come next. However, in working through these phases, Johnson was able to enter into the discourse of the *making* of architecture and recast the unique mission he had established at the Museum of Modern Art, that of passionately promoting the art of architecture. In the decades from the 1970s until his death in 2005, what counted most were his intelligence, his curiosity, his fearlessness, his liveliness, his deep and broad knowledge, his sharp wit, his resistance to piousness, his critical judgment, and his sense of *réel politique* in the recognition and cultivation of emerging architectural genius that has advanced and elevated the field.

fig. 30 Helmut Jacoby rendering for Kline Biology Tower, Yale University, New Haven, Connecticut

fig. 31 Sculpture Gallery, Philip Johnson estate, New Canaan, Connecticut, 1970, interior

Notes

1. Philip Johnson, "What Makes Me Tick," lecture presented at Columbia University, September 24, 1975, published in Johnson, *Philip Johnson: Writings,* foreword by Vincent Scully, introduction by Peter Eisenman, commentary by Robert A. M. Stern (New York: Oxford University Press, 1979), 260–265.

2. See Philip Johnson, "House at New Canaan, Connecticut," *Architectural Review* 108, no. 645 (September 1950): 152–159.

3. Philip Johnson, "The Seven Crutches of Modern Architecture," informal talk presented at Harvard University, December 7, 1954, published in Johnson, *Writings,* 140.

4. Johnson, "Seven Crutches," 140.

5. Quoted in Hilary Lewis and John O'Connor, *Philip Johnson: The Architect in His Own Words* (New York: Rizzoli, 1994), 37.

6. Quoted in Selden Rodman, *Conversations with Artists* (New York: Devin-Adair, 1957), 1: 54.

7. *Philip Johnson: Architecture, 1949–1965,* introduction by Henry-Russell Hitchcock (New York: Holt, Rinehart and Winston, 1966), 11. William J. Jordy considered the Boissonnas House to be one of the "most significant ventures in movement in Johnson's recent work," manifesting the "principles of Japanese domestic architecture which adds up similar units in dynamic movement." Jordy placed in this same category the "complexity of plan and ceiling in the New Harmony shrine" and the "often literally moving detail of the newly opened Four Seasons Restaurant in the Seagram Building." See his essay on "The Mies-less Johnson," *Architectural Forum* 111, no. 3 (September 1959): 115.

8. Philip Johnson, "Retreat from the International Style to the Present Scene," lecture presented in Scully's survey course modern architecture, Yale University, May 9, 1958, published in Johnson, *Writings,* 89.

9. Quoted in Rodman, *Conversations with Artists,* Philip Johnson, 2: 64.

10. Johnson, "Retreat," 89.

11. Ibid. By 1956, Johnson had also completed the Leonhard House, in which the main pavilion was almost an exact transcription of Mies's 1935 sketch for a mountain house.

12. Johnson, "Retreat," 86–87.

13. Ibid., 93.

14. Ibid., 94.

15. Ibid., 95.

16. A year later, in an informal talk at the Architectural Association in London, Johnson called the Idlewild building the "bird that really could not get off the ground" (November 28, 1960, published in Johnson, *Writings,* 110). By this time he had become censorious of Saarinen and much more self-assertive. In the same talk, speaking of Saarinen's American Embassy in London, Johnson said, "I do not like it.... It is Mies–modern, but instead of using a steel H, he has taken a single shape. It is multi-repeating on pins. There is no top, bottom or corner. All my corners, tops and bottoms are becoming stronger and stronger" (Johnson, *Writings,* 111). However, in the 1958 lecture, Johnson had found Saarinen's skating rink at Yale to be "one of the most wonderful places to sit in that I have ever been in," and he admired the fact that he had "thumbed his nose ... at the tradition of structural integrity" while "most of the rest of us are still stuck thinking of structure as something to handle as a theme in design. [Saarinen] doesn't" (Johnson, "Retreat," 96).

17. Johnson, "Retreat," 95.

18. Ibid., 89–90.

19. Phyllis Lambert, "Stimmung at Seagram: Philip Johnson Counters Mies van der Rohe," in *Grey Room,* Summer 2005, pp. 39–59.

20. Peter Blake, "A Conversation with Mies," in *Four Great Makers of Modern Architecture: Gropius, Le Corbusier, Mies van der Rohe, Wright. A Verbatim Record of a Symposium Held at the School of Architecture from March to May 1961* (New York: Columbia University, 1963), 94.

21. Philip Johnson, "Whither Away—Non-Miesian Directions," lecture presented at Yale University, February 5, 1959, published in Johnson, *Writings,* 230.

22. Ibid., 228.

23. Ibid., 227.

24. Ibid., 228.

25. Ibid., 232.

26. Quoted in Lewis and O'Connor, *Philip Johnson,* 37.

27. Johnson, "Whither Away," 235.

28. Ibid., 236.

29. Ibid.

30. Ibid., 234.

31. Ibid.

32. Ibid., 232.

33. Ibid., 237.

34. Ibid.

35. Ibid., 238.

36. Ibid.

37. Ibid., 239.

38. Ibid., 238.

39. Philip Johnson, "Whence and Whither: The Processional Element in Architecture," *Perspecta* 9/10 (1965): 168.

40. Ibid., 171.

41. Ibid., 172.

42. Ibid.

43. John Peter, "Conversations Regarding the Future of Architecture," excerpts from tape-recorded talks with Ernest Kump, Gordon Bunshaft, Eero Saarinen, Philip Johnson, Mies van der Rohe, Walter Gropius, and Richard J. Neutra (Louisville, Ky.: Reynolds Metals, 1956), sound recording. A varying description was given by Philip Johnson in "100 Years, Frank Lloyd Wright and Us," talk presented at the Washington State Chapter of the American Institute of Architects, Seattle, March 1957, published in Johnson, *Writings,* 197–198.

44. Johnson, "What Makes Me Tick," 260–265.

45. Ibid., 264.

46. Ibid., 263.

47. Ibid., 262.

48. Ibid., 263.

49. Ibid.

50. Ibid., 265.

51. Johnson, stated in "Whither Away," 227, and in almost all subsequent texts.

52. Cf. Henry-Russell Hitchcock's introduction to *Philip Johnson: Architecture, 1949–1965,* and the open letter to Johnson that Robin Middleton wrote in lieu of a review of the same book, published in *Architectural Design* 37 (March 1967): 107.

53. Johnson, "Where Are We At?" in *Architectural Review* 127 (September 1960): 173–175, published in Johnson, *Writings,* 103. The role of Johnson's partners cannot be discussed here, yet it is remarkable that Richard Foster, formerly Johnson's student, to whom he dedicated *Philip Johnson: Architecture, 1949–1965,* was his partner in the 1960s, while John Burgee, with ten years of experience with large-scale projects at Naess & Murphy and C. F. Murphy in Chicago, joined Johnson in 1968 and was his partner until 1991.

54. Judith Dupré, *Skyscrapers* (New York: Black Dog and Leventhal, 1996), 8.

Reaction Design

Mark Wigley

There are only a few basic things to know about Philip Johnson. Number one—he walked fast. He was always on the move, eager, restless, impatient. It is not just that he hated stasis. All regular speeds of movement were his natural enemy. As he got older he seemed to move more quickly because his speed seemed more and more unreasonable, unnatural—inhuman, even. The guy really moved. And for him, walking was the very meaning of architecture. The fast walk was a very serious matter. It already defined a different approach to architecture.

Number two—he had very good suits. Cut close to the body yet presenting their own clearly defined geometric structure. Very crisp suits. Or, rather, a single crisp silhouette, since the suit was always more or less the same through the years. I imagine that only one tailor made them, and he specialized in holding that effect of a quasi-aristocratic distance from the movements of fashion. And the purpose of a suit is exactly that, to hold the line, absorbing all the complex irregularities and movements of the body. The best suits, as Johnson's surely were, have their own complex and resilient structure, such that it is the suit itself that relaxes in the face of change, and it is the relaxing of the suit that relieves the person wearing it of any responsibility to either stiffen or soften. It is the suit that does the walking and the talking. In the case of Johnson, this seemingly unchanging, strong yet soft, self-supporting structure holds up a highly animated face. Johnson's forever talking head dances around on top of the crisp suit, or rather the stable suit holds up an ever-moving sphere, which in turn holds up the all-important glasses. The fast-moving figure is basically a highly mobile pair of trademark glasses. These two thick black circles are not just the trademark of Johnson. Their polemical echo of the glasses of the most influential architect of the century establishes the trademark of the very figure of the architect. When designing the glasses for Cartier to produce in 1934 Johnson was already aiming to become indistinguishable from the trademark. So it is the trademark of the architect that moves at great horizontal speed through the world, authenticating every word launched out of the opening just below the lenses as architectural, while tireless legs keep striding purposively on to find a new target.

In the years before the glasses, the younger Johnson wore softer, lighter suits, particularly when traveling in Europe to prepare the International Style exhibition, as befits the eager tourist leaving behind the hard-edged business outfits and manners of New York. But they quickly give way to the single suit as Johnson mastered the art of constantly traveling as the way of life even when at home. After the completion of the Glass House, there were two distinct looks. There was the metropolitan suit, to which his body was just an accessory to keep the suit and glasses in the correct relationship, and the close-fitting country shirt, typically worn with great ease in New Canaan, especially in front of people who were dressed formally, as people would often do in treating the Glass House as a pilgrimage site. Johnson would happily flaunt informality in the country just as he flaunted his formality in the city—as if the house itself had taken over the role of the all-important suit in representing him and liberating his body.

So here you have the suit, the single mobile suit holding up the talking head, which you see in countless images that don't really need to be seen because they are so iconic. More precisely, it is a single image that gets steadily perfected. As Philip got older, the suit remained the same but his neck got increasingly narrower, so it seemed as if the head lifted higher and higher, and almost seemed to spin around as it became more spherical. In the photos from the last years, his face became more and more a cartoon, the diagram of a face. The face became a caricature of itself. The glasses seemed to get bigger and bigger. It is not that his head was getting smaller or that the glasses were getting bigger. Rather, layers of detail were steadily leaving the face. From the moment the glasses arrived, details started to fall away. The two black circles literally took over the face. The hair was discarded very early. Lacking geometry, it was irrelevant to the system. There was soon an edited version of Philip Johnson that could more efficiently do his trademark work.

So there are these two important things to remember about Philip Johnson: he walked very fast and he had good suits. If you put the two together, you get a lean figure moving quickly forward—no curves, yet streamlined. All extraneous details edited out to reduce drag. A kind of streamlined box with a sphere on top with two black circles hovering over an ever-operational mouth. So really a set of glasses and a mouth in the end, like a cartoon where the artist discards all of the other details just to leave the eyes and the mouth along with a single remaining hint of the outline of the face. As the figure relentlessly moves, the mouth launches a continuous staccato commentary on what the exaggerated eyes keep taking in, and soon the description of what is seen and what should be seen become one; descriptions become prescriptions.

If you take this image of a man walking very fast in a sharp suit, a man who is a suit with glasses, a suit that walks and talks fast, and if you believe that what it is to be modern is to be on the move, to move forward, to embrace the horizon, then Philip Johnson is the very image of the modern. In other words, this personal performance, this kind of mobile drapery over a lean body with the exaggerated efficiency of the clothing, face, and mouth, makes it seamless for him to promote the modern at the museum of the modern. Self-promotion becomes one with the promotion of a movement. Johnson deploys personal speed as an advertisement of modernity.

So it is easy, then, to see his subsequent embrace of a seemingly more decorative postmodern architecture as a backward move—moving as quickly as usual, but in the opposite direction, accumulating the kind of details on his buildings that he has so systematically removed from his body. A retrograde move for devotees of the modern but modern in his own mind precisely by reacting against his own definition of the modern, remaining modern by moving on, catching up with the latest thing, even if that thing had once been left behind. Not by chance, in turning away from the modern outside the museum of the modern, Johnson regained the appearance of power. Any sense that some sort of crime was being committed in falling from the purity and efficiency of modernity was at once deepened by, and deepened, the myth of control. Despite the clean-cut and resilient silhouette, the figure was porous. Johnson's power was the power to absorb. It was more reactive than proactive. In fact, he depended on his harshest critics, and even on the lurking thought that his embrace of superficial ornament, seen as a crime through the usual regrettably superficial reading of Loos, might intimate deeper personal complications of norms.

Having watched the figure seamlessly move from modern to postmodern, it was not a surprise to finally see him reacting against the reactions in the late 1980s, and it was precisely in this moment, as he returned to the Museum of Modern Art for the last time, that I got to know him while curating an exhibition of calculated confusions of structure and ornament by a small emergent gang of designers. The singular and obvious mission was to move beyond the postmodern in its countless guises, returning to the aesthetics and institutions of the modern but inserting into the modern itself an internally tormented modernity, a gently tortured purism in the hope of unlocking a wider unpredictable discourse.

To figure out what this move meant, and what it meant for me, and what it might have meant for Philip, I think you need to know one more basic fact about him. There are only these three key facts. One, the walking speed. Two, the suits. And three, the sensitivity. He was very sensitive—in every sense. First, in being able to quickly detect things, like a barometer able to pick up almost anything in the air at the very moment it starts to arrive, responding to that which is arriving even before it has fully arrived. But also sensitive in the sense of being fragile, vulnerable. A man with a history of breakdowns, literal and metaphorical, familiar with both anguish and delight. An architect who weeps, in both pain and pleasure. How often do we talk about architects who cry? What would that mean? The traditional figure of the architect never even smiles. We talk about emotions, but it would be bad for us to actually have them. Yet the highly edited, smooth face of Johnson, this refined modern facade, leaks from the inside out. Since good architecture usually leaks, perhaps we need to encourage the idea of sensitivity in an architect. But Johnson is also sensitive in the sense of being touchy, reacting immediately. These sensitivities are of course interrelated. Philip Johnson is a sensitive system: detecting things, absorbing them, analyzing them, and reacting to them. Not so much moving through the world as taking it in and being propelled forward by the act of digestion itself.

Now, combining these three points, we have the singular image of Johnson as a resilient streamlined figure, a walking, talking suit, endlessly moving forward, being imperceptibly affected by everything around, and the reaction being part of the movement, even its very engine—a resilience driven by vulnerability, then. Not so much walking purposely as on the run. In moving so quickly he stays just out of reach, even within his sentences. Each phrase moves briskly on. No punctuation in the middle to slow things down as it races impatiently toward the point. Always quick and always a point. In fact, Johnson was all points, his default setting being that of the manifesto in even the most casual conversation. Observations were launched as provocations, all descriptions as formulas. He continuously reacted to the work of others and polemically refused originality, such that his best designs are treated as surprising exceptions, aberrations even. He was a thoroughly flawed individual who was able, presumably through sheer quantity of commissions, to generate embarrassingly good work as an exception to his otherwise systematically reactive character. An architect who designs by reactions, only by reactions, seems to be practicing a lesser form of our craft, merely modifying the work of others rather than generating new ideas, propelled forward only by reactions and at a speed born of reactivity. That is at the heart of the standard accusation: that Philip Johnson moved too quickly from model to model, that he was the very definition of derivative, a word that can be delivered only as a slur. And this second-hand work was associated with political negligence, with an insatiable hunger for power, so aesthetic crime and political crime are treated as one. The architect moves quickly to escape a succession of crime scenes, but as the witnesses, we are quick too, quick to judge, seeing the practice of reaction sliding into the reactionary and then further into the unforgivable. It is so very easy to criticize Johnson. He is such a convenient target, allowing such a wide range of people to credit themselves with moral, political, aesthetic, and technical superiority. We should be so grateful for somebody who offers such easy comfort, elevating all of us in our own eyes.

But the standard scenario, the Johnson we knew, the architect as criminal, is far too reassuring. Johnson, with his culture of reactivity, was not the clear-cut enemy. In fact, the whole association of modernity with forward movement, of modern and progressive, is suspect. After all, wasn't the whole official defense of "Modern Architecture," in the hands of the most polemical architects and their key writers, that the "new" architecture of the twenties was simply the moment that architecture finally caught up to the steel and glass innovations of the mid-nineteenth century? This was exactly the argument made by its leading propagandists. The fact that the architecture was seventy years late was not an embarrassment, apparently. Quite the opposite. The time was finally right, as if there was a calibration of the appropriate distance between architecture and contemporary technology. Indeed, the promoters of so-called modern architecture aligned it with the openness of steel-and-glass construction, but the practice of art nouveau that was being polemically rejected actually deployed that quality more radically. The new architecture was as much a resistance to the no-longer-new technology as it was a product of it. No longer nervous, the architect was finally in a position to domesticate the existing technological environment. The title of the most influential manifesto was *Toward an Architecture*, not *Toward a New Architecture*. To be modern is simply to move toward what has already happened, to move quickly but to arrive just after the train has left. In other words, modern is a reaction. It is not the contemporary but a reaction to the past in order to be behind again, but by the right amount. As the speed of technological change increases, architecture lags behind in ever smaller delays. Perhaps architecture moves relative to the speed of change rather than toward specific developments. But the mission is clearly never to catch up, just to remain visible in the rear-view mirror.

In this sense, modern is neither progressive nor regressive but is the very attempt to assume a kind of neutrality in time—modern not as the impulse toward the future, not even as the present, but as the recent past. It is an image of the past, a kind of edited version of recent history. Modern as a historical statement then, a writing of history. The architect edits the past in order to launch a particular image toward the future, as if through a kind of slide projector, where something of what is behind now appears in front. What it is to be modern is to edit. It is a defensive reaction. Most of architecture may be a form of reaction in this sense. Architecture might even be a kind of allergic reaction, not a creative invention by designer but a type of reaction within in the organism of the city. Architecture might just be the name for a kind of defensive response that does not even require the figure of the unwitting architect, an allergic reaction that develops within the biology of cities themselves, a kind of hardening of particular shapes and forms of organization into a limited set of lasting images. What if architecture is not invented or even constructed as such but is actually a form of pruning, a form of editing? What if buildings are just editing machines? If you listen to our descriptions of buildings, that seems to be exactly how we imagine them to operate. Designers steadily limit a series of options to leave only a series of calibrated sequences. A window, to state the obvious, is not the opening up of a view, but the removal of countless possible views. What if the theory of modern architecture in all of its sophistication, and the sophisticated scholarship and artistry of its propagandists, was nothing more than a particular theory of editing?

If so, Johnson would emerge as an exemplary figure in his quick-step reactive mode. Even his laugh, and he laughed a lot, was edited in order to be editing in its effect. It was a very quick laugh. The mouth would open extremely wide and a kind of gleeful cackle would emerge from somewhere within, rising rapidly, and suddenly cut off when it reached high altitude, the stopping being more dramatic than the start. The stop being the point. The laugh came from the brain rather than the body. It was a comment, part of the conversation, a form of talking. Like everything else, it had to be cut to do its work. Likewise with the design work. All of the forms were edited down into a clear pattern, a kind of formula, and some kind of drapery was added, and then even the drapery was edited. The didactic geometries were always softened by some kind of elemental drapery, especially in his most Miesian work. And it was that softening that was actually the key to the work. Johnson was good with geometry and drapery. Drapery seduces and comforts, but it also hides, especially hides. Yet the exact nature of the drapery that defined Johnson and his work tends to be overlooked. For all the talk of dark secrets, there is not enough reflection on the veils. This allows a series of stories to be told about him, almost all of which he initiated and which are almost impossible to resist repeating, endlessly replaying his image with minor variations in a kind of Warholian grid.

Clearly, Philip Johnson is not gone. The godfather of American architecture keeps producing the same excesses of praise and criticism that he attracted his whole life. It was his special gift always to be able to elicit this intense yet ambivalent reaction. From the moment in January 1931 that he was asked to direct an exhibition at the Museum of Modern Art at the precocious age of twenty-four until his death not quite four months after he retired at the daunting age of ninety-eight, Johnson rattled institutions and ideas. To his credit, he is unlikely to be treated kindly in official memory.

There was always as much to criticize as to praise in Johnson, yet most of the inflated reaction says more about the people reacting than about him. One of his key roles was to act as a highly visible screen onto which people could project their fantasies—a role he seemed to enjoy, since it paradoxically granted him a kind of privacy. The most public figure in architecture—who literally lived in a glass house

and was endlessly explicit about his ambitions, tactics, and limits (and eventually his sexuality)—was finally elusive. His smooth speed of mind and word only served to create a seamless shelter for ever-present vulnerabilities.

From the beginning Johnson constructed himself as a public personality, a media figure, with a combination of boyish enthusiasm, relentless intelligence, and strategic brilliance. Every act was calculated for effect, and before long he was an institution in his own right. Immediately after curating the pivotal 1932 *Modern Architecture: International Exhibition* at MoMA in partnership with the historian Henry-Russell Hitchcock, he was appointed the inaugural director of the museum's department of architecture. The relationship between architecture, its collection, and its exhibition immediately changed with the innovative launch of the first such department in the world. Architecture could now be positioned and promoted differently. Johnson quickly turned the department into the arbiter of quality, operating like the editor of a polemical magazine: The museum would serve as an activist medium rather than as a mausoleum. Exhibitions were launched like salvos in a battle. Circles of practitioners, critics, collectors, clients, and a newly cultivated public hovered around this new scene created by the rich, young aesthete from

fig. 1 Andy Warhol, *Gold Marilyn,* 1962. Silkscreen ink on synthetic polymer paint on canvas, 83 1/4 x 57 in. (211.5 x 144.8 cm). Museum of Modern Art, New York, Gift of Philip Johnson

Cleveland who had no formal training in the field he now presided over.

Johnson is unthinkable outside of this role at MoMA, and the museum is unthinkable outside of him. He curated so many of the pivotal exhibitions, designed some of its most admired spaces, and was the donor of thousands of key paintings, sculptures, prints, drawings, posters, and books. Johnson was usually ahead of the museum, and he remains so. His influence is so great that we still need him to enter the building: The image on our membership card is a detail of Andy Warhol's *Gold Marilyn Monroe* of 1962, donated by Johnson the same year (fig. 1). The gift woke up the museum to the contemporary American art it had been ignoring, and in 1969–72 Johnson's massive donation of pop and minimalist works established the core of the museum's holdings in the area, with pivotal works like Rauschenberg's combine-painting *First Landing Jump* of 1961. Having started with a Paul Klee painting he bought from the artist when visiting the Bauhaus in 1929, Johnson kept gathering momentum as a collector, particularly with the collaboration of David Whitney, his life partner from 1960 on. If one were to reassemble all the gifts to MoMA along-side all the remarkable works that will now remain on display at his house in New Canaan, Johnson's collection would rival any in the world and attest to his knack for presciently identifying key figures, works, and tendencies.

In the architecture world Johnson's keen feel for the pulse is equally admired, but the reviews of his own work are mixed. The designs are usually seen as derivative, which is how he described them himself, repeatedly flaunting his overarching principle of getting the job. He had the same influence on the interpretation of his own work as on that of others. There is a surplus of unimpressive works, yet Johnson was a much better architect than his insistent confession of fickleness and superficiality would suggest. We have to greatly admire any designer who leaves us the Glass House (1949), one of the most celebrated buildings of the last century; Pennzoil Place (1976), which redefined skyscraper design; the subtle brilliance of the Four Seasons Restaurant interior (1958); and the pre-Columbian galleries at Dumbarton Oaks (1963), with their nuanced play of interlocking geometry and light (fig. 2). Many other exemplary works could be singled out, but Johnson's self-deprecating wit once again acts as a shelter, a preemptive defense against critics. His infamous chasing of successive styles overlooks the consistent qualities in the work, the steady pursuit of sensuous efficiency and an expertise with the calibrated processional experience of space. The tension between the minimalist empty glass box of the house in New Canaan and the interior decor of its antithetical closed Guest House is emblematic of the way his work continually absorbs the dual influences of Mies van der Rohe's minimalism and the simplified yet rich classicism of the late eighteenth-century English architect John Soane. The result is a paring down to basic elements, then a seductive elaboration within the surface of the reduced elements. The work was always minimalist in the sense of capturing and communicating a diagrammatic idea, even if that idea involves a complexity of geometry or decoration.

Johnson cultivated the very same quality in conversation and polemic. He was an astute reader of situations, able to cannily reduce everything to a charming and efficient sentence. In the late 1980s he invited me to put together an exhibition at MoMA, and I will never forget his clarity and humor, the boundless enthusiasm and laughter of a child. It was as hard to keep pace with him walking briskly along 53rd Street as it was to keep up in a conversation.

He was fascinated by the latest innovations yet easily encouraged to reminisce. He was a walking archive, with vague memories of the recent past and precise memories of the 1920s. Everything was driven by an impatient desire to cut through to the key issues or sensations. At the time he was propelled by an active disinterest in the discourse around postmodernism that had captivated him for some years. The sense that the discourse was finally moving again was his only elixir. Johnson was yet again a catalyst, inserting himself at the center of the scene to help push things along, embracing the latest wave of experimentation while using the implied promise that he would equally easily embrace a subsequent move as a thin but effective defensive layer.

The exhibition was about work that had already happened over the previous decade, strong work that needed to be acknowledged in the museum of record, which is what MoMA had long become, in complete opposition to its more provocative role in 1932. It was an exhibition of recent history, even if the point was to clear space for new but undefined experiments. It focused on a small group of highly experimental architects in the act of crossing the threshold from paper threats to built threats, crediting objects with considerable but uncertain force. All of them would go on to produce remarkable and diverse buildings. But more important, the intention was to open up a new way of talking about buildings, the seemingly simple objects that architects love with all the care we are supposed to show toward people but rarely do. Johnson clearly relished the thought that the future could be made less clear, that an object could so easily become as contradictory, twisted, and uncertain as a person.

Johnson was passionately in love with his field and in so many ways better than his reputation, the reputation he so carefully constructed. Yet we cannot forget his appalling affair with fascism that overlapped and interrupted his early years at MoMA. Johnson had more than just a personal sympathy with the far right. He attempted to found a political party, attended one of Hitler's rallies, enthusiastically followed the invaders into Poland, and wrote in support of the Reich. He was not just seduced by authoritarian power but tried to be active in its consolidation. In a strange way, this well-known episode has ultimately been treated as less offensive than his self-described weakness for style, which again reveals more about the field than it does about him. Architects rarely see themselves as ethical role models. The discipline feigns blindness to its complicity, and perhaps it has to in order to operate at all. But the nuanced work has yet to be done to identify the exact relationship between Johnson's actions and his work. Rather than scandal or analysis, all we have ended up with so far is an implicit association between the dictatorial power that attracted him and his own influence on the discipline as the "godfather," along with his infinite comfort consorting with the plutocracy. One crime scene is quietly associated with another.

This image of power is inseparable from Johnson's generosity. He was famously supportive of the generations before and after him, which is almost unheard of in the field. He helped connect architects to clients; underwrote organizations, research, and publications; and even gave direct financial aid to some designers. He collected architects like paintings and photographed his collection. A series of images of groups of the chosen designers after meetings behind closed doors magnified the image of power, even though he was more propped up by his protégés (Peter Eisenman, Frank Gehry, etc.) than he was responsible for their success. Johnson's actual role was to be the symbol of power that allowed the whole system to operate, even if he had very little ability to control anything. This is a role unlikely to be filled again. It defines a time, now passed, when a single figure, a single museum department, a single institution, or a single book could wield so much influence. A figure like Philip Johnson is as redundant in today's dense culture of overlapping global networks as it was crucial in the last century.

Johnson was in the unique position of being able to confuse the roles of patron, designer, and curator. The immediate steep rise in the value of the aluminum stock that had he received from his parents at the age of eighteen allowed him to experiment. He hired Mies and Lilly Reich to do the interior of his apartment in Manhattan in 1930. Ten years later, after setting up many commissions for others and trying to escape his political blundering, he finally decided to be trained as an architect and was immediately able to act as his own patron, building a house for himself in Cambridge during his time at Harvard. The sophisticated design echoed the courtyard house schemes of Mies and was successfully presented as his senior thesis project in yet another confusion of roles. Like the Manhattan apartment before and the Mies-inspired Glass House later, the domestic space was used as a key site for the endless salons that incubated him as a public figure. He wore each house like an ostentatiously crisp, tailored suit to be admired more for the way it had been chosen from a particular line than for its actual design.

This pleasure in the supposedly subordinate variations in a line reveals a deeper affinity with Warhol than their friendship and collaborations might indicate. The two were great collectors because they were great shoppers. While Warhol turned commercial objects and personalities into icons, Johnson treated the world of design objects as something to absorb, analyze, and tweak in subtle variations. Other architects were his readymades. Yet he was strangely reluctant to copy himself, allowing some lines to develop in his work for a short time but avoiding Warhol's hypnotic seriality in order to polemically represent nothing in particular other than tasteful choice and change itself. What didn't change was him—a remarkably resilient figure whose distinctive silhouette became clearer with each shift of enthusiasm.

In the end, all talk of Philip Johnson is brought to a stop by the remarkable Glass House, a landscape project that goes far beyond its inspiration in a house by Mies as a manifesto of reaction design. Its beauty lies in marshalling so many different elements to construct the effect of emptiness. Its brilliance transcends the personal soap opera of its architect or any discussion of the originality of copies in our culture. We are left with a design that finally shuts up everyone, including its restless designer.

Yet the relentless gleam of the great glass incubator in New Canaan that kept Johnson going as he became more childlike with each decade might finally be too much of a distraction. What, for example, if the rarely discussed Dumbarton Oaks extension of 1963 is the key work? What if this reaction to an existing building is the decisive one? Looking at the plan, it seems too simple to be celebrated, too obvious, but if we are judging a kind of minimalism, the word simple, even simplistic, is no longer negative. Looking at the interior effect, it seems not simple enough, too rich to be celebrated, even too much gold. But are we so sure? Perhaps the reluctance of the field to discuss such a project, let alone celebrate it, has to do with our reluctance to leave behind the very narrowly defined image of modern architecture that Johnson and Hitchcock edited down for us. That is to say, our negative judgment is driven by a strong desire to keep going backward. But what if we allowed ourselves to move forward, just for a moment, and appreciate such a work? Our fear of this work, and I believe it is a fear, is a fear of seduction by that which lies just outside the rules, outside the law. The gallery is some kind of frozen yet sensuous space, an erotic refrigerator. One can feel the abstract coolness but also the endless refinement of the surfaces negotiating the complex play between inside and outside. It is a sophisticated variation of the Glass House, a reaction to people's reaction to the reaction to Mies, and it helps us to see how the seemingly antithetical figures of Mies and Soane could have been linked, and were in fact always linked before Johnson made the connection, with their polemical confusion of drapery and stone that goes back to the very heart of the classical tradition. Our fear of seduction by this project might therefore be an anxiety about the pleasures felt by the so-called heroic figures of modern architecture, in particular Mies van der Rohe, whose ostensibly minimal interiors are actually lush, colorful, and refined—intensely rich in fact. From the intricately veined marble planes of the Barcelona Pavilion onward, the minimalist effect is paradoxically linked to the sense that the richness of the surfaces is not just intense but excessive, and vice versa. The same nervous defense that systematically effaces Lilly Reich's critical role in the design of those spaces effaces the unique quality of the spaces. In embracing the sensuous refrigerator, Johnson brings out a secret. The master of the reactive simplification ultimately complicates things for us.

All this just to say that when the most prominent person in our discipline is devoted to restless change and the pleasures of the surface, and is an actual criminal, then it is too easy to keep everything in its place. Johnson as criminal is an all too convenient prop for our aesthetic morality. The pleasure of ornament remains a crime, despite the manifest and multiple sensuous pleasures enjoyed and fostered by the role models of the modern. Pleasure itself remains an enemy, along with a whole range of emotions. Johnson is a reactionary figure to be sure, but our own reaction to him is perhaps even more reactionary. The privileging of his aesthetic crime over the political by our field is damning—to such an extent that the nuclear reactor in Israel could win the AIA Honor Award a couple of years before Dumbarton Oaks without debate. Johnson now drapes a reactor core itself, and so much more besides. But our avoidance of the drapery and the theatrics of atonement again say so much more about us than about him. Johnson is a mirror to our field, providing an image of ourselves that is disquieting but accurate, an image of architecture as a form of reaction, even as a reactionary art. This is not offered as a defense of Johnson. On the contrary, it is an accusation, a self-accusation. To resist the nervously edited narratives of the past, letting the unspoken finally come out, we need to read Philip Johnson more thoroughly, and we need to be able to enjoy the best of the work in the designing, curating, writing, and talking. We may wish to be freed from his carefully edited scripts but also feel unable to do it. There is clearly a lot of work to be done, but also a lot of pleasure to be had. If discussions of Johnson and his legacy keep bringing us up short, suspending us on a threshold we dare not cross, this at once ethical and aesthetic hesitation may mark the beginning of a rethinking and even a wholly different kind of discussion about our discipline. If so, we will owe one last debt to the figure who is, and hopefully will remain, disquieting.

fig. 2 Dumbarton Oaks Museum, Washington, D.C.

THEORY.

Philip Johnson:
Romanticism and Disintegration

Peter Eisenman

The beginning and the end of American modernism as seen through the lens of Philip Courtelyou Johnson's two bookend exhibitions at the Museum of Modern Art

In the summer of 1962, I was on my second excursion through Europe with Colin Rowe, who at the time was between the end of his teaching obligations at the University of Cambridge and what was to be his prolonged stay at 106 Cayuga Heights Road in Ithaca, New York.[1] We were, as I remember, on our way from Carcassonne to Toulon, where the parents of a student/friend of ours had a summer villa. We stopped on the way at Le Pradet, where Le Corbusier did a house for Madame de Mandrot. We learned from its then owner, a French farmer, who invited us in, that the Germans had used the house as a hayloft during the occupation. As we looked around the modest furnishings of the house's present occupants, I spied on a table what I knew to be a rare first-edition hardback copy of the book by Henry-Russell Hitchcock and Philip Johnson, *The International Style: Architecture Since 1922* (fig. 1). Although I had seen photographs of the dust jacket and contents (hence my recognition of the book), I had never seen one in its original state, neither in the flesh nor in any library. I should say that, by 1962, I was well into my insatiable passion for collecting books and periodicals on architecture from the 1920s and 1930s. You must then imagine the fever pitch of my desire to possess this book. I was also suddenly reminded of the Rowe dictum, that if a book has not been taken out of a library in ten years, it was somehow permissible to steal it. Rowe's caveat had referred specifically to the book by one of the authors in question, Hitchcock's 1929 book *Modern Architecture: Romanticism and Reintegration* (fig. 2). I had seen this book on Rowe's own library shelves with its institutional dark blue buckram rebinding and its RIBA imprimatur on the inside front cover with several dates stamped on a small loose-leaf page certifying that, according to Rowe, after ten years its rightful owner might no longer note its absence. Now here, in front of me, was a trophy that the unknowing owner proudly had on display because his very own house was pictured in its contents. Was there any way I could connive to remove this book as Colin had done some years earlier with another of Hitchcock's tomes? After some futile conversation with the owner in my minimal French, I gave up my quest and we moved on empty handed. Years later, Rowe would trade his Hitchcock book with me, and it remains in my possession, as well as the two versions of the Museum of Modern Art catalogue for the exhibition *Modern Architecture: International Exhibition* and the *International Style* book, also a first edition but acquired elsewhere.

This prolegomena introduces the two books that served as my introduction to Philip Cortelyou Johnson. A look at the shift in argumentation and conception in these two books is significant in order to comprehend a strategy that characterizes Johnson's career, bracketed by the 1932 *Modern Architecture: International Exhibition* and the *Deconstructivist Architecture* exhibition of 1988 (figs. 3, 4). The title of this essay, "Romanticism and Disintegration," attempts to weave another narrative between the two exhibitions by highlighting a common subtext of both exhibitions and their subsequent publications. In adapting the title of Hitchcock's *Modern Architecture: Romanticism and Reintegration,* and substituting one of its terms with its antonym, disintegration, this essay questions the tidy assimilation of the formal and the aesthetic, which will be central to Johnson's covert strategy in the two exhibitions.

The difference between Hitchcock's *Modern Architecture* and Hitchcock and Johnson's *International Style* is apparent from their titles. Despite Hitchcock's authorship of both, and the short three-year gap in their publication dates, the question that must be asked is: Why would a conservative pedant like Hitchcock, even by Alfred Barr's critical standards, change within three years what was an uncapitalized "international style" to a capitalized International Style?

First, it is known from Terence Riley's excellent chronology that Hitchcock and Johnson were working on parallel publications before there was any idea of an exhibition.[2] While Hitchcock attributes the term International Style to Alfred Barr, another explanation is also possible. It is clear that Hitchcock was the primary contributor to both texts, and, as Riley would have us believe, part of the change in what was initially conceived of as a slight updating with better images of the 1929 book was due to Alfred Barr's not so subtle critique of that book. Hitchcock's ensuing writings reveal him to be a conservative pedant, as I was to find out living a floor above him in Cambridge in the fall of 1962 and spending several besotted evenings in his presence, listening to him rattle off fact after fact of an obscure

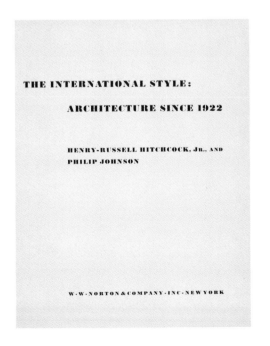

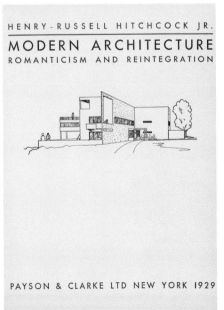

fig. 1 Henry-Russell Hitchcock, Jr., and Philip Johnson, *The International Style: Architecture Since 1922* (1932), title page

fig. 2 Henry-Russell Hitchcock, *Modern Architecture: Romanticism and Reintegration* (1929), title page

fig. 3 Exhibition catalogue for *Modern Architecture: International Exhibition,* Museum of Modern Art, New York, February 9, 1932–March 23, 1932

history of architecture as he filched bottle after bottle of my prized 1947 vintage Aloxe Corton. Hitchcock, in my opinion, was incapable of change.

As Jeffrey Kipnis related to me about a discussion he had with Johnson, it was Johnson, not Hitchcock, who brought about the radical change in approach, and this change in turn raises certain questions—such as Kant versus Nietzsche, aesthetic versus formal—that will become crucial in understanding Johnson's two exhibitions and that characterized his entire attitude toward architecture. Johnson was a patrician esthete who, despite his privileged background, became conversant with many of the important issues of his day. While Johnson had read Nietzsche in German, he was in fact more Kantian in his cultural pursuits, especially in his appropriation of the idea of art as a critical form and thereby freed from the forces of common opinion. Yet it is not only Johnson's reinterpretation of Kant's defense of an autonomous capacity for avant-garde art that accounts for the profound shifts implied in the transformation of what was called Modern Architecture in 1929 into the International Style by 1932. And it was no mere accident or whim that a new, seemingly innocuous yet potent title, *International Style,* was coined for the 1932 book and exhibition.[3] It was Johnson who packaged with almost cunning unconsciousness what was initially to be a rewrite of the 1929 book that would appear only in German; later, as if by an afterthought, came the catalogue and exhibition. It was to introduce European modernism to what was hoped would become America's new style.

The change in the titles of the books is significant—from the 1929 *Modern Architecture* to the title of the first commercial edition of the 1932 exhibition catalogue, *Modern Architects,* to its final title, the *International Style.*[4] It is my contention here that it was Johnson and not Barr, as Riley suggests, who is in some way responsible for the word substitution, which would become pivotal in framing America's reception of largely European modernist buildings. The shift from the term modern to the seemingly equivalent term international—replete with its leftist connotations—is in fact denatured by Johnson through the simple, subtle addition of the word style. If *reintegration,* from the subtitle of Hitchcock's *Modern Architecture,* portended some psychological construct, no such implication is operative in the term style. It was probably Johnson who thought that Hitchcock's idea of reintegration, of function and form after the individual eccentricities of the nineteenth century, had too much latent ideological content. But it was not Hitchcock who changed his lifelong tendency to be a documenter to become a nascent ideologue. First, Hitchcock had no such ideological intention in his use of the term reintegration. Second, his first use of the term International Style may have occurred on page 162 of *Modern Architecture,* where Hitchcock writes, "It is enough to call the architecture of the New Pioneers the international style of Le Corbusier, Oud, and Gropius."[5] The lowercase term "international style" did not suggest anything more than something that might group the varied nationalities of the aforementioned Swiss/French, Dutch, and German architects. As Riley demonstrates, Johnson's prolific correspondence during the planning of the exhibition contributed the capitalization of International Style, and Johnson's own introduction to Riley's *Exhibition 15* reiterates his claim to have "prophesied a few of the prophecies that now seem prescient."[6]

While the polemical rhetoric of the exhibition and the book was purportedly directed toward academicism and the academy, an alternative interpretation can be proposed, which would suggest that it was not so obvious that the academy was in fact the enemy. Rather, the enemy could be said to be embodied in the political and social resonances of the term modern. For example, there are casual references to Le Corbusier as a "sociologue," a term loaded with enmity. But what is left unsaid is equally important. There is no mention of the term "modern movement" as a gathering of international architects united in their pursuit to produce affordable living environments for Europe's working class, or, where housing is discussed, there is no mention that it is *social* housing, as would be clear from the context, layout, and organization of the buildings. As Riley points out, all of the projects displayed in model form were single-family residences, whose guest and servant quarters reiterated their retreat from the concerns of a populace well into the grips of the Great Depression. Yet it was clear to all by the late 1920s that modern architecture was above all an icon of left-leaning (if not in some cases explicitly Marxist) political movements, particularly in Germany and Russia. And it would certainly not be on aesthetic grounds that the Nazis closed the Bauhaus in 1933, given the significant building commissions that had been awarded to some Bauhausler by the Nazi regime. Therefore, it did not take much insight for Lewis Mumford to write in 1932 that the "phrase 'the international style' emphasizes all the wrong things architecturally ... individualism must now be expressed through the collective enterprise." He continued: "Capitalism could favor an organic architecture only by way of escape. Communism will favor it directly by way of growth."[7] Mumford's not so subtle critique was directed at Johnson and his complacent elitism (and that of his not so elite fellow travelers). But while opposed in principle to Johnson's conception of the exhibition, he nevertheless consented to curate a section of the exhibition on housing and have his name listed as an author on the catalogue.

As Walter Benjamin was to say in "The Work of Art in the Age of Mechanical Reproduction," his famous essay of 1938, "The logical result of fascism is an aestheticizing of political life."[8] In fact, the aesthetic understood as "l'art pour l'art" has been a continuing problem for an understanding of form in architecture, so much so that it stigmatizes the important difference between the formal and the aesthetic.

Central to my argument here and below is precisely this distinction. In short, the aesthetic relies on the truth of what is seen, while the formal is nested within what *is;* the latter is autonomous from ideas as truth in perception. The aesthetic is about the facts of perception, while the formal is about what lies both under and hidden in perception: one is a physical response to visual stimuli, the other mental; the one is about shape, the other structure.

In this context it remains ironic that the subtle shift away from the political and ideological aspects of modernism, through the agency of individualism (hence the revised title of the 1932 trade publication as *Modern Architects*), style, and aesthetics, can in retrospect be understood as a political gesture by Johnson. In some sense Johnson's draining of modern architecture of its leftist politics created the very aestheticization of architecture—the very creation of architecture as simply a style—which would return in postmodernism, a style that functioned as an ideal container for its intensely capitalist agenda.

It is then not without some irony that Johnson adopts a similar strategy, which is the conflation of two terms to mean something quite other than their separate meanings, again to undermine another ideological movement in favor of an aesthetic

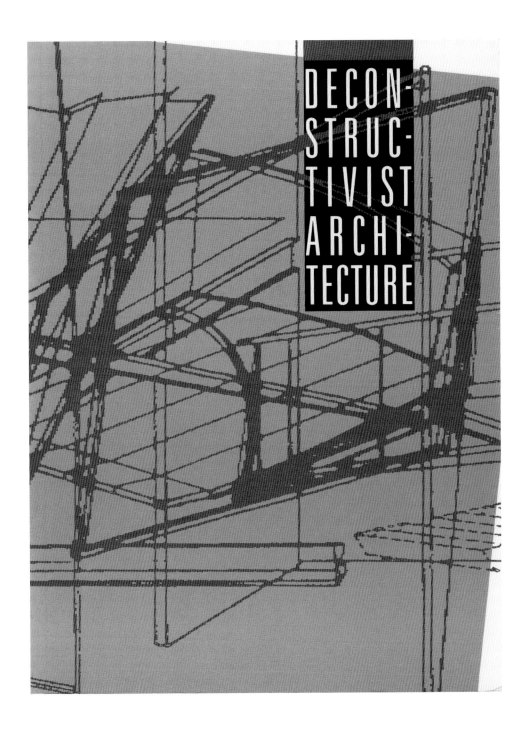

fig. 4 Exhibition catalogue for *Deconstructivist Architecture*, Museum of Modern Art, New York, June 23, 1988–August 30, 1988

one. In the winter and spring of 1987–88, two young Chicago architects, Paul Florian and Steven Wierzbowski, proposed an exhibition called *Violated Perfection* to Aaron Betsky, who was to have curated it. Betsky in turn brought the idea to the attention of Johnson.[9] The dynamism and energy of the selected architects and their work appealed to Johnson. Their cast of characters was more or less the same as those who would be included in what became Johnson's 1988 exhibition, *Deconstructivist Architecture.* While it was publicly rumored that MoMA had rejected the exhibition's title, Johnson personally mentioned to me that it was he, and not the museum, who could not abide the title *Violated Perfection*. While Johnson was determined to stage another avant-garde exhibition (little did he know, nor was it his intention, that this exhibition would signal the end of pastiche postmodernism), he was equally determined to have another curator and another title. For reasons unknown, Johnson ruled out Betsky and *Violated Perfection;* it is possible that the title was too strident or too overt in its critique of postmodernism. Johnson's search also discarded Jeffrey Kipnis as curator, as Philip told me, on aesthetic rather than theoretical grounds. Finally he hit upon a relatively unknown New Zealander, Mark Wigley, who ironically was staying for several weeks with Kipnis. Wigley had written his doctoral dissertation on Jacques Derrida and the philosophy of deconstruction.

With Johnson's now familiar and instinctive sleight of hand, the portmanteau confection *deconstructivist* was hit upon as the new title for the exhibition. It was assumed that the neologism was produced from a combination of the terms deconstruction and constructivism, as was clear not only in the title, but also by the fact that the exhibition included an introductory room on Russian constructivism. The twist, as Mark Wigley says in the catalogue, is in the "de" of deconstructivist. He says that the projects can be called deconstructivist because they draw from constructivism, yet they constitute a radical deviation from it. According to Wigley, they are not -isms because for him it was not a new style. Wigley, in an obvious reference to the 1932 exhibition, says that the projects do not simply share an aesthetic. To say that these remarks at the time seemed disingenuous is too easy. What was interesting is not what Wigley said but rather the context for Johnson's reorganizing the terms deconstruction and constructivism, with which, much like the conflation of "style" with "international" he skillfully denatured a seemingly ideologically charged theoretical construct.

Like Wigley, Johnson's introduction is transparent in this regard in explicitly disavowing the parallels between the two exhibitions, stating that deconstructivist architecture is neither a new style nor a new movement. Yet *Deconstructivist Architecture* is related directly to the formal innovations of constructivism in its diagonals and fragmentation, while the "warped" images—and architecture is expressly considered in terms of its image—are played against the "pure" images of the International Style. Deconstruction has no place in Johnson's introduction. Rather, it is the token acknowledgment of deconstruction in drawing on Wigley's dissertation that facilitated its denaturing, as did the gesture toward the "International" claims of modern architecture in the 1932 exhibition.[10] Deconstruction would, in Wigley's subsequent introduction to the exhibition catalogue, be mentioned largely in passing. Wigley suggested that the exhibition and its projects did not derive from, nor were a mere application of, the mode of contemporary philosophy known as deconstruction. He argues that deconstruction is often intentionally misunderstood as destruction, dissimilation, or demolition, as in the work of Gordon Matta-Clark, the taking apart of construction. Rather, the works selected for the *Deconstructivist Architecture* exhibition, Wigley says, owe their heritage to the formal experimentation of Russian constructivism. While Johnson would never have considered constructivism for his International Style exhibition because of its affiliations with Russia and more explicitly with communism (the only two projects from the USSR in the 1932 exhibition are tepid facsimiles of what was happening in the West), here its use to bury the term deconstruction and its contemporary critique of Western culture within another totally different ideological framework is quite ingenious. First of all, of the architects included in the exhibition, only two or three had any relation to constructivism as a background for their thinking. Second, from the supposedly formal vocabulary of constructivism, images were deftly extracted from their ideologically charged social milieu; this decontextualization remade of them purely aesthetic objects. That such denaturing, such masking of deconstruction as an ideology of the left, by virtue of its homologous relation to constructivism, can produce an aesthetic or a new style is what seems to be at stake for Johnson.

This idea of denatured—in the chemical sense of the term—theory is important in the context of Johnson's entire ideology. In *Deconstructivist Architecture,* theory could be lodged, if not hidden, within a historical framework, rather than underpinning the very conceptualization of the exhibition. The difference between the formal and the aesthetic is largely obscured, and in this context, because that difference is a theoretical one, Johnson would not allow its nuances to become conscious. It is reasonable here to speculate on Johnson's preternatural dislike of theory. He disliked theory and theorizing probably because he much preferred history and historicizing. This gave him what amounted to a free pass, that is, an aesthetic free play. It can be well documented that Johnson's bias toward the aesthetic is also a bias toward history as opposed to theory. His impatience with theory was certainly colored, and perhaps misguided, by the sentiment that theory is an instrument of the left. Nevertheless, a constant debate over the role of theory was part of our ongoing lunchtime conversations. To say he was not aware of these differences between history and theory, or for that matter between the formal and the aesthetic, would be not to acknowledge Johnson's capacity for humorous and casual dissimulation.

Now, after his death, it is important for me to say the following things that perhaps I could not have said to Philip when he was alive. First, Johnson's bias toward the aesthetic in the context of the two exhibitions not only denies ideology but becomes ideological in itself. Second, his attempts to drain the political implications of modern architecture and to denature both deconstruction and Russian constructivism in favor of an aesthetic removed from its cultural context were political gestures. Such a strategy, implemented twice, casts doubt on the official lines of explanation. For me, the idea of disciplinary integrity always involves some condition of both autonomy and the formal. These two conditions must be considered outside of any label such as art for art's sake in that they provide charged edges by which a discipline engages with culture as a whole. The fact that these concepts are often conflated with the aesthetic not only is Johnson's strategy but also reflects in part on our society's own biases in favor of the visual.

It is in this sense that the irony of my use of the term denature is critical. If ingested, denatured alcohol can do two things. It first may blind; this could be metaphorically blinding one to our cultural hegemony of the visual, which is the medium for the rapid reception of a style. At the same time, denatured alcohol is the same poison that may keep one from drinking alcohol in the first place, suggesting here that denatured theory in some sense prevents that very same consumption of theory.

The *International Style* and *Deconstructivist Architecture* titles can be seen both to characterize Johnson personally and to reflect his entrepreneurial talent for breaking taboos. As Glenn Lowry, MoMA's director, said to me in conversation, "The museum can no longer do what *you* want it to do."[11] Founded as an avant-garde institution, it is perhaps now primarily the site of what the avant-garde has become in today's culture: blue chip and old master fodder for blockbuster exhibitions. Whatever Johnson's ambivalence to theory, commercialism was certainly never the motivation that animated his sponsorship of these two exhibitions. They were, in the most generous and perhaps obvious sense, of *his* era. Spanning from modernism to postmodernism in a more nuanced and personal sense, these exhibitions represented Johnson's unrequited battle with the status quo. His ultimate triumph in staging this pair of exhibitions is, on the one hand, the founding of a style in 1932, and, on the other, the disintegration of a style in 1988. This, for one architect to do in his lifetime, is no mean accomplishment.

Notes

1. My first trip in Europe with Colin Rowe occurred in the summer of 1961 during what was called the "long vac" from the University of Cambridge. Beginning in Holland, we went down the Rhine through Switzerland, crisscrossing Italy. Seeing Florence after Rome; exiting through Turin and up through France to Paris. If the first trip was essentially north-south, the second trip, a year later, was east-west, with Vienna the turning point for our return.

2. There were three different catalogues/books. The first listed three authors: Hitchcock, Johnson, and Lewis Mumford. It was entitled *Modern Architecture—International Exhibition* and published in 1932 by MoMA as the official catalogue. A trade edition was published by Norton, also in 1932, as *Modern Architects*. A third volume, also published by Norton in 1932, was the now famous *International Style: Architecture Since 1922*. The subtle movement from Hitchcock's *Modern Architecture* of 1929 to the Johnson-Hitchcock text *The International Style* of 1932 has been analyzed in detail by Terence Riley in his book *International Style: Exhibition 15 and the Museum of Modern Art* (New York: Rizzoli, 1992).

3. Riley cites that at one point the book was even called "The New International Style." See Riley, *Exhibition 15,* 90: "In an October 1930 letter to Johnson, Otto Haesler refers to Hitchcock and Johnson's working title: 'The New International Style, 1922–1932'" (Haesler to Johnson, undated response to Johnson's letter of September 2, 1930, MoMA).

4. While frequently referred to as the International Style exhibition, both the exhibition and the catalogue had the same name: *Modern Architecture: International Exhibition.* Catalogue by Henry-Russell Hitchcock, Philip Johnson, and Lewis Mumford (New York: Museum of Modern Art, 1932). The book also was published as *Modern Architects* (New York: Museum of Modern Art and Norton, 1932). The discrepancy between the two titles is due to an arrangement between the publisher and the museum: "Some of the books produced by the Museum and bound in paper cover for sale at the museum were by the firm for publication, hard bound in cloth and sold through the bookstores" (from a typescript entitled "An Account of the Early Days of W. W. Norton and Co.," Howard P. Wilson, W. W. Norton Editorial Archives, Columbia University). *Modern Architects* was the title of the trade version of the catalogue.

5. It must be remembered that the title of the first Bauhaus book, published in 1925 and written by Walter Gropius, was entitled *Internationale Architektur.* The difference between architecture and style is important in this context. For a more detailed account of this term, see Riley, *Exhibition 15.*

6. Ibid., 5.

7. Lewis Mumford, letter to Frank Lloyd Wright, February 6, 1932, Mumford Papers, University of Pennsylvania. Cited in Riley, *Exhibition 15.*

8. Walter Benjamin, *Selected Writings,* ed. Marcus Bullock and Michael W. Jennings, vol. 4, 1938–1940 (Cambridge: Belknap Press, 1996–2003), 269.

9. Betsky was teaching at the University of Cincinnati but had friends in Chicago at the Art Institute who may have introduced him to Florian. In any case, the book *Violated Perfection* was published two years later, in 1990.

10. Mark Wigley, *Derrida's Haunt: The Architecture of Deconstruction* (Cambridge: MIT Press, 1993), based on Ph.D. diss., 1987, University of Auckland, New Zealand.

11. At the Museum of Modern Art in New York in 2005.

Philip Johnson and the Rhetoric of the New: *Panta Rhei* versus the Avant-Garde

Ujjval Vyas

Philip Johnson's death provides an occasion for revisiting his work and life, reaffirming previous judgments or perhaps challenging them. But to praise or condemn without understanding is to do neither.

Interpreting Johnson's work and life is as much about our own views about what is valuable in architecture—or, more appropriately, our aspirations for achievement in architecture—as it is about assessing the man or his work. Whether we are talking about him as a critic, historian, or practitioner, all interpretations of Johnson and his work should address two basic issues in addition to the standard problems associated with historical and architectural interpretation. The longevity of his involvement in architecture, and the fact that his views about the human condition were highly divergent from the common pool's, make interpreting Johnson and his work especially difficult. The rich and sometimes maddening complexity of his life and work is daunting in itself, but the added complications of an intellectual view which many in architecture cannot understand or view as anathema create a chasm that will not be easy to cross.

Like other complex and intellectually gifted figures who witness the waxing and waning of ideas and movements during a long and eventful life, Johnson is best interpreted within his historical and intellectual context. Interpreting Oliver Wendell Holmes, Werner Heisenberg, or Henry Kissinger poses the same dilemma: they are easy targets for overly simplified or moralistic judgments. Holmes thought pacifism silly and didn't believe in human rights as an adequate or coherent basis for the law; Heisenberg was a fervent nationalist and commonly considered a Nazi collaborator; and Kissinger is more hated for his political activity than respected for the knowledge of history and diplomacy that informed his decision making. Like the great jurist, physicist, and diplomat, Johnson has become too complex, too challenging of the common verities.

A closer look at each of these figures is unlikely to convince the ideologically driven interpreter or critic. A pacifist is unlikely to be moved by Holmes's complex views, distilled in a letter that, "all 'isms' seem to me silly—but this hyperaethereal respect for human life seems perhaps the silliest of all."[1] And those who see every German remaining willingly in Germany during the Nazi era as a collaborator might not be inclined to change their opinion given the lesser known fact that Heisenberg was instrumental in engineering a foiled attempt on Hitler's life at great risk to himself. Certainly those who have made hay in hindsight out of Kissinger's decisions fail to understand that diplomacy is not primarily the business of imposing moral virtue on other states but rather the need to maintain the state in an uncertain and changeable world. And yet Holmes, Heisenberg, Kissinger, and even Johnson have their admirers.

The enormity of the actual lived experience of such figures, among which Johnson finds easy acceptance, means that they have seen multiple generations come and go. They repeatedly have seen fads, movements, ideologies, creeds, and sects rise, then founder, and then return in new guises. In this regard they know all too well the sound and fury signifying nothing protected under the aegis of the "new." The confusion surrounding Johnson and his work, in large measure, stems from a fundamental misunderstanding of his relationship to the new. Clarifying this confusion will allow us a more general apparatus by which to consider the value of Johnson's work and his exercise of authority within the world of American architecture.

Johnson began promulgating the "new" in architecture in the 1920s; he was instrumental in bringing certain European trends to America, particularly the International Style in the 1930s; he was vital in establishing a Miesian aesthetic; he was one of the first to support the experimentation in form by mid-twentieth century architects like Edward Durell Stone, Minoru Yamasaki, Eero Saarinen, and Louis Kahn; he was the first major architect to speak out for historic preservation in the 1960s; in the 1970s he became an important backer of Robert Venturi and the related experiments with form associated with postmodernism; and in the twilight of the century he helped establish the New York Five and deconstructivism while aiding the elevation of Frank Gehry to matinee idol status.

On the other side of the coin, Johnson was among the first to reject modernism—and especially Mies's formal strictures and muddled tenets. He had little time for the self-inflationary rhetoric of social-cause architects and was simply bemused by those who created self-glorifying theories of architecture by plagiarizing badly from other disciplines. And although he was often identified with a variety of younger architects of the passing generations, he never became a convert to any theoretical or ideological position proffered by these architects—often to their great consternation.

How can we rectify this seemingly opposite set of facts? The answer lies in understanding that Johnson (like Holmes) did not believe in Truth. Johnson rejected any attempt to create an architecture or a politics based on claims to Truth. For him, this made no sense either philosophically or as the basis for his own work. Instead of the truth of content, he believed only in the beauty of form. There were no true forms, only beautiful forms. Romanesque forms were no more or less true than Incan or Miesian or blob architecture. All of these could produce beautiful or ugly architecture depending on the skill, sensitivity, and prowess of the designer. Like a chef who is fascinated by new ingredients and techniques, Johnson was interested in maintaining or even expanding the range of possible forms.

In fact, Johnson rejected any theory that brought in that tired deus ex machina—the zeitgeist—that is the commonplace prop of the avant-garde. To give only one example of this rejection we can look to an interview he gave to Heinrich Klotz and John Cook in 1973. In my view, this interview remains the single best introduction to Johnson's worldview. In the interview, Klotz thought it important to accuse Johnson of being "monumental," a term of approbation to Klotz and a synonym for creating or glorifying authoritarianism. Klotz tried to castigate Johnson for using forms that should not be used if one understood properly the true zeitgeist.

PJ: It isn't the monumentality that's wrong. It's the architect that's wrong. Baalbek isn't wrong! Let's go back to what the real criticism is of the Kline Biology Tower at Yale: it's dark; it's out of scale. I understand words like that. It's too tall for its square. The cylinders come down in an inexorable way that makes you feel you'll be killed if you go between them, as you would indeed at Luxor. But you [meaning Klotz] don't think Luxor, or maybe you do think Luxor, is too heavy. I don't know.

HK: If it would be built today, I would object to it.

PJ: Ah, you see, I don't have this prejudice about today. To me there is no today. To me there are just wonderful things and not-wonderful things.[2]

Earlier in the essay Johnson put it even more bluntly: "No, I was never an avant-garde man. It never interested me."[3]

The avant-garde validates itself and new forms through a confusion of certitude with certainty. Certitude—an overwhelming feeling that one is right, does not in fact equal certainty. The avant-garde aims to create the true forms of the time by asserting special powers of perception for all those who convert. The religious analogies are obvious, especially at this time in history. Fundamentalism has serious ethical problems, not the least of which is its easy belief that a few eggs must be broken to achieve true enlightenment, salvation, or whatever utopian and dystopian scheme is being proselytized. Like nationalism, sectarianism, or the politics of identity, the avant-gardists can brook no skeptics. They see their position as inevitable to all who have eyes to see.

It has been commonplace, almost to the point of banality, in the last two centuries to assume that the artist must be a fanatic to number among the greats. Hyperbole, apocalyptic rhetoric, self-inflationary grandiloquence, and simplistic assertions constitute the most effective signs of greatness. Such fanaticism can occasionally lead to great formal experimentation: counter-Reformation fanatics produced wildly inventive baroque forms. And while Johnson knew that aestheticized fanaticism could sway the mob, he also knew it was possible to enjoy the increase in the formal vocabulary of architecture without caring one whit for the fanatical beliefs.

Johnson fully embraced Heraclitus' view that "all things change"—*panta rhei,* in ancient Greek.[4] From this perspective, the new is inevitable not because it is true but because change is inevitable. The new has no particular path or goal; change is neither progress to a glorious future nor a return to a glorious past. And since the winds of change are constant, one must constantly struggle to navigate and be open to the possibility of changing one's judgments. And to be open to change, one must be skeptical about one's own dearest beliefs. To Johnson the chasm between certitude and certainty could never be crossed. In Johnson's world, it was almost impolite to cross the chasm. Others could do this and it might be amusing, pathetic, or even sad in the way an evolutionary biologist might feel about a staunch follower of intelligent design. Johnson was never able to play the role of the fanatic believer, and this has been held against him for far too long. His devotion was not one particular set of forms but to the full gamut of possible forms for architecture, an architecture with a capital A.

Even those who thought Johnson was at one time solely committed to modernism were deeply mistaken. Witness the statement he made in a letter to his parents in 1944: "And the house I am doing for them is turning out to have a French

18th century plan with romanesquoid exteriors. What would you think? I am afraid I shall be excommunicated from the modern brotherhood. I better not publish the house anyhow."[5] The functionalist or social betterment aspects of European modern architecture were completely lost on Johnson from the very beginning. In point of fact, a close examination of Johnson's activity in the 1920s and '30s would show that the architects he promulgated most assiduously were also dismissive of the functionalist and social engineering aspects of the new architecture. Certainly his preference for Mies and even greater admiration for J. J. P. Oud were based on a shared concern with beautiful architectural form and a rejection of functionalism and social engineering.[6]

Johnson was committed to increasing the possibility of elegant architecture in the world. He was voracious to see, experience, and build to add to this catalogue of elegant forms. All his authority was directed at stopping a particular set of forms from controlling architecture and thus reducing the scope of possible forms. This is the reason he often championed formal attempts that appeared in the aggregate to be contradictory. The strategy was to use his personal and cultural assets to initiate an increase in formal experimentation. As often as not, the new that he backed came with the baggage of the avant-garde or some other theory of art or society. This hardly mattered to him as long as there was a potential for the creation of beautiful architectural form. This is why Johnson was such an unusual guardian of American architecture: instead of keeping people out of the room, he made sure the door would not close.

Notes

1. Richard A. Posner, ed., *The Essential Holmes: Selections from the Letters, Speeches, Judicial Opinions, and Other Writings of Oliver Wendell Holmes, Jr.* (Chicago: University of Chicago Press, 1992), 113. The quotation comes from a letter to Harold Laski dated September 27, 1921.
2. John W. Cook and Heinrich Klotz, *Conversations with Architects* (New York: Praeger, 1973), 47.
3. Ibid., 28.
4. See, for example, the speech given at the Smith College symposium "Art and Morals" on April 23, 1953; his use of the phrase *panta rhei* as an epigram introducing his own work in "Philip Johnson," *A + U* (Architecture and Urbanism), April 1992, 10–14; transcript for a public interview conducted in Chicago on October 24, 1995, under the auspices of the Chicago Architecture Foundation; and finally, see my *The Intellectual Foundations of Philip Johnson, Ph.D. diss.* (Ann Arbor: UMI, 1996), 50–56.
5. From a personal letter from Johnson to his family in Cleveland dated July 13, 1944; Philip Johnson Manuscripts (Mss. 3766), Western Reserve Historical Society Archives, Cleveland.
6. See, for example, Philip Johnson, "Architecture in the Third Reich," *Hound and Horn* 7 (October–December 1933): 137–39. For a more general understanding of why and how Johnson came to hold such a position, see Vyas, *Intellectual Foundations of Philip Johnson,* chapters 2 and 3.

Working Out Johnson's Role in History

Mark Jarzombek

In 1977, Peter Eisenman wrote a remarkably clear and insightful article on Johnson ending with the words, "Johnson's writings, like a glass box, have the transparency of our time. It will remain for history to reveal their opacity."[1] I would like to dedicate my thoughts to the theme of that opacity, given for the moment the presumption that that is where history locates itself. I do not, however, intend to get entangled in Johnson's frustrating cleverness, much less revel in his opacity, which can only bring out the usual trying fluctuations of admiration or disgust. I am interested in addressing the relationship between ego and architecture as something that goes beyond Johnson. Is there something historical in Johnson that lies outside the overproductions of his ego and its associated seductions? Is there a history of ego that is bigger than Johnson's? Is there something clear in all the opacity?

In answering these questions, I would like to state at the outset that I see Johnson as a figure in the crisis of the post-Enlightenment, as someone who operated in the service of that crisis, unbeknownst to him, however, operating because of the cunning of history, and not because of his own cunning. And it hinges, I admit, on a perhaps all-too-delicate illusion. One illusion, if you will, meeting the other, one opacity meeting the other. Johnson's claim that he was a "Mies *Schüler*" needs no confirmation, but it could be an entry point into a philosophical problem that needs to be further unpacked.[2] What Schüler means philosophically is explained by Immanuel Kant in his *Critique of Judgment,* where he describes that at the heart of a "school," in the sense of a "school of Rembrandt," was the genius who furnished the "rich material" that others need to think over, discuss, and emulate.[3] According to Kant, "Because a genius is a favorite of nature and must be regarded by us as a rare phenomenon, his example produces for other good heads a school, i.e., a system of teaching according to rules."[4] These rules, he argues, are not set in stone and should not be aped; nor should we appeal to mannerism in studying them. Kant links the work of the Schüler with another type of work, the work of the genius, namely opus. An opus is a series of works produced over time in the cycling of experience and cognition. An opus, in the Kantian sense, was more than just a compilation of one's artistic efforts, but something with *Schwergewicht* that enabled those in the "school" to condense these efforts into rules that can be studied, imitated, and learned. Opus is thus a form of history, and in reverse, history finds itself in opus. As a diagram, one can think of being and history as intersecting circles with opus the overlapping region. Opus was opacity that lent itself over time to clarity, and here you can see why I picked out Eisenman's clever phrase.

On the surface Johnson's turn away from Mies was the turn away from being a Schüler, from someone living in the "reflected glory" of Mies, as he writes, to a person with an opus all his own, someone with his own opacity. We also have to remember that in 1959 Mies had a one-man show of his work here at Yale. We also have to remember Le Corbusier's *oeuvre complète* came out in the mid-1950s and that Le Corbusier clearly stood in the long line of artists and musicians who were self-consciously opus-makers, the first being Beethoven, who already two years after the publication of *Critique of Judgment* began to identify his compositions with opus numbers. Le Corbusier, one could say, brought the Kantian imperative directly into the midst of the modernist project.

Johnson was well aware of the oeuvre complète series and even wrote a review of it in 1953.[5] But there are hints that things are not going to work out as planned. In the review, Johnson wrote: "After being known for thirty years as the leader of the international school of design, . . . [Le Corbusier] now in full vigor steps out into space sculpture, breathtaking and unanalyzable."[6] This says little about Le Corbusier, a lot about Johnson. How do we analyze Johnson against the grain of the desire for unanalyzability?

Being unanalyzable is Johnson's pretension and Johnson's ultimate discovery. It is the semicolon in the flow of historical development. It coincides not only with a disengagement of modernism but also with a disengagement from the modernist self, and it comes from that date forward in the form of the self put-down. My work, he reiterated, is "frankly derivative" in many ways. This is, as we know, not because Johnson discovered humility. On the contrary, Johnson became the first architect of note to resist the Nietzschean imperative and in the process discover a fracture in the modernist edifice that allowed the insertion of a psychoanalytical presence. It is an opus unmoored from Enlightenment ego, becoming both wounded and self-wounding. The lack of differentiation with Mies slides into hyper-differentiation, resulting in a type of postmodernized Oedipalesque tragedy in which the erstwhile teacher-husband turns out to be a father figure, creating perhaps a Lacanian "false being" (Seminar XV), the product of a reflection that interlocks for ever more mature production and pathological reenactment. "You have to thumb your nose [at your father]," Johnson writes in 1960, "in order to exert your own poor little ego." For this reason, "My stand is violently anti-Miesian. I think that is the most natural thing in the world just as I am not really very fond of my father."[7]

One could read the Munson-Williams-Proctor Institute (1960) as an enactment of this radical undoing of Mies (fig. 1). Everything that was once elegant and transparent has become mute and tomblike, frozen over in spiteful granite. It is a memorial/antimemorial to Mies, a purposeful misreading as well as a representation of Oedipal self-disgust. It is clearly one of the most preeminent psychoanalytically marked buildings of the twentieth century, so complete in its articulations that it outranks even the work of Adolf Loos.

It is irrelevant, to my argument, whether there is psychoanalytical veritas to this. Apart from his relationship with Mies one could mention the death of Johnson's parents and changes in his love life, but it is not my role to determine the "realness" of this sign, its potential causes, pathologies, or diagnosis. What is just as "real" is the presence that Johnson makes for it in making architecture, as a trope of unanalyzability, which we can match not by analyzing it, not by explaining it

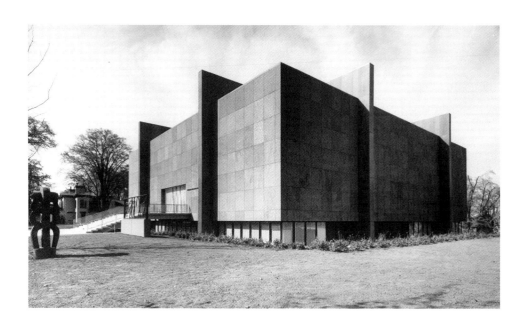

fig. 1 Philip Johnson Associates, Munson-Williams-Proctor Arts Institute, Museum of Art, Utica, New York, 1960

away, but by accepting it as a sign that indicates the larger problem of architecture's missing signifier.

We thus find not the beginnings of a predictable opus, but a post-opus work, opus having been rendered impossible—except in the form of opus envy—by the eruption of a psychoanalytical subject. But if the special effect of *jouissance* has freed the subject from the strictures of the social code, freed it from the obligations of opacity, and destabilized the historial world, it has also magnified its tremblings. Johnson's work henceforth promises neither a discourse of progress nor one of modernist acceleration, nor can it rely on the conventions of eclecticism. His new particular historicism can be likened to a type of photographic overexposure to the historical referent, which means that we should refrain from trying to correct the exposure, to sharpen the image. We have to respect the contrived splitting of the I into Self and False Self.

For this "project" to work from a philosophical point of view—in other words, for it to be "not architecture"—and yet for all practical and sociopolitical reasons have the appearance of architecture, one more, essential, step was required. In order to produce something that was not opus but only its ghostly over-illumination, Johnson had also to renounce Arbeit, not any old Arbeit, but Arbeit as understood by Kant, who, in the *Critique of Judgment,* set up a contrast not only between the work of the genius and the work of the Schüler, but also between opus and Arbeit. Opus is elevated, whereas Arbeit is mercenary; the one yields a civilizational possibility, the other is a necessary, often unpleasant, reality. That the dialectics of work resides at the heart of all post-Enlightenment discourses of architecture, I would say Johnson somnambulistically understood as the historical cunning set before him. Thus the insistence from the mid-1960s on the casualness of design, on "FUN." In 1975, Johnson wrote: "John Burgee and I have had fun in the last few years with shapes and funnels, plazas, 'gozintas,' indoor streets, sloped sides and/or roofs."[8] The interesting thing about both Arbeit and opus is that both are definitely *not* fun. Asked why he chose the Caprarola plan for a model of one of his houses, he answered "Why not?"[9]

Now this part of the equation brings us to the question of class. I am not talking about Johnson's wealth or his privileged position, and not even about his late-in-life seemingly "honest" admission about being part of what he called, oddly enough, the "elect."[10] I am more interested in his insistent self-representation as a person who does not need to appear to work in the sense that what he produces is work *ohne* Arbeit. This is a quasi-aristocratic pretense—with resonances back in the baroque—that is better understood as a cultural trope more by Europeans than by Americans, and brought into modernism by the likes of Wassily Kandinsky, who painted while dressed in his coat and tails. This is not the same as amateurism; it is not the same as being a "gentleman architect," but something altogether more powerful and more devious, its edges leaking out in curious statements like "Architecture helps me fight the interminable boredom of bourgeois culture."[11] In a strange way, one could take one of Johnson's earliest designs, the 1949 "House for Millionaire with no Servants" as a type of leitmotiv for his later attitude. There are, of course, servants, but they are rendered invisible in a politics of economic segregation. Once again, this is not a question of economic privilege but a question about the ongoing crisis of Arbeit, especially as it applies to architecture in the modern world, and Arbeit that was abjected from the Enlightenment system, and that haunts architecture to its core, making it easy to redeem authenticity in the name of doing "no work." The resultant false consciousness exerts its pretense toward legitimacy by sublimating work into fantasy where the irrepressible curse of Arbeit reidentifies itself in the form of play, sexuality, and disguise.

We should not, however, miss the fact that Karl Marx made a whole philosophy out of redeeming the legitimacy of Arbeit, a discourse that was carried forth into the 1970s by Christopher Lasch in *The Culture of Narcissism: American Life in an Age of Diminishing Expectations,* published, relevantly, in 1978, at a time when theory of a leftist sort was attracting the interest of young architects. A Laschian-styled critique of Johnson would point out that our culture of diminished expectations would celebrate Johnson's open-endedness in order to legitimate and disguise the falsity inherent in its false liberalism.

As attached as I am to Lasch's position, I have to admit that there is something more complex here in the discussion of Johnson, for labor can also mean civilizational labor, as in the difference between, for example, Philip Johnson and Louis Kahn, and Philip Johnson and Peter Eisenman, where both Kahn and Eisenman also undo Kant, but by emphasizing the difficulty—laborious difficulty, I should add—of getting to a design. Johnson undoes Kant by turning the dial not to a fantastical excess of Arbeit, but to an excess of ease. But we have to remember that he had to work hard at reminding us at how easy it all is. Johnson's critics long ago pointed to the "facileness" of Johnson's work and to its purported stylishness, but they failed to understand that this facileness was more than just a cultural trope, but philosophically legitimate in the deconstructions of the Enlightenment, even if it is a distasteful symptom of false consciousness. It works, however, only if it is contrived so as to not land us back in the realm of opus. Johnson has to work hard at not working and thus delivers the undeliverable.

Let me give an example. In discussing the AT&T building in 1977 he writes that for the scale and human references of the base of the building he used Brunelleschi, but he added a question mark after the word, as in "Brunelleschi?" and surrounded the word in parentheses. It is a punctum that expresses Johnson working to show the lack of effort.

> *The middle a shaft from the twenties (Raymond Hood?) and the top a broken pediment complete with cornice (late Roman?).*

We see in this phraseology the very moment in which history is evoked in order to disappear, the very moment in which a discipline is acknowledged only to be transformed into semiotic play, the very moment in which intellectual work confronts the crisis of civilizational *Arbeit*. Johnson gives us the three question marks to make sure that we get the picture and to tease unsuspecting readers into thinking that the humanist subject has been retrieved, when in actuality it is being stripped of relevance. One could almost say that the work of architecture requires a type of *Überarbeit*.

My point is not a negative one, however. Johnson has accomplished something quite startling. In the name of architecture, almost everything that one would think important to its disciplinary formation, namely Being, History, along with Opus and Arbeit, is expelled in the name of architecture's survival. Being has been replaced by False Being, and History by Historicism; Opus and Arbeit are excluded from the site of production. Their dialectic has, in essence, been deconstructed.

As I tried to stress, Johnson's poison has its own chemical makeup and its own corrosive force, its own "science," if you will, its own consistency. It is not, one can say, meaningless and trivial, but a regime like any other, purposefully unrequited, saturated with relations to power, structuring the effects of pleasure, and generating an endless supply of possibilities—human relationships included—to disguise its profoundly constricted reflections. For this reason it fitted all too well with the corporate world of the 1970s; for this reason, intuited more than expressed, many younger architects in the 1970s found no inspiration in Johnson. For them he was the deadened afterlife of the implosion of modernism, floating weightlessly through time.

I am, however, trying to redeem a value in this by inverting the inversion and arguing, to say it bluntly, that architecture is wedded—even now, in a sad but true way—to the traumatic dislocation of work in the Enlightenment brought on by the splitting of Being from non-Being and opus from Arbeit. It needed the right man at the right time.

And so we stand before the uncertainty of what his architecture actually is. Once detached from philosophical representation, and then reattached by way of compensation to the reality of its failure, Johnson seems to show that architecture can exist only as a reflection against that which it thinks it is. All of this challenges the way we write Johnson into architectural history; his architecture evokes a possibility of history, but of what type of history we are not sure, except that it is decidedly impossible. My interest in these remarks is to state that architecture can never escape from the negativity that gave it the set of disciplinary rules by which it came to have its history. Johnson allows us to reestablish contact with the primacy of that negative history, which, having been detached from philosophy's higher aims, floats awkwardly away through modernist time, never measuring up and never wanting to measure up, never truly alive and yet not quite dead, either. It is in this context that we should seek Johnson, both as a theory and, just as important, as a practice of architecture.

Notes

1. Peter Eisenman, "Behind the Mirror: On the Writings of Philip Johnson," *Oppositions* 10 (1977): 12.

2. Philip Johnson, *Philip Johnson: Writings,* foreword by Vincent Scully, introduction by Peter Eisenman, commentary by Robert A. M. Stern (New York: Oxford University Press, 1979), 171.

3. Immanuel Kant, *Critique of Judgment,* trans. J. H. Bernard (New York: Hafer, 1951), 152.

4. Ibid., 162.

5. Johnson, "Correct and Magnificent Play," Review of *Le Corbusier, Complete Works V. 1946–1952,* ed. W. Boesiger; from *Art News* 52 (September 1953): 16–17, 52–53.

6. *Philip Johnson,* 201.

7. Johnson, Speech, Yale University, February 5, 1959, in ibid., 227.

8. Johnson, "What Makes Me Tick," Lecture, Columbia University, September 24, 1975, in ibid., 265.

9. Stover Jenkins and David Mohney, *The Houses of Philip Johnson* (New York: Abbeville, 2001), 175.

10. Johnson, "A Conversation Around the Avant-Garde," in Robert E. Somol, ed., *Autonomy and Ideology* (New York: Monacelli, 1997), 45.

11. Ibid., 46.

The New Canaan Estate:
A Gallery

fig. 1 Da Monsta, 1995

fig. 2 Da Monsta, 1995

fig. 3 Da Monsta and Library/Study

fig. 4 Library/Study, 1980

figs. 5–6 Library/Study, 1980

fig. 7 Ghost House, 1984

fig. 8 Calluna Farms, c. 1890/1910

fig. 9 Popestead, c.1920

fig. 10 Lake Pavilion, 1962

fig. 11 Lake Pavilion and
Lincoln Kirstein Tower

fig. 12 Lincoln Kirstein
Tower, 1985

figs. 13–14 Painting Gallery, 1965

figs. 15–17 Sculpture Gallery, 1970

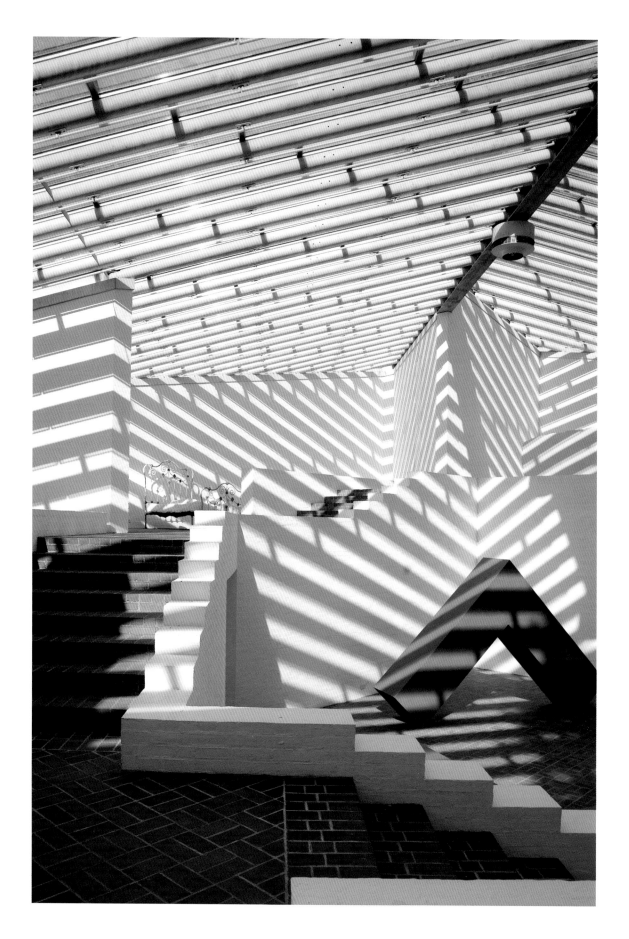

fig. 18 Sculpture Gallery, 1970

fig. 19 Glass House, Pool, and Guest House

fig. 20–21 Glass House, 1949

fig. 22 Glass House interior;
chairs, ottoman, and lounge chair
by Mies van der Rohe with
Lilly Reich

fig. 23 Glass House interior; at
right is Elie Nadelman, *Two Circus
Women* (1930)

fig. 24 Glass House, 1949,
bathroom

fig. 25 Glass House, 1949

Contributors

Beatriz Colomina is professor of architecture and founding director of the program in Media and Modernity at Princeton University. She is author of *Privacy and Publicity: Modern Architecture as Mass Media* (MIT Press, 1994) and *Domesticity at War* (MIT Press, 2007), editor of *Sexuality and Space* (Princeton, 1992), and coeditor of *Cold War Hot Houses: Inventing Postwar Culture from Cockpit to Playboy* (Princeton, 2004).

Peter Eisenman is Louis I. Kahn Visiting Professor of Architectural Design at Yale University and principal of Eisenman Architects in New York. His books include *Written into the Void: Selected Writings, 1990–2004* (Yale University Press, 2007), *Eisenman Inside Out: Selected Writings, 1963–1988* (Yale University Press, 2004), *Blurred Zones: Investigations of the Interstitial* (Monacelli, 2002), *Giuseppe Terragni: Transformations, Decompositions, Critiques* (Monacelli, 2003), *The Formal Basis of Modern Architecture* (L. Müller, 2006), and *Diagram Diaries* (Universe and St. Martin's, 1999).

Kurt W. Forster is Vincent Scully Visiting Professor of Architectural History at the School of Architecture at Yale University. He founded and directed research institutes at the Getty Research Center in Los Angeles and the Canadian Centre for Architecture in Montreal. He cowrote *Frank O. Gehry: The Complete Works* (Monacelli, 1998), *Massimo Scolari: Il ponte di Cesare sul Reno secondo Palladio* (Centro Andrea Palladio, 2002), and *Exploring Boundaries: The Architecture of Wilkinson Eyre* (Birkhäuser and Springer, 2007), and coedited *Theorie der Praxis: Leon Battista Alberti als Humanist und Theoretiker der bildenden Künste* (Akademie, 1999).

Mark Jarzombek is associate dean of MIT's School of Architecture and Planning and professor of the history and theory of architecture. His books include *On Leon Battista Alberti: His Literary and Aesthetic Theories* (MIT Press, 1989), *The Psychologizing of Modernity, Art, Architecture, and History* (Cambridge, 2000), and *Urban Heterology: Dresden and the Dialectics of Post-Traumatic History* (Lund, 2001). He cowrote *A Global History of Architecture* (Wiley and Sons, 2006).

Charles Jencks is an independent scholar, architect, and author of numerous books, including *The Iconic Building: The Power of Enigma* (Frances Lincoln, 2005), *The Garden of Cosmic Speculation* (Frances Lincoln, 2003), *The New Paradigm in Architecture* (*The Language of Post-Modern Architecture,* 7th ed., Yale University

Press, 2002), *Le Corbusier and the Continual Revolution in Architecture* (Monacelli, 2000), *The Architecture of the Jumping Universe* (Academy, 1995), *The New Moderns* (Academy and Rizzoli, 1990), *Post-Modernism: The New Classicism in Art and Architecture* (Rizzoli and Academy, 1987), *What Is Post-Modernism?* (St. Martin's and Academy, 1986), *Kings of Infinite Space* (St. Martin's and Academy, 1983), and *The Language of Post-Modern Architecture* (Rizzoli, 1977).

Phyllis Lambert is an architect and the founding director of the Canadian Centre for Architecture in Montreal. She was the director of planning for the Seagram Building. She is editor of *Mies in America* (Abrams, 2001), *Fortifications and the Synagogue: The Fortress of Babylon and the Ben Ezra Synagogue, Cairo* (Weidenfeld and Nicolson, 1994), and *Viewing Olmsted* (CCA and MIT Press, 1996), coeditor of *Opening the Gates of Eighteenth-Century Montreal* (CCA and MIT Press, 1992) and *En chantier: The Collections of the CCA, 1989–1999* (CCA, 1999).

Reinhold Martin is associate professor at the Graduate School of Architecture, Planning, and Preservation at Columbia University, and a partner in the firm Martin/Baxi Architects in New York. He is a founding editor of the scholarly journal *Grey Room*. He is the author of *The Organizational Complex: Architecture, Media, and Corporate Space* (MIT Press, 2003).

Detlef Mertins is professor of architecture and chair of the architecture department at the University of Pennsylvania. He is editor of *The Presence of Mies* (Princeton, 1994). He has contributed revisionist interpretations of modern architecture, as well as essays on contemporary architecture, to a number of books, including *NOX, FOA's Arc, Hejduk's Chronotope, Monolithic Architecture, AT-INdex, KMPB, Interact or Die, Walter Curt Behrendt, Zaha Hadid,* and *Burckhalter and Sumi.*

Joan Ockman is professor of architecture and the director of the Temple Hoyne Buell Center for the Study of American Architecture at Columbia University's Graduate School of Architecture, Planning, and Preservation. She edited *Architecture Culture, 1943–1968: A Documentary Anthology* (Rizzoli, 1993), *Out of Ground Zero: Case Studies in Urban Reinvention* (Prestel, 2002), *The Pragmatist Imagination: Thinking About Things in the Making* (Princeton, 2000), and *Architecture, Criticism, Ideology* (Princeton, 1985), and coedited *Architourism: Authentic, Escapist, Exotic, Spectacular* (Prestel, 2005).

Emmanuel Petit is assistant professor in the School of Architecture at Yale University. He is working on a book entitled *Irony: The Theoretical Unreason of Postmodern Architecture.*

Terence Riley is director of the Miami Art Museum and previous chief curator of architecture and design at the Museum of Modern Art in New York. He is author of *The Un-Private House* (MoMA and Abrams, 1999), *On-site: New Architecture in Spain* (MoMA and D. A. P., 2005), *Light Construction* (Museum of Modern Art and Abrams, 1995), *Yoshio Taniguchi: Nine Museums* (Museum of Modern Art, 2004), and *The International Style: Exhibition 15 and the Museum of Modern Art* (Rizzoli,

1992). He edited and coedited many books, including *Frank Lloyd Wright, Architect* (Museum of Modern Art and Abrams, 1994), *Filter of Reason: Work of Paul Nelson* (Rizzoli, 1990), and *Mies in Berlin* (Museum of Modern Art and Abrams, 2001).

Vincent Scully is Sterling Professor Emeritus of the History of Art in Architecture at Yale University. He was a 2004 recipient of the National Medal of Arts. He is author of *The Shingle Style: Architectural Theory and Design from Richardson to the Origins of Wright* (Yale University Press, 1955), *Frank Lloyd Wright* (G. Braziller, 1960), *Modern Architecture: The Architecture of Democracy* (G. Braziller, 1961), *American Architecture and Urbanism* (Praeger, 1969), *Architecture: The Natural and the Man-Made* (St. Martin's, 1991), *Earth, the Temple, and the Gods: Greek Sacred Architecture* (Praeger, 1969), *Louis I. Kahn* (G. Braziller, 1962), *New World Visions of Household Gods and Sacred Places* (Little, Brown, 1988), and *Pueblo: Mountain, Village, Dance* (Chicago, 1989).

Michael Sorkin is professor of architecture and director of the graduate program in urban design in City College of New York's School of Architecture, Urban Design, and Landscape Architecture. He is principal of the New York–based architectural practice Michael Sorkin Studio and contributing editor to *Architectural Record* and *Metropolis*. For ten years he was the architecture critic of the *Village Voice*. His books include *Variations on a Theme Park* (Hill and Wang, 1992), *Exquisite Corpse* (Verso, 1991), *Local Code* (Princeton, 1993), *Some Assembly Required* (University of Minnesota Press, 2001), and *Starting from Zero: Reconstructing Downtown New York* (Routledge, 2003). He edited *Against the Wall: Israel's Barrier to Peace* (New Press and Norton, 2005) and *Analyzing Ambasz* (Monacelli, 2004).

Robert A. M. Stern is the dean of and J. M. Hoppin Professor of Architecture in the School of Architecture at Yale University. He is founder of and senior partner in the firm Robert A. M. Stern Architects in New York, and he is author of many books, including *New Directions in American Architecture* (G. Braziller, 1969), *George Howe: Toward a Modern American Architecture* (Yale University Press, 1975), and *Modern Classicism* (Rizzoli, 1988). He cowrote *New York 1880* (Monacelli, 1999), *New York 1900* (Rizzoli, 1983), *New York 1930* (Rizzoli, 1987), *New York 1960* (Monacelli, 1995), and *New York 2000* (Monacelli, 2006). In 1986, he hosted the eight-part PBS documentary "Pride of Place: Building the American Dream."

Kazys Varnelis is director of the Network Architecture Lab at the Graduate School of Architecture, Planning, and Preservation at Columbia University. He is a member of the founding faculty at the School of Architecture, University of Limerick, Ireland.

Stanislaus von Moos teaches at the Accademia di architettura in Mendrisio, and was professor of modern art at the University of Zurich from 1983–2005. He is author of *Le Corbusier: Elements of a Synthesis* (MIT Press, 1979), *Le Corbusier: l'Architecte et son mythe* (Horizons de France, 1971), *Venturi, Rauch, and Scott Brown Buildings and Projects* (Rizzoli, 1987), *Venturi, Scott Brown and Associates: Buildings and Projects, 1986–1998* (Monacelli, 1999), *Nicht Disneyland und andere Aufsätze über Modernität und Nostalgie* (Scheidegger and Spiess, 2004), *Fernand*

Léger: La ville. Zeitdruck, Grossstadt, Wahrnehmung (Fischer Taschenbuch, 1999), *Turm und Bollwerk: Beiträge zu einer politischen Ikonographie der italienischen Renaissancearchitektur* (Atlantis, 1974).

Ujjval K. Vyas is an independent scholar, a practicing attorney, and a principal of the interdisciplinary consulting firm Alberti Group, which specializes in policy, strategy, and research in the building industry.

Mark Wigley is dean of the Graduate School of Architecture, Planning, and Preservation at Columbia University. In 1988 he curated, with Philip Johnson, the MoMA exhibition *Deconstructivist Architecture*. He is cofounder of *Volume Magazine* and author of *The Architecture of Deconstruction: Derrida's Haunt* (MIT Press, 1993), *White Walls, Designer Dresses: The Fashioning of Modern Architecture* (MIT Press, 1995), *Constant's New Babylon: The Hyper-Architecture of Desire* (010 Publishers, 1998).

Index

education of Johnson and, 167; International Style and, 62, 173, 221; relations with Johnson, 61

Barr, Margaret Scolari, *61*, 67n5

Batista, Fulgencio, 94

Bauen in Frankreich, Bauen in Eisen, Bauen in Eisenbeton (Giedion), 173, 174, *174*

Bauhaus, 30, 62, 65, 173, 214; closed by Nazis, 224; *Internationale Architektur* (Gropius), 229n5

Baxter, William F., 131

Bayer, Herbert, 174

Beatty, Hamilton, 65

beauty, 162, 163, 216; Erotic Frigidaire and, 139; fascist aesthetics, 87; of form, 231; Medusa myth and, 150; Nazi cult of, 88; taste and, 168. *See also* aesthetics

Beethoven, Ludwig van, 235

Behrendt, Walter Curt, 160, 186n14

Ben-Gurion, David, 95

Benjamin, Walter, 20, 117, 224

Bergson, Henri, 15n17

Berlin, 66, 115

Berlin Diary (Shirer), 137

Bernini, Giovanni, 29

Beton als Gestalter [Concrete as Form Giver] (Hilberseimer), 174

Betsky, Aaron, 226, 229n9

"Beyond Utopia: Changing Attitudes in American Architecture" (film), 4

Blackburn, Alan, 6, 86

Blake, Peter, 120, 121

Bodenschatz, George K., 101

Bodenschatz, Karl, 101–2, 109n54

Bodenschatz, Viola, 58n59, 101–3, *104–5,* 109n54

Boissonnas (Eric) House (New Canaan, Conn.), 31, 191, *193,* 206n7

Bonaparte, Napoleon, 41, 42, 43, *43*

Bontempelli, Massimo, 53

Borromini, Francesco, 147

Bottai, Giuseppe, 42, 57n27

Boulez, Pierre, 44, 58n34

Bourdieu, Pierre, 124, 125, 162–63, 168

Bramante, Donato, 168

Brancusi, Constantin, 180

Breton, André, 57n28

Breuer, Marcel, 142, 178, 198

Britain, 87, 137–38, 153; critics of Johnson in, 205; lists of great men in, 139–40

Britton, John, 56n6

Brockway, Merrill, 3

Bronfman, Samuel, 92, 94

Brown, Charles E., 29, 131

Brown, Frank E., 25, 26

Bruggen, Coosje van, 44

Brunel, I. K., 139

Brunelleschi, Filippo, 147, 168, 237–38

Bunshaft, Gordon, 3, 142

Burgee, John, 21, 123, 184, 203, 207n53, 236

Bush, George H. W., 114

Bush, George W., 113, 119n4

Butler, Samuel, 65

Camus, Albert, 2, 6

"The Candid King Midas of New York Camp" (Jencks), 138, 150

capitalism, 10, 85–86, 136, 224; Coughlin's denunciation of, 98; Jews identified with, 87, 91, 94; listomania and, 140

Castro, Fidel, 95

Cathedral of Hope (Dallas, Tex.), *99,* 99–100, 109n50

Céline, Louis-Ferdinand, 92

Century Club (New York), 144

Century of Progress International Exhibition (Chicago, 1933–34), 68, 99

Chapel of the Rosary (Matisse), 93

Charlie Rose Show (television program), 4, 75

Chicago: AT&T office in, 126; International Style show in, 99; Lake Shore Drive apartments, 72–73, *73*

Chicago Tribune Competition (1922), 32

Choisy, Auguste, 49, 58n46, 146

Chomsky, Noam, 138, 139

Church, Frederic Edwin, 40–41

churches, 192–93, 194, 198. *See also* Cathedral of Hope (Dallas, Tex.); Crystal Cathedral (Garden Grove, Calif.); Roofless Church (New Harmony, Ind.)

CIAM: A Decade of New Architecture (Giedion), 179

Ciano, Count, 42

Citicorp building (New York), 32

Ciucci, Giorgio, 57n29

civilization, 142, 175

Clark, Eleanor, 25

class, social, 163, 233, 237

classicism, modern, 179–80, 214

Clauss & Daub, 62

Clay, Paffard Keatinge, 181

Clouds of Magellan (Lassaw), 89, *89*

Cobb, Henry, 14n8

Cohen, Jean-Louis, 14n8

Columbia University, 62, 101, 124, 144, 203

The Coming American Fascism (Dennis), 87

communism, 5, 42, 86, 224

Complexity and Contradiction in Architecture (Venturi), 125, *181,* 181–83, *182,* 185

Congrès Internationaux d'Architecture Moderne (CIAM), 170, 173, 178, 179, 188n40

constructivism, Russian, 33, 35, 44, 226, 227

"Conversations Regarding the Future of Architecture" (Johnson), 202–3

Cook, John, 231

Cook, Peter, 149

Le Corbusier, 27, 29, 49, 191; Beistégui

Florian, Paul, 226
Florida Southern College (Wright), *26, 26–27*
Ford, Henry, 152, 153, 154
Fordism, 122, 127
formalism, 182, 184
40 Under 40 exhibition, 124
Foster, Richard, 21, 207n53
Foucault, Michel, 84
The Fountainhead (Rand), 101
Four Seasons Restaurant (New York), 2, 11, 201;
    Bar Room, *196*; as elite meeting place, 144,
    146; interior, 214; Rothko mural and, 92–93.
    See also Seagram Building
Frampton, Kenneth, 50, 124
Freud, Sigmund, 150
Friedrich, Caspar David, 51, 52, 59n53
Fujikawa, Joseph, 72
Fuller, Buckminster, 20, 68, 72, 194
functionalism, 20, 30, 62, 124, 185; architecture
    as art and, 125; CIAM and, 179; form and, 161;
    Giedion and, 173; modern aesthetics and, 162;
    "organic" style opposed to, 178; social better-
    ment and, 233; style in opposition to, 160

Galaxy series (Kiesler), 90, *92*
Galbraith, John Kenneth, 138
Gandy, Joseph, 57n31
Gaudí, Antonio, 33, 147
Geddes, Norman Bel, 62
Gehry, Frank, 14n8, 21, 35, 136, 148; on AT&T
    building roof, 116; in Eight Deconstructivists,
    142; houses, 9, 43–44, *44*, 58n34; as Jewish
    friend of Johnson, 89; Johnson's emulation of,
    20; portrait with Johnson, 33, *33*; as protégé of
    Johnson, 4, 215, 231; studio house for Ronald
    Davis (design), 44; Venice Biennale and, 145
genealogy, Nietzschean, 84, 89
genius, Kantian view of, 234
Gerald D. Hines College of Architecture
    (Houston), 8
German-American Bund, 152
German language, 186n12, 223
Germany, 85, 87, 101, 102, 152–53, 224
Ghosh, Amitav, 110
Giedion, Sigfried, 11, 101, 109n52, 182; *Bauen
    in Frankreich,* 173, 174, *174*; *CIAM: A
    Decade of New Architecture,* 179; on "flimsy-
    effeminate" style, 178–79; International Style
    and, 172–76; *Mechanization Takes Command,*
    175, 186n7; "Modern Architecture: Death or
    Metamorphosis?", 170; "New Monumentality"
    and, 179–80; "Nine Points on Monumentality,"
    180; on "Playboy Architecture," 170–71, 179;
    Space, Time and Architecture, 170, *171,* 174,
    179, 180, 185; style battle and, 176
Gill, Brendan, 19
Glasarchitektur (Scheerbart), 68

Glaser, Milton, 130
Glashaus (Taut), 68, *70*
Glass House, 19, *54,* 208, 214, *260; Architectural
    Review* article on, *48, 50, 70,* 190; bathroom,
    259; circular forms in, 22–23; expansion of
    compound, 30; exterior views, *68, 255–256;*
    furniture, *257;* historicism and, 83; iconic
    status of, 82; as imitative work, 20; interior
    views, *50, 74, 257–258;* Johnson's comments
    on, 68, 71; in landscape ensemble, 34, *45,
    255;* liberation of individual and, 9; in *Life*
    magazine, *70;* lists of Great Men and, 146;
    "Miesian" aesthetic of, 4, 146, 216; mirror
    effects and, 53; model, *71;* networking at, 95,
    120, 121, 134n4; night views, *51,* 52–53, *69,
    196;* as pilgrimage site, 209; reaction design
    and, 216; Scott Brown on, 189n54; sculpture
    in, 90, *90, 258;* space defined in, *77,* 77–78;
    television and, 10, 68, 73–75; variants on,
    149; Venturi on, 181, *181,* 182. *See also* New
    Canaan estate/compound
Glass House on a Hillside (Mies van der Rohe), 68
Glass Room (Mies van der Rohe, Reich), 68
Godard, Jean-Luc, 57n28
Goebbels, Joseph, 138, 153
Goering, Hermann, 102, 109n54
Goethe, Johann Wolfgang, 82, 197
Goetheanum (Steiner), 34
Goff, Bruce, 142
Gold Marilyn Monroe (Warhol), *213,* 214
Goldberger, Paul, 14n8, 120, 143
Gonzaga, Federico, 39
Goodyear, A. Conger, 86
Gores, Landis, 21, 56n1
Gothic architecture, 197
Gottlieb, Adolph, 91
Goya, Francisco, 51
Graham, Dan, 71
Les grands initiés (Schuré), 140
Graves, Michael, 14n8, 75, 123, 126, 142
Grays, 123, 124, 125
Greece, classical, 20, 23
Greenwald, Herbert, 72, *72*
Gropius, Ise, 50
Gropius, Walter, 5, 21, 109n50, 191; functional-
    ism of, 20; house in Lincoln, Mass., 50, *50;*
    international style of, 223; *Internationale
    Architektur,* 229n5; *Monument for the March
    Dead, 99,* 100, 109n50; Nazism and, 138;
    praised by Johnson, 139, 142; style rejected
    by, 175
Guest House, *45, 74, 75,* 182, 214, *255;* remodel-
    ing of, 74; sculpture in, 89, *89;* sculpture
    in and around, 90, *91;* television in, 79n14;
    vaulted ceiling in bedroom, 191, *192. See also*
    New Canaan estate/compound
Guild House (Venturi and Rauch), 181, *182*

aesthetics of, 88, 141; architects and, 138; Bauhaus closed by, 224; Bodenschatz family and, 102; Céline and, 92; classicism associated with, 180; as critique of capitalism, 87; Hitler Jugend, 98, 152; Johnson's past and, 120; Nuremberg rallies, 6; sexual thrill of, 141. *See also* fascism; Hitler, Adolf

Negri, Antonio, 132, 133

neoclassicism, 180, 187n17

neomodernism, 18

Nervi, Pier Luigi, 194, 198

network theory, 132, 133

Neumeyer, Fritz, 14n8

Neutra, Richard, 62, 99

New Canaan estate/compound, 4, 6, 202, 209; *Architectural Review* publicity for, 38; art collection at, 214; as autobiography, 44–45, 46, 58n41; Brick House, 22, 28–29, 34, 197; Calluna Farms, *247*; Dog House, 4; Ghost House, 45, 74, *246*; Lake Pavilion, 197, *198–99, 248*; landscape at, *137*; Library/Study, *243–45*; Lincoln Kirstein Tower, 35, 45, 74, *248–49*; map of, *46*; milieu of clients and, 54; monumental historicism and, 83–84; as museum of personal memories, 9; Painting Gallery, *250–51*; pool, 34, *255*; Popestead, *247*; sculpture gallery, 115, 203, *205, 252–54*; Visitor's Booth (Da Monsta), 36, 45, 74, *241–43. See also* Glass House; Guest House

New Empiricism, 178, 179

New Left, 123

New Monumentality, 179–80

New York City, 8, 23, 129–30; Asia House, 183; Citicorp building, 32; Lipstick Building, 32, *32*; McGraw Hill Building, 64; Pennsylvania Station, 28; skyscraper architects and, 63–64, *64. See also* AT&T headquarters building; Four Seasons Restaurant; Lincoln Center; Seagram Building

New York Five, 123, 124, 139, 145, 231; as elite group, 142; Johnson's "Listomania" and, 10

Newman, Arnold, 53

Newman, Barnett, 91, 108n41

Niemeyer, Oscar, 95, 189n62

Nietzsche, Friedrich, 2, 87, 94, 167, 223; on critical history, 101; on death of God, 96; elitism of, 141; influence on the arts, 161; on monumental history, 82–83, 84; Rothko influenced by, 93; stream of German thought and, 142; superman concept, 139, 140; on will to power, 20, 140

nihilism, 92, 96, 101, 123, 139, 140; aesthetic taste and, 163; architectural whimsy and, 181; Johnson's contradiction and, 149; modernism and, 161

"Nine Points on Monumentality" (Giedion, Sert, Léger), 180

Nocturnal Discoveries (Bontempelli), 53

"Non-Miesian Directions" (Johnson talk), 197

Nowicki, Matthew, 142, 194

Number One Shell Plaza (Houston), 117

Oberhammer, Hans, 65

Objects: 1900 and Today (exhibition), 9, 64, *65*

Octopus Project (Johnson and Gehry), 34, *34*

"Of the Delicacy of Taste and Passion" (Hume), 162

"Of the Standard of Taste" (Hume), 161–62

oil economy, 110–11; as fetish, 112–13, 114, 115, 119n3; violence and, 117, 118

Olana (F. E. Church estate), 40–41, *41*

Oldenburg, Claes, 44

O'Leary, L. K., 127

"On Architectural Formalism and Social Concern" (Brown), 184–85

Onassis, Jacqueline Kennedy, 121

Oneto (George C.) House (Irvington-on-Hudson, N.Y.), 24, *24*, 191, *191*

opus, 12, 234, 235, 236, 238

Ortega y Gasset, José, 20

Oud, J. J. P., 5, 12, 60, 173, 179, 180; Amsterdam Town Hall project, 178, *178*; international style of, 223; Johnson and, 62, 139, 142, 233

Owen, Robert, 29

Owens, Craig, 49, 106n5

Owl in a Gothic Window (Friedrich), 51, *52*

Padavic, James, 29

Painting Towards Architecture (Hitchcock), 91

Palazzo Ruccellai, 183

Palladio, Andrea, 36, 57n19, 168

Paris: Musée d'Art Moderne, 179–80, *180*; Navy Building Office, *180*; UNESCO building, 198; World's Fair (1937), 178

Park Güell (Gaudí), 147

Parkinson, Mrs. Bliss, 121

Parthenon, 60, 147

patronage, 1, 39, 84, 92, 121; modern architecture as style and, 176; synagogue commissions in postwar America, 89

Paxton, Joseph, 99

Pazzi Chapel, 127

Pei, I. M., 3

Pelli, Cesar, 142

Pennzoil Place/Twin Towers (Houston), 8, 10, 110–18, *111, 118*, 123; atrium, 114, *114*; executive office, *112*; facade detail drawings for, *116*; minimalism of, 149, *149*; as sculpture, 203–4; situation and function as skyscraper, 32; skyscraper design redefined by, 214

Peres, Shimon, 95, 137

Pérez Alfonzo, Juan Pablo, 117

Perret, Auguste, 180

Pétain, Marshal Philippe, 138

Peter, John, 202

Illustration Credits

The photographers and the sources of visual material other than the owners indicated in the captions are as follows. Every effort has been made to supply complete and correct credits; if there are errors or omissions, please contact Yale University Press so that corrections can be made in any subsequent edition.

Page x: Maria von Matthiessen, courtesy Research Library, The Getty Research Institute, Los Angeles, California (980060)

Page 13: Emmanuel Petit

Vincent Scully essay: fig. 1, from H. Lewis and J. O'Connor, *Philip Johnson: The Architect in His Own Words* (New York: Rizzoli, 1994), 15; fig. 2, Digital Image © The Museum of Modern Art/Licensed by SCALA/Art Resource, NY; fig. 3, Collection of Earl of Plymouth, Oakley Park, Great Britain. Scala/Art Resource; figs. 4, 5, 13, and 14, Ezra Stoller © Esto. All rights reserved; fig. 6, Photo © Steven Brooke; figs. 7 and 8, The Museum of Modern Art, New York, NY. Digital Image © The Museum of Modern Art/Licensed by SCALA/Art Resource, NY; fig. 9, Vanni/Art Resource, NY; fig. 15, Photograph Collection, Art Library, Yale University; fig. 17, Yale University Archives; fig. 18, Richard Payne; fig. 20, Photo by Hugh Halestooke; fig. 21, © Manuel González Olaechea y Franco; fig. 23, Vincent Scully; fig. 24, © Todd Eberle

Kurt W. Forster essay: figs. 1 and 2, Kurt Forster; fig. 3, Oscar Savio, from M. Praz, *La casa della vita* (Milan: Adelphi, 1969); fig. 4, © Langdon Clay/Esto. All rights reserved; fig. 5, © Peter Aaron/Esto. All rights reserved; figs. 6, 7, and 8, Mike Dolinski; fig. 9, Photo: Ole Woldbye, By courtesy of the Trustees of Sir John Soane's Museum; fig. 10, © Laura Padgett; fig. 15, from A. Andreoli, *Il Vittoriale* (Milan: Electa, 1993); fig. 16, Sergio Anelli, from A. Andreoli, *Il Vittoriale* (Milan: Electa, 1993); fig. 18, Ezra Stoller © Esto. All rights reserved; fig. 19, Robert Damora; fig. 21, Photo by Hulton Archive/Getty Images; fig. 22, © The State Hermitage Museum, St. Petersburg; fig. 23, © Luca Vignelli/Esto. All rights reserved; fig. 24, Photo by Arnold Newman/Getty Images

Terence Riley essay: figs. 1, 2, 3, 5, 6, 7, 8, and 9, Digital Image © The Museum of Modern Art/Licensed by SCALA/Art Resource, NY; fig. 4, Photo by Atelier Rudolph Desandalo, Brno/Digital Image © The Museum of Modern Art/Licensed by SCALA/Art Resource, NY

Beatriz Colomina essay: figs. 2, 14, and 20, Ezra Stoller © Esto. All rights reserved; fig. 3, Alexandre Georges; fig. 5, Photo at top of page by Arnold Newman/Getty Images; fig. 6, Akademie der Kunst in Berlin, Bruno Taut Archive; fig. 7, Photo by Arnold Newman/Getty Images; fig. 10, Photo by Thomas McAvoy, from M. Geller, *From Receiver to Remote Control: The TV Set* (New York: New Museum of Contemporary Art, 1990); fig. 11, Photo by Frank Scherschel/Time Life Pictures/Getty Images; fig. 12, *Life Magazine*, March 18, 1957; fig. 13, Photo by Frank Scherschel/Time & Life Pictures/Getty Images; fig. 15, Photo by Arnold Newman/Getty Images; fig. 17, from J. Zukowsky, *Mies Reconsidered: His Career, Legacy, and Disciples* (New York: Rizzoli, 1986); fig. 18, from *House & Garden*, February 1952

Joan Ockman essay: fig. 1, © David Diao, courtesy of the artist; fig. 5, Paul Rocheleau; figs. 6 and 10, Ezra Stoller © Esto. All rights reserved; fig. 7, © Robert Schezen/Esto;

fig. 8, from D. Whitney and J. Kipnis, *Philip Johnson: The Glass House* (New York: Pantheon, 1993); fig. 9, from E. Bitterman, *Art in Modern Architecture* (New York: Reinhold, 1952); fig. 11, © 2008 Austrian Frederick and Lillian Kiesler Private Foundation, Vienna; fig. 12, Image courtesy of the Board of Trustees, National Gallery of Art, Washington/© 2008 Kate Rothko & Christopher Rothko/Artists Rights Society (ARS), New York; figs. 13 and 14, from S. Nodelman, *The Rothko Chapel Paintings: Origins, Structure, Meaning* (Austin: University of Texas Press, 1997); figs. 15 and 16, Courtesy of the Avery Architectural and Fine Arts Library, Columbia University, New York; fig. 17, Photo by Arnold Newman; fig. 18, Wisconsin Historical Society; fig. 19, from *Domus*, July–August 1980; fig. 21, Erich Lessing/Art Resource, NY; figs. 24 and 25, Courtesy, Rare Book and Manuscript Division, Butler Library, Columbia University, New York

Reinhold Martin essay: fig. 1, Richard Payne; figs. 6 and 7, Photographs by Paul Hester, from F. Welch, *Philip Johnson and Texas* (Austin: University of Texas Press, 2000)

Kazys Varnelis essay: fig. 1, Photo by Ben Martin/Time & Life Pictures/Getty Images; fig. 2, © Vitali Ogorodnikov/Emporis.com; figs. 3 and 4, © Peter Mauss/Esto. All rights reserved; fig. 5, Photo by Ted Thai/Time & Life Pictures/Getty Images; fig. 6, Courtesy Pierogi Gallery

Charles Jencks essay: figs. 1, 3, 5, 6, and 7, Charles Jencks; fig. 2, Squire Haskins; fig. 4, Portrait by Timothy Greenfield

Detlef Mertins essay: figs. 1, 2, and 3, Courtesy, Beinecke Rare Book and Manuscript Library, Yale University; figs. 4 and 5, Courtesy of the Philip Johnson family; fig. 6 and 7, from F. Schulze, *Philip Johnson: Life and Work* (New York: Knopf, 1994)

Stanislaus von Moos essay: figs. 3 and 20, Courtesy gta-Institute, ETH, Zurich; fig. 7, © Fondation le Corbusier; fig. 19, Photo by Ted Thai/Time & Life Pictures/Getty Images

Phyllis Lambert essay: fig. 1, Digital Image © The Museum of Modern Art/Licensed by SCALA/Art Resource, NY; figs. 2, 3, 4, 5, 6, 7, 12, and 16, Ezra Stoller © Esto. All rights reserved; figs. 8, 10, 19, and 21, Louis Checkman; figs. 13 and 23, Alexandre Georges; fig. 18, Saul Leiter

Mark Wigley essay: fig. 1, Digital Image © The Museum of Modern Art/Licensed by SCALA/Art Resource, NY; © 2008 The Andy Warhol Foundation for the Visual Arts/ARS, NY; Marilyn Monroe™ is a trademark of Marilyn Monroe LLC; fig. 2, Ezra Stoller © Esto. All rights reserved

Peter Eisenman essay: figs. 1 and 2, Courtesy, Beinecke Rare Book and Manuscript Library, Yale University; figs. 3 and 4, Digital Image © The Museum of Modern Art/Licensed by SCALA/Art Resource, NY

Mark Jarzombek essay: fig. 1, Photo by Dmitri Kessel/Time Life Pictures/Getty Images

Gallery: All images © Paul Warchol Photography, Inc.

278